Diverging Tracks

Diverging Tracks

American Versus English Rail Travel in the 19th Century

Trevor K. Snowdon

McFarland & Company, Inc., Publishers
Jefferson, North Carolina

LIBRARY OF CONGRESS CATALOGUING-IN-PUBLICATION DATA

Names: Snowdon, Trevor K. 1955– author.
Title: Diverging tracks : American versus English rail travel in the 19th century / Trevor K. Snowdon.
Description: Jefferson, North Carolina : McFarland & Company, Inc., Publishers, 2019 | Includes bibliographical references and index.
Identifiers: LCCN 2018052627 | ISBN 9781476671543 (softcover : acid free paper) ∞
Subjects: LCSH: Railroad travel—United States—History—19th century. | Railroad travel—England—History—19th century. | Railroads—Social aspects—History—19th century.
Classification: LCC HE2751 .S56 2019 | DDC 388/.22094109034—dc23
LC record available at https://lccn.loc.gov/2018052627

BRITISH LIBRARY CATALOGUING DATA ARE AVAILABLE

ISBN (print) 978-1-4766-7154-3
ISBN (ebook) 978-1-4766-3245-2

© 2019 Trevor K. Snowdon. All rights reserved

No part of this book may be reproduced or transmitted in any form or by any means, electronic or mechanical, including photocopying or recording, or by any information storage and retrieval system, without permission in writing from the publisher.

Front cover image © 2019 Givaga/iStock

Printed in the United States of America

McFarland & Company, Inc., Publishers
Box 611, Jefferson, North Carolina 28640
www.mcfarlandpub.com

To Ian Carter, former chair of Sociology and
professor emeritus, University of Auckland, New Zealand—
a man with a razor-sharp mind, whose teaching was
both profoundly illuminating and truly inspirational.

Table of Contents

Preface   1

Introduction   5

One. Nineteenth Century England: A Very Strange Railroad System in a Very Strange Society?   11

Two. The Carceral Experiences of the 19th Century English Railroad Passenger   51

Three. Nineteenth Century America: A No Less Strange Railroad System in a No Less Strange Society?   93

Four. Traveling with the Passenger on the 19th Century "Classless" American Railroad   144

Five. The Safety of Railroad Travel in 19th Century England and America   195

Six. The "Railroading" of Consciousness in the 19th Century   236

Conclusion   269

Chapter Notes   273

Selected Bibliography   293

Index   295

It takes an endless amount of history to make even a little tradition.
—Henry James, *The American Scene*

It requires years of research for a moment of synthesis.
—Fustel de Coulanges

Preface

During the last 150 years transportation historians have not been sparing where superlatives describing the historical significance of the advent of railroads are concerned. But like the historians who came after them, many who actually witnessed the advent of railroads viewed it as a monumentally significant development and one likely to completely transform the fabric of Western civilization in the foreseeable future. And it did.

In this book, it is my intention to focus *comparatively* upon the advent of railroads in Britain (principally England) and America in the 19th century. In certain important respects, the advent of railroads in these two national contexts did not take a remarkably different course, whereas in other respects it did; to the extent that, ultimately, two entirely different *national styles* of railroading—railroad construction, railroad technology (locomotives and carriages, for instance), the commodified forms of railroad passenger traveling experience, railroad administration, and railroad operations—emerged. And, if nothing else, this study ought to make it apparent that although we can speak meaningfully of the advent of railroads in a generic sense; yet, in every national context, I would argue, the newly emergent railroad system inevitably acquired, and acquired multifariously, a national style.

This national style of railroad development and of railroad systems will, to a considerable extent, reflect key aspects of culture or of the dominant culture. But it will also reflect—often to some considerable extent, as we shall see in the comparative examples of England and America—key elements of social structure, and especially the form of social stratification in society at large. Furthermore, this national style of railroading may reflect not only key values and significant aspects of social structure; it may also encapsulate and exemplify some of the predominant ideologies of the age (some key values *emblematic of national ideology,* if you like)—even if myth underpins them—which the societies in question identify with. Moreover, the national style of railroading that emerges may not only have an ideological underpinning reflecting a nation's self-image; it may represent a conspicuous, even a pre-eminent (microcosmic) exemplification of that national self-imagery, as we shall see in due course. However, I think some comments on the railroad literary tradition are in order before I "get up steam."

Historically, the advent of railroads and their development has fascinated and sometimes bemused veritable legions of (mostly male) researchers and authors. Consequently, there exists today a mammoth literature addressing the multidimensional historical trajectories of this technological juggernaut through time and space, society and culture. However, the mainstream of railroad history literature is characterized by the fact that authors within it tend almost invariably to talk past each other—as if there is nothing worthy of discussion or debate. Nor is there, apparently, much requiring protracted analysis. Indeed, it must be the only field of scholarly endeavor within the broadly conceived field of historical studies where that is so. In fact, having read many hundreds of books in both the transportation history and railroad history fields, yet I cannot recall ever having come across any author taking another to task assiduously in respect of this or that point. That is a sad indictment of the body of literature constituting the genre in question. Moreover, this is a field of intellectual endeavor in which descriptive commentary rather than analytical rigor prevails.

But one book within this literary tradition which has always struck me as being both theoretically informed and thematically powerful, as well as analytical in its approach—and thus seemingly out of place within this literary tradition—is Wolfgang Schivelbusch's award-winning *The Railway Journey* (just a small paperback); which ought to be considered a "classic" in this genre, despite my giving Mr. Schivelbusch a tough time in my narrative. His book seems to be an outlier where the mainstream literature is concerned. And, interestingly, it is a book seldom acknowledged within that mainstream literature, let alone engaged with analytically, critically, or discursively.

In *The Railway Journey*, Schivelbusch, in a series of snapshot-like essays, attempts to capture some of the most significant aspects of the advent of railroads at the moment of their introduction and shortly thereafter. He focuses upon subjective experience, viewed through the lens of a commodification of motion and problematized as an industrialization of time, space, and consciousness. But these interesting formulations—which promised to move railroad history in the direction of a "phenomenology" of railroads, as well as towards more general "philosophical" reflection upon the historical significance of their advent and the psychological dimension to that—were never capitalized upon by other thinkers in the field. Consequently, they have long remained ungerminated seeds. But I do pick up that gauntlet here.

Why am I interested in the advent of railroads? Certainly, I did not move into this field of knowledge with either the self-consciousness of the stranger or the apprehensiveness of the interloper. After all, I had researched and written a doctoral thesis in the early 1990s which attempted to articulate the advent of railroads with a concept of modernity. And over a period of around 20 years subsequently I have been continuing to research 19th century British and American railroad history, albeit with different thematic orientations in mind than those that guided my doctoral thesis. So, I do not tour "Railroadland" as a foreigner without a passport.

And, being a railroad enthusiast in only the scholarly sense, I should like to think I approach my research object dispassionately; though perhaps a little too dispassionately and clinically for the liking of some writing in this field. In fact, because I do not consider myself to be either a railroad "enthusiast" or a railroad "romantic"—being either can be problematical when it comes to writing railroad history, although British authors seem to be more seriously afflicted than their American counterparts—I do at times feel like somebody who has never owned a cat or a dog writing a book about the psychology of pet-keeping in a very cold and clinically detached way.

Indeed, some of the railroad enthusiasts and romantics out there will no doubt perceive me to be something of a "grim reaper," as I mow down at least a few of their most cherished generalizations, bosom-held mythologies, gilt-penned evangels, and steam-exuding sacraments. But the world needs its grim reapers, just as it needs a messiah or two from time to time. And if my "apocrypha" dismay some railroad enthusiasts and romantics, then I apologize in advance for having disenchanted their fairytale kingdoms and jealously-guarded fiefdoms in Railroad Fantasyland.

Finally, I should like to append a note on narrative style where the writing of history is concerned. Many historians seem to assume theirs is a legislative role, to a point—they attempt to tell us how it was, or even how we ought to think about how it was in times past. And although most historians stop short of equating the verity of what they write and how they arrive at it with the objectivity of scientific research and the hard data it gives rise to; yet, most historians would, I surmise, want to say that the writing of history is remarkably different from the writing of a novel, for instance.

However, the historian brings particularistic interests, a unique set of values, a unique biography, a uniquely "hued" ethos, a uniquely cultivated intellect, a unique imagination, and a unique consciousness more generally to the writing of historical narrative. And that makes the writing of history a much more subjective enterprise than many historians would want to concede it is. Bearing in mind, moreover, that where the "fictive" aspect to the historical narrative is concerned, historians always select, classify, categorize, and "censor" *what they can find out* about this or that subject. Consequently, their narratives inevitably leave out more history than they include.

But let us not lose sight of the fact, either, that what the reader brings to the text is a no less uniquely configured spectrum of values, interests, and attributes, which shape what is read, and how it is read, irrespective of what the author of the text intended. Consequently, the text is "negotiated" as much as it is read. Indeed, the writing and reading of a text always entails a negotiation of sorts between writer and reader. And it is this negotiation—of the meaning of the text—and, more especially, the highly subjective authorial creation of it where the writing of history is concerned, that necessarily gives the latter a "fictive" quality, strictly speaking.

Hence, I see the writing of history as more like art than science. Indeed, I prefer to view the writing of history as more like painting a scene than "writing up" an experiment, and more like an Impressionist painting than a conventional landscape. Indeed, the writing of history is a form of impressionism and the historian should never lose sight of that fact. But nor should the reader be duped into thinking that apprehending a "work" of history is necessarily very much different to apprehending an Impressionist painting. Indeed, to "steal" a line from Albert Bushnell Hart, I must admit of my offering here that 'tis only a mosaic at best.

Introduction

> I cannot express the amazed awe, the crushed humility, with which I sometimes watch a locomotive take its breath at a railway station.... What manner of men they must be who dig brown iron ore out of the ground and forge it into THAT.
> —John Ruskin

If the rise of industrial capitalism necessitated the expansion and intensification nationally—in both England and America—of transportation systems, yet that opened vast areas of entrepreneurial opportunity for capitalists with especial interest in the transportation of both freight *and people.* Indeed, in the immediate pre-railroad era *the transportation of people* (by coastal shipping, canal, river, and road) in both England and America had already become a significant sector of the economy in both countries.

If the Industrial Revolution in England (arguably it lagged by a few decades in America until after the Civil War) engendered the creation of affluence on an unprecedented scale; yet, it also impacted powerfully upon the social structure of England, creating a new, burgeoning middle-class, essentially. It also took the consumption of goods and services to another scale, while also stratifying the consumption of goods and services more elaborately than had previously been the case. Hence, there was a proliferation of *status-symbolizing* goods and services, tailored for conspicuous consumption by the upper-classes and those aspiring to gentility (the middling classes). As for the lower social classes, they were consumers of relatively basic goods and services, or were not even catered for at all in respect of some goods and services. The commodification of travel in England was certainly implicated in these developments, and of seminal interest here.

In America, comparatively, the ideology of republicanism had somewhat "ironed out" social structure by the time railroads emerged. Social structure was still discernibly pyramidal, but social class distinctions were not as glaring, nor as "institutionalized" as in England. Of course, the Negroes were not even considered to be part of social structure in many parts of America at that time; nevertheless, their servitude, and marginal citizenship (and even human) status facilitated a fundamental racial divide upon which were predicated essential elements of the broader (white) social structure.

The consumption of goods and services in America was not as stratified as it was in England, either, and was relatively inclusive—even the Negroes were not necessarily excluded from the consumption of most goods and services within the broader economy. Indeed, what differentiated American "publicly-accessible" transportation systems from the English counterparts, in the immediate *pre-railroad* era (the early 19th century), was that the concept of "public" transportation in America (negroes aside, for the most part) at that time *excluded very few people comparatively*.

In early 19th century England coastal shipping, canal transportation, and the "public" coach were all forms of passenger transportation *largely* inaccessible to the lower social classes. Indeed, in England these lower social classes were virtually excluded altogether from using the coach, if only because coach travel was priced beyond their means. And if they could avail themselves of transportation on coastal ships and canals, yet such transit (as "deck" passengers) could, nevertheless, be in quite miserable, even degrading circumstances. So, even before the railroad age the concept of "public" clearly had different import, where *access to* "public transportation" was concerned, in England and America respectively.

In America, republicanism did tend to obviate exclusivity where the forms of commodification in the field of transportation were concerned. However, that is not to say there were not different (passenger) classes available to people traveling by coastal, river, or canal vessels because such (passenger) class distinctions did exist in America—bearing in mind the coach was not very amenable to stratifying its accommodation, anyway. But even if there were passenger classes where American waterborne transportation systems, for instance, were concerned; yet, virtually nobody (negroes aside in some places) was *completely excluded* from traveling by those means in America, nor was anybody *calculatedly* "degraded" during such travel.

Compared to American transportation capitalists of the same era, the English counterparts *seemed* almost blind to the entrepreneurial opportunities which catering to the lower social classes presented—as Americans liked to point out at the time—so besotted were the English with the ideological imperatives underlying the "culture" of long-standing, institutionalized, social class distinctions. But it is important to understand that the English "victimization" of their lower social classes, where the consumption of goods and services more generally was concerned, was simply reflective of the class structure (and its more general dynamics) that prevailed at the time.

Many railroad historians seem to have a vested interest in conserving the railroad as a *unique* historical phenomenon; which might help us to understand why many of them are remiss when it comes to identifying qualities which the railroad *has in common with* less glamorous—from their standpoints—technologies, industrial production systems, institutions, and other cultural artifacts. Many of those historians are also, apparently, "nationalists," albeit often without realizing it. And the latter is one reason for the dearth of comparative approaches, historically, in respect of *national railroad styles*. But it could also be because very little of that history is written by sociologists, for instance, most of whom would be awake to the fact that railroad systems necessarily have a sociological aspect to them. Another reason for the lack of comparative studies in this field is that relatively few, perhaps very few, railroad historians step outside their own national railroad history tradition to develop a facility for comparing national railroad systems, such as the English and American systems in the 19th century. Furthermore, the deeper you delve into a nation's railroad history, the more apparent it becomes—or at least it ought to—that you need to know a lot about the history of the country concerned, and not just about its railroad history, to adequately understand the latter. Yet, perhaps many railroad historians fail to appreciate that.

One essential element of my methodology here is to make considerable use of travel narratives penned by English men and women who toured America in the 19th century and used the nation's railroads. However, I also use the content of those narratives to assist understanding of American railroad systems more broadly—that is, within the context of 19th century American society, culture, economic values, and nationalist ideology. And I should like to think that element of my methodology considerably enriches the narrative and gives it, if nothing else, an entertainment value it might otherwise lack.

There were many, possibly hundreds, of travel narratives penned by 19th century English visitors to America. The best summary of them, and the best bibliographical source for them, seems to be Henry T. Tuckerman's *America and Her Commentators, with a Critical Sketch of Travel in the United States* (1864). However, Tuckerman's work consists only of snippets; during my research I read dozens of such 19th century (English) travel narratives in their entirety, numerous of them being multi-volume works.

Tuckerman suggested that from the close of the war of 1817 there was an "inundation" of English travel narratives: "Wherein the United States, their people and prospects, were discussed with a monotonous recapitulation of objections, a superficial knowledge, and a predetermined deprecation, which renders the task of analyzing their comparative merit in the highest degree wearisome." Tuckerman was right about the wearisomeness; but, since I never had occasion to read anywhere near as many travel narratives as he slogged through, I can empathize only to a point—he evidently read hundreds of such narratives, since his study included other (than English) foreign travel narratives, reached back into early colonial times, and even had a good sampling of the travel narratives of the Americans who were the first to tour their own country and write about it.

However, Tuckerman evidently had scant knowledge of England and the English, since, several times in his book he refers to the English as "cockneys"—certainly at the time he was writing (1864) a "cockney" was unequivocally an East Londoner. Nevertheless, Tuckerman, having surveyed what was a very extensive field, arrived at the conclusion that the "swarm" of English travel narratives "abusive of America, upon calm reflection, appears like a monomania"; he also noted that "equally preposterous was the sensitiveness of the (American) people to foreign criticism." In that connection, one notes Dickens, even before he did his own American tours, had "latched onto" the "merriment." Indeed, in the *Pickwick Papers* he has one of his characters say: "Have a passage ready (for him) taken for 'Merriker.... And then let him come back and write a book about the 'Merrikins as"ll pay all his expenses, and more, if he blows 'em up enough."

However, in the early 19th century some English tourists thought their "kith" had been unreasonable in their appraisals of America. Indeed, not all English tourists "blew up" the 'Merrikins. Cobbett, for instance, in his 1818 work on his American travels, thought works in the same genre penned by his countrymen were either too generous or too critical. However, many of the criticisms leveled at the Americans by the English "anthropologists" and "zoologists" were no doubt accurate and fair-minded, despite the "legendary" English chauvinism. In fact, American historian Albert Bushnell Hart, said in his highly regarded (edited) epic, *American History Told by Contemporaries* (1901):

"One of the largest forces for an *accurate* knowledge of America is the body of travels chiefly by foreigners."

But, where American responses to the foreign criticism of their country were concerned, it was not just that they were a hyper-sensitive lot. In *The American People: A Study in National Psychology* (1909), Maurice Low wrote: "The American loves to read about himself and is eager to see himself from the point of view of the foreigner, although he does not always agree with him." Furthermore, it did not seem to occur to many (American) critics of travel narratives penned by foreigners that the latter were among the foremost means by which they, and many other Americans, "discovered" their own country and its regional "idiosyncrasies" (from earliest colonial times, in fact). Furthermore, the foreign criticism may be thought of as salutary in one respect at least—it inspired an American literary response, which began to probe issues bearing upon the concept of national self-identity.

In chapter one of this book I offer up a tentative "phenomenology" of the nineteenth century railroad. I then discuss some of the perplexities the advent of the railroad gave rise to, including those stemming from its role in engineering not only the railroad system, but also the passengers and their movements through railroad systems. I also attend to the railroad's role relative to modern conceptions of "traffic" and mass mobility. I then proceed to explain why the English railroad companies instituted both passenger classes and the compartmentalization of carriages, tying that analysis to considerations of cultural values, social structure, and ideology.

In chapter two the focus is largely upon description and analysis of the English railroad passenger class system and the compartmentalization of carriages, and some of the perplexities and dilemmas arising therefrom within nineteenth century English railroad capitalism. The concepts of social structure, social class, passenger class, along with the invocation of the concepts of "discipline" and the "carceral," frame that analysis.

In chapter three there is protracted analysis of what I cast as the "American character" in the nineteenth century; the foci of that analysis some prominent American values, nationalist ideology, more generally, and social structure. I then tie such considerations to the American railroad companies' preference for the "open" and uncompartmentalized form of passenger carriage. But there were peculiarities, idiosyncrasies, and anomalies characterizing the "American style" of railroad administration, operation, and travel in the 19th century, and they are addressed in due course.

In chapter four I focus upon foreign travelers" encounters with the nineteenth century American railroad system. Indeed, we look closely at the constituent elements of 19th century American railroad systems to draw out the signal features that marked off the American railroad traveling "style" from the English counterpart.

In chapter five I attend analytically to the health and safety issues which arose in relation to railroad travel in the nineteenth century in both England and America. Such considerations throw further light upon the differences between the English and American railroad styles, but address other issues as well—such as how safe, comparatively and absolutely, railroad travel in the 19th century was.

In chapter six I attend to some of the "psychological" consequences, and more general impact upon "consciousness," of railroad systems and railroad travel in the nineteenth century. So, although the central concern of this study is to *differentiate* the 19th century English and American national styles of "railroading," yet at certain consequential levels of analysis there were points of convergence that ought not to be overlooked—especially since some of them inform the attempt to adequately frame a phenomenology of 19th century railroad travel. I also undertake a protracted analysis of the phenomenon of "railroad reading" in that concluding chapter.

A short conclusion ties all the loose strands together and summarizes the argument.

Finally, just a word concerning linguistic usage. I have generally opted for the term "railroad" as against "railway," except when directly quoting a contemporary (often English) source which uses the term "railway." However, the term "railway" was quite widely used in 19th century America, even if "railroad" was dominant in common usage; so, occasionally, when *directly quoting* an American source which employs "railway" I do not alter the word to "railroad."

I generally refer to "locomotives," not "engines"; and I generally refer to locomotive drivers as "enginemen"—in early days in America the locomotive was sometimes called the "motive."

When referring to England, I generally use the word "carriage" to describe the passenger rolling stock, which is the term the English used; but the term "car" is generally invoked when I refer to American passenger rolling stock, which was the term preferred by Americans.

I generally use the term "station" when referring to English passenger stops. But because both "station" and "depot" were used widely in America, I tend to follow the usage in the source I happen to be quoting, paraphrasing, or referring to. Otherwise, I use "station/depot" when referring to American passenger stops. In both national contexts, "terminus" is also used as appropriate.

I use the term "baggage" instead of "luggage," unless the latter is included in a direct quotation.

I generally use the terms "England" and the "English" when referring to the English nation. But, occasionally, I refer to the "British" when talking about the inhabitants of the British Isles, more generally. And I sometimes refer to the "United Kingdom" as well, although only when citing statistics which were compiled in respect of England and Wales exclusively.

When I use the term "America," I mean the United States of America. When I use the term "states," that is a reference to the constituent "states" which comprise the United States of America as opposed to the "Federal Government"—for instance, "all states were opposed to that Federal Government policy." Furthermore, when addressing matters of governance, I avoid the use of "government" in a generic sense, always specifying whether I mean the "Federal Government" or "State" government(s).

I draw attention to these usages simply because in a comparative study like this you must make some choices when linguistic usage arises as an issue; and the usages opted for need to be consistently applied so as not to confuse readers. Hopefully, the usages I have opted for here do not offend or confuse anybody.

ONE

Nineteenth Century England: A Very Strange Railroad System in a Very Strange Society?

> In very few countries are class distinctions carried to a more ridiculous and unseemly height than in England. A querulous anxiety about caste is one of the most strikingly disagreeable characteristics of English society.... Countless are our degrees of gentility, and endless our subdivisions of respectability, and in no other land is poverty so unequivocally regarded as a crime.
> —"Class Distinctions," *The Bristol Mercury*, January 1, 1842

> Perhaps the most repulsive thing an English traveler meets with in America is the want of distinction in classes. On the railroad, there is but one class and one price.
> —Thomas Nichols, *Forty Years of American Life*, 1864

Introduction

In this chapter, it is my primary intention to consider some of the peculiarities of the English "character," and of the English social class structure in the 19th century, so that we might better understand why a system of *passenger classes* and compartmentalizing of carriages was adopted by the English railroad companies in the 19th century, as well as why English railroad travelers, who could afford so to do, preferred to travel in compartments.

In 19th century America, by way of comparison, *railroad* passenger class discriminations were rare before the Pullman era—notwithstanding some glaring discriminatory practices regarding certain categories of persons (negroes and immigrants)—and throughout the 19th century the "ordinary" car in America was the "open" (non-compartmentalized) and "classless" type.

In most European countries at the time of the advent of railroads there had been a very long history of institutionalized social class distinctions. Indeed, apart from the more obvious dimensions to hierarchical society such as wealth and poverty, dominance and deference, status, honor and servitude, different social ranks were to be both socially and spatially separated from each other in most circumstances. Nineteenth century English society was precisely a "species" of this "genus."

A key objective in this and the chapter following is to establish the form of the English railroad *passenger class system*, then to contrast it with the American system in chapters three and four. Indeed, the contrasts, when they are drawn between the two systems, will become apparent and dramatic in chapters three and four, where I make considerable use of 19th century travel "logs," penned mostly by 19th century English travelers in America, to embellish what would otherwise be a fairly "pedestrian" description of the American railroad passenger traveling experience, and of American railroad systems in the 19th century.

However, I do not attend in quite the same way to American tourists" impressions of English railroad passenger conveyance at the time. That is a methodological peculiarity of my approach, although I doubt the omission has any real bearing on the tenor or substance of my argument. Nevertheless, an article which appeared in an English newspaper in *1869* is instructive, to a point, where the American view of English railroad systems was concerned:

> An American in England misses the sleeping cars, the ladies' cars, the smoking-cars, and one or two more traveling comforts to which he had been accustomed, which may be cheaply and advantageously introduced, and which are only withheld because of the *fine old English prejudice against novelties*.[1]

But if the English were generally perceived by Americans to be somewhat conservative in outlook and "straitjacket-*ed*" in behavior, yet Englishman, William Hardman, concluded, towards the end of his tour of America (1884), that in the Great Republic: "Traces of old English manners and customs still survive among them which have long since been lost to us."[2] But such "oddities" were most likely to be encountered in cities like Boston or Philadelphia, which did, indeed, retain "flavors" of pre-revolutionary "Englishness."

But what the American would have found especially odd, and quite possibly amusing when traveling in England in the second half of the 19th century, were the fundamentally different English railroad *passenger class system* on the one hand, and the English upper-class preference for carriage compartments on the other. And, all considered, our American would most likely have agreed with an English newspaper's American correspondent writing in 1875, who thought English people had "no idea of the real superiority of the American over the English (railroad) system."[3]

But we are beginning to step ahead of ourselves here. And what *this* chapter is about, essentially, is understanding the English, and especially the English "character" in the 19th century—so that we might then be able to understand why the English had the kind of railroad traveling preferences (passenger classes and compartments, most notably) which marked them off from the Americans at the time.

But before we can address any such "posers" analytically, some conceptual/analytical matters need to be addressed. For a start, we need to understand exactly what a railroad journey in the 19th century entailed. And what is required, in that regard, is a "phenomenology" of railroad travel itself; explication of which ought to draw out some of the signal features of railroad travel relative to those modes of transportation which it superseded or relegated. So, what is a railroad?

The Railroad as an Industrial Production System

I contend that the railroad must be seen, first and foremost, as an industrial production system possessed of many of the hallmarks of both the factory and the industrial production line. This is not a novel conceptualization of 19th century railroad capitalism, since Wolfgang Schivelbush, in his seminal, *The Railway Journey*, attends to the "industrialization" of the passenger during a railroad journey, as well as to the impact the advent of railroads had on the industrialization of consciousness more generally in the 19th century. However, I should like to think the argument forthcoming here transcends Schivelbusch's relatively constricted account of the industrialization of the railroad traveler; notwithstanding that there are numerous points of difference between his and my own approach to this fascinating and, indeed, undervalued and thus much neglected dimension to sociocultural and psychological history. But, that aside, Schivelbusch generalizes, and perhaps to a questionable degree, since the processing of railroad passengers in the 19th century, not to mention their accommodation during railroad travel, could differ remarkably from one national context to another, as shall be evinced from this and the chapters following.

However, Schivelbusch aside, even early on some English people who had witnessed the advent of railroads understood the "industrializing" aspect to railroad passenger travel. John Ruskin, notable mid–Victorian art and architectural critic, although he could be melodramatic in his appraisal of the negative impact railroads would have on the face of Britain did, nonetheless, have a good appreciation of the industrial character of the railroad, as well of the implications of railroad travel for the passenger, and of railroad systems for the environment. Indeed, he understood both the *industrial* and *factory-like* qualities that the production of a railroad journey encompassed. And he was one of the first, and among the few in his time, to have appreciated the fact that the railroad traveler—as "consumer"—was simultaneously enmeshed in an *industrial production system* which was producing the commodity (transit) at the same time it (the commodity) was being consumed by the traveler. Ruskin did not state the fact of the matter so; but his writings, if you penetrate below the "melodrama," clearly indicate he had a substantial grasp of this stark reality.

Another very percipient observer of early railroad passenger travel, American writer Henry Thoreau, observed, similarly, that railroad travel reduced men to "chattel, who could be transported by the box and the ton"[4]—this was not pure metaphor.

One might also note, in this connection, it was not uncommon by the late 19th century for American railroad executives to conceive of their railroads as akin to giant machines. And in that conceptualization, thereby, to visualize a production process which, in its expanse, and incorporating thousands of functionaries as it did, approximated to (and thus prefigured) the modern (mechanical) assembly line in terms of both its systemic rationality and its elaborate division of labor alone. Indeed, the *production* of a railroad journey does have many of the characteristics of such an assembly line process. It is just that *nobody thinks about it that way*.

The early 20th century American radical sociologist, Thorstein Veblen, also had a good grasp of what a railroad was and what it entailed. He remarked upon the fact that it was "of the nature of a mechanical process," that "people are required to adapt their needs and motions to the *exigencies* of the process," that "the service is standardized," and that "schedules rule throughout."[5] However, that could just as easily pass as a description of the conditions attending the "manufacture" of a Big Mac in a McDonalds restaurant today. So, at that level of analysis, the similarities between the production of a railroad journey and that of a Big Mac are not remarkably different—indeed, there is not much difference, at a certain level of analysis, between the production of a Big Mac and the Ford motor vehicle assembly line, either.

However, for the moment, let us move on to consider the following statement: "The division ought to be so ordered as to prevent the possibility of communication between the different classes, so that the members of one class might not be seen by those of any other." This could well have been an imperative for the engineering of early Victorian English railroad termini and stations (as we shall see in the chapter following), as well as for the conditions of conveyance for different passenger classes—perhaps an assertion arising during a Great Western Railway Company Board meeting in the 1840s. But it is, in fact, a statement of the Prison Architect to the County of Essex rationalizing a signal feature of prison design in 1819.[6] Yet, it *was*, also, a fundamental premise underlying English railroad passenger travel in the 19th century, and especially so during the early period.

Indeed, the commodification of railroad travel in Victorian England was wedged between the rationalizing imperatives of the bureaucratically administered, factory-like, industrial production process on the one hand, and some observance of the existing social class boundaries on the other. To some considerable extent this chapter, at that level of analysis, is an exploration of how that tension was resolved in England. But, before advancing to that enterprise, let us, for a moment, consider several factors, all of which bear upon that phenomenon, starting with the concept of "mass transportation."

Mass Transportation and the Enhancement of Personal Mobility

The railroad was, arguably, the first mode of vehicular mass transportation in the industrial age. And that itself led to rationalizations which effectively disciplined the passenger. The number of railroad passenger journeys undertaken in the UK in 1861 was almost 163.5 million, representing, at the time, an average 5 to 6 journeys annually per person. And, at that time, almost half of all railroad company revenue was derived from passenger and mail carriage (the latter a very minor portion of the total).[7] Furthermore, excluding season ticket holders, passenger travel in the UK. increased nearly tenfold in the period 1850–1885.[8] If nothing else, surely these statistics are an indication that the phenomenon of mass transportation had arrived *in the industrial age.*

However, Jack Simmons concluded that the steamboat earlier, rather than the railroad, effected the first instances of mass transportation, pointing to the resort steamboat traffic on the southeastern coast of England to underpin the argument. He noted, of that coastal steamboat traffic: "They carried their passengers by hundreds at a time, instead of tens. They first demonstrated the meaning of mass transport, its capabilities for the future; they, not the railways.[9]

The notion that transporting *hundreds* of people at a time represents an instance of "mass" transportation is questionable. And how could anything as "class-exclusive" as that (steamboat) traffic was qualify as "mass" transportation, anyway? Surely the concept of "mass" is predicated upon the possibility of broad accessibility and normally does imply general access. That aside, one notes the coastal steamboat traffic in question was seasonal and confined to movement between not very many places at all. Again, where travel is concerned, ought a "philosophy" of "mass" transportation perhaps need to account for the (national) geographical extent of the phenomenon? Or does it make sense to describe the occasional movements of upper-class people between a few points on the coast, in a few little corners of Britain, and only in summer, as constituting instances of "mass" transportation?

Simmons' argument is also untenable, if only because the steamboat excursion traffic in question was not of such a volume that one could justifiably refer to it as entailing instances of "mass" transportation. Having said that, in 1835 steamboat excursionists from London to Gravesend numbered over 670,000.[10] And steamboat passenger traffic in other European countries was also significant before and during the early railroad age.

Yet, in Britain by the 1840s there were organized railroad excursions which moved tens of thousands of people to the same destination in the matter of a few hours. Furthermore, within the space of six months in 1851 many hundreds of thousands of people took a train to *one event*—the Great Exhibition. The Exhibition eventually admitted "shilling people," many of whom traveled to it third-class on the railroad.

But mass transportation was not just about excursion traffic, of course. Indeed, the advent of the railroad took the enhancement of "personal mobility" into an entirely new dimension. So, let us consider a few facts, in that regard, compiled by that lustrous sociological source of mid–Victorian England, Henry Mayhew. Firstly, Mayhew draws attention to the fact that in the year ending June 1849, 60.3 million passenger journeys were undertaken in the United Kingdom. Secondly, he noted that between mid–June 1845 and mid–June 1849 passenger journeys on United Kingdom trains almost doubled—from 33.7 million to 60.3 million. Thirdly, by June 1849 there were 78 passenger-carrying railroads in the United Kingdom.[11] However, as Mayhew himself pointed out, reasonably astute statistician that he was, the concept of the "passenger journey" in these statistics can be misleading; since, by his own example, a gentleman traveling from London to Greenwich daily could alone account for 730 passenger journeys annually. However, relatively few people (like that gentleman) at that time had "season" or other "concessionary" (discounted multi-journey) tickets, and only the wealthy could afford them. The truth is Mayhew had no idea how many people did use the railroad at that time. However, even allowing for the "frequent user" qualification Mayhew draws our attention to, yet 60.3 million passenger journeys in the UK by 1849 is an impressive statistic, and certainly belittles the earlier steamboat excursion statistics.

The concept of "mass transportation" aside, there is no doubt that personal mobility had already been enhanced considerably before the advent of railroads. That enhancement related to both greater accessibility to public transportation and a marked increase in the regularity of its use. The former is to imply that public transportation in Britain not only became more affordable, but also less exclusive and thus more genuinely "public," though not absolutely so, as we shall see in the next chapter. Nevertheless, the extent to which transportation had become "public" implied that a "cultural" shift had occurred; not just in terms of social class accessibility, but also where the travel of women, for instance, was concerned.

By the early 1830s about 15 times as many people were availing themselves of stagecoach transportation than had been the case 40 years earlier.[12] And apart from the sociocultural factors underpinning the expansion of that "traffic," several other factors ought to be considered: roads had improved considerably; quality roads were beginning to link to form networks; developments in coach technology had made for more comfortable coach transportation; coach speeds had increased considerably, especially those of the mail and other express coach services; and the rapid expansion of industrial capitalism had increased the amount of business-related travel undertaken (much coach travel was between commercial and manufacturing centers).

But despite all the improvements within the coaching industry, yet the coach passenger's traveling experience still had to be reckoned with alongside what the railroad eventually came to offer. Speed was the key difference. Even the "express" mail coaches were hard-pressed to average over 12 mph, while the weather could impede the progress of a coach more than that of a train.[13] And despite the improvements in coach technology there were still "rough" rides—even when coaches had a reasonably sophisticated suspension system, that itself often produced a motion akin to that of a rolling ship, resulting in "sea-sickness" for some. However, that was a problem on the early English railroads, too, although the oscillations were probably not as bad as in the coach. Nevertheless, they were significant enough to be remarked upon in the media: "Most travelers are aware of the extremely unpleasant motion experienced on English railways, which keep the sitter in a state of constant lateral oscillation, as well as the occasional pitching, and the hard vibration in carriages which are not stuffed and lined." The author of this (1845) article suggested such problems resulted from the "top-heaviness of the carriages and the insufficiency of base," and he suggested that if the carriages were twice the length and on six wheels, then both lateral and vertical oscillation would be prevented. In support of the argument the author pointed to German and Danish carriages of the recommended design in which "No movement or vibration is experienced, even in the second-class carriages, and that persons can read and write in them with as great facility as on firm ground, even at the highest velocities." The author also pointed out that the only English adaptation at the time of the recommended principle was to be found on Irish lines, adding: "The small boxes to which horse transit was limited ... are not adapted to our improved capacities and advancing knowledge."[14]

But let us return, for the moment, to the theme of mass transportation. Three factors, essentially—aside from those already mentioned—indicated that the railroads had indeed effected the first means of mass transportation in the industrial age. One was the architecture of terminals, which were increasingly designed to engineer the "mass" flow of pedestrian traffic into and out of both termini and train carriages. The second was the adoption by the railroad companies of Edmondson's ticketing machine. And, finally, the advent of a third passenger class more than hinted at the notion of "mass," since I contend nothing which is very exclusive ought to be considered a "mass" phenomenon.

Peculiarities of terminal architecture—such as bridges, concourses, subways, flow control barriers, waiting-rooms, and circulation areas—were not only signs that the age of mass transportation had arrived; but they also signaled the arrival of pedestrian traffic *engineering* more generally.[15] But to be able to manage such traffic flows effectively—of both passengers and freight—was something which probably took even the best-managed railroad companies years or even decades to master. Furthermore, managing *through* (passenger and baggage) traffic took traffic engineering to another level of complexity altogether, especially when multiple routes, railroads, and companies were involved.

In Britain in the early period the engineering of traffic into and out of, through, and circulating within the railroad passenger station or terminal hardly solved "overnight" all the problems it was a response to. Sometimes the number of travelers was simply beyond the capacity of the facility regardless of how well engineered its pedestrian traffic systems were. In other cases, the parsimony or lack of vision of some companies served to undermine rationally engineered pedestrian traffic systems at termini and stations, and sometimes the solutions had more to do with "common sense," as an English newspaper article in 1879 noted:

> Tickets are as difficult to procure as ever. There are few stations where there is not an unseemly scramble for first place at the wicket.... There is no reason in the world why the tickets should not be on sale at all hours of the day, and at booksellers" shops as well as at stations.[16]

At the time this was written the suggested outlet (and many others) for buying tickets had been available in America for decades—even in the 1860s American hotels, for instance, generally had a facility for purchasing railroad tickets to virtually anywhere the trunk railroads went at that time.

The Advent of Railroads and the Concept of "Traffic"

"Traffic" is a modern concept. And today administering traffic flows is very much an "engineering" problem. *The rail road and traffic upon it gave rise to the first attempts to engineer vehicular traffic in conjunction with signaling systems.* In fact, arguably it is only with the advent of railroads that there develops a concept of "traffic" with all its "modern" connotations. So, it may be thought that traffic problems and the first systematic attempts to regulate (engineer) traffic on a large scale took place with the advent of railroads.

However, strictly speaking, it could be argued otherwise. Even in ancient Rome, for instance, there were serious problems with "traffic" in city streets, which is one reason why several emperors introduced stringent laws restricting and controlling vehicular traffic, and otherwise regulating street activity—the underlying rationales of traffic regulations in those times were usually to conserve the roads and minimize disorder, apart from which traffic control was not really a province of engineering expertise at the time, anyway.

Furthermore, even in Tudor England London streets were often fraught with "traffic" problems. One cause was the narrowness of many urban streets,[17] apart from which people dumped rubbish in them often. But at that time the London authorities never really had any effective means for dealing with traffic problems and that remained the case across the centuries.

So, it is not as if railroad operations themselves gave rise to the first serious traffic *problems* in history or even to the first attempts to seriously address such problems. Having said that, it could be argued that with the advent of railroad "traffic," *traffic* itself for the first time became conceived of as an *engineering* problem. And, therefore, attempts to effectively coordinate and control railroad traffic led to the development and applications of systematic means of so doing and, ultimately, to administrative and technological (mechanical and electronic techniques such as signals and the telegraph, for instance) in that connection.

The railroad companies had to deal with traffic multi-dimensionally—traffic along the lines; traffic *systems* for the movement of freight, sometimes including picking it up from the consignee's premises and delivering it to the door of the recipient; passenger traffic into, through, and out of termini and stations; the baggage traffic of passengers; and, later, through travel, which represented as much of an engineering as it did an administrative and operational problem. In fact, it is in respect of these railroad traffic perplexities and attempts at their resolution that we get an early glimpse of the formative relationship between engineering and management.

Traffic along railroad lines was incredibly difficult to manage safely in the early period, especially once locomotives came to the fore (some early public railroads used horse power initially and many used horse power as back-up for years), given that: often there was a single track used by traffic going in both directions; people and other hazards had to be kept off the line to facilitate traffic flow; trains had hardly any means of braking effectively in an emergency; signals were performed by humans, semaphore used in the early period; there were no means of communication between a traffic control center and enginemen, nor could enginemen in different locomotives on different parts of the track communicate with each other; and even communication between the enginemen on a train and the guard or conductor was extremely limited. Indeed, in the event of a "traffic" problem suddenly arising, perhaps foreseen by a mail guard or brakeman sitting atop a carriage, there was not much they could do about it except jump for their lives if necessary!

And if freight trains did not put passengers at risk to the same extent in the early period—notwithstanding that, often, English third-class carriages were hooked up to freight trains—they were often operated at night, which, given all the constraints mentioned above, introduced another degree of risk where traffic safety was concerned.

But of more consequence for my purposes here is the railroad companies' "engineering" of *passenger traffic* into, through, and out of their facilities during a railroad journey. And let us not lose sight of the fact that a railroad journey, regardless of how one may wish to romanticize it, initiated the passenger into an industrial process conducted within a factory-like, industrial production system. Indeed, engineering passenger traffic flow along this industrial production system (a completed railroad journey was the product or what was "consumed") was not a straightforward matter of moving passengers from one point on the compass to another. In fact, it was made much more complicated than that in England because of the number of passenger classes and concomitantly stratified amenities. Indeed, passengers were often not only separated into several types of (passenger class) accommodation on the train, but separated from each other within the terminal or station precincts as well on the same basis—often they had separate waiting-rooms and other amenities (such as having to get their tickets from separate ticketing windows at the station), as well as using different concourses to get from the waiting-room to the train. However, sometimes the third-class passengers were not even admitted to station facilities proper, but, like cattle, were "herded" and "corralled" in "pens" in the freight area.

All the problems arising from the above dimensions to passenger traffic flows became more pressing as passenger volumes increased dramatically, more trains were running, schedules became tighter, and congestion somehow had to be avoided both on the lines and in the stations.

Eventually, such was the volume of freight and pedestrian traffic in the vicinity of metropolitan railroad stations in Europe and America that terminal architecture, and both vehicular and pedestrian traffic, were necessarily drawn into broader urban planning regimes; and, sometimes, but more especially so in America, the broader public interest was subjugated to railroad company power and privilege in such events—as in the commonplace of railroads running up the main streets of cities and towns in America. And, given the urban problems (including traffic), which railroad development engendered, it may be thought of as having contributed something to the development of urban planning, more generally (if only by default)—because of the pressure railroad systems put on the broader urban environment wherever their activities were intensive and expansive enough to demand remedial action.

On the other hand, railroad companies contributed (directly or indirectly) to the development of urban planning because of their large-scale demolitions in urban areas. And although in cities like London demolitions and the resulting displacement of people had preceded the railroad age, yet, the railroad companies often demolished and displaced on another scale, cutting swathes through cities and displacing people in their many thousands. Ultimately, that pressured local authorities to become more proactive in constraining and managing (railroad company) demolitions and displacements, and thus to take the concept of urban planning more seriously than had hitherto been the case.

Where railroad pedestrian traffic engineering was concerned, the resolution of the problem it posed was not without engineering precedent, though arguably we find the precedents in somewhat unlikely places. In Victorian Britain around mid-century, Joseph Paxton had, for a while, almost something of a monopoly of laying out urban and municipal parks, and he often designed his parks with quite elaborately engineered traffic circulation systems—bearing in mind that some London parks quite literally had thousands of carriages traveling through or around them each day, not to mention the flow of pedestrian traffic. At Birkenhead Park, for instance, Paxton provided for through traffic across the park, pleasure traffic within the park, and a separate circulation system for pedestrians.[18] But if this kind of (park) engineering of pedestrian and vehicular traffic flow had a rational foundation to it, yet its precedents were more aesthetically than "rationally" founded—the gardens of the Blenheim estate in the late 18th century, for instance, extended over more than 200 acres with carefully contrived, intersecting walks.[19] Of course, people were not taking sight-seeing strolls through railroad termini, so the engineering of pedestrian traffic through the latter had necessarily to differ from the engineering of the leisured pedestrian's perambulations in "engineered" parks.

However, the English railroad "traffic engineers" were probably not as lateral in their approach to solving pedestrian traffic issues as the French. In France Haussmann's radical and controversial "make-over" of Paris entailed routing some railroad pedestrian traffic from termini directly into commercial and leisure centers—prefiguring modern mall design—rather than engineering railroad pedestrian traffic principally to prevent congestion or to facilitate rapid exit from station precincts, although his solutions probably incorporated such considerations as well.[20]

Regardless of whether contemporaries approved of Haussmann's dramatic transformation of Paris, his historical significance resides in the fact that he was one of the first people to view the organization of the city as a technical (engineering) problem to be resolved. And it is difficult to imagine Haussmann designing anything as "irrational" as the Vanderbilts' Grand Central Terminal (America), which had separate waiting-rooms for the New York Central, Harlem, and the New York and New Haven Railroads, apart from which it was necessary to first exit the building to transfer from one of those railroads to another.[21]

The engineering of pedestrian traffic flows through the Crystal Palace during the Great Exhibition of 1851 must also have posed something of a challenge—one imagines Paxton (apart from his role in the design of the Crystal Palace) would probably have played a role in designing pedestrian traffic flows there, too, given his experience in pedestrian traffic engineering, the number of exhibits in what was a relatively constricted space, and the pedestrian traffic volumes. In fact, I have read a lot of literature pertaining to the Great Exhibition of 1851, yet I do not recall ever reading of pedestrian traffic congestion at the Exhibition, so the (pedestrian) traffic engineering must have been good. Indeed, railroad companies may have learned something from it.

But railroad traffic engineering (of both the rail "road" and through railroad facilities such as termini and stations) also had a lot to do with safety, not just motion. The bureaucratic form of managerial administration which emerged within 19th century English railroad capitalism entailed various disciplinary regimes, some of which *targeted* the passengers, while others impacted them. But the administration of railroad operations necessarily had this disciplinary underpinning to it; if only because of the nature of the industrial process which production of the commodity (travel) engendered, along with all the safety issues which arose in relation to that. The passenger simply could not stand beyond those disciplinary regimes nor be unaffected by them, since they were necessary for the establishment and maintenance of fundamental "boundaries" within the industrial production system in question. On the London and Birmingham in the early period, for instance, people were not even allowed onto the platform to see off friends and family, while the "commission of other nuisances" on the platform was also prohibited.[22] But there were significant national differences—to be discussed in much more depth in due course—at the point where railroad pedestrian traffic engineering and discipline merged.

Passenger Traffic, Safety and Discipline

Other factors, apart from the industrial nature of the production process, impinged upon the question of passenger discipline. Timetables, for instance, simply by their existence—regardless of their fictional quality in the early period—effectively imposed a discipline of conformity (to them) on the would-be passenger. In that connection, it may be argued that the advent of railroads contributed more to the raising of time-consciousness in the 19th century than did any other technological or institutional development, even if it were to be conceded that the factory had already effected that, to some extent at least, before the advent of railroads.

In fact, being a member of a leisured class had always elevated such people above the pettiness of minute time divisions and the imposition of fixed schedules. Indeed, the timetabling of consciousness, which regular railroad travel required, was problematical primarily for those whose lives had never been governed by temporal disciplinary regimes—"time discipline" was often a central element of factory "culture," but *rigid* time conformity no doubt required a considerable psychological adjustment for the bourgeois and aristocratic traveler not accustomed to the temporal disciplines of factory culture. And although people of the (English) upper classes changed their clothing in accordance with the time of day or the nature of a regular activity (dinner or morning calls, for instance), yet this was a relatively relaxed kind of time-discipline compared to that which the railroad system demanded of the passenger. And the timetabling of consciousness, first impressed upon the English (middle and upper-class) public on a grand scale with the advent of railroads, ought to be considered a significant factor in the emergence of modernity. Indeed, the railroad timetable became for many a bourgeois railroad traveler what the *Book of Hours*—which effected a synchronized liturgical discipline—had been to the 13th century nobleman and his family. And no doubt from 1841, when Bradshaw's national (monthly) railroad timetable guide first appeared, it quickly became for many as portably indispensable as its sibling, the gentleman's pocket-watch (women did not carry watches very often, it seems).

But if this new-fangled industrial time-discipline was an imposition on the upper-middle and aristocratic classes, those people could hardly justify an aversion to such structure, control, and discipline, especially since their privileged positions in society were predicated upon those very foundation stones. Of course, there were aspects to railroad travel which the aristocracy especially objected to and attempted to resist initially, and they will be addressed at length in the chapter following. However, after the initial period of resistance, the aristocracy and the upper-classes more generally accommodated themselves to the "exigencies" of railroad traveling, eventually habituating to the most objectionable elements of it. And this was clearly made easier by the fact that England was a very structured society in terms of its "caste system." People were used to giving or receiving orders, while the protocols of appropriately deferent and "proper" conduct were built into the culture of etiquette practiced by the "respectable" classes. There were also work ethics; religious ethics; temperance and moral uprightness ethics; the peculiarly English obsession with earnestness, seriousness, respectability, rational recreation, and so on—all these values with a disciplinary regimen embedded within them.

As for the lower social classes, most of them knew their "place" in society, so when they were catered for at all by the English railroad companies in the early period they probably expected to be treated like livestock or cotton bales, as they often were. Hence, their experience of railroad discipline was qualitatively different to that of the middle-

and upper classes of society, as we shall see in due course; nevertheless, there were some aspects of railroad discipline which all English railroad travelers were subject to.

Indeed, both the railroad company's timetables and its regulations eventually extended the notion of "iron" from the technology to the English passenger traveling experience. And, as already indicated, this new disciplinary regime was not accepted or embraced uncritically by all. Nevertheless, English travelers very quickly adjusted to the disciplinary imperatives of the railroad companies. In fact, not only was the English railroad passenger able to easily accommodate to the "exigencies" of railroad discipline eventually—which is not to say that it did not *initially* occasion some vociferous complaint, as we shall see in the next chapter—but many English travelers eventually came to associate this discipline with safety and security of travel. Hence, when they went abroad, to America, for instance, they could initially be quite perturbed by the relative absence of the various manifestations of railroad discipline ("coddling") they had become used to at "home." Indeed, one English tourist (in 1864) was disarmed by the fact that "When you enter a station (in America) you see no porters from whom to make an inquiry, nor is there any person whose business it is to find you a seat.... No one whose duty it is to prevent you from breaking your neck by getting in when the train is in motion."[23] Clearly this gentleman had become accustomed to being "coddled" at English railroad stations. Another English traveler, writing around 1880, noted: "A very free and easy style prevails on the American train. People stand outside on the platform (between the cars while the train is in motion), walk from one car to another while the train is in motion, (and) consult their individual inclinations in every way."[24]

Indeed, the English bourgeois or aristocratic railroad traveler would have been astounded to discover on the Kansas Pacific Railroad that enginemen would stop their trains in the middle of "nowhere" so that passengers could take "pot-shots" at buffalo from car windows. And they would have been shocked to see "passengers" riding on the cow-catcher so that they might take pot-shots at anything they thought merited a bullet.[25] The Englishman, Foster Zincke, traveling in America in the mid–1860s, was surprised that his train made unscheduled stops in the wilderness to pick up people, or even just to take up a parcel or a letter. On another occasion, he asked a conductor when the next scheduled refreshment stop was. He was informed that no such stop was scheduled in the short term: "(But) I will at 11 o'clock stop the train at a house in the forest where I sometimes have supper myself." In due course, the train was stopped at the house, just Mr. Zincke and the conductor taking a twenty-minute repast while all the other passengers waited patiently for them![26]

Some English tourists had arrived in America with a certain degree of anxiety where the prospect of railroad travel was concerned, having read about the alleged reckless speed and a willful disregard of all rules and regulations on the American railroads. The American enginemen often allowed people to ride on the locomotive, especially in the West, where discipline seems to have been relatively lax and often unenforceable so long as the conductor was complicit. But the practice of allowing people to ride on the footplate was not uncommon in England up until mid-century, either,[27] although the "privilege" was probably restricted to prominent people and those connected to railroad company management—I.K. Brunel, for instance, was known to frequently take people with him on the footplate, until the Great Western Railway Company became less flippant concerning who might have access to the locomotives, as well as seeing a need to restrict the "irregular" movements of locomotives. Indeed, reflecting upon the early days of railroad travel in England Acworth (1890) recalled: "Fifty years ago, a place on the foot-plate of an engine was looked upon much like the box seat of a stage coach. A well-known passenger could have it for the asking, and half-a-crown might secure it for a stranger."[28] But that was before railroad companies in England universally adopted disciplinary regimes which would have forbidden such practices.

Railroad safety remained a critical issue for decades in England. The companies were usually very slow to adopt new safety technologies or other safety measures. Consequently, they were subject constantly to public, media, and state inspectorate criticism in those respects for almost half a century. Writing in 1842 Sydney Smith contended that most English railroad companies were quite flippant on the matter of safety. He suggested the situation would change only after somebody of "rank" had been killed: "The first such person to perish will produce unspeakable benefit to the public." Viewed in historical context, this was quite an extraordinary statement from a prominent and highly respected gentleman, thus indicating there was a problem and that negligence was part of it. In fact, it seems that for decades English railroad companies tried to effect passenger safety, and safety more generally, largely by means of discipline—of both railroad servants and passengers.

The lines of some English railroad companies—as in America, as we shall see—had reputations for being notoriously unsafe. In England that was certainly so in respect of the Eastern Counties in the mid–1840s, regardless of whether the company was negligent or just "unlucky" with a run of accidents. And one might have thought Churton a major shareholder in the company (perhaps he was!) judging by the extent to which he went in "to bat" for it in his 1851 railroad guide. There, he suggests that, due to "some early casualties," a "most discreditable notoriety," which "engendered a sort of mania among the traveling public for exaggerating every trivial irregularity into a most formidable and momentous occurrence," had accrued to the company.[29] Well, what can one say but that the bridge from notoriety to legend is not a long one to cross, and that "mud" does stick?

In Britain from 1846 passengers could gain financial compensation for pecuniary loss and suffering arising from railroad accidents. But it seems that had little impact on the railroad companies, since state inspectors (of English railroads) continued to identify serious safety issues, while the companies continued to plead poverty, or to appeal to "superior" knowledge and authority when it came to the question of putting recommended new or proven safety devices and protocols in place.

Another issue bearing upon matters of safety and discipline was the practice, in the early period, of locking first- and second-class passengers in their compartments—the compartment will be discussed at length in the next chapter. But clearly this policy could have tragic consequences in the event of a serious accident or fire. From the mid–1840s English state officials were advising companies that it was imprudent to lock people in compartments, but the practice continued for quite some time and figured as an aggravating factor in subsequent accidents.[30]

All 19th century English railroad companies were empowered to fine passengers for a range of offences, as well as their policemen having powers of arrest in some circumstances. One company fined somebody 20 shillings for smoking a cigar in a railroad carriage. And people traveling in a (higher) passenger class than they had paid for were also fined—as much as forty shillings on the London and Birmingham in 1839. Furthermore, some Scottish companies claimed the right to be able to fine passengers for swearing at railroad servants or at other passengers. But despite the punitive sanctions passengers still tried to beat some of the regulations. For instance, railroad company officials were always on the lookout for "smuggled" lap dogs, which most companies charged a minimum of 10 shillings to transport and probably would not have permitted in passenger compartments[31]—257,474 dogs (and 267,249 horses) made (legitimate) railroad journeys in the UK in 1861.[32]

The point of this diversion on safety and discipline has been to draw attention to the fact that the early English railroad companies had some unique traffic engineering problems to deal with, that safety issues were integral to both their conceptualization and attempted resolution in the early period, and that discipline of the passenger was *the first recourse* for resolving such perplexities.

As passenger traffic increased and intensified it became necessary to find some more efficient means of ticketing other than having countless clerks doing it manually. There needed to be a ticketing system which could keep pace with the exponential development of passenger traffic on the one hand, and which conduced to effective surveillance of the passenger's movements on the other. Enter Edmondson's ticketing machine—Edmondson was assisted by a watchmaker in developing his machine.

This technology did not simply speed up the issuing of tickets. It also (because of the information on the ticket when issued) enabled enhanced surveillance of some aspects of passenger travel—because passenger classes could be matched to ticket colors that enabled *easy* detection of people trying to travel in a class other than that they had paid for, while serial numbering made for even closer surveillance in respect of each passenger journey. But serial numbering and color coding of tickets not only assisted attempts to discover deception on the part of passengers, they also enabled checks on the honesty of ticketing and other clerks.

We tend to take for granted, in this age of computerization, the extent to which its multifarious applications effectively check the honesty of employees in all kinds of situations, apart from its broader applications in the causes of surveillance, security, the profiling of consumers, and other aspects of market research and data gathering. However, when all cashiering and accounting was done manually—and because of the scale of it in some enterprises—it often took a long time to detect cases of fraud or theft. Furthermore, to be able to pinpoint exactly where in the system such frauds or thefts were occurring and then prove, without doubt, who was responsible was a formidable task. Indeed, to be able to do all of that in the absence of modern forensics and auditing techniques was obviously very difficult.

In the early days of his London omnibus service (in the 1820s) Shillibeer discovered that his conductors were robbing him of at least £20 a week. To solve this problem, he spent £300 on a machine which could be fitted to the steps of an omnibus to record the number of passengers (treading on a plate entering and leaving the vehicle). After a two-week trial, the machine on the trial bus was smashed by "persons unknown" (but undoubtedly disgruntled conductors) with sledge-hammers—so it was back to the "drawing-board" for Mr. Shillibeer.[33]

Dee Brown contends that in America there was a time when people quite commonly jumped on the train at the last minute without a ticket so they could negotiate a fare with the conductor, who usually pocketed it.[34] Several years after the Civil War a number of leading American railroad companies undertook a secret investigation, which disclosed that about *two-thirds* of all cash fares paid on their trains was "ripped off" by conductors, some of whom pocketed up to $75 on a single trip.[35] From 1869 the Union Pacific was aware that its conductors were syphoning off a lot of money through taking kickbacks, giving unauthorized discounts, and giving free passes away "willy-nilly."[36] On the other hand, sometimes American railroad company policy (unwittingly) abetted conductors (and ticket agents) to swindle *the public*, as the following indicates:

> Applicants for tickets are expected to offer the exact amount of the fare, and it has been legally decided that agents and conductors are not bound to make the change; and anybody demanding change may be expelled using "due force," as though payment of the fare had been refused.[37]

Hoyt contends that conductors were very important people in America until Cornelius Vanderbilt cut them down to size. In fact, it was Vanderbilt who "spoilt the party" for many conductors by introducing the concept of selling tickets only on the platform rather than allowing conductors to do it on the train. In that connection, Vanderbilt had noticed that some of his conductors were doing extraordinarily well for themselves, notably a Mr. Phipps, who had somehow come to own 25 houses in Rochester, 15 in Syracuse, and 5 in New York City (a property portfolio worth about $300,000). Vanderbilt had Mr. Phipps summoned to his office where he enquired of him how it came to pass that a conductor on $1,000 a year owned so much real estate. Phipps admitted his "indiscretions" with the "odd" passenger fare. But he quite rightly pointed out that what he had filched was a drop in the ocean compared to Vanderbilt's own stock-watering rackets and, being a reasonable man, Phipps offered to hand over $300 and "call it square."[38]

Rational ticketing systems also allowed for a better system of reservations—of compartments and seats. However, in Britain the railroads by no means instituted the "reserved seat." This facility had been available for centuries where stage-coaching was concerned, but it was evident in other institutions as early as the 17th century: "By 1662 Bowman had a named pew in the church; he sat at pew 21, while his wife, sitting with the women, had number 17."[39] Indeed, even well into the 19th century church pews could be leased or purchased in both England and America much as a modern apartment in a block can be. And as Keith Thomas points out, English parish church pews had a "deep symbolic importance, since they represented a highly visible, public ranking of an individual's worth and standing." But at that time (the 17th century) there were probably other institutions where "reservations" were accepted. However, this was apparently not true of the coffee house which, in the mid–17th century, was quite a new social institution, not the least because *no seat could be reserved, and no man might refuse your company in the coffee house.*[40]

Where the early English railroads were concerned, the reserved compartment and seat facility was not solely a means of more rationally organizing and accommodating passenger traffic. It was also part of the "culture" of rationalizing multiple *social class* distinctions into just two or three *passenger class* distinctions during railroad travel;

each class characterized partly by certain "privileges" or an absence of them—for many decades third-class passengers could not reserve seats, although for many years some English companies did not even provide seats for third-class passengers, obliging them to stand for the duration of their journeys. But the reserved seat facility was also integral to the culture of administrative discipline of the passenger—it facilitated orderly seating arrangements.

To this point, then, we have looked at some of the administrative and operational problems which confronted the early English railroad companies; notwithstanding that many of the same problems confronted the American railroad companies, but were—as we shall see in due course—responded to differently by them.

The English railroad companies considerably enhanced personal mobility, but that gave rise to problems pertaining to the mass transportation of people. Hence, in Britain the "engineering" of passenger travel, and of pedestrian traffic through railroad production systems, engendered railroad administrative and operational regimes *characterized by an emphasis on discipline and surveillance of the passenger*, but essentially with the safety and security of the passenger in mind. And this was to be typical of railroad travel on the Continent as well, as against the more "relaxed" style of railroad administration and operations which emerged in America at the same time.

But apart from the safety and security of the English railroad passenger being a foremost rationale for the *national style* of railroad administration and operation which emerged in England, two other very important factors shaped the form of 19th century English railroad passenger traveling experience. One was the "character," if you like, of English middle- and upper-class people, the other (not unrelated, of course) the English social class structure. So, let us now consider the English "character" in the 19th century, and relate it to the (stratified) forms by means of which the 19th century English railroad companies tended to commodify railroad passenger travel; before moving on to look, in the same connection, at the English social class structure in the 19th century.

Peculiarities of the English "Character" in the 19th Century

Towards the end of her travel log (1887), recounting her travels in America, well-to-do Englishwoman, Catherine Bates, impugned the English character in terms which her upper-class English contemporaries must have found truly chilling. She conceded that: "England is eminently a country of insular prejudice, ignorant obstinacy of opinion, and a dogmatic conventionality." She went on to suggest: "The English think of foreigners as a very poor imitation of the real thing. We have a general monopoly, including, as some foreign cynic observes, the shortest and most direct route to the Kingdom of Heaven." However, she thought these impaired qualities of the English redeemable to a point, since: "No doubt this quality of mind, rotten and intolerant in itself, lies at the bottom of the dogged determination and almost brutal strength of the English character." Was she finished? No. She continued: "We may sneer at political corruption in America, but are we ourselves so absolutely immaculate in this line? We may call their liberty "license"; but they may fairly retaliate that a good deal of English prudery hides a considerable amount of English hypocrisy." As an afterthought, a few pages later, she disclosed her most admirable maxim: "Speak boldly and honestly, or do not speak at all."[41] However, there was much more to this "rotten and intolerant" quality of mind than Bates accounts for here—Bates is not rated among the Victorian social psychologists or sociologists, but probably ought to be!

Understanding the predominant English values and virtues—especially those of the English upper-classes—pertaining to the era in question may considerably assist our understanding of several things: why, in contrast to America, a conspicuous passenger class system became seemingly indispensable on English railroads; why the English upper-classes had a preference for compartmentalized carriages; and why the early English railroad passengers put up with relatively severe, over-arching railroad company administrative and disciplinary regimes, bordering on the "carceral," for decades.

We might begin such reflection by alluding to the key virtues of Protestant morality, which really constituted the "hub" of what came to be known as the "staidness" of the Victorian English; and especially so when it had a self-righteous "Puritanism" grafted onto it (more typical of the middle than upper-classes, it must be said), which added another layer—of Stoicism—to the staidness. This "puritanical" quality of mind was itself stratified, the middling classes under its sway often referred to as "evangelicals," while Methodism was the (transmogrified) version of it most compellingly inflicted on the lower social classes.

One source has described "Victorian piety" (obviously, the middle-class version) as the piety of "the comfortable, the easy-going (and) the unworried"; a piety "which was placed on the piano and dusted every morning by the servants," and "which wrapped up its ideas in mufflers of soft, warm, cozy words like "little" and "meek," and, softest and most favored of all, "lowly."[42]

But the religiously inspired values accounted for here had possessed a dynamism of their own. Indeed, earlier they had become largely divorced from their religious roots and acquired a (secular) "sanctity" of their own, the ether arising from which came to permeate "respectable society" in the Victorian era.[43] Indeed, four such key "offshoots" of the "ascetic" Victorian "character" were civility, respectability, seriousness, and rationality. But politeness and refinement were also important qualities in the same connection.

- **Civility** incorporated: knowledge of what good manners were and when to demonstrate them appropriately; being approachable, agreeable, affable, obliging, and reasonable, but not imposingly or patronizingly so, especially in inappropriate social contexts; and generally demonstrating a public persona which accorded with the general expectation of what being a "gentleman" or a "lady" required—Hibbert suggests that in 1824 a man earning £150 a year was entitled to call himself a gentleman,[44] although his conduct would have had to be consistent with that expected of a gentleman.
- **Respectability**[45] entailed: sobriety; thrift; good manners; a concern for dress and other aspects of the publicly projected self-image; respect for the law; and chastity, honesty, and uprightness in business affairs. As Altick points out, even somebody from a lower station in life could effect some upward

mobility, perhaps even to be considered part of an elevated "in-group" so long as he was "respectable." Respectable people also usually maintained a "barbed-wire" fence around themselves called "privacy," which could only be relaxed or retracted, or penetrated by others, in accordance with strictly defined social situations and circumstances. However, many of the above (respectability) values were common to both aristocratic "class culture" and the "culture" of "upwardly-mobile" bourgeois types.

- The **serious** person was, in addition to all or most of the above, puritanically opposed to vanities and frivolities, largely devoid of humor, and intolerant of others" inanities, indulgences, and frivolities.[46] Moreover, "serious" people almost invariably had "serious" pursuits and interests, and their chosen forms of recreation were ostensibly entirely "rational."
- The **rational** person embraced most if not all the values identified above with the "respectable" and the "serious" person. But he was also extremely self-disciplined and often earnestly engaged in self-improvement of one form or another. Furthermore, not uncommonly he wished to impose his value system more generally—to bring the lower social classes within its orbit and under its yoke, thus subjecting them to its peculiar disciplinary regime, with the noble aim of making them more "rational" and, ideally, as rational as he was!

According to one source, the unique feature of Victorian society was that middle-class patterns of behavior were grafted onto the honorific code of the aristocracy or gentry to produce the broader concept of "gentility"; which was, by this view, one of the most effective instruments of social control ever devised.[47]

But there were other clearly signposted lines of demarcation in Victorian society, such as that between men and women, and the number of "strands of barbed wire" used to separate the sexes usually increased the farther up the social scale one went. These divisions were predicated not just upon a gendered division of labor and associated ascribed social and domestic roles, but extended way beyond both. Indeed, the period 1850–80 has been described as:

> An age when women were still given to blushing, swooning, profound and graceful curtsies, wrote a slanted hand—delicate penmanship to distinguish them from men (they crossed and re-crossed their letters, and were greatly addicted to postscripts)—and their attire was less rational (crinolines, bustles, chignons, and other absurdities).[48]

All the qualities and characteristics sketched above collectively constituted *some of the values* which were embedded in the psyches of the people the early railroad companies *desired to attract* to their railroads as (first- and second-class) passengers. And it is with this knowledge in mind that we begin to negotiate the peculiarities which came to govern English railroad company provision of passenger accommodation—at least for people of the middle and upper *social classes* in Victorian society. And foreigners certainly found the English very strange people in some respects, not the least concerning the latter's "rigidity" and "frigidity." Heine, for instance, said of the English: "The English blockheads—God forgive them! I often regard them not at all as my fellow beings, but as miserable automata—machines whose motive power is egotism."[49]

The English and Their Fetish for Privacy

As a preliminary to looking much more analytically at 19th century English railroad passenger traveling experience in the next chapter, and further to what has already been said about the English character in the 19th century, perhaps something ought to be said about the English upper-class obsession with privacy; and especially so concerning the tendency of such people to often prefer social "*dis*-engagement" beyond certain circumscribed social contexts and situations. And this is important, not the least because it enables us to *begin to understand* why the English upper-classes preferred to travel in compartments.

The English upper-classes valued privacy immensely. They were opposed to the introduction of Peel's police force in 1829—even though they might be thought the classes most likely to benefit from its existence—because it would undermine the privacy and liberty of the individual.[50] And the English upper-class fetishism for privacy sometimes did reach "psycho-pathological" heights. The fifth Duke of Portland, for instance, not only traveled in his own carriage on a railroad flat wagon (not unusual at the time); but he was, apparently, so very coy about being seen on his way to the station that he traveled along a 1.5-mile-long tunnel from his home to where he caught the train at Worksop.[51]

One Englishman who had "gone native" in America noted that the Englishman is shy and private. And that he builds a high wall around his house and garden to keep out the eyes of the public, whereas the American builds a fine house and lays out a handsome garden that others may see and enjoy them. However, that had not always been the case in America. In colonial times gardens were often able to be "privatized" because of landscape features on a private property or the use of trees and other flora to shelter and thus hide gardens: "Salem gardens had always been kept out of sight, enclosed with hedges, high fences, and tree lines and out-buildings, rather than being open to gratify passers-by. Instead, the best of them afforded a private park for their private enjoyment."[52] However, republicanism and notions of democracy may have brought about a change where the accessibility of private gardens was concerned.

However, the *English obsession with privacy even had sartorial manifestations*. Perhaps that was epitomized in the ladies' "poke bonnet," which first appeared in 1804 and was described by one English publication at the time as "repulsive"—it became known pejoratively as a "coal-scuttle bonnet." However, similar bonnets had been known much earlier in colonial America (New England). By 1830 the English poke bonnet had so increased in size that no part of the head could be seen at all apart from the face, which could only be seen if the viewer was standing immediately in front of the lady wearing it. We know this had more to do with the quest for privacy than simply seeking anonymity when out, since women (especially of the upper-classes) were easily recognizable to their acquaintances by their carriages, clothing, gait, or accompanying servants or children. But when used as a "hiding place" the poke bonnet certainly exemplified its effectiveness as a "technology of privacy." In America Harriet Tubman put it to good use for the disguise of slaves escaping along the Underground Railroad,[53] although the American colonial "prototype" had served the same function for women, since it allowed them to nod off in church, *usually* unseen: "Mr. Whiting doth pleasantlie say from ye pulpit hee doth seeme to be preaching to stacks of straw with men among them."[54]

In the private realm of the Englishman's "castle" well-to-do and aristocratic people felt able to cast off the mask of strict self-control otherwise required by the protocols of civility and good manners in public. Indeed, it was only in the private domain that people could reveal their "true" selves. And this is one reason why servants invariably answered the door and calling cards were left or sent—people did not like to be "caught short" where the protocols of personal presentation and social interaction were concerned.

But to turn now to railroad travel, and to align the Englishman's quest for privacy with his preference for railroad carriage *compartment* accommodation, the reality was that it was unrealistic for privacy-obsessed, upper-class English people to be allocated a railroad carriage each to safeguard their privacy; but the compartment was the next best thing, and not a bad compromise. And even in the compartment absolute privacy was still possible for the "artful," since would-be compartment "invaders" could be deterred by purchasing all the seats in the compartment; giving the impression you had some highly contagious disease—such as influenza—or by having a coughing fit; glowering at the intruders; otherwise being objectionable or disagreeable; telling the would-be invader that your wife and children are "just coming" and, therefore, that the entire compartment is taken; spreading baggage all over the seats to give the same impression; or bribing a railroad official to ensure that there were no intruders—during her sojourn in England Nathaniel Hawthorne's wife, Sophie, very quickly mastered the art of driving would-be "room-mates" out of *her* railroad compartments.

We shall, in due course, consider—in a much more analytical way—some of the reasons English middle- and upper-class people preferred to travel in railroad carriage compartments rather than in "public" carriages, as their American counterparts almost invariably did and without feeling "hard done by." And this peculiarity—of the English railroad passenger—was by no means simply reducible to "snobbery,"[55] as made apparent above. But, rather, as Alexis de Tocqueville pointed out in the 1830s, "the whole of English society still runs on aristocratic lines"[56]—although "snobbery" and claims to "status honor" may overlap, they are by no means the same thing.

However, "snobbery" and "reputation" were, nevertheless, *sometimes* significant factors where the upper-class experience of early railroad traveling in England was concerned. The experience of Augustus Hare and his family highlight both. Hare, described by one commentator as an "acidulated snob whose snobberies grew with the years," traveled often with his mother. Initially, his mother had refused to travel by rail at all, before condescending to travel in her own carriage lashed onto a flat wagon before, finally, being coaxed into a carriage compartment. However, when traveling to London Hare's mother ensured that they were always set down on its outskirts, since *she did not want to be known to have entered London on the railroad*. And this was not at all uncommon for people of her social class at the time. In fact, this practice was known, in those early days of English railroading, as entering the metropolis "by land" (as if the rails somehow disconnected the train and the passenger from the planet)—surely only the upper-class English could have invoked such a ridiculous notion?

Given these psychological propensities, it should not really surprise to find such people wishing to be run about the country in isolated little boxes called compartments and commonly very aloof of those they had to share them with. Indeed, an American writer (in 1863) advised American tourists in England to use third-class (open) carriages, since there was, he thought (but I think he just "got lucky," as will become evident in the next chapter), no difference in comfort between second- and third-class carriages. And, furthermore, he found third-class passengers "unpretentious, talkative and friendly," whereas first- and second-class passengers tended to be "obnoxious," or "insolent and encroaching."

Railroad Guidebooks and Railroad Etiquette

In Victorian Britain people of the middling and upper-classes fetishized traits, rituals, behaviors, and dress that people of their social class were expected to display appropriately. These outward symbolic representations of the social class dimension to their sense of identity were intended to enable other people to identify them as being, if not members of the same social class, at least not inferiors. But the knowledge of class symbolism and how to display it appropriately was not "innate." It had to be learned. To some considerable extent that type of knowledge was inherent to the socialization process for the social classes concerned. But it was often problematical in instances of upward social mobility, when aspirants to a new social status had not been socialized so—this was no less so in America after mid-century, where the newly rich parvenu had trouble penetrating the insular, long-established (upper) social class barriers in some American cities (in America by the 1870s "intermarriage" had apparently confused the boundaries between the "Old Guard" and the "New Class").[57]

In England, social class "filters" regulated the flow "upwards" of people. They were permeable enough to allow a select few to move up to the highest echelons of society, but not so permeable that the flood gates were opened. Entrance to "higher" strata could be enabled because an individual had established such renown for himself that the privilege of being admitted to "society" could be extended to him. But, just as often, it was a case of aristocratic families having to marry a daughter or son "down"—marrying into "new money," sometimes out of financial necessity and, thereby, socially elevating the "incumbent." But whatever the case, the newly-elevated person still needed to learn the appropriate behavioral codes, their demonstration of which confirmed their eligibility to participate in "high society."

That is one of the reasons why etiquette books emerged and became popular in the 18th and 19th centuries—etiquette books served to objectify and formalize what had previously been knowledge peculiar to the socialization processes of very exclusive social strata. Indeed, the emergence and proliferation of such books was sure testimony to the dynamic (new) phenomenon of "upward (social) mobility" and the culture of "gentility" associated with it, and that was so even in parts of America.

With the advent of railroad travel in England, the middling and upper classes had to accommodate their social class peculiarities and ritualized behaviors to the railroad passenger experience, whereby social class distinctions were rationalized by being compressed into just two or three passenger classes. On the other hand, the railroad presented passengers of the middle and upper classes with novel amenities and experiences for which often there were no established social class protocols. Consequently, "correct" etiquette had to be developed to deal with the perplexities arising from these new situations, but without such new "devices" seriously undermining the prevailing social class distinctions. Surtees, for instance, published a *Hints to Railway Travelers and Country Visitors to London*, full of instructional details concerning such information as how to hold your ticket and other indispensable strategic knowledge one ought to be aware of when traveling by rail.[58] But Surtees was far from being the first to write an etiquette book for the railroad traveler; apart from which the railroad passenger *guidebooks*, which proliferated from the 1840s, also often afforded the railroad passenger much advice concerning railroad traveling *etiquette*. Furthermore, popular journals, such as the *Penny Magazine* and the *Athenaeum*, often published itineraries for day excursionists. And, indirectly, though directly as well occasionally, they shaped passenger behavior (etiquette, if you like), if only by drawing the excursionists" attention to "wholesome" and "improving" sights and experiences, rather than informing as to which were the best "watering holes" and "bawdy places."

In America, with the advent of the first transcontinental railroad in 1869, there followed a proliferation of railroad guidebooks, many of which were, at least in part, didactic in an etiquette sense. Indeed, there seems to have developed a culture of "correct" passenger behavior, strictly speaking, although this seems to have occurred only after a burgeoning, affluent social class had emerged, and Pullman services had become well-established (from the early-1870s). Indeed, during that era American advisers on railroad manners proffered advice to the well-to-do traveler concerning: what kind of clothing to wear, what types of cosmetics ladies should use, how to direct the Pullman porter, and how to behave appropriately at a dining-carriage table.

Some of this advice, apart from the etiquette dimension to it, was quite practical; and especially so for tourists who had never dined or slept on a train before, did not know how to "dress" for breakfast and dinner on a train, had never encountered a maid in the form of a black man (Pullman porter), did not know whether to tip railroad servants, and so on. And this kind of literature (incorporating etiquette, strictly speaking) was still around in America in the 1920s:

> A man may, if he chooses, make acquaintances on a journey, and a woman also, though with less frequency and freedom.... As a usual thing, it is best for a young girl traveling alone to avoid all communication with strangers, as she cannot know into what complications it might lead her.[59]

However, Americans were never as "transfixed" by the demands of etiquette as the English middle and upper classes, as one would expect to be the case in a society where individualism (one should not confuse or conflate the concepts of "individualism" and "privacy") was a so much more prominent value in society.[60]

Indeed, if 19th century English society was one in which social classes were conspicuously divided; yet, the more exclusive social classes towards the top of the "ladder" were very homogeneous, nevertheless. In fact, European revolutionaries of the 19th century, who pinned their hopes on the raising of *working class consciousness*, may well have envied the relatively cultivated consciousness of the adversary (classes) and, in most cases, they probably greatly underestimated it—as indicated by Marx's rather simplistic concept of class "polarization," whereby the (ideological) "walls" between the middle and working classes, for instance, were assumed to be paper thin.

But where individualism is concerned, it is not as if this driving value was absent in 19th century *English* society, either. It was simply more constrained than it was in American society; and this was due, at least in part, to the fact that the homogeneity of the English middle and upper social classes, along with a certain coherency which aligned them in important respects, constrained individualism to a point. Which is to say that in 19th century English society individualism, taken beyond a certain point, could appear "unseemly" and inconsistent with prevailing notions of "respectability"— especially when linked to "money-making." Indeed, that was why, in England, the possession (by "self-made" men of the middle classes) of immense wealth could be as much a barrier to penetrating the highest echelons of society as it was an "entry ticket."

But let us focus upon the "guidebook" for the moment. The guidebook has a long and interesting genealogy. It was known in the ancient world where, often, it was to be found in the form of an official document—sometimes even a "classified" document intended for restricted circulation.[61] In the Medieval period the guidebook became even more common, especially in connection with pilgrimages to local shrines and reliquaries, or to the Holy Land. But, later, during the Renaissance, there also developed more secular versions of it—providing strategic information for merchants, as well as incorporating travel itineraries for the leisured classes.

The guidebook, in its strictly secular orientation, became even more prolific in the 18th century as the "Grand Tour" became institutionalized as part of the socialization and "education" of young gentlemen, an escape for bored aristocratic ladies, or "therapy" for those needing to travel for health reasons. But the guidebook was often a "supplement" to a human guide; the former usually providing interesting facts, both historical and geographical, about the (foreign) places traveled to, while the human guide was more useful for practical, everyday things—such as where to sleep, eat, hire horses or carriages, present letters of credit, cross borders, and so on.

By the 18th century, English travelers had, apparently, become very reliant on guidebooks; although we should expect a people, whose upper-classes were as subject to codes of etiquette as the aristocratic English were, to be remarkably lacking any degree of initiative and self-sufficiency, and thus to need guidebooks in "strange" situations. Indeed, in the mid–19th century Karl Marx's "left-hand" man, Engels, remarked upon this peculiar trait of the English; noting that "John Bull," the Englishman, stayed in his steamboat cabin from Rotterdam to Cologne, and only emerged to satisfy what aesthetic sensibility he allegedly had as and when his guidebook compelled him so to do.[62]

But it was not entirely a question of lack of initiative or any sense of adventure which confined the English traveler to the dictates of his guidebook. Good maps were not as freely available as they are today, and road signage was often lacking, too; and once off the main roads local knowledge needed to be tapped into—notwithstanding that local people encountered during travel in 18th and 19th century Britain were often clueless concerning how to get to where one wanted to go. Furthermore, in Britain before the mid–19th century travel agents, who might have provided a detailed itinerary along with maps and precise "navigational" instructions, were rare.

Nevertheless, in the 19th century English road travelers could have recourse to one of a range of "Road Books," the best-known of which were *Paterson's Roads* and *Cary's Traveler's Companion*. The first edition of Paterson's appeared in 1785 and the work ran through 18 editions 1785–1832. These books must certainly have been in demand, since Bovill (1959) remarked upon how easy it still was, even then, to obtain one of the old editions "at almost any second-hand bookshop."

Such guidebooks provided fairly detailed itineraries of all the roads served by the mail and "ordinary" stage-coaches; and they also identified toll gates, bridges, waterways to be traversed, prominent country houses and the names of their owners, and other useful information—including where your coach started from, where you might leave it to reach your destination, how to reach any town or village in the countryside having alighted from the coach, and the location of posting-houses from which horses or a chaise could be hired.[63]

Henry Cole, who among other things, was one of the organizers of the Great Exhibition of 1851, has been described by a biographer as a "personal railway maniac." This "mania" apparently induced him to write several railroad guides.[64] One of them, the *Railway Traveler's Chest*, was a cunningly contrived pamphlet which, when unfolded, revealed a sort of map of where the railroad ran down the center of the page with items of interest graphically represented on it[65]—a form of map which is quite common these days. And, as the railroad guide developed, it became quite different to the road guides of former times. After all, the railroad passenger followed a fixed, immutable trajectory during a journey, and all stops were programmed in advance, with no chance of stopping the train to take in this sight or that before continuing the journey. So, what use was a railroad *guide* if everything was predetermined?

As we have seen already, railroad guide books could offer some advice about passenger "etiquette." But they also routinely offered up descriptions of scenery along the way, pointed out prominent landmarks, and drew attention to engineering and other features of the railroad itself. In fact, by mid-century English railroad guidebooks were, arguably, the exemplars of a "technologically-induced ecstasy" genre at the time. They were often full of descriptions of the "heroic" achievements of railroad engineers, who had mastered every obstacle nature had placed before them in constructing the railroad in question. Perhaps Churton's guides, better than any other, exemplify this phenomenon—with their metaphorical and hyperbolic excesses, and mind-boggling statistics (such as how many million bricks *exactly* were used in the construction of this or that tunnel, or *exactly* how many tons of iron were used in the construction of this bridge or that viaduct). In fact, describing the engineering of the railroad itself became a feature of some of these guidebooks—effectively, such descriptions were advertisements for the railroad. And, in that regard, we might consider such books as one of the precursors of one of television's most loathed advertising techniques—the "infomercial."

After mid-century, English railroad guidebooks almost invariably offered advice to the passenger concerning what was appropriate conduct (etiquette, in effect) during a railroad journey. This dimension to such books was usually unabashedly didactic. *The Railway Traveler's Handbook* (1862), for instance, very much tended towards being a railroad traveler's etiquette book. It was divided into three parts—before the journey, on the journey, and after the journey. And a reviewer of the book suggested that those not "au fait" with the "ins and outs" of railroad travel might derive "a good many useful hints from the work." The work offered such salutary advice to the railroad traveler as the following: although you may have conversed as freely with a person (on the train) as though you had known him twenty years, you would not be justified in accosting him in the street subsequently; "up" signifies towards London or any other large city or terminus, "down" from such places—it was added that these words are so familiar to railway officials that even when a person is asking information respecting the trains these technicalities *must* be resorted to, if he desires to make himself intelligible. The work also made it apparent just how confusing railroad travel could be for people unaccustomed to it, by noting of such people: "If they alight at a station on one side of the line, they cannot understand why, when departing from the station, they have to cross to the other side."[66]

The guidebook also took off in America. And there, too, guidebooks were often full of inflated accounts of the engineering of the railroad itself. *Harper's Guidebook* (1855), for instance, said of the New York and Erie: "It crosses mountains deemed impossible; it goes over valleys which timid men said it would cost millions to fill in; it leaps valleys where bold engineers paused, shook their heads, and turned back." But this was no different to what the English guidebooks were full of at the time. And, as already alluded to, in America the opening of the first so-called transcontinental railroad—which started in the Midwest—afforded huge opportunities for guidebook writers and publishers. Indeed, within a few weeks of its opening there was a proliferation of guidebooks for travelers on it—George Crofutt claimed to have sold half a million copies of his *Great Transcontinental Railroad Guide* during the 1870s. However, in America what could be seen from the train often did not correspond with what the guidebooks stated could be. One traveler recorded that he could not see any of the landmarks allegedly visible from the train, concluding they must have been "discerned in a vision" by the guidebook authors, while a bridge, which was supposed to be the "grandest feature of the railroad," our cynical traveler found to be "rickety."

Dee Brown, who evidently studied quite a few of these American railroad guidebooks (as, indeed, I have), found them to be characterized generally (like their English counterparts) by a "melodramatic" quality and thought most of them comparable in style to the "dime novels" of the period. He also noted that many (ostensibly autobiographical) travel narratives of the late 19th century were often inaccurate because some of their content had been uncritically "uplifted" from railroad guidebooks. Indeed, Brown draws our attention to the fact that Walt Whitman wove numerous guidebook phrases into his *Passage to India*![67]

However, I found that some of the American guidebooks written in the 1870s through the 1890s were of a very high caliber, and no doubt very useful to the tourist in the West (some of those published by the railroad companies themselves, or penned by their agents, were among the very best). That said, many of the rest did not differ very much one from another, and there seemed to be a lot of plagiarism—which extended beyond content to the formatting (structure and style) of the text.

Railroad Traveling and the Concept of "Status Space"

Let us move on to look a little more analytically at the phenomenon of the English railroad passenger in the 19th century, having considered earlier his affinity with and preference for structure and discipline.

Social psychologists talk about the concept of "personal space," whereby discomfiture arises if this space—immediately surrounding the body, but not necessarily of the same dimensions in all cultural contexts—is trespassed upon, *regardless of the social standing* of the individuals concerned. But it is my contention we might also talk about *status space*—a similar concept, except that it is *sociocultural distinctions and conventions* which determine the boundaries of individual space. In fact, the concept of "etiquette" may be closely tied to the concept of "status space." And what may be denoted by the concept of "status space" could extend from one person's right or privilege to occupy a space to the exclusion of others, or even to the exclusion (from designated spaces) of entire communities by one section of the population.

But whatever the extent of the "status space" under consideration, it may become powerfully institutionalized and symbolic of broader power asymmetries within society. However, the processes of monopoly and exclusion concerned may be complex and subtle, and extend across a wide range of social situations. These processes of monopoly and exclusion may be enforced by law or simply by constraints in the form of social norms, protocols, or etiquette.

On the other hand, the *inclusive* character of "status spaces" may itself invite constraints in the form of sanctions. For instance, London University was refused a Royal Charter in 1827 because it *admitted* Catholics, Jews, and other non–Anglicans. A similar example relates to the apparent "denominational" circumscription of railroad traveling space by the directors of the Enniskillen and Londonderry Railway in Ireland in October 1849—the directors refused to provide a special excursion train because it was in relation to a *Catholic* religious ceremony.[68]

And let us, for a moment, use religion as a vehicle for further exploring the notion of "status space" as a prelude to its application to 19th century railroad passenger travel. In the late 16th century some English churches had benches marked "For the Poor" while the wealthy had private pews which were often numbered and for which they paid an annual rent to occupy—Jeremy Bentham, writing in 1817, thought the Anglican Church not really interested in admitting the poor to communion unless they "can pay for a pew."[69]

Pew rights also obtained in pre–Revolutionary France and in 19th century America. In France an annual rent was paid for the pew, although the "owner" of the pew could trade it like any other commodity,[70] while in America in the 19th century pews were usually sold by auction—the English tourist, George Combe, noted in 1841 that: "When an American church is built the pews are generally sold by public auction." And he noted of one newly opened church that 196 pews were auctioned at from $401 to $1,200 each (self-evidently one would have had to be quite well-heeled to be able to afford a seat in *that* church). In fact, the privatized church pew would seem to have been one American pre–Revolutionary institution which was not impacted by republicanism and notions of democracy. From earliest colonial times, in fact, "spots for pues" were sold and known commonly as "pitts." Their owners often designed and built them with direct, private access to the "pew" from a door in the meeting-house wall, often the door having the owners" name painted on it in large white letters. Since the occupants of the pew were often invisible to the minister, because many had "towering partition walls," they did not even have to face him." Indeed, Earle quotes a little colonial girl's first encounter with one of these pews: "What! Must I be shut up in a closet and sit on a shelf?"[71]

In England by the late 1830s questions were being raised as to the legality of renting church pews, or otherwise treating them as if akin to real estate and thus amenable to privatization. An 1839 judgement by the Chancellor of the Diocese in the Consistory Court of Chester found that pews "belong not to individuals, but to the parish," but that parish officers could assign pews to people according to their status in society. And that (legal) ruling questioned the practice of renting or selling (as akin to a leasehold-type arrangement) church pews: "We find pews claimed by a kind of prescriptive right, which right has no existence. We find pews sold, when no legal sale can be effected. We find pews let, when the persons have no right to let them. Pews devised by will, where the parties had no property right to them."[72]

We see, then, how the concept of "status space" may operate formally in an almost institutionalized kind of way and even in what might seem to be the most unlikely contexts, such as Christian church culture, and even in the exemplary 19th century democracy, America.[73] And it is with this concept of "status space" lurking in the background—as a basic premise, if you like—that we begin the quest to unravel the rationale underpinning the advent of railroad *passenger classes* in Britain in the 19th century.

Although the way third-class passengers were treated on English railroads—when they were catered for at all during the early period—might seem reprehensible to us, when we come to look at it closely in the next chapter, yet, viewed in historical context, it was unexceptional. It simply reflected the way in which social class discriminations more generally not only "worked" but were institutionalized in the broader society (not losing sight of the concept of "status space" here, either).

Indeed, why should English bourgeois reformers have complained about the fact that third-class railroad passengers had been bundled into freight or livestock wagons? Had it not been the case that for centuries the traveling poor paid their farthings or pence for the privilege of riding on the lumbering freight wagons which plied the country roads or to sit atop the freight on canal barges? So why should the railroad companies have treated them any differently? Were they not just following historical precedent and current practice where treatment of the poor traveler was concerned?

So, before we consider the *status distinctions* which emerged in early English railroad passenger travel, it is important to realize that their emergence and institutionalization was quite unexceptional at the time. In fact, they fell into line with countless other social class-based forms of differentiated commodification and consumption at the time, many of which had genealogical foundations extending a long way back historically—such as the church pew. So, let us sample next a few instances of this historical phenomenon as we find them prior to or contemporaneous with the advent of railroad passenger conveyance, just so that we have an unambiguous sense concerning the historical context of what is being addressed here. And these, albeit cursory and fleeting historical investigations, indicate sufficiently that the discriminatory practices encountered by English third-class railroad passengers in the early period were no different to the indignities and forms of exclusion which they experienced in the highly-stratified society at large.

Commodification, Consumption and Social Class

In late 17th century England subscribers to the proposed publication of a book were either "first-class," in which case they were individually honored with the dedication of a plate and their arms engraved underneath, or they were "second-class," in which case they paid a much lesser amount for a standardized edition with no personalized embellishments of the book (they were normally the majority of consumers).[74] And, generally speaking, literate poor people could not afford to buy new books at that time, and neither were there free public libraries. However, although the cost of books (and newspapers), even in the mid–19th century, could be prohibitive, yet people did form clubs and societies to purchase such commodities collectively and shared them.

On the Bridgewater Canal in 1801 it was stipulated that "no improper company can go in the boats." That aside, a part of the boat was reserved for "superior" passengers and provided with a stove, tables, and convenient seats, while passengers of a "lower description" were sent aft and paid about two-thirds of the fare paid by the "superior" passengers. But the passengers of a "lower description" would, nevertheless, have been quite "well-to-do" people. And such canal excursions at the time often allowed for three cabin classes (priced in one case at 2s/6d, 1s/6d, and 1/- respectively).[75] However, on the Manchester-Chester Canal in the early 19th century the barges were divided into two "compartments"— the "parlor" and the "kitchen"—at two prices.[76]

On the mail coach three passenger classes normally prevailed: inside, imperial (outside), and beside the coachman (box seat), the latter sometimes a coveted position despite exposure to the elements. In fact, well-heeled gentlemen did not necessarily choose the inside option, aside from which those traveling imperial (atop the coach) could be sightseers (especially tourists, who could obtain information from the coachman about the sights), fresh air maniacs and "outdoors" types, claustrophobics, antisocial people, or coaching enthusiasts. The box seat, the prized spot, was often vied for by coaching enthusiasts and adventurous young gentlemen hoping to be given the reigns now and then[77]—"amateur" coach driving became something of a fashion for "gentlemen" in 19th century England.

Concerning English mail coaches, clearly the *inside* passengers paid more to be protected from the elements and have a more comfortable ride, although obviously few "ladies" would have wished to brave the outside of the coach, nor would have the elderly or infirm. Furthermore, whereas the mail coach could go faster (not the least because it was smaller and lighter) than an ordinary coach that meant it usually carried only four inside passengers, whereas an ordinary, lumbering English day coach could carry up to 16 people inside[78] and up to a dozen outside. The poor could not afford coach travel.

In 1830 licenses for selling beer were abolished, so there was immediately an enormous proliferation of "pubs." But many of those pubs initially stratified themselves in accordance with the prevailing class structure so that they serviced drinkers of different social classes. On the other hand, a single pub of the 1830s could have up to six entrances, each leading to a different drinking "compartment" corresponding roughly to the different social class "qualifications" of drinkers. And in many pubs not compartmentalized so, yet there were metal or glass "snob screens" on the bar to accommodate privacy fetishists, so that they did not have to look at the people sitting next to them, or at anybody except the bartender. So, even in the pub, generally thought to be one of the most leveling and congenial of English institutions, yet the early Victorian Englishman could demand and be granted both his class privilege and his privacy.[79]

A concert advertised to celebrate the installation of a new organ at St. Philip's Church, Sheffield, in October 1840 offered three "classes" of seating for the performance: Reserved (7s), First-class (3s.6d.) and Second-class (2s.6d)[80]—not an unusual classification at the time for such performances (concerts and the theatre). In fact, in the early 19th century classical music concerts were essentially a class-based activity, essentially because access to them was subject to "filtering" both by the (high) price of tickets and the subscription facility. And even though by 1830 accessibility to such concerts had been broadened, yet it was considered by some that tickets priced at less than five shillings (way beyond the means of working-class" people) "degraded" the art.[81]

By 1855 London had thirteen public baths. They offered first- and second-class bathing and associated facilities—waiting rooms, dressing rooms, and *private* baths. Of course, separate provision for men and women cut across these class distinctions[82] and no doubt certain social classes would have been excluded altogether from the use of such facilities.

In 1864 the Taunton Commission Report graded all secondary schools into three categories essentially on the basis of the social classes they catered for. And this gradation was probably quite similar in terms of its underlying premises to those which underpinned the different standards of passenger accommodation offered by railroad companies—people usually paid for the best "accommodation" they could afford, whether it was a railroad compartment or carriage, or a son's education (notwithstanding that very few children of the lower social classes, unless "sponsored" by a wealthy patron, had any chance of obtaining secondary education in Britain at the time).

Even asylums in England (and on the continent) catered to different social classes or separated and treated people differentially within the institution based on social class. In Germany Nietzsche, for instance, when diagnosed at a Jena hospital (in 1889) as requiring hospitalization in a psychiatric clinic, was admitted to the facility in question as a "second-class" patient because his mother could not afford to pay for "first-class" treatment and care[83]—asylums were similarly stratified in Britain at the time.

Death was no leveler (throughout Europe) at the time, either. In Vienna (earlier) at the time of Mozart's death there were different classes of funeral; Mozart given a third-class funeral, which did not include the use of the nave or chancel in the cathedral, but only access to a chapel, while the service took the form of a *low* mass.[84] And the "commodification" of death and attendant rituals was similarly stratified in England in the 19th century.

But this brief consideration of social class distinctions during and before the Victorian era is a mere gloss on what was a remarkably pervasive sociocultural phenomenon at the time, spanning virtually all forms of commodification and consumption (of goods and services). But the irony is that where exclusivity was concerned *there were often no conspicuously sign-posted boundaries at all.* In fact, the Victorian English were quite expert at devising strategies to effect monopoly and exclusion—exclusivity of social space and consumption in other words—without "sign-posting" it. Indeed, there were numerous cunning strategies devised in that regard, some of them quite historically long-standing.

The most basic strategy was to simply price something high enough to ensure that only very wealthy or well-to-do people could avail themselves of it. For instance, initially high fares were used to preserve exclusive passenger traffic on the London and Brighton Railway. However, later, under new management, fares were reduced and cheap excursions available—so that on Easter Monday, 1862, for instance, 132,000 passengers arrived at Brighton Station from London by means of a two-hour railroad journey.[85]

Another means by which exclusivity could be ensured was to incorporate an exclusive society or club—as was often the case where classical music and choral society performances were concerned—with admittance to performances restricted to subscribers; the subscriptions themselves inflated sufficiently to ensure that only very "well-off" people could afford them (furthermore, often subscriptions or membership could only be obtained on the recommendation of an existing member).

Holding ostensibly public events in what were, effectively, private spaces was where the English fetish for "club culture" came into its own. Indeed, Flanders asserts that by the 18th century clubs were an integral part of the "civilizing process" in Britain, and that by the mid–18th century there may have been as many as 20,000 men meeting every night in London alone in some form of organized group.[86] Nor should we lose sight of the fact that first-class railroad travel, for instance, was effectively to become a member of an ad hoc exclusive club for the duration of a railroad journey.

Related was the strategy of requiring people to book for something in advance, so that undesirable people might be excluded—initially, the Liverpool and Manchester Railway Company, for instance, required would-be travelers to order their tickets 24 hours in advance and to supply name, address, place of birth, age, occupation, and reason for travel, so that "unsuitable" persons might be excluded.[87]

Another cunning strategy, especially to effect relative exclusivity of attendance at events, was to offer different opening hours with correspondingly differentiated admission charges. For instance, in 1865 the South Kensington Museum offered *free* admission on Mondays, Tuesdays, and Saturdays, whereas admission was charged on Wednesdays, Thursdays and Fridays—the underlying assumption (probably correct) was that the lower social classes would take advantage of the free admission days, while the "better" people would take the paying-day options, happy to pay to be separated from their perceived "inferiors."[88]

Yet another strategy for effecting exclusivity at exhibitions and the like was to charge a very high admission fee for the opening day, then a lower one subsequently, and an even lower one as the exhibition drew to a close. This was precisely how "consumption" (of the spectacle) was stratified at the Great Exhibition of 1851—the opening day was a very exclusive affair as were the first few weeks, the "hoi polloi" only gaining affordable (one shilling) entry during the later stages of the Exhibition. But that was customary practice where such events were concerned.

In view of this brief diversion, then, it seems reasonable to suggest that, when we come to look closely at the passenger class distinctions which emerged on the 19th century English railroads, we ought not to think of them as at all exceptional; but, rather, that they were consistent with broader processes of commodification and consumption in Victorian society.

Early Railroad Passenger Conveyance

Arguably, Thomas Gray, in his *Observations on a General Iron Way* (1802), was the first to envision substantial passenger carriage by means of railroad in England, as well as being the originator of the concept of a national railroad *system*. His book, which was widely read, had run to five editions by 1825.[89]

It appears that the Swansea and Mumbles Railway (1807) was the only passenger-carrying railroad in Britain before the Stockton and Darlington (1825).[90] But these were both horse-powered railroads, of course—initially the latter company used a mix of horse and locomotive power. And although the Stockton and Darlington was intended to be primarily for coal conveyance, yet the passenger numbers—even when horse power alone was employed—immediately pointed to a new (lucrative) opportunity which had clearly not been envisioned:

> The number of passengers obtained, even during the time when horse power alone was employed, soon became important, and is said to have increased thirty-fold since the opening of the communication.... Previously there had been hardly traveling enough to support one coach three times a week (between the two localities); where now (1836) there are from 150–200 persons daily along the line.[91]

The point is that when the first steam-powered railroads came into existence their potential as a means of passenger transportation was hugely undervalued by all but a few visionary people. In fact, passenger travel on English railroads in the earliest period—even when it was planned for carefully rather than being an afterthought—was not necessarily seen as "core" business for quite some time. The Liverpool and Manchester directors, for instance, were no doubt delighted—but also surprised, one imagines—that in the first six months of the railroad's operation it carried over 200,000 passengers. After all, the company's first prospectus had dedicated only 32 of 2,000-plus words of puffery to the potential of passenger traffic and passenger revenue,[92] although that may have been partly so as not to alarm the coaching interests. And although the London and Birmingham (a little later) had projected that half its revenue would be derived from passenger traffic, yet the first year of operation reaped the company five times as much revenue from passenger as against freight traffic.[93] But even when the early railroad companies had come to realize the potential of passenger conveyance as a revenue earner, yet they still did not immediately realize the full extent of its commodification possibilities. Suburban commuting and the excursion business remained underdeveloped fields of enterprise for many years. And the neglect and mistreatment of third-class passengers—for decades by many companies—could hardly be considered "enlightened" if the aim was to make money.

In America, by way of contrast, it seems that passenger conveyance figured prominently in the earliest proposals to build railroads. By 1828 New York, Maryland, South Carolina, and Pennsylvania had all commenced railroad construction and all the projected railroads were conceived of as "passenger railroads," and that at a time when the viability of locomotive power was still moot—arguably, the South Carolina Canal and Railroad Company was the first to start scheduled passenger operations in America using a locomotive (December, 25, 1830).[94] However, it has been suggested that in America passenger conveyance on some early railroads only came to the fore because "some routes simply would not have withstood large tonnages of freight moving over them,"[95] hence, passenger conveyance provided a practical and remunerative revenue supplement in the short term. Nor in America was there a class structure imposing enough to exclude the conveyance of the lower social classes as a source of revenue and profit.

Commodifying Railroad Passenger Travel in Victorian England

But let us move on to look at the peculiar stratification system which emerged on the English railroads from early on. And in so doing attend to how the English railroad companies resolved the problem of providing something approximating to a "publicly-accessible" passenger conveyance system in what was a highly-structured society. But let there be no confusion concerning the true nature of the passenger's status, nor should we allow "romantic" notions in that regard to obscure or misrepresent the true nature of the railroad passenger's traveling experience in 19th century England. Earlier, I stated that the true nature of the railroad system was industrial; and, moreover, that it had many characteristics of the industrial factory system. Now it is time to follow through on those premises.

A much-aggrieved Jack Simmons informs us in one of his books that in 1988 English Rail committed what apparently seemed to him an unconscionable act when it "translated" the concept of "passenger" into the new-fangled concept of "customer." Simmons, having put on the sociolinguist's "trencher," described this as a "plain misuse of language," for a "customer," according to Simmons, also means "someone sending a consignment."[96] The reality is that a passenger effectively consigns him- or herself from A to B with the assistance of the railroad company—something both John Ruskin and Henry Thoreau realized, around 150 years ago. But this is the kind of argument only a railroad romantic could conjure up,[97] though allowing for its intended political import at the time.

What I find interesting about early English railroad companies, where passenger conveyance was concerned, was how they commodified passenger travel in a hierarchical society, characterized by finely tuned (more so than we realize today) and powerfully institutionalized social class distinctions. In fact, English railroad travel in the era concerned necessitated—as it was commodified and consumed—significant rationalizations of broader social class distinctions, effectively collapsing and compressing them into ad hoc status distinctions (1st, 2nd and 3rd passenger classes).

For the upper social classes, this had a profound impact at the subjective level, for these new status distinctions (railroad passenger classes) cut across the traditional niceties of upper social class privilege and exclusivity. Hence, English railroad capitalism effected new, stratified commodities—or styles of consumption, if you like—in the field of personal mobility; which, effectively, coerced members of the upper-classes most notably into accepting them for the duration of a railroad journey if they wished to avail themselves of the convenience of the railroad. Indeed, the advent of the railroad in England eventually (as Smiles put it): "Put an end to that gradation of rank in traveling which was one of the few things left by which the nobleman could be distinguished from the Manchester manufacturer and bagman."[98] However, that is somewhat simplistic and erroneous to a point.

Nevertheless, we might properly consider the advent of the railroad—railroad capitalism more precisely—in England to have been one of the first and most exemplary of industrial/technological developments to seriously "gash" the English social class structure and to do so in accordance with the rationalizing imperatives of (industrial) capitalism more generally. There resides the single most important effect of the advent of the railroad in 19th century England where passenger conveyance was concerned.

According to Jack Simmons, the word "class" was never applied to coach and wagon transportation in Britain. He argues that the Grand Junction Railway Company was the first to use the word "class" to describe *passengers*.[99] However, it needs to be made clear that neither the Grand Junction nor any other English railroad company intended the concept of "class" to apply to anything other than the carriage or compartment accommodation (though sometimes to other amenities provided by the company as well) being offered. Hence, a "first-class passenger" was one who traveled in a first-class carriage or compartment, but the passenger himself was not "first-class" in any other sense.

Furthermore, even if the word "class" had not been used in road (or canal and coastal shipping) transportation before the railroad age—although my own research indicates it was—it does not follow that passenger accommodation discriminations were absent. Indeed, they were not! And that is the point—even the dopiest philosophy student understands that just because something is not accounted for in terms of a familiar or preferred name (like "class") it doesn't mean that it does not exist.

The above example is indicative of more general deficits where the writing of English railroad history is concerned—namely, the conspicuous absence of conceptual-analytical rigor and dynamic discursive activity. Indeed, you are more likely to find *that* in the writings of 19th century commentators on English railroad history than in the works of many contemporary English writers on the subject.

In fact, a basic passenger class distinction was made on all forms of public transportation before the railroad age, and initially the railroad companies followed it. This was the distinction between "outside" and "inside" or "covered" and "uncovered" passenger accommodation. On coastal shipping and canal boats this distinction was rendered as that between "deck"/"steerage" and "cabin." On the coaches, it really was as simple as the distinction between "inside" and "outside"—in the early 18th century it seems that the inside coach passengers paid about twice as much as the outsides.[100] And it may well have been the case that many of the "macho" men who chose to ride atop the coach and brave the elements were more niggardly than they were manly.

When locomotives were first harnessed to passenger carriages on the Stockton and Darlington the inside passengers paid one and a half-penny per mile, the outside passengers a penny a mile.[101] On the Liverpool and Manchester in the early period "everything connected with the passenger department was copied from the coaches"[102]—

including the "inside" versus "outside" distinction, once enclosed carriages materialized. In fact, the early Liverpool and Manchester Railway carriages—fashioned after the French diligence system—were designed to carry 16 inside and four outside.[103] And even as late as 1838 coaches on some lines still had *seats* on the roof for those who preferred riding outside,[104] while the practice of putting baggage atop carriages—also in emulation of coaching practice—persisted on some railroads until 1860.[105] But the key point here is that exposure to the elements (or otherwise) was the most fundamental passenger class distinction in evidence both before the advent of railroads and during their formative period.

Another basic passenger class distinction which predated the railroad age was that between "express" and "slow," and this distinction was known in both road transportation (coaching) and on the canals in England.

In *The Railway Station* (1986) its authors note that it was at railroad stations that the different social classes were most likely to be provided with brief windows into each other's lives, while also noting that railroad stations were in some respects designed to avoid such encounters as much as possible.[106] Indeed, railroad passenger classes concentrated, compressed, and effectively rationalized social classes during the course of travel. The passenger class boundaries were arbitrary, since they were purely "administrative divisions" and "commodity forms." Hence, they did not so much separate this or that class, but, rather, they "bundled up" social classes into passenger classes during the production and consumption of differentiated (travel) commodities. And once we understand the processes involved here, then we begin to understand why people of the upper social classes initially refused to use the railroad carriage (or compartment) at all, or even to use the railroad station in the early period.

Exclusivity and Railroad Travel

In America, on the Northeastern seaboard from the late 1820s, competition for passenger traffic on river and coastal shipping routes was very intense. In 1829 the ruthlessly competitive Cornelius Vanderbilt (who went on to be a no less ruthless railroad magnate), having cut his costs as much as he could to rival his competitors, cunningly contrived to gain an advantage over them by offering something new (for America, apparently)—exclusivity! In 1829, he advertised that on his *Caroline* passengers would be able to avoid "the pressure of a crowd of ten shilling passengers." Indeed, it seems people got nothing more on the *Caroline* than they had previously on a Vanderbilt vessel, except for being separated from the "ten-shilling passengers," for which "privilege," in this "classless" society, they were apparently happy to pay "through the nose."[107]

When passenger accommodation discriminations occur, regardless of the transportation mode under consideration, often the key factor in the situation is exclusivity. The early 20th century sociologist, Georg Simmel, rationalized that phenomenon rather tidily:

> What the traveler buys with his first-class ticket is the right to join the exclusive company of those who pay such a higher price to be separated from the second-class passengers. Thus, the well-to-do individual can acquire an advantage simply by spending more money, *without necessarily receiving a material equivalent for his expenditure*.[108]

A second key factor in the situation, where consideration of 19th century English railroad passenger classes is concerned, is that railroad passenger classes did not correspond to social classes. Rather, they were *rationalizations* of them. Which is to say that the complexity of the English social class structure had to be rationalized during railroad travel simply because its complexity could not be reproduced by the railroad companies, which commodified railroad travel in the form of just two or three basic commodities (essentially first-, second-, and third-class passenger accommodation), although, as we shall see in the next chapter, further discriminations were made within and beyond those tidy categories.

The reason railroad passenger classes are so troublesome is precisely because they are often held—by railroad historians, in particular—to be analytically parallel to social classes. That is a serious mistake. And we can redress the error, to some extent at least, by making a distinction drawn by the early 20th century German sociologist, Max Weber—a distinction between "social class" and "social status." In that connection, it is extremely important to understand that the passenger classes offered by the Victorian railroad companies were simply stratified commodities. Each of those commodities had travel as its fundamental quality. But value was added to that fundamental quality and the resultant embellished forms of consumption were the passenger classes—not forgetting, either, the role of "exclusivity" in the commodification process. Indeed, the passenger classes were also differentiated social *status* (as opposed to social *class*) categories—at least for the duration of a railroad journey. Furthermore, they also conformed, as accommodation spaces, to the concept of "social space" enunciated earlier.

Essentially, there were four dimensions to the embellishment of the commodification and consumption processes characterizing the differentiated railroad passenger classes in Victorian England. The first accounts for the fact that value was often added in an obvious material form—relating to the architecture and furnishings of the carriage and compartment, for instance, so that there were degrees of comfort. Secondly, there was (relatively privileged) access to a superior grade of amenities at the station and to superior service (or any service at all) for those traveling first- or second-class. Thirdly, these forms of "added value" imply a *higher* cost, which the consumer had to pay for the preferred commodity. And, fourthly, a scale of costs (for the differentiated forms of a basic commodity, travel in this case) itself implies a differentiated degree of exclusivity attending the consumption of each (embellished) form of the basic commodity.

Once all of this is understood, then it becomes apparent that there is no necessary connection between social class and railroad passenger class—except insofar as railroad passenger classes effectively *rationalize* social class distinctions during travel. The various passenger classes, then, ought to be thought of as "status" categories and "commodity forms," access to which *may* be determined by financial means, which *may* in turn tell us something about the social class position of the traveler. But the passenger class *itself* may tell us very little about the social class position of this or that traveler. After all, a member of the aristocracy and a well-to-do shopkeeper, for instance, might have finished up sharing a first-class compartment in a first-class carriage. On the other hand, a niggardly senior clerk and an itinerant "pure finder" (a collector of dog droppings which were sold to tanners) might be found in the same third-class carriage. That is the point. It may seem subtle, even idiosyncratic, but it is important.

The Architecture of 19th Century English Railroad Carriages

Travelers on the first English railroads would certainly have found some aspects of the experience familiar. An early traveler on the Liverpool and Manchester, for instance, identified the middle section of his carriage as resembling the body of a coach; that those at either end of it resembled a a "chaise" and had two-seater "coupe" bodies; while another carriage was described as being akin to an "oblong square of church pews."[109] Furthermore, during the earliest period the ticket office was sometimes located at an inn proximate to the railroad, the inn-keeper occasionally doubling as stationmaster. And when purpose-built stations began to appear the earliest of them often had familiar domestic or agricultural (the barn) associations—perhaps the only influence on the earliest stations deriving from the road transportation industry was the structure's roof (some turnpike tollhouses had a roof extending across the road so that the coach had cover during a stop).

The early railroad carriages designed for the conveyance of people of some means were basically mail coaches on flat wagons.[110] However, one design feature unique to railroad carriages was the door handle which opened the door by being pulled upwards—railroad companies were the first to patent this idea.[111] However, the architecture of the early railroad passenger carriages intended for the conveyance of third-class passengers was more original, although it was little or no different often to the rolling stock designed for the conveyance of livestock or freight in the earliest period.

There certainly was some continuity from the architecture of the coach to that of the early railroad carriages and compartments; and where passenger class distinctions were concerned, too, the early railroad companies simply followed coaching practice—initially by instituting the crude discriminatory criterion of "inside" versus "outside"" accommodation, and later with the introduction of "express" services. In fact, in the mid–1830s some companies offered a seat at each end atop first-class carriages for those who liked to travel "outside." And even in the early 1840s some people (usually adventurous boys) were still able to ride on the roofs of carriages with the guard[112]—like the coaching counterpart, the early railroad guard sat atop the "coach." Furthermore, in the early period the railroad guard—like the coach guard—carried a horn which he blew to signal the approach, arrival, and departure of trains (bearing in mind that the train whistle had not been invented at that time, nor were huge bells positioned on the English as they came to be on American locomotives).[113] In fact, for years on the Liverpool and Manchester trains left the terminal stations to a "lively tune performed by a trumpeter at the end of the platform."[114] Also following coaching practice, the baggage was, in the early period, stowed on the roof of the carriage. And before the railroad companies began to impose a discipline upon the passenger some people thought that they could catch the train just as they had often caught the coach at a crossroads or some other prominent place by waving an umbrella at it to bring it to a halt. But during the early period there were many other "carry-overs" from coaching practice and the "culture" of road transportation apart from those already mentioned. For instance, the gauge of the first railroad was taken from the standard width of road wagons. And in the earliest period the passengers were to be conveyed by private coach along the railroad, the coaching (or freight) company concerned paying the railroad company a toll for using the way (instead of paying such a toll to a turnpike trust as would otherwise have been the case).

So, the practice adopted initially by the early railroad companies, where use of the way was concerned, had simply been to follow turnpike practice. Hence, the railroad was accessible to almost any (freighting, passenger, or other commercial) concern prepared to pay the user toll—it is not always clear whether people rented railroad wagons, supplied their own if they were to be regular users, or both systems prevailed in that early period. Whatever the case, treating the railroad as if it were a public highway was an irrational phenomenon. That became increasingly apparent as traffic intensified, especially given the relatively primitive traffic control systems in place at the time. In fact, confusion, congestion, and accidents resulted from the absence of an effective, centralized, administrative and operational authority to effect rational and safe traffic flow and control; apart from which, it became quickly apparent to the boards of directors of the early railroad companies that they could make a lot more money if they monopolized the carriage of freight and passengers themselves, rather than allowing other people to "rake off" such income.

What really set off the English railroad passenger system from the American counterpart, even in the earliest period, was the stratification of passenger traveling experience into several passenger classes. Even at the ceremonial opening of the Liverpool and Manchester Railway, passenger carriage accommodation was stratified (even if it was a free journey)—the Duke of Wellington had the most lavish carriage of all, those carriages on either side of it were "grand" but not quite so lavish, and the remaining carriages in the procession constituted a third degree of comfort,[115] even though they carried dignitaries. That extraordinary event aside, in the early period *the* most basic discriminatory criterion employed in the constitution of passenger classes was the distinction between open and closed carriages. But it was sometimes reducible to a distinction between day and night travel—night carriages were usually closed and cost more to ride in than did open carriages.[116] However, first-class carriages were, almost from the outset, invariably closed. And except for excursions, the open carriage (for second- and third-class conveyance) was the exception after 1844.[117]

In England, some of the first enclosed carriages had no suspension and hard benches for seats. In fact, one of the earliest passenger carriages, the *Experiment*,[118] was described at the time as being like a "chicken hutch on wheels," while some early passengers described their having ridden in chaldrons—a "chaldron" was the common type of mineral wagon (though originally it was a variable *measure* of bushels) and such carriages were self-evidently cauldron-shaped.[119]

In England during the early period, while carriage and compartment furnishing was still quite crude, relative access to the means of illumination and ventilation constituted other basic criteria for passenger class discriminations within closed carriages. When oil lamps were introduced in carriage compartments in the early 1840s, some companies provided two half-lamps per first-class partition, but just one half-lamp for second-class.[120] But companies could be entirely remiss when it came to lighting, some apparently still offering none by mid-century—gas lighting on trains was first employed on the Great Western in 1862. As for third-class passengers in closed carriages, they often found themselves pitched into darkness with no means of illumination whatsoever.

Where ventilation was concerned in the early period, second-class carriages were often "open," so ventilation was not a problem, whereas the closed first-class carriages usually had louvre windows to effect ventilation—but it was quite a few decades before ventilation systems were devised that prevented smoke and other fumes entering the carriage. As for the earliest "enclosed" third-class carriages, they afforded only very limited ventilation relative to the number of people often crammed into them—but all of this is discussed more protractedly in the next chapter.

Americans in England usually found the passenger class system and railroad compartment (once both had developed) somewhat strange and oppressive, but rationalized these "curiosities" variously. One American correspondent suggested in 1868: "The Englishman has never yet given up the idea that he is running a stage-coach, and he calls his car a coach"—undoubtedly fair comment. Another American thought English carriages and rolling stock "not to our taste," but that they "were in keeping with the solid respectability of the (English) national taste"—we have already teased out the (social class) filaments underlying such a view.

Schivelbusch has suggested that the principal reason Americans preferred to travel in a "large room" while their European counterparts preferred to travel in "little cells" (compartments) was because of the difference in the average travel distance in the two contexts; Schivelbusch suggesting, furthermore, that the American train, like the steamboat, had to provide all the amenities the public might require during the course of a journey where stops were infrequent and station facilities Spartan.[121] But this is largely nonsense, especially where the *early* railroads were concerned. In America, the early railroads were to be found mostly on the Northeastern seaboard, in the South, either in the coastal areas or close to the major river systems to which they were indispensably articulated, while the Baltimore and Ohio was the nearest the early railroads got to penetrating the interior initially. Many of these early American railroads were originally not very long at all (many of them under 20 miles in length) and not a few of them were impractical, rickety, "rip-off" schemes built primarily as "hit-and-run" jobs to fleece money (large subsidies for construction) out of gullible state legislatures, or they were simply constructed incompetently and managed no less so. Those points aside, it was not really until the Pullman era began in America—from the 1860s—that trains had the kind of amenities Schivelbusch refers to. Furthermore, in America short-line railroads often only became more extensive when profits enabled add-ons, when amalgamations or takeovers occurred, or when articulations were otherwise effected.

But many of the early American railroads were intended to be short-line roads. In fact, articulating all these silly little railroads from one state to the next was partly the rationale for the numerous state railroad conventions in the 1840s. Indeed, the irrationality of many states' railroads (one could hardly talk about a "system" in respect of them) befuddled the state legislatures tasked with trying to put all the bits and pieces together—especially when multiple companies became insolvent at around the same time, while there were often gauge discrepancies, too—to effect something approximating a "system." In fact, in America it was often only "consolidations" effected by railroad corporations which enabled the emergence (hence, by default rather than by design) of extensive, coherent, rational railroad systems facilitating through traffic. But that was also true of Britain to a point.

But let us return to the peculiarities of the English. Hamilton Ellis noted the curious tendency of English railroad companies to wedge a first-class compartment between two second-class compartments in the one carriage. And he thought this was primarily to enable the upper social classes to travel with their servants in easy reach.[122] But this is probably not a very satisfactory explanation of the architectural form in question because, for decades, compartments were locked and movement between compartments physically impossible while the train was in motion—so servants would have been inaccessible and thus of no use, anyway. Nor should it be assumed that servants traveling with their employers always traveled second- rather than third-class. And Ellis may have confused this architectural form with the "family saloon," which was eventually introduced by some companies, and which did accommodate servants in the same carriage—but in a separate compartment—with their employers.

That aside, English carriages usually contained either all first- or second-class compartments. And it is my contention that placing a first-class compartment between two second- class compartments, when that occurred, had something to do with the relative claims to status honor of the passengers traveling in those respective classes. And one should note, in that connection, that on *ceremonial* occasions involving royalty, for instance, the royal carriage was normally placed in the *middle* of a procession, notwithstanding that the situation might be different in processions such as military expeditions or the like. So, it is important to make it clear that I refer to *ceremonial* occasions here as the analogy.

However, the "higher status" of the first-class railroad passenger was publicly affirmed not only by the architectural form and other signifiers of the compartment/carriage configuration described above; but also by a first-class compartment only carriage being placed between two second-class compartment only carriages. In both instances, the accommodation of the first-class passenger conspicuously signified his superior status. Indeed, we should not lose sight of the fact that not only was Victorian society characterized by multiple gradations of social class, but also by an infinitude of signifiers of social class position which had to be visual to be both identifiable and meaningful.

On the other hand, the very same point applies to the second-class passengers relative to the third-class passengers, since, for many decades, third-class carriages were normally attached to goods trains. So, if the second-class passengers did not have the same "superior" traveling comforts and conspicuous status of the first-class passengers, at least they were part of a *passenger* rather than a *goods* train (a distinction elaborated upon in the chapter following). And, again, the difference was both visual and conspicuous, notwithstanding that the appearance of the third-class carriages alone, apart from their being attached to a *goods* train, was usually itself visible and conspicuous testimony to the third-class passengers" status (as "inmates" of goods carriages rather than passenger carriages). Schivelbusch draws a signal observation in this connection, though without following through on it: "The fact that the members of different classes traveled on the same train, moved by the same power, did not render them social equals, but it was ever present in their minds."[123] Indeed, it was important both to passengers and the railroad companies that the relative claims to "status honor" of travelers in the respective passenger classes be conspicuously "signposted."

Apart from the use of carriage architecture, carriage classes, compartment classes, compartment architecture, and train classes such discriminatory processes and categorizations as were employed by 19th century English railroad companies could be further reinforced by painting carriages and compartments different colors—to commensurate with their passenger class status. In fact, this was common in the early period and it was not just to help passengers *identify* their carriage at the station.

Hamilton Ellis, in describing 19th century English railroad passenger classes, suggested first-class was "high caste," second-class "low caste," and third-class "outcast." These are certainly entertaining metaphors, but somewhat misleading, nonetheless; since I have indicated that both first- and second-class passengers had their claims to relative "status honor" conspicuously signposted by the railroad companies through the architecture and color coding of carriages and compartments, as well as by other means, not the least of which was being formally classified as *passengers* rather than miscellaneous *goods* (on many early English railroads "third-class" seems to have been a euphemism for "miscellaneous goods," as we shall see in the chapter following). Furthermore, one notes that in England the distinctions between first- and second-class passenger experiences were never as dramatic as those between second- and third-class. And another reason it is dubious to consider third class "outcast"—despite its exigencies and ignominies, and its resemblance to freight conveyance—is because those of the lower social classes who could afford third class railroad travel had their own claims to status honor over and against the much more numerous body of the lower social classes unable to afford railroad travel at all for decades. Indeed, as Alfred Williams noted of railroad travel many decades later: "It is a common saying among work people of all sorts that third-class riding is better than first-class walking."[124] So, even those traveling third-class by rail had a claim to relative status honor over and against those who had no choice but to walk.

In 1845 only around 17 percent of English railroad travelers were third-class passengers (although that figure rose to 77 percent by 1875). But those third-class passengers who could afford to commute by rail in 1845 were, indeed, the *better off* of the working classes—the "aristocracy" of the working classes, if you like. In fact, in 1854 around 80 percent of the 250,000 daily travelers into London still went on foot,[125] indicating relatively few of the lower social classes used even suburban omnibus services, let alone train services where the latter were an option—Flanders points out that in the 1830s London's two million inhabitants were crammed into an area 6.5 kilometers north-south by 10 kilometers east-west, which meant that many people were only an hour's walk from the countryside.[126]

In the next chapter, I look more analytically at 19th century English railroad *passenger* classes. Furthermore, I shall draw out the signal characteristics of the national style of railroad passenger conveyance in 19th century England in such a way that it establishes the groundwork for—indeed, a platform from which to approach—a similar analytical treatment of the 19th century American railroad passenger and American railroad passenger travel in a comparative point of view.

Two

The Carceral Experiences of the 19th Century English Railroad Passenger

On our Great Western Railway, how admirably are the gradations of society preserved. The thirty-shilling aristocrats lull upon luxurious couches, securely protected from wind and weather; the one-and-twenty-shilling shopocrats sit upon uncovered seats, exposed to all the skyey influences; whilst the twelve-shilling mobocracy, coming under the denomination of the swinish multitude, are appropriately packed off with the pigs in the luggage train! Nor does the distinction end there. The two former classes are whirled the whole distance in four hours; whilst those to whom time is, emphatically, money, are detained on the road for twelve hours.
—"Class Distinctions," *The Bristol Mercury,* January 1, 1842

I very much doubt the legality of locking (compartment) doors and refusing to open them. In all other positions of life there is egress where there is ingress. Nothing, in fact, can be sillier or more mistaken than their over-officious care of the public. But why stop here? Why are not strait-waistcoats used? Why is not the accidental traveler strapped down? Why do contusion and fracture remain physically possible? Is not this extreme care of the public new?
—Sydney Smith, "Letter," (to the) *Morning Chronicle,* May 21, 1842

Introduction

In the two quotations above we have—notwithstanding some other significant points of difference—the essential qualities which marked off English railroad passenger travel from the American "species" for much of the 19th century. And it was these essential qualities of the English railroads—passenger classes and compartments—which inclined English people, who had visited America and experienced something radically different there, to expatiate upon the decided superiority of American railroad passenger cars when they did. It is true some English tourists found the American cars to be "unaccommodating" in certain respects. But almost universally they found certain advantages in the American railroad system where key aspects of passenger accommodation were concerned.

The 19th century English railroad capitalists had a remarkable tendency to stratify their passenger conveyance operations. However, in one respect at least it was not so remarkable, since it was, after all, and as we saw in the previous chapter, consistent with the stratification of commodification (the forms of the provision of goods and services) and consumption processes in Victorian society more generally, as well as microcosmically representing—albeit in simplified, somewhat distorted, and (for many) disconcerting form—the template of the elaborate social structure which was the hallmark of English society at the time.

This peculiar social structure, as alluded to previously, was especially noteworthy for its multiple gradations and infinitude of related discriminatory criteria, ranging from the idiosyncratic, petty, and sometimes pathetic in the extreme in the treatment of the poor, to the grandiose claims to status honor of the titled aristocracy and the "great enthroned one." Accordingly, the English railroad companies did not conjure up a simplistic passenger class stratification system based on just first-, second-, and third–class carriages, for that clearly would not have satisfied the seemingly insatiable English fetish for stratifying and re-stratifying, classifying and re-classifying, everything and everybody. Consequently, the English railroad capitalists came up with station classes; train classes; variously stratified amenities at stations and termini; carriage classes; and compartment classes. Indeed, multiple classes within classes to the point that it all becomes quite mind-boggling for the student of railroad history seeking to fathom it. But I should like to think I have managed to "tease out" the key elements of this "smorgasbord" of seemingly idiotic gradations.

Yet, if they do seem idiotic to us, these gradations of Victorian railroad passenger travel certainly had a rational underpinning—from the standpoint of those who designed them, that is. And when "grafted onto" the peculiar value system (determined by ruling class ideology), upon which English society at the time was founded, not only do they make some sense; but, considered within that broader context, the rationale for 19th century England's *national style* of railroading more generally also becomes intelligible.

But one more thing ought to be said about the Victorian social class structure to this point; which is that understanding its peculiarities and idiosyncrasies, in all their minutest and most obscure manifestations, would entail a formidable scholarly challenge for anybody. And even though, being an historical sociologist, I have read many interesting works which probe the Victorian class structure, yet no single work that I am aware of adequately penetrates, explicates, and explains the darkest depths, byways, and workings of this strange beast, so difficult is it to pin down for a "snapshot." Nevertheless, let us proceed to look now at the traveling experience of the 19th century English railroad passenger *relative to* the class structure of Victorian society.

Classes, Classes and More Classes

The experience of railroad traveling commenced, of course, inside the railroad station, if there was one, which was not always the case in the early period, nor was it for quite some time in some localities. But where it existed, and especially so in the case of the larger station or terminus, the Victorian railroad station concentrated people of different *social* classes and, in the process of concentrating them, it "shuffled" them

Two. *Carceral Experiences of the 19th Century English Railroad Passenger*

into just two or three *passenger classes* representing the different forms in which the basic commodity (travel) was "packaged," with various kinds and degrees of "added value." One might even say the English railroad system at that time reshuffled the broader social class pack in an ad hoc way—a point discussed in the previous chapter, but further developed here in due course.

Initially, as indicated above, there were even different classes of station: first-class stations, for instance, which were principal stations and the only ones express trains stopped at; second-class stations, on the other hand, were generally second-class by default—they were stations which all or most passenger trains stopped at. But there were also private stations for members of the aristocracy.

In the early period, there were also different classes of train. First-class trains ran more frequently than other classes of train, thus offering a greater choice of departure (and arrival) times for those fortunate enough to be able to afford them.[1] They also normally ran at times much more convenient for travelers than did other trains, and they were often express trains, stopping only at principal stations and commanding right of way along the track. On the Liverpool and Manchester as early as 1831, for instance, all first-class trains had become express trains, while *second-class* trains stopped at all stations. Clearly, a train which had to stop at more stations took longer for the journey in question; but, that point aside, some companies did deliberately run second-class trains slower than first-class trains. Furthermore, second-class trains could also be held up for some time in sidings, since they had to give way to first-class trains, apart from which, often, they had goods wagons attached to them, which may have had to be uncoupled or unloaded. However, the difference between first- and second-class trains, in terms of journey times, was not necessarily that great. But the difference between both *first- and second-class trains* on the one hand, and *third-class trains* (to be described shortly) on the other, was significant and remarkable, and especially so where the length of journey times was concerned. In 1841, for instance, the London and Birmingham Mail (a first-class) train took 4¾ hours for the journey between the two cities, whereas the third-class train took 8½ hours.[2]

The first-class train normally afforded only first-class carriage accommodation, although the (compartment) accommodation within the carriage could itself be stratified into six-seater or the more exclusive and pricier four-seater compartment.

The second-class train was also known as a "mixed" or "composite" train, and that was so when it provided for both first- and second-class carriage accommodation; although, technically, it was also "mixed" if it had goods wagons attached to it. In the early period, such a train's second-class carriages could be "open" and often were; but once they were enclosed and compartmentalized, then both the first- and second-class carriages on these second-class trains normally contained only six-seater compartments. Hence, the difference between first- and second-class accommodations on those (second-class) trains was usually a difference between the quality of compartment furnishings, rather than how many people the compartments accommodated.

Another key difference, often, between first- and second-class trains, was that on first-class trains seats were usually numbered and allocated on a rational basis, whereas on the second-class train one may have had to behave in an undignified manner to obtain a desirable compartment or seat. The numbering of seats was relatively novel at the time, perhaps only to be found elsewhere in churches—where compartmentalized pews were sometimes numbered—or in respect of private boxes at the theatre. However, the numbering of seats in first-class compartments was an ambivalent phenomenon from the "well-to-do" passenger's viewpoint—although it afforded the privilege of a reserved seat, yet it prevented "colonization" of all the other seats in the compartment to prevent other people getting into and sharing it with you (since somebody else may have had a reserved seat in the same compartment). But that was hardly an insurmountable problem, as an American newspaper correspondent noted in 1868: "I have had a whole compartment for my family for 200 miles for a shilling put into the hands of the conductor. It needed no words. He wanted the money and understood its language perfectly."[3]

First- and second-class trains thus differed essentially regarding speed, traveling time, right-of-way, convenience, comfort, and degrees of exclusivity. However, it is to be noted that the fact first-class trains were express trains indicated they often traveled greater distances and were thus available—in the early period—only between major centers separated by some considerable distance.

The key difference between the second-class train and the third-class train was that the latter was a "mixed" train of a different kind. In fact, in the early period it was usually a "goods" train to which third-class carriages were attached, although it seems the third-class carriages used by some companies during the early period, if not "goods" or "livestock" wagons, did not differ very much from either—the Great Northern certainly used cattle trucks for excursion traffic in 1851. And although second-class trains were known to also have goods carriages attached to them, yet a second-class train was a passenger train with some freight carriages attached to it, whereas the third-class train was a freight train with some passenger carriages attached to it. The difference may seem subtle, but it is very significant, nonetheless, if one thinks about it. Indeed, Usher argues that in the early period the people transported on third-class (freight) trains were not even classified as "passengers." It was passenger service only insofar as people were being transported, although the reality was that they were treated as if goods or livestock.[4] The London and Birmingham, for instance, at one time carried third-class passengers only on trains that hauled livestock and empty wagons. And a Board of Trade inquiry of 1842 found that third-class passengers had, indeed, been accommodated in livestock wagons and on luggage trains[5]—this was no great revelation at the time, since many companies did it and everybody knew about it. Furthermore, when the lower social classes were catered for in the early period they were often loaded and unloaded at goods sheds, not stations.[6]

But this treatment—of the lower social classes—must be rationalized in historical context. The road freight wagon had been the traditional mode of transportation for the poor and the coach had never been accessible to them, so the railroad companies were probably not sure how to deal with them, or even whether they ought to be catered for at all. In fact, when in 1839 the eminent engineer, Robert Stephenson, told a Select Committee on railroads that the laboring classes had not much benefited from them and that ought to change, that was considered a radical stance. In fact, some companies had no interest in provision of third-class travel; and eventually offered it only begrudgingly, and often under compulsion (by the state). Typical was the attitude of the Great Western, whose Secretary commented in 1839 upon the possibility of offering a third-class facility: "I think they (the directors) will probably send carriages once a day, perhaps with merchandise: carriages of an inferior description, at very low speed for the accommodation of those persons, and at a very low price; perhaps, too, it may only be done at night."[7] In 1840 this facility was introduced on the Great Western, the category of third-class (goods) train effectively added to the first- and second-class (passenger) train categories.

But some companies operated for decades without offering any third-class service at all—the North London until 1875—although that may have had a lot to do with the relative social class exclusivity of their catchments, which may have precluded the need for a third passenger class or have made it unremunerative.

I suppose what is surprising, under the circumstances, is that the railroad companies bothered to cater for the lower social classes at all. The Great Eastern, for instance, was loath to let them use its fine urban stations, since it considered they did not pay enough to merit it. Indeed, the company proposed instead to turn out the "workmen"s" trains onto "some cattle pen siding," where a large platform would be set aside for their use.[8]

But there were also "political" elements opposed to the enhancement of the mobility of the lower social classes; after all, the 1830s and 1840s constituted an era of considerable agitation from "below" in England and an age of revolution across continental Europe. So, that, too, may have shaped the thinking of the directors of some railroad companies.

Anecdotal evidence from the early period suggests third-class trains were deliberately run as slow as possible to encourage people to pay more for a higher class of train.[9] That may have been the case, but not necessarily so. It seems more likely that often, because these trains were essentially *goods* trains, they frequently went into goods sidings so that goods wagons could be coupled or uncoupled, loaded or unloaded, and the amount of time needed for that in each instance had to be accounted for relative to the working schedules of the lines in question. And it would make sense for a company, allowing for all kinds of contingency, to conservatively calculate the time required for each such stop—for coupling and uncoupling, shunting, loading and unloading of freight, and so on. Once so scheduled, the train was then locked into that schedule, which had to fit into the overall traffic regime of the line before the telegraph and other sophisticated communications systems had become widely adapted for use by the railroad companies. Furthermore, goods (third-class passenger) trains had to give way to higher classes of train, including even goods trains with higher priority—and that, too, could mean a long wait in a siding in the early period. But, again, essentially because of a very limited administrative and operational communications facility.[10]

The "goods" trains, which carried both freight and passengers, were very dangerous in the event of an accident, especially a collision, since the freight carriages were usually placed at the rear of the train. And in a collision their combined (loaded) weight could crush or smash to pieces the relatively flimsy passenger carriages in front of them.[11] But there were numerous other hazards for third-class passengers in the early period, one of which was outlined in a letter to a newspaper in August 1840, the company concerned the North Midland Railway. The letter complained that: "Passengers needed to be better protected from injury by fire…. Pieces of cinder, almost of a white heat, and about the size of a walnut, are continually descending among the passengers in the open carriages."[12]

In 1841 the Board of Trade reported that only two companies continued to convey third-class passengers by "goods" train.[13] But that seems to have been somewhat premature and overly-optimistic, if intended as a "prognosis," since even in the 1870s third-class *trains* still existed and they were all:

> Universally slow, started at the most inconvenient hours, and did not enjoy the advantages, except in a few cases, of through communication with other lines; nor did the (third-class) passengers enjoy the privilege of being able to purchase (discounted) daily return tickets for long journeys.[14]

The English Railroad Station

Let us move beyond the "analytics" of passenger classes to look now at the English railroad station, since it is where the process of industrializing, classifying, and otherwise processing the traveler commenced.

Much of what has been written about English railroad stations has been penned by architectural historians or railroad enthusiasts and romantics with an interest in them. The basic premise I start from here in my evaluation of the railroad station is to identify it as a "technology." The study of buildings very seldom springs from what I would have thought an elementary fact. Namely, that a building is, first and foremost, a *technology*. That ought to be obvious even regarding the kinds of building people live in, but it is even more glaringly so the more functionally specialized the building. Apart from regarding any building as a technology, we must understand it as also entailing an *engineering* of space, human motion through that space, the control of light and air, and so on. One theorist who fully understood the status of the building as both a technology and a work of engineering was Lewis Mumford. Mumford described the modern commercial-industrial building in his time as: "An establishment devoted to the manufacture of light, the circulation of air, the maintenance of uniform temperature, and the vertical transportation of its occupants."[15] Of course, all these various engineerings were intended to optimally facilitate human use of the technology (the building), and there was usually an economic rationale to that. Nor did Mumford doubt that the building is characterized essentially by engineering: "As the building more and more takes on the character of the machine, so does its design, construction and operation become subject to the same rules that govern a locomotive."[16]

The concept of "station" has many interesting historical permutations, one of which is that in late 17th century France a "station" was a church which a religious procession visited.[17] But other curious permutations on the concept will be alluded to in due course. In England in the early 1830s, railroad "station-houses" were mostly sheds at the smaller stopping places, while "even the termini were poor structures."[18] But once traffic volumes—of both passengers and freight—escalated it became necessary to lay out stations and termini on a much more rational, indeed, engineered basis, and to control traffic flow through them with a high degree (for the time) of calculated rationality and engineering applications. In fact, the more sophisticated and complex early railroad termini were often designed by engineers, since it was taken for granted that the problems to be resolved were essentially of an engineering nature; although, to some extent, that was also the outcome of a limited professional "struggle" between engineers and architects in which the former often prevailed during the earliest period. There again, many architects were not prepared to compromise their "dignity" by designing factories or other industrial plants, since they did not consider such buildings to entail architecture—at least not by their lofty definitions of it (many architectural historians and critics at the time took the same view).

The engineering problems of the early termini, where passengers were concerned, related essentially to: pedestrian traffic flow, streaming, concentration (in waiting-rooms), access to platforms, and entry to carriages. But all that had to be designed relative to the commodification of passenger travel—into different passenger classes—which further complicated it. Indeed, where passenger traffic was concerned, initially the early termini had to be designed with separate station entrances, booking-halls, waiting-rooms, and routes onto the platforms for the different passenger classes. But systems also had to be developed for handling baggage and freight, as well as to effect a rational division of the labor of railroad servants relative to the various tasks to be performed, and duties to which responsibility had to be assigned—this complexity cost money, which was one reason why railroad travel was more expensive in England than America throughout the 19th century.

As English railroad capitalism "matured" in the first half of the 19th century, the administrative form typifying it was highly bureaucratic, and the discipline of the passenger that engendered was reinforced by the architecture of both stations and carriages. Hence, the discipline of the passenger was a fusion of bureaucratic administration on the one hand and the engineering of space and human movement through it on the other, both integral to the production of the commodity (travel) and its consumption.

The engineering of railroad passenger space and accommodation then, apart from conducing to the disciplinary requirements of the railroad company, had also to re-stratify the social classes relative to the commodity forms offered—the different classes and other gradations of passenger travel—whereby passengers were sorted into "status spaces," as discussed earlier.

The fact it was unusual for any institution to concentrate the social classes so—as the early railroad station did, even though it differentially streamed as it concentrated them—is indicated by the fact that both the *Cornhill Magazine* and Hippolyte Taine commended the railroad station as an excellent place to observe a broad cross-section of the Victorian social class structure, as well as the "mannerisms" and etiquettes characteristic of the different classes; while W. P. Frith's painting, *The Railway Station* (1862), was acclaimed for also capturing this aspect of the metropolitan railroad station.[19]

In the very early period there had been no station waiting-rooms at all—just separate "pens" on the platform for first- and second-class passengers—which were usually accessed by separate pedestrian walkways (goods sheds and livestock pens often sufficed for the third-class passengers in the early period). When waiting-rooms emerged they were provided only at termini and larger stations. However, by the late 1830s the single waiting-room was considered unacceptable by the upper social classes. Hence, waiting space was stratified and enclosed relative to the passenger classes (usually just first- and second-class at that time), although gender differences could result in a further division of these passenger class enclosures.

The public waiting-room was a novel phenomenon and a source of perplexity for some people, especially women traveling alone. Indeed, even by the mid–19th century the rules of chaperonage were still very strict in England—an unmarried woman (of the middle and upper classes) under thirty could not go anywhere or be in a room, even in her own house, with an unrelated man unless also accompanied by a married gentleman or a servant.[20] And since unchaperoned "ladies" loitering in public places were usually assumed to be offering "passenger accommodation" of another kind it was absolutely necessary, therefore, that the railroad companies provided separate waiting-room space for women—so that their status as travelers was unambiguously clear. Indeed, as Mayhew showed in his wonderfully meticulous, extended account of the social stratification of prostitution services in Mid-Victorian London, some prostitutes were very well dressed and could easily have been mistaken for "ladies of class" (visually at least).

Before the railroad age, women of the upper classes had seldom traveled beyond their local areas, and most of the travel they did undertake was in the form of "morning calls" (in the afternoon!). Indeed, one might reasonably have expected the "range" of that most resilient of Victorian bourgeois female institutions, the morning call, to have been extended somewhat by the advent and increasing aristocratic and bourgeois female use of railroads. That aside, before the railroad age women of the middle and upper-classes living within 20 or 30 miles of London would seldom have visited that city, in many cases not even as often as annually.

Where the waiting-room was concerned, waiting itself was not new, since travelers had always had to wait for coaches. But the gentleman traveler would normally have retired to an inn to await the coach, perhaps to imbibe a "bracer" before embarking upon his journey, while the lady traveler of means would normally have awaited the coach in her own carriage, which was the "proper" thing to do. However, in the early railroad period people of the upper classes often had to wait for the train in the station waiting-room. But, as indicated, eventually these facilities were often both passenger class- and gender-differentiated, and by 1845 some railroad companies had extended the separate female waiting-room facility to the provision of "Ladies Only" carriage compartments. However, that ran against the general trend, which was to integrate the sexes during railroad travel. Nevertheless, such separate-sex facilities, even if short-lived, probably did much to encourage bourgeois women to use the railroads in the first place, as well as reassuring their husbands and fathers that doing so was "proper."

To some extent, eventually the advent of luxurious railroad company-owned station hotels, often attached or adjacent to stations, resolved the problem of the "public" waiting-room for upper-class men and women. Some of these railroad hotels were very exclusive affairs, often intended, or at least parts of them were, to have the same status as private clubs, and to have a club atmosphere.

Female use of the railroad may have resulted in a shift in clothing fashion eventually as well. The crinoline and the hooped skirt were not quite such "mindless" (self-) impositions as we might think, since they made it clear that the wearer was a member of a leisured class who did not do physical work. Furthermore, the production of such sartorial embellishments employed a lot of people. In fact, the textile "yardage" used in the hooped skirt or (multi-layered) petticoats worn around 1850 would have clothed 14 women in the 1920s,[21] so there was certainly a lot of (fabric) "bulk" involved; while crinoline manufacture, too, employed a lot of people in the metal industries. And perhaps the contemporary railroad companies' greatest oversight, in this regard, was not to inflict upon female travelers encumbered so a surcharge for the extra "baggage."

But certainly women's dress of this kind was not at all conducive to railroad traveling—such dress encroached imperialistically beyond the wearer's own seat, while "puffy" sleeves could also encroach, much to a fellow passenger's annoyance.[22] And since the early railroad carriages were fashioned after the coach, perhaps what the author of a 1745 tract (entitled *The Enormous Abomination of the Hoop-Petticoat*) had to say on the matter applied no less to the early railroad age—he complained that wearing this "prodigious garment takes up too much room," and that it becomes "a perfect publick nuisance in the streets, in coaches, and at church."[23]

But just how difficult it must have been traveling by rail in the early period when outfitted so is attested to by a much more recent "case." In the early 1980s the Italian fashion journalist, Anna Piaggi, spent six months traveling by train because the exaggerated crinolines she liked to wear would not allow her to fit through the door of a plane[24] (in the early period railroad carriage compartment doors were probably often just as narrow). But if the practicalities and exigencies of railroad traveling induced a change in Victorian female attire, the cause of dressing more sensibly was certainly given a nudge by Queen Victoria; whom, in an open letter addressed to the ladies of England in 1863, stated her disapproval of the crinoline—there were safety issues, too, since "overwrapped" women had been known to become entangled in carriage wheels or blown under horses in the street.[25] Likewise, there was probably some risk of them being blown off station platforms and onto the tracks.

English Railroad Station Architecture

In ancient civilization architecture was used to extol the greatness of a ruler or to express religious sentiment and to honor the gods. Samuel Florman has suggested that every man-made structure, no matter how mundane, has a "little bit of cathedral in it," since man cannot help but transcend himself as soon as he begins to design and construct.[26] John Ruskin suggested that even the simplest structure produces a visual impression upon those who use it or look at it, and that both the form of the architecture and the materials used in its construction reveal much about the builder and the society in which he lives. Lewis Mumford concurred, suggesting that buildings are essentially "documents."[27] Of course, what such "documents" reveal to posterity may be considerably more than their builders imagined might be the case. That said, we should not lose sight of a relationship which often obtains where certain types of architecture are concerned—a relationship between architectural pretension on the one hand, and the power and authority it symbolizes on the other. More generally, we should not lose sight of the fact that architecture, especially "monumental" architecture, often has glaringly ideological import.

In 19th century Britain monumental station architecture was used to express both the power and prestige of the railroad companies concerned. But just as often it was an element in a broader public relations exercise. Indeed, the monumental station was often intended to be an addition to a long-established city's grand, architecturally tasteful buildings. But the use of architecture by railroad companies was a no less effective public relations tool in provincial towns, where the architectural "delight" (the station and its environs) was intended often to serve as a majestic "gateway" to the "place," thus enhancing the prestige and presence of the railroad company, as well as supposedly enhancing the civic pride of such towns[28]—in Britain even small companies could be quite extravagant in their architectural embellishment of stations. In fact, Edgar Jones has argued that, increasingly during the 19th century, architecture became an advertising medium as well as an indicator of corporate status.[29] That was undoubtedly true of the principal architectural works associated with many early English railroad companies, but it was a little different in America, as we shall see in subsequent chapters.[30]

The English guidebooks, published for the use of railroad travelers during the first few decades of railroading are full of references to railroad architecture (and feats of engineering along the railroad), which often read like advertisements for the railroad companies concerned. But was "publicity" all that monumental station architecture was about?

Because the railroad traveler was implicated in a factory-type, industrial production process, the railroad companies had to "package" the railroad traveling experience—for the upper social classes, especially, for whom industrial process was novel—in such a way that both the industrial plant and the industrial quality to traveling were presented and managed ways in which accounted for "delicate sensibilities." Station architecture was also used both to dignify the industrial dimension to railroad travel and to reassure the timid traveler. Indeed, as two architectural historians have noted: "The distinguished diplomatic mush, which cloaks the front of St. Pancras Station, decisively and safely shields the tender eye from the rigors of engineering within."[31]

But there was more to it than that. The entrance to such stations was a "gateway" in other than the usual sense—it was a point (symbolically) separating the engineered, industrial space of the railroad system from what lay beyond it, and was thus a peculiar contribution to softening the "psychological" adjustment which the traveler needed to make within this engineered, industrial, closely administered environment.

John Ruskin was clearly a very perceptive critic of contemporary architectural forms and, for my purposes here, one might draw attention to two premises which often informed his appraisal of architecture. Firstly, he argued that all buildings show people as either "gathering" or "ruling"—arguably, the railroad companies were implicated in both (at least during passenger travel where the latter was concerned). Secondly, he argued that all architecture presupposes some effect on the human mind; that premise inclining him to argue, furthermore, that architecture and architectural decoration may be used to "disguise disagreeable necessities."[32] Moreover, Ruskin was adamant that there was such a thing as "improper" appropriation of architectural styles and motifs, and furthermore, that there were injudicious, even insipid, applications of them. And he seemed to be especially splenetic in his condemnation of "monumental" station architecture.

But it is not altogether clear why Ruskin singled out railroad station architecture for criticism against a backdrop of industrial architectural buffoonery more generally at the time—Ruskin referred to the "impertinent folly" and the "strange and evil tendencies" of decorating railroad stations. But perhaps Ruskin homed in on station architecture because in his time the railroad was emerging as a national arterial system with the termini and stations its nodal points—such nodal points the system's ugly "gargoyles," while the emergent railroad system itself was the "Roman Nose" of industrial capitalism and demonstrably symbolic of its broad environmental impact. But, like almost everybody else in his time, Ruskin could not afford to miss the train—in fact, he *did* compromise himself by riding thousands of miles in a first-class compartment aboard one of "the loathsomest forms of devilry now extant," as he once described the railroad.[33]

But Ruskin was hardly a "lone wolf" when it came to "howling" about the misappropriation of classical architectural forms and their incorporation in railroad architecture. Pugin thought the colossal Greek portico at the entrance to Euston Station "useless decoration" applied to "gigantic piles of unmeaning masonry."[34] But even in relatively recent times the same phenomenon has been assailed by architectural critics. Hersey, for instance, has attacked "classical formalism"—by which he meant the mindless repetition and variation of forms for their own sake, irrespective of their literary, associational, and poetic meanings, and irrespective of their mythical origins. And Hersey poses an interesting question. "Why do architects erect columns and temple fronts derived ultimately from Greek temples when ancient Greek religion has been dead for centuries, and when the temples themselves were not even buildings in the sense that they housed human activities?"[35] And this was the question Ruskin seemed to be asking almost a century and a half earlier.

Hersey goes on to point out that in origin the word "ornament" has little to do with beauty. Rather, it applied originally to something which had been equipped or prepared in a distinct way for a ritual or symbolic function or purpose—as in "fitting out" a hunter, soldier, or priest. Hence, an ornamental temple was one which had been prepared to honor the gods by means of sacrifice. Such places were never intended to be beautiful, but to elicit a sense of dread in their beholders (Nietzsche, too, had something to say on this matter, and very much along the same lines).

In classical architecture, there were "hierarchies of decorum"; and the degree of stateliness, and the amount and form of decoration, was often commensurate with the status of the client or patron.[36] But it would also have undoubtedly been determined by the god or gods being honored in the case of a temple. On the other hand, concepts such as "Greek," "Roman," and even "classical" are abstractions, and thus amenable to being over-generalized, especially so the moment one starts legislating about their appropriate meanings and applications. After all, both Greek and Roman civilizations flourished for centuries, their cultures changed dynamically across those time spans as one would expect, and both inherited much from other cultures and civilizations which both preceded and coexisted alongside them (or were politically—but not necessarily culturally—incorporated within them). Furthermore, there never was a Greek nation in the ancient world, but only ever a heterogeneous collection of political entities which did not necessarily—and often did not—share identical genealogical foundations where "culture" was concerned. But let us not get lost in the historical detail.

Indeed, all that said, let us return to the question as to why 19th century architectural critics singled out railroad station architecture—as Ruskin and others did—for especial criticism. To begin with, one might recognize a line of descent running from ornate domestic chimneys and fireplaces through the classically-embellished, smoke-spewing chimneys of the satanic mills to the castellated railroad tunnel entrance, railroad station portico, and even to the "prettied-up" (painted and ornamented) mobile boiler which the locomotive was. In fact, in the late 18th and 19th centuries we find peculiar architectural embellishment to have been a more general feature of commercial-industrial culture in Britain. Indeed, there were many commercial interests in the 18th and 19th centuries—potteries and dock companies, for instance—which used architectural "pretension" to dignify or enhance the public image of the industry or business concerned. And, more generally in the 18th century, mills sometimes had impressive classical features such as arches and Doric columns—Edgar Jones suggests some such buildings could easily have been mistaken for a substantial townhouse with a typical Georgian façade. And some "satanic mills" of the early 19th century even had elegant engine houses and ornate chimneys.[37]

So, we begin to see that in the 19th century the incorporation of classical themes and motifs in industrial architecture was hardly confined to the building of railroad stations and termini. In fact, it popped up in the most unlikely places—the same was true of America, as will be evinced in subsequent chapters. And, in reflecting upon why Ruskin and his contemporaries singled out railroad station architecture for especial criticism, I want to look, albeit briefly, at some of these broader appropriations (mis-appropriations as Ruskin would have viewed them) of classical architectural styles and motifs and their applications in commercial-industrial settings in late 18th and 19th century Britain.

To begin with, the architecture of gasworks often incorporated classical themes, the triumphant Doric column a popular chimney form for such works. Iron works and other such industrial plant were also "housed" in architecturally ennobled buildings—for instance, in the early 19th century the Bute Ironworks at Rhymney had a pretentious, Egyptian-style façade. Nor should we overlook the canals, which could feature tunnel decoration, though not typically—for instance, the eastern portal on the Sapperton Tunnel (1789) on the Thames and Severn Canal had a classical façade complete with Roman Doric columns. Another point of note is that the Victorians were sensitive to, but usually silent about, bodily functions. Not surprisingly, then, sewage works were both camouflaged and dignified architecturally—Bazalgette's Crossness Sewage Works (1865) had "extremely ornate ironwork with an Italianate Romanesque interior."

Apart from camouflaging distasteful and unpalatable industrial process, dignifying various forms of industrial capitalism, or simply reflecting the "aesthetic" excesses of generously indulged engineers and architects, Victorian architectural pretense could be underpinned by other motivations as well. Pubs, which generally catered to the lower and middling social classes, were often places of "the greatest architectural elaboration." But why? Presumably this was to help give them a "moral tone" or dignity which they clearly did not possess. In fact, the trend of dignifying pubs by architectural means spanned a range of architectural styles—Swiss Cottage and Chalet, Italian and Gothic Revival with romantic gables and ornate interiors to the fore. Institutions such as lunatic asylums were also apparently in need of similar ennoblement—St. Ann's Heath Lunatic Asylum in Surrey (1871–84), for instance, had quite lavish Gothic decoration.[38] In America the architectural embellishment of the "disagreeable" was similarly manifest in "institutional" architecture—South Carolina's State Asylum was described, by Hamlin, as a "masterpiece of Greek Revival architecture," while he described the Utica Insane Asylum (1838) as given a "quiet dignity, distinction and beauty" by its monumental Greek Doric portico.[39] Architectural embellishment was sometimes used for jails as well in America—for instance, the Philadelphia Jail (1835) was of Gothic design, though the debtor's wing was Egyptian!

In England in the early 18th century, the third Duke of Richmond built a magnificent stable block for his hunters and racehorses "complete with Doric columns and a triumphal arch." And in the early 19th century the grandstand at Epsom racecourse was "all Doric columns."[40] But did it get any stranger? It certainly did at London Zoo, founded in the 1820s; the first generation of animal houses there apparently resembling nothing so much as an "eclectic English village or gingerbread suburb." Yet, the first Elephant House was a little thatched pavilion with Gothic windows, but was eventually replaced by something which apparently looked like a terraced row of gabled country cottages. The Camel House was an ornate villa surmounted by a clock tower. And by 1864 the monkeys, in their Beaux Arts Pavilion, could spit at the visitors through ornamental arched windows, while the Giraffe House was a type of "Tuscan barn" which would have been immediately recognizable by a Venetian Renaissance villa owner.[41] What did John Ruskin make of those oddities?

However, when it came to architectural embellishment of railroad stations certainly it was not only the architectural critics who were complainants. In a letter to a newspaper in October 1838 the correspondent impugned the spending of shareholders' funds on lavish architectural ornamentation of stations: "Why should we, subscribers in Lancashire, pay for noble and beautiful buildings at London and Brighton, or London and Colchester? The best railway ornament that I know of ... is not a capital of either the Dome, Ionian, Tuscan or Corinthian Order, but a capital dividend."[42] And so the Philistines struck back! Indeed, the previous year *The Morning Post* had "raised its eyebrows" concerning the £7,000 worth of masonry at the mouth of the Primrose Tunnel, as well as at the £30,000 worth of railroad company portico at Euston Square.[43]

Symes and Cole have suggested that during the early period of English railroading, the four main south-eastern companies used architecture as an image-enhancing strategy at a time when railroads still faced opposition from various foes.[44] To my mind, that seems a reasonable enough assertion. Yet, all the rationales invoked, hitherto, to explain the peculiarities of much station architecture during the early period of railroading may be insufficient.

If people like Ruskin and Pugin would question the legitimacy of applying classical architectural forms to Victorian industrial and commercial architecture, then to be consistent they might have questioned why a "fluent" knowledge of Greek and Latin—and other aspects of Greco-Roman culture—remained not only conspicuously extant in Victorian culture, but an essential part of the education and cultivation of genteel folk like themselves. To take this "logic" to its conclusion, one might ask why the Victorians read anachronistic literature like the Bible or Shakespeare so enthusiastically (not to mention Thucydides and Tacitus) and "ornamented" their personas by being able to mindlessly quote the stuff? Which brings us to a key point. Was the use of Greco-Roman culture by railroad companies, for instance, as "mindless" as some contemporaries would have it? I suggest not.

Let us not overlook the fact that for many decades the railroad companies were only interested in first- and second-class patronage of their services, and that they catered only somewhat patronizingly and unwillingly to the "hoi polloi." The second-class passengers could be a "middling" lot. But I think most people who could afford to regularly avail themselves of the "first" passenger class would have been from the upper-classes in society, many of whom would have been classically schooled (to some extent at least, formally or otherwise), and often have had leisure interests with some classical associations—literature, art, architecture, history, and the (Latin) Linnaean system of biological classification. Hence, one might view the use of classicism in railroad architecture as an attempt by the railroad companies to ingratiate themselves to such well-heeled and (classically-) "cultivated" consumers. And when considered in this light the architectural oddities and eccentricities in question may not have seemed as alien and irrelevant to many contemporaries as they seemed to John Ruskin or as they might seem to us.

In that connection, then, familiarity was assumed by the railroad companies not to breed contempt. Indeed, in the same connection one notes the spacious entrance halls were sometimes in emulation of the great halls of aristocratic manors which could accommodate banquets on a grand scale. But reassuring the (well-heeled) traveler entailed the more widespread use of familiar architectural imagery by railroad companies—for instance, the Midland's Grand Hotel at St. Pancras had a Big Ben look-alike clock tower,[45] while Churton noted that the Brighton Station refreshment room was "fitted up in the style of a handsome London coffee house," and that the covered passage at the London Bridge Terminus was "similar to the Lowther Arcade in the Strand."[46]

Indeed, this use of architecture (as well as the subtler classical embellishments), rather than being mindless, could be viewed as clever and "cunning" advertising on the part of the railroad companies concerned. After all, the image production which much modern advertising engenders links commodities with all manner of historical entities, events, and places; but such associations often quite meaningless to most people, and often leaving one scratching one's head and asking oneself, "what was that all about?" Indeed, it is remarkably common today for the promotion of a commodity, or of a corporation associated with it, to entail invoking all kinds of "strange" historical imagery—almost invariably completely perverting any historical context in the process—simply to add "dignity" or an "aura" to the commodity or corporation in question. And if some Victorians thought there was something "profane" about the appropriation of classical architectural forms, by industrial capitalists or other commercial interests to ennoble their enterprises, then arguably that was because they were not—as we today are—inured to the appropriation by capitalism of historical imagery and iconography in the quest to market goods and services. In Victorian times, classical architectural forms "captured" in this way often had precisely that kind of utility. But even though this was a novel phenomenon at the time, contemporary objections to it become interesting if only because they materialized at all—clearly the likes of Ruskin and Pugin did not know a good advertisement when they saw one!

In the same connection, another cunning strategy employed by some English railroad companies was to try to convince the locals that the railroad came as a friendly power, and to do that by incorporating iconic aspects of local culture in their armorial devices. Of course, the fact railroad companies had armorial devices at all tells us something about their ennobling self-images. That aside, the ideological tactic in question—whereby iconic aspects of local culture were incorporated in railroad company armorial devices—was intended primarily to impress upon the "local" a sense of familiarity, or even that the railroad rightfully belonged in the locality and that it was integral to both the local economy and the environment. Perhaps the exemplar of this phenomenon—and there are numerous examples of it—was the armorial device of the Leeds and Thirsk (1845). The three divisions of its shield on the coat of arms displayed: (1) a sheaf of corn, highlighting the role of the railroad in the local agrarian economy; (2) a fleece—a symbol which the company "pinched" from the arms of Leeds, so it was both familiar to the locals and further reinforced the railroad's tie to the local agrarian economy; and (3) a fish—Thirsk was noted for its trout streams.[47]

Catering to the Aristocracy

During the early period, aristocratic types often preferred to travel in their own carriages lashed onto flat wagons. The fact that railroad companies usually bent over backwards to accommodate this practice indicates the aristocracy remained a potent force in early Victorian society, although upper middle-class people also availed themselves of this facility, and it seems to have become quite the fashion for those able to afford it. Indeed, whereas the *aristocratic* use of the flat wagon facility had its roots in exclusivity, for upper middle-class people using it was more of a fashion (in emulation of the aristocrats). The companies even provided carriage "docks" for these people, which facilitated the efficient loading of carriages, presumably without their occupants needing to alight from them. But the anxiety experienced by the upper-classes, which led to their traveling in their own carriages lashed to freight wagons, apparently had a long pedigree—in 1683 Ralph Thoresby noted in his diary that he was "fearful" of being confined to the coach for so many days with "unsuitable persons."[48]

People traveling in the way described above could be charged a first- or second-class fare and a surcharge for conveyance of the carriage as well, depending on the pricing protocols of the railroad company concerned. If horses were transported, then there was sometimes an additional charge for that.

MacDermot noted that on the Great Western during its first few years the people wanting to travel in this way were "exceptionally numerous"—indicating that the "new" wealthy and non-landed aristocracy availed themselves of the facility. And MacDermot claims the only reason these people eventually gave it up was because the railroad compartments became much more comfortable than their carriages.[49] That it is a reasonable explanation, since railroad passenger carriages were eventually designed to minimize shock and vibration, whereas (railroad) flat wagons did not need to be mechanically engineered so. Exposure to the elements on flat wagons (especially driving winds) may also have eventually discouraged their use by private carriage travelers.

People who traveled in their own coaches and carriages lashed onto flat wagons were not just guarding their privacy or reclining in what might have been superior comfort (in the earliest period, at least) and with more "personal space" than would otherwise have been the case, or simply participating in a "fashion." In fact, people could do things in their own vehicles which they could not do in a railroad carriage compartment shared with other people. The Duke of Wellington, for instance, used to get changed in his carriage.[50] And this was a time when people of the upper-classes conformed to strict dress codes and were expected to change costume—often several times a day—in accordance with the occasion or time of day. The Duke of Wellington was still able to travel in this way—in his own carriage lashed to a flat wagon—in the early 1850s. He avoided using compartment accommodation on trains for as long as he could, excepting his ride in a railroad carriage at the opening of the Liverpool and Manchester Railway, and in 1843 when he was obliged to ride in one while accompanying the Queen on a railroad journey.

However, from the outset provision of this facility must have been a great nuisance for the railroad companies, since the time taken to load and unload these carriages would have been significant, and thus needed to be factored into operational schedules, even though on many company's lines carriages had to be at the embarkation point at least fifteen minutes before departure (servants and baggage went in the railroad carriages). All considered, it was probably not even profitable for the companies to provide such a facility.

However, one should not ignore the similarity between riding in your own carriage on a flat wagon behind a locomotive and the road transportation practice of traveling "post chaise"—a kind of carriage/horse "rental" service, where you changed (rented) horses every ten miles or so. The only real difference was that with the carriage on the train the train was the "horse," and it did not run out of legs or breath and, therefore, have to be changed every ten miles or so. Indeed, the people using this facility probably thought of themselves as traveling "post," especially since they may have hired horses at either or both ends of the railroad journey. And traveling by post-chaise had probably never been only about speed—it also precluded sharing carriage accommodation, as coach travel necessitated, and hence ensured privacy.[51]

In England in the early period the quests for comfort, convenience, exclusivity, privacy, and to participate in a "fashion" seemed to be the summary factors underlying the practice of traveling in one's own carriage on a railroad flat wagon. However, the comments of Augustus Hare—the "acidulated snob" we met in the previous chapter—concerning his family's journeys around 1850 afford insight into the social pressures which kept the upper-classes out of railroad compartments for so long. When he and his mother did finally come to use the "ordinary railroad carriage (but first-class, of course)," yet they still had themselves set down outside London (as mentioned earlier) so that they did not enter the metropolis by railroad; but not only because railroad travel itself was stigmatizing for such people at that time, but also because—according to Augustus Hare—it was "so excessively improper sitting opposite strangers in the same carriage."

But let us move on to look at some other peculiar forms of conveyance which some railroad companies made available to wealthy people in the early period. During the 1840s some companies provided "family saloons," which were first-class carriages—an entire carriage, in fact, but still compartmentalized, including a compartment at one end for the servants, and space at the other end for the mounds of baggage.[52] The Manchester and Birmingham, in its early years, allowed the liveried servants of aristocrats to travel in their own compartments on first-class trains but at second-class fares.[53] In 1879 Charles Darwin, when taking his family to the Lakes District for a holiday, splashed out on a private carriage for the journey.[54] So, these "family saloons," or something similar later on, were apparently accessible to anybody able to afford them.

In the early period, there was also something known as a "special." If some important person missed his train or had to go somewhere in a great hurry, then he could charter an entire train—the "special." Indeed, the "special" was common on some lines in the 1840s.[55] But even as late as 1881 Charles Darwin, again, was able to hire a private train for a journey from Bromley to Cambridge.[56] And even very late in the 19th century an aristocratic English fox-hunter could hire a private train and have it draw up on the track at a point near the meet, where his stud groom would have his horses waiting for him.[57] One notes, furthermore, that the "special" figured in fiction, notably in Conan Doyle's *The Vanishing Train* (1924), in which Mr. Caratal "absolutely refused to consider (sharing) it for an instant—the train was his," he said, "and he would insist upon the exclusive use of it." But in the early period it seems some companies may have compromised safety in the provision of "specials." In May 1845, both an engineman and the Superintendent of Locomotives for the Edinburgh and Glasgow Railway Company were charged with culpable homicide in respect of the death of a man who had hired a special train. He had negotiated the price down from ten to five pounds. But the (one-carriage) special train had neither a guard nor tail-lamp and was rammed from behind by another train in the accident concerned.[58]

The aristocracy, and members of the other upper-classes in Britain, were initially loath to use the railroad compartment, even though it might accommodate only four people and was thus fairly exclusive. They liked their privacy and they valued their privilege. The idea that a perceived social "inferior," even if a very "well-to-do" or "cultured" person, was treated just as they were could be unpalatable. The "stranger" was also to be avoided. But if the aristocracy was slow to fully appreciate the benefits railroad travel might confer, yet once its members attained such realization, they used the railroad to their advantage, both personally and as a social class.

Indeed, where commuting was concerned, the English aristocracy was eventually able to cultivate its own variant upon it with the aid of the railroads, thus enabling more frequent visits to their estates by those who often had to reside in a large city, such as London, in connection with their business or political activities—typical in this regard was the Duke of Norfolk, whose Arundel estate in Sussex became much more accessible (with the advent of the railroad) from his London residence, Norfolk House. Indeed, one source suggests the advent of the railroad invented the possibility of the "country house weekend" for these wealthy classes.[59] But, strictly speaking, that is incorrect—what the railroad did do was make far-flung country house retreats much more accessible.

Likewise, in America the railroads could hardly be thought of as having instituted a similar type of "commuting"—from an urban center to a country village or rural "estate"—for the upper-classes in the great "classless" society; since, on the north-eastern seaboard, for instance, steamboats along the Hudson River and elsewhere, rather than the railroads, first effected that development. However, railroads eventually made commuting (for magnates) from quite far-flung places up the Hudson River practicable.

Surtees, in *Plain or Ringlets*, cast the rural aristocracy as a mostly sedentary class until the advent of railroads, which enabled its members to rub shoulders with each other in London clubs. In fact, prior to the "club age" many members of the aristocracy did not know each other unless they were members of the House of Lords or related through marriage. The enhanced mobility which the railroads afforded, along with the increasing fashion and extension of London "club culture," assisted the welding of class consciousness within the waning aristocracy. But it also enabled the newly emergent capitalist and professional classes in the same way, facilitating the forging of strategic economic and political links between them, as well as between these newly-aligned (parvenu) social classes and the aristocracy.

First-Class Passenger Travel and Carriage Accommodation

First-class passenger accommodation entailed a rationalization of social classes, since even first-class accommodation represented a standardized commodity. And the standardized service offered in the form of first-class carriage and compartment accommodation was set at a level which the upper social classes could only view, from their lofty social pedestals, as a rather low common denominator." Nor should one overlook the fact that, historically, and especially on military expeditions—as opposed to ceremonial occasions where the situation was different—the "train" followed in the wake of the "great one." But, alas, now the "great one" was a machine, and no matter who the (self-declared?) dignitary he had to ride behind it as part of the "train."

Consequently, those people (especially the aristocracy) who sniffed pure ozone high up in the stratosphere initially demanded extraordinary privileges from the railroad companies—such as their own private stations or that facility whereby they could travel in their own coaches or carriages lashed to flat wagons—even as late as 1848 some companies were still prepared to *build* private stations for powerful and influential members of the aristocracy,[60] while members of the aristocracy were still able to *use* private stations as late as 1867, and in some instances for decades after that date. But eventually members of the aristocracy had to accommodate themselves to the exigencies of public transportation if they wished to take full advantage of railroad travel. But let us move on, to look now at the actual passenger accommodation within the carriages.

On some English railroads during the early 1830s three higher levels of passenger accommodation within the carriage were offered under the rubric of first-class. The following, based on one company's offering, is intended to be representative rather than put forward as universal or even a common standard. However, it gives a sense of the phenomenon in question. On this railroad, there was the extra-luxurious, first-class coach with first-class, four-seater compartments (eight shillings); next, a slightly inferior first-class coach which offered first-class, four-seater compartments (six shillings); and, finally, first-class coach with first-class, six-seater compartments (five shillings). The next step down—and significant in terms of comforts provided—was the second-class compartment (three shillings and sixpence) in a second-class carriage. By way of contrast, the London and Birmingham (1837–44) had a slightly different scale of provision—there were, effectively, five passenger classes due to discriminations made within two of the classes. Hence, there were two first, two second, and one third class.[61]

By the mid–1830s first-class compartment accommodation typically provided the passenger with cushioned seats, padded backs, and elbow rests. And by mid-century the first-class passenger was usually accommodated within a spacious compartment, although excessively "petticoated" or "crinolined" women, along with all the baggage they often carried with them, could cramp it somewhat. That aside, the first-class passenger was allocated a personal space, sufficient to allow bodily spread and comfort, and it was usually privatized—to a point—by means of dividing arm rests. The compartment was normally carpeted and tastefully lined, and often also had an adjustable means of ventilation, some form of artificial lighting, and sometimes extras such as foot warmers. And when advertising on trains was introduced (mid-century), first-class passengers were spared this assault on their senses, since initially advertisements were inflicted only on second-class passengers, it seems.[62] As for toilets, they did not become available on ordinary passenger trains until 1882—first-class passengers on the Great Northern the first to have the honor during the course of a railroad journey[63] (notwithstanding that the Pullman sleeping cars available years before that date on the Midland Railway would have had separate men's and ladies' toilets in them).

Foot-warmers had become available to most first-class passengers by mid-century. These early foot warmers were made of iron and about two-and-a-half feet long, nine inches wide, and four inches deep. Like a "hot water bottle," they were filled up with boiling water. Of course, in very cold weather they very quickly cooled down and became "foot freezers," apart from which they sometimes leaked. And during a long journey it could be difficult or impossible to get them refilled or replaced, so they may not have been any great comfort to the traveler.[64] Such foot-warmers may have been around for centuries, since in colonial New England women and children had portable foot-stoves filled with a box of hot coals to warm their feet during lengthy church sittings in winter, and that may have been something brought to America from England.[65]

By way of contrast, in mid–19th century France first-class railroad carriages were often not only carpeted, they also commonly had an elaborate system of pipes—containing hot water—to warm the passengers" feet in winter. And in America from very early on passenger cars were furnished with stoves—presumably there must have been firewood stacked somewhere in the car, unless it was transported there from the tender, nor is it clear whose job it was to keep the stove fire going. Whatever the case, the author of an 1879 English newspaper article, who had enjoyed the warmth provided by a stove in American carriages, remarked that: "The foot-warmer, which is the nearest approach to the heating of railway carriages our civilization (the English) has yet attained, gets cold before we have traveled 30 miles."[66] He went on to praise the stoves in the American cars. But these stoves were often a source of complaint as well, especially from English tourists, as we shall see in the chapters following. They were also a terrible hazard when accidents occurred, which was quite often on American railroads. For instance, a disaster on the (Chicago) Lake Shore Railroad in December 1867—involving the derailment of an express train traveling at speed, and which resulted in almost 50 deaths—highlighted the risk of stoves in passenger carriages:

> The horror of the situation was sufficient without that which instantly became added by the igniting of the splintered wreck from the overturned stoves.... The dry wood of the car burned like a heap of kindling.... Nearly fifty human beings roasted ... committed to the flames without hope of rescue.[67]

Perhaps there is a certain irony to the fact that stoves, which were clearly a fire hazard in the event of an accident, were almost obligatory on American trains in the early period, whereas many American companies were loath to use oil lamps (for illumination) in the cars for quite some time—even after they had become a standard household fixture—because they supposedly posed a fire risk.[68]

Perhaps the only other issue that needs to be addressed here concerning first-class provision is to consider its economic viability for the companies. Edward Dorsey (1887) stated that by then: "It is safe to say no railway in England now makes any money from its first-class travel."[69] I have no doubt he was correct in that assessment, since he would have done his homework. And I think almost every company would have been subsidizing—in some cases for decades—first-class passenger conveyance by means of correspondingly elevated freight rates and similarly elevated second- and third-class passenger fares. Indeed, while researching this book I came across innumerable 19th century (book and article) assertions that travel on English railroads was generally overpriced, if not exorbitantly so; and that, in an international comparative context, railroad passenger travel in England was more expensive than anywhere else in the world, and certainly more expensive than in America. However, the English companies generally spent more on safety measures, on quality track construction, and station and other facilities, and their passenger class system was also an imposition.

If Edward Dorsey was correct, in his assertion that first-class passenger provision did not pay, yet perhaps he might have suggested that, even at that time (1887), it was effectively subsidized by the passengers traveling in second- and third-class. The astute contemporary railroad commentator, John Francis, suggested that this was evident (where passenger duty payable to the state was concerned) as early as 1832—he pointed out that the government duty on railroad passengers at that time was a half-penny per mile for every four passengers, although without reference to the passenger class. That meant, as Francis noted so insightfully, that: "While the rich man, traveling in the first-class train for pleasure, paid to the state three-and-a-half per cent upon his fare, the poor man, hurrying on the business which supported his household, paid twelve-and-a-half per cent."[70] But these passenger duties may have been lower or even non-existent in many countries where railroad travel was cheaper than in England, and that too may have been an explanatory factor in the international comparative context where passenger fares were concerned.

Second-Class Passenger Travel

Our statistical friend, Henry Mayhew, noted that 1845 through 1849 second-class passengers got more numerous every year, and that they were three times more numerous than first-class passengers by 1849.[71] But where second-class passenger provision was concerned, there is not a lot to be said here. In the early days on the Liverpool and Manchester, for instance, second-class carriages had been "little better than cattle trucks," with no seats, no partitions, and sides about three feet high—consequently, it was not uncommon for people to fall out.[72] Beyond the earliest period, second-class passengers tended to be accommodated in closed carriages, which were normally compartmentalized.

Writing in 1846, Robert Ritchie took the view that English second- and third-class carriages did not compare favorably with their French and Belgian counterparts.[73] Indeed, by mid-century the English second-class compartment was often not carpeted, lined, or cushioned, while the means of ventilation and illumination were relatively rationed—relative to first-class provision, that is. And it was not until the late 1850s that foot-warmers became available to second-class passengers. But perhaps Surtees put things in perspective—to a point—when noting in 1844 that "a second-class railway carriage (obviously a closed one) is infinitely better than the inside of an old stage coach."[74] In general terms, after mid-century the difference between first- and second-class passenger experience was marked essentially in respect of carriage or compartment furnishing, and access to amenities and services during travel.

The Architecture of the English Railroad Carriage Compartment and Its Carceral Character

One of the most curious features associated with the advent of railroads in England was the development of, and the passenger preference for, the compartment, although other European countries also embraced the compartment. Even in the 1870s, despite the anxieties and fears of some, there was still "great enthusiasm" for it as against the "American style" of (open) carriage. Among the reasons Acworth offered to explain why many English people came to prefer compartments was that they were just "plain stupid" or wanted "to escape crying babies and nuisance children."[75] These may well have had something to do with it, but they hardly serve as adequate explanations for something which, I suspect, had a much deeper *psychological* underpinning to it, as well as there being several (explanatory) sociocultural factors impinging upon the issue.

People could easily monopolize a compartment by means of the tactics discussed earlier. And no doubt some frequent travelers very quickly reduced that to an art form. However, such illicit compartment usurpation could be legitimized (by the guard or conductor), as also indicated earlier. Indeed, according to an 1869 newspaper article: "The traveler in England ... pays a few shillings to the guard for the privilege of having two or three seats instead of one. The guard, who has reduced this means of swindling the railway company to a system...."[76] In the same connection, one notes that on transatlantic ship crossings at around the same time it was possible to order one or two berths in your cabin so as not to have to share it.[77]

In addressing the peculiar English preference for the compartment several factors need to be broached. One is the architecture of the compartment itself. And the question arises as to whether there were architectural antecedents of the compartment familiar to the upper-classes and which, therefore, had some bearing upon its emergence as a preferred architectural form within English railroad capitalism.

The coach might *seem* to be the obvious architectural influence, as already indicated, but that was not necessarily all there was to the matter. After all, just because the coach seemed to the early railroad company proprietors the "logical" form the architecture of the railroad carriage ought to take, that does not explain the ongoing preference for the compartment as against an open style of carriage.

One possible antecedent which ought to be considered in the latter connection is the church pew. In the "better" churches in the more affluent areas the pew was not a seat, but often a "compartment" which was "owned" or rented by individuals or families. Sometimes these church compartments were enclosed by obtrusive walls, which ensured privacy and exclusivity as well as the convenience of rendering its "inmates" invisible to the preaching clergyman—hence, its architecture was very conducive to their dozing off invisibly during lengthy sermons. And, apart from being possibly one immediate ancestor of the railroad compartment, the (compartment) church pew may also be considered an ancestor of the modern corporate box."

In that connection, we might also entertain the idea that the "private box" at the theatre may have had some influence on the development of the railroad compartment. However, although most well-to-do people went to church, yet many stayed away from the theatre and other "frivolous" entertainments in an age of extreme seriousness and evangelical earnestness. So, I should be inclined to think the church pew and the coach more likely antecedents of the railroad compartment than the theatre box.

Another possible influence on the architecture of the compartment—and even if not a direct architectural influence, yet it may have inclined the bourgeois and aristocratic passenger to identify the compartment with it (as a comfortable, cozy, private, self-contained, and familiar space)—was the "inglenook" (chimney corner). This was an alcove, often found in the large homes of the very well-to-do. It was, in effect, just a very small room (strictly speaking, a recess), usually with some comfortable chairs and a fireplace, and often it was the warmest, coziest, most intimate, and most favored little "corner" in a large house, and very conducive to being "privatized."

Other considerations, where the upper social class preference for compartments was concerned, draw us in the direction of psychological factors. Perhaps the early socialization of the (upper-class) child was one in which it did not have much social interaction with anybody apart from family and servants. Hence, the child's nursery space and, later, the "run of the house," were domains it experienced in relative social isolation (even parents of these upper-class children often had very little to do with them). Furthermore, the socialization process in question was one which did not often expose the child to public spaces, public events, or strangers, while the child often had governesses or tutors rather than going to school—until into its teens if a boy and often not at all if a girl. And even when the child did venture out, yet the "public" the child encountered was invariably an upper social class bubble hermetically sealed off from the rest of society, while the child's "presence" on such social occasions was carefully circumscribed and subject to constraint—it often was very much a case of speak only when spoken to.

Given such processes of socialization, it should not surprise that people of the English upper social classes had serious inhibitions and anxieties attending their use of public transport, which extended to having to share a railroad compartment with just 3 to 5 other people unknown to them. And many of the people under consideration here were probably not only maladjusted, but quite possibly psychologically and socially impaired.

However, it was not just this form of obligatory social interaction (sharing compartments) which perturbed the upper social class traveler, it was also the confined space in which it occurred. This confinement put serious constraints on the amount of "personal space" allocated everyone within the confines of the compartment, a forced spatial intimacy which exacerbated the social "imposition." And this was the point at which "personal space," and what I defined earlier as "social space," had to be mediated. And that tension was very problematic for upper-class English railroad travelers.

The truth is there is no simple answer to the question as to why the early English railroad companies compartmentalized their carriages or why most "well-heeled" passengers preferred the compartment to the open carriage. However, for the early railroad companies ensuring the patronage of the upper social classes necessitated that the commodification and consumption of railroad travel, by such people, be characterized by some degree of both relative exclusivity and privacy. I would suggest it was also desirable that an architectural form that was familiar and which they felt comfortable with was provided.

On the other hand, from the outset English railroad administration was notably bureaucratic and disciplinary. In fact, the two (railroad discipline and the passenger "box") may be articulated, and that "hand-in-glove" articulation will become of more interest here in due course. Indeed, we might identify a certain harmony of interest between the well-to-do passenger's desire for relative privacy and exclusivity, and the railroad company's bureaucratic and disciplinary imperatives (in the early period passengers were locked in compartments). And what mediated these two spheres of interest, essentially, were, at least ostensibly, considerations of safety and security. So, it is not too difficult to theorize how the carriage compartment may have come to be favored by both the railroad companies and the well-to-do passenger on that rationale alone. However, if the railroad carriage compartment was the best available "compromise" that could be made in accommodating the well-to-do passenger, yet it was neither universally welcomed nor unproblematic.

At the head of this chapter I offered up a quotation from Sydney Smith's[78] 1842 letter to a newspaper in which he complained about the over-officiousness of the railroad companies, and in which he lampooned their insistence on locking people in compartments. He went on, in the same letter to the *Morning Chronicle*, to point out that "outside" coach passengers had never been tied to the roof to prevent them falling off, nor had packet passengers been locked in their cabins to prevent them from falling overboard and drowning. He also suggested that many well-to-do women avoided using the railroads precisely because of this "abominable tyranny and perilous imprisonment." Smith's diatribe is surely one of the greatest verbal assaults launched against the English railroad companies during the Victorian era, and there were many such assaults. And it inclines one to wonder what he would have made of the world we live in today, with all its institutionalized variations on the multi-faceted theme of "political correctness"— an insidious phenomenon which even George Orwell, the inventor of "Big Brother," had not really anticipated in its fullest guise. And perhaps the genealogical foundation of "political correctness" was, indeed, the phenomenon of locking people in railroad carriage compartments for their own safety!

The isolation of the railroad passenger—locked in a compartment with strangers and with no escape—induced a wave of paranoia during the 1850s/1860s when, quite exceptionally it must be said, people were sometimes robbed, assaulted, or "done to death" under such circumstances. But I have more to say about that later. For now, we note that the architecture of the early railroad carriages—for those well-heeled enough to pay for compartment accommodation—was indeed amenable to a severe disciplinary regimen, and that during the early period the passengers were almost invariably locked inside their compartments, the doors of which afforded the only form of egress, there being no internal corridor within the compartment carriage.

No doubt most English railroad companies would have argued that this was necessary in the interest of, if nothing else, preventing people disembarking while the train was in motion, and more generally to ensure the safety and security of the passenger. And that would have been a valid argument, especially during the early period. For there were, at that time, frequent occurrences of people jumping off while the train was in motion—often to chase hats (these were passengers in open carriages, however)—with no appreciation of how dangerous that was. And there is no doubt that people locked in compartments and closed third-class carriages would, at least occasionally, have been silly enough to do the same thing if able to. In that connection, one notes an 1839 newspaper article which referred to the continued "foolish temerity of persons in attempting to get out of the carriages while at full speed to recover articles." The article mentioned a man who did so while the train was running at 30 mph., but "fortunately for himself he was precipitated into a pond."[79]

By mid-century most companies were leaving the non-egress (but emergency only—there were two doors for compartments) door unlocked. However, as Mark Huish of the London and North Western pointed out in his medal-awarded paper on railroad safety presented to the Institution of Civil Engineers in 1852, people still (dangerously) hopped out of this compartment (emergency) door occasionally for whatever reason, usually onto the tracks and all too frequently with unfortunate consequences for the "escapee." Furthermore, Huish stated that at that time only one company still refused to have this emergency form of (one compartment door unlocked) egress available.

So, by around mid-century people locked in compartments may not have been as helpless in accident situations as was generally understood to be the case. In fact, it may have been that many passengers did not even realize one compartment door was unlocked. And, given the foolish propensity of some passengers to "misuse" this facility, perhaps the railroad companies had no real interest in publicizing (after mid-century) the fact that one compartment door was usually unlocked during travel.

Nevertheless, this concern for the passenger (locking them in compartments), which was ostensibly safety-driven, inevitably engendered a carceral approach to his or her care during a railroad journey. And right up there with Sydney Smith's memorable diatribe is the following extract from a newspaper article in 1863, which no less brilliantly captures the carceral dimension to the experience in question in a unique "phenomenology" of the (English) train of the time:

Two. Carceral Experiences of the 19th Century English Railroad Passenger 75

> A cruelly inexorable machine, composed of a set of closed boxes, chained together without the least communication with each other, dragged on by an irresistible force, along an inévitable iron path.... One of them may break, or get on fire, or jump off the line; but the engine and the engine driver need know nothing of what is going on, and may drag it mercilessly to destruction. Each of the boxes, too, is divided itself into smaller boxes, which are part, indeed, of the same construction; but, like adjoining prison cells, have no further communication with each other. The prisoners who occupy these cells may have no means of communicating with their neighbours, and they have not even the relief of knowing that they can apply, in the case of necessity, to their gaolers; for the gaolers are prisoners too, and are shut up by themselves—it may be several boxes off.[80]

So, the carceral dimension to the compartment was not just a matter of its secure closure, but also a matter of the passenger's inability to communicate anything to anybody (apart from their fellow compartment inmates) in the event of an emergency.

However, by the 1860s the latter dilemma had ceased to be a problem on American railroads, since, as English tourists using American railroads at that time noted with admiration, the American system incorporated a means by which any passenger could communicate to the engineman that the train needed to be stopped urgently. Yet, this American system had its own problems. The author of an 1868 article in *The North American Review*, in noting the reluctance of English railroad managers to adopt the rope and bell emergency stop system used on American railroads at the time, thought that reasonable, since, according to him, on American railroads it was "pulled improperly oftener than otherwise."[81]

To a point, the English "well-to-do" probably got the degree of relative exclusivity and privacy many insisted upon while railroad traveling during the early decades in England. But at what cost? After all, and as Americans liked to point out, the quest for privacy and exclusivity resulted in their being imprisoned in compartments for the duration of a railroad journey, only to be "paroled" when it was time for them to alight. Of course, paradox turned to tragedy on occasion, one of the worst tragedies in this accident "genre" occurring on the similarly carceral French railroads in the early 1840s: "A terrible accident on the railway between Paris and Versailles occurred on 8 May 1842. The train caught fire and some fifty-five passengers were burnt alive. None of them could climb out, for they had all been locked into their compartments by the railway officials."[82] That disaster was one factor which subsequently inclined the English companies to leave a compartment door on one side unlocked.

However, if the compartment represented an elevated risk to the European passenger in the event of an accident, yet the presence of the stove in the American cars no less elevated the risk to the passenger in such an event. Indeed, there was not a lot of difference between eventually being burned to death because one was locked in a compartment and being burned to death because the car stoves turned the wooden cars into incinerators in a matter of seconds.

Eventually, the design of passenger carriages on many European railroads was radically revised and there developed the type with an internal corridor—with access to compartments from the corridor. But that was a long time coming in Britain. However, Schivelbusch has suggested that, with this transformation of the architecture of the English railroad carriage, the carceral dimension to railroad traveling was by no means lessened, just altered—for now the guard could walk through the carriages, exercising close surveillance of them, so that he became akin to the prison guard who controlled the cells from his central tower.[83] However, most English upper-class railroad passengers, rather than viewing that as an imposition, would have found it as reassuring as having their nanny tuck them into bed at night. Indeed, such enhanced security offset rather than increased the anxieties which the former type of (compartment) carriage had given rise to; hence, this new system of surveillance reassured—if not coddled—English passengers, as they liked to be the case, even if not quite so carcerally as before.

Yet, many English people did not realize just how carceral the compartment experience was—essentially because they had habituated to it—until they traveled on American railroads. We get an excellent sense of that from the experiences of numerous English tourists to America, for whom "escape" from the English railroad compartment into the "public" car of the American railroads seemed almost like a cathartic release and relief for them—but only once they had accommodated themselves to it, which was not easy in some cases. And they would not have been so comfortable with it were it not for the surveillance of the perambulating conductor, which they invariably found extremely reassuring, even if many American conductors in the early period were bumptious, obnoxious, or even thuggish.

Furthermore, the majority of English tourists to America whose travel narratives I have read commented upon how safe America was, relatively, for a woman traveling alone. That arises so often as an observation—in both the women's and men's travel narratives—that one is left wondering if, in England at the time, it was possible for a woman to go anywhere without being insulted,"propositioned, indecently assaulted, or even ravished in public places. Therese Yelverton said: "A woman is secure in America from any unforeseen insult, at all hours, and in all places."[84] And Lady Hardy thought that the lack of privacy in American passenger cars (a degree of privacy which the English railroad compartment had, by way of contrast, provided) was "compensated for (in the American car) by safety from attacks of lunatics, thieves, or ruffianism."[85]

This raises a very interesting issue, concerning just how safe for women railroad compartment travel was in the first 50 years of railroading in England. Based on my own research, the conclusion I have reached is that there was little for anybody—including women—to fear; but there was a popular myth, underpinned by very real anxiety and fear, pertaining to the dangers for women traveling alone in compartments which they had to share with male strangers. But the news media also seemed to subscribe to the myth in question, and thus further fueled it by publishing assertions, such as that below, extracted from a letter to the editor of a Scottish newspaper in 1875. The letter argued that compartments were undesirable because: "They do not provide safety from outrage to females, while all acknowledge that safety is obtained in the open apartments of third-class carriages." The correspondent went on to say that compartment carriages "should be tossed among the rubbish of a darker age"; and he suggested adopting American-style carriages, both for the security of numbers it afforded the passenger and because of the surveillance of the roving conductor.[86]

But the myths pertaining to English railroad (compartment) travel safety "migrated." An American correspondent (for a Californian newspaper) claimed (1868) that women were not safe when traveling in English railroad compartments: "It is not a month since an outrage was committed upon a helpless woman while riding through a tunnel." The correspondent went on to allege that such incidents were "not very uncommon."[87] Furthermore, the author of an 1864 English newspaper article, in alluding to the well-publicized attack on a Miss Moody in a railroad carriage compartment (in July 1864), and to another case of indecent assault (on two sisters in a compartment, even though there was another gentleman—apart from the offender—in the compartment at the time!), also referred to "The wanton outrages to which females are daily subjected in the streets, in omnibuses, in railway carriages...."[88]

It is difficult to determine whether such assertions were valid at the time. All I can say is that my research of 19th century English newspapers, during which I spent some time researching the incidence of crime (and not just assaults on women) in connection with railroad travel or railroad amenities, failed to uncover very much at all where such alleged crimes were concerned; nor did my research of Old Bailey cases in the same connection (assaults on women in railroad carriage compartments) turn up very much.

The greatest fears entertained seemed to be in relation to women traveling alone in compartments with men (strangers) who might have sinister intent. And although hardly any cases of sexual offences occurring in railroad compartments were heard at the Old Bailey, for instance, that may have been because many such incidents were not reported. In fact, where the Old Bailey was concerned I could find only three cases of alleged sexual offences in railroad carriages in its records from the time of the advent of railroads through to the late 1880s. At the Old Bailey in November 1859 a man was charged with unlawfully assaulting a woman, but that was in a third-class carriage on an excursion train. And it seems he did little more than put his hands on her knees through her clothing. Nevertheless, he was found guilty, and although recommended to mercy by the jury he was "sent down" for one month. In February 1860, a man was charged with indecently exposing himself to a woman in a carriage on the South Eastern Railway. But it is not clear whether this incident occurred in a compartment, apart from which it was dismissed on a technicality, anyway. And in July 1864 a man was indicted for indecently assaulting a woman in a railway carriage on the North Kent Railway, though details of the case were not documented beyond that.[89]

Nevertheless, it seems that during the 1860s female compartment travelers were afflicted by a wave of paranoia—women demanding not to have to share a compartment with a lone male who might turn out *not* to be a gentleman; while lone gentlemen travelers, for their part, sometimes refused to share compartments with lone female travelers lest they be falsely accused of indecent assault![90]

If "outrages" against women during railroad travel in Britain were as common as some (media) sources—such as those mentioned above—suggest, then there may well have been any number of reasons why such incidents were not reported to the police. However, if such (allegedly numerous) offences were not reported to the police, do not figure prominently in the annals of criminal cases, and were not commonly reported by newspapers, then it inclines me to wonder how our informants (mentioned above) could justifiably make the assertions they did about how unsafe railroad traveling was for English women. They may well have been correct, but I have my doubts that women—and especially women traveling in railroad passenger compartments—were as unsafe as such sources suggest they were.

But strange things happened to men, too, in railroad carriage compartments. In 1850 a lady entered a first-class compartment with a two-month-old baby girl. She left the train at Shoreditch, ostensibly of necessity and just for a few moments, leaving the baby in the arms of the gentleman sharing the compartment with her, with whom she had not previously been acquainted. The woman was never seen again. The baby was wearing apparel "of a good and expensive description, and was wrapped in a silk cloak lined with ermine." There was a letter inside the baby's clothes, inside which were two ten-pound notes (a very large sum at that time). The letter stated that the child was "the offspring of persons of the highest respectability," and that if its "finder" made known publicly where it would be raised, then its owner would return to collect it one day—how reassuring for the "finder" of the foundling!

Apart from the peril people locked in compartments faced in the event of an accident or fire, I suspect it was only on very rare occasions that people had found themselves locked in compartments with others who turned out to be lunatics or had criminal intent. Very occasionally people were robbed or even "done to death" in compartments—but only about once a decade, if even that frequently. But we might also note that at the time in question the development of some "technologies" quite possibly played upon the fears of railroad compartment passengers—technologies such as "Patent Railway Safety Pockets" (detachable pockets that could be tied or sewn on under skirts for securing valuables).[91] But if this safety technology was intended to be a safeguard against pickpockets, then why call it a patent railway safety pocket—as if the station or railroad were the only places peoples" pockets were likely to be picked? Having said that, pickpockets were known to target railroad stations. They were often smartly dressed but seldom took the train, and when they did it was usually a crowded excursion train. However, the truth is there was nothing new about the Patent Railway Safety Pocket, since pockets had always been detachable, and that only changed from about 1860, which is precisely why it was possible that "Lucy Locket lost her pocket, Lucy Fisher found it," as the age-old nursery rhyme informs us. In fact, curiously enough dress-pockets sewn into the skirt of a gown were coming into vogue at around the same time the Patent Railway Safety Pocket appeared.[92]

The Carriage Compartment and Conviviality

Wolfgang Schivelbusch has suggested that aloofness when traveling in a 19th-century English railroad compartment was largely due to people having lost the ability to engage in elementary conversation in such circumstances—he compares the English railroad compartment passenger (unfavorably) to the earlier, relatively more gregarious (so he alleges) stage-coach passenger.[93] But if earlier, and indeed contemporaneous stagecoach travelers, did interact more during the course of a journey than did railroad compartment passengers, then that probably related to the fact that a coach journey was, apart from whatever else, both an adventure and an ordeal, where everything was less predictable (less "rational"), and more could go wrong than was the case with the pre-determined and fixed route of march of the railroad with its firmly-scheduled stops. And since, generally, a coach journey was slower than a railroad journey over the same distance, coach passengers spent longer in the coach with each other than would have been the case if traveling by railroad. Furthermore, most railroad journeys in England in the early period were self-evidently quite short and did not take very long, barring mishap. By comparison, on longer journeys coach passengers would most likely share meals and accommodation in the relatively intimate setting of the inn, apart from which they had to share in all the relative exigencies of coaching—weather problems; making up or losing time; the detour because of the impassable road; the rude, crazy, or drunken coach driver; the lame horse; the broken axle; the wheel that had come off; and so on. Indeed, Count Kielmansegge, a foreigner touring England in the 1760s, remarked upon an initial "deep silence" among coach passengers, which slowly fell away as the exigencies of the journey—weather and road conditions—occasioned conversation. Another tourist, in the same decade, rather than having to endure silence in the coach, had to bear a passenger who chatted "like a magpie,"[94] but perhaps only after the ice had thawed. In fact, on a long-distance coach journey, passengers were probably subject to the same compulsion to fraternize as would be half a dozen modern people stuck in an elevator for half an hour. Having said that, Germaine de Stael, writing in the early 19th century, remarked that the (upper-class) English were: "As shy and ill at ease with each other as they are with strangers (I think she meant foreigners); they only speak to one another if introduced."[95]

Something has already been said about the Englishman's fetish for privacy. But if being confined (locked) in a small space (a railroad carriage compartment) with strangers was something of a novelty, yet it was also disconcerting for many. But that would have been so where coach travel was concerned, too. After all, it must have been very difficult when sitting opposite people in a coach or railroad carriage compartment to avoid eye contact, let alone conversation. But this is apparently what happened often enough. One would imagine that normally there would have to be exceptional circumstances for avoiding conversation altogether in a public coach on a journey of any length, or for not noticing somebody whom you knew in the coach, such as when Charles Darwin, on a coach trip from Birmingham to Shrewsbury pretended not to know Mr. Hunt (very difficult in the confines of a coach one would imagine) for whatever reason. But the appearance of Mrs. Hunt put paid to that: "I shook hands with vast surprise and interest, and opened my eyes with astonishment at Mr. Hunt, as if he had dropped from the skies."[96]

Schivelbusch fails to adequately analyze the reasons why stage-coach passengers interacted more (than railroad compartment passengers) comparatively if they did, while on the other hand accepting uncritically the testimony of some early novels as affording reliable evidence of what did occur on the coach. Perhaps some people rode atop the coach because they were anti-social; or, on the other hand, because they wanted to chat with a down-to-earth and worldly person like a coach driver! Furthermore, some tourists probably chose to ride atop the coach because the driver—given the local knowledge that most coach drivers would have had—would no doubt have been a mine of information where "sightseeing" was concerned.

But let us re-focus on early railroad travel. The aloofness of the English compartment passenger is not reducible to a single factor. Recall that earlier I argued railroad companies had to shrink and condense the English social class structure to just two or three passenger classes. So, whatever other reasons upper-class passengers may have had for remaining aloof of their fellow compartment "inmates," yet during the early period those fellow inmates, though able to afford first-class compartment accommodation, were by no means of the same social class as those they shared the compartment with—that is glaringly obvious when a member of the aristocracy shared a compartment with non-aristocratic fellow passengers, such as prosperous wholesalers or "jumped-up" clerks. But they also had to share other facilities (at stations) with those people, bundled together, as they were ad hoc (for the duration of a railroad journey). Having said that, when people of the upper-classes did use the station in the early period it seems that at smaller stations these "better sort of people" were often invited to await the train in the stationmaster's office.[97] But, as indicated earlier, some members of the aristocracy demanded private stations for their exclusive use—sometimes as the price the railroad company had to pay for encroaching upon their estates.

But we should not think that everybody who used the railroad compartment disdained the company of others, and especially so the company of members of the opposite sex. In that regard, I suspect the railroad compartment availed people of "opportunities" which had their antecedents in the confined spaces of the coach. Indeed, a German coach traveler in England in the 18th century remarked upon such "opportunities," which were, apparently, manifest in mail coaches (which usually traveled at night)—he was referring not only to "a dangerous exchange of glances," but also to a "scandalous entanglement of legs."[98] And, even earlier, Michel de Montaigne had noted that in his time (late seventeenth century France) ladies could receive some "gratification" from the motions of a coach: "The shaking and trembling of their coaches arouses and solicits the ladies,"[99] and who knows with what consequences?

Anthony Trollope's biographer, Victoria Glendinning, suggests that, like most men of his period, Trollope found railroad compartments "sexually exciting." But not so waiting-rooms, apparently, for by the mid–1860s he had come to positively loath some aspects of railroad travel—he knew "no hours so terrible" as those passed in "hideous, dirty, and disagreeable" waiting-rooms, and wondered why "stationmasters do not more frequently commit suicide."[100] Clearly no eye contact "copulation" was to be had with the opposite sex in waiting-rooms at that time!

We do not know to what extent romantic "episodes" occurred in English railroad compartments in the 19th century and the best we can do is to conjecture in that regard. But *if* there was a lot of sexual harassment of women during railroad travel, yet there may also have been numerous mutually consenting engagements in the privacy of compartments. In fact, it seems to me the railroad compartment, which an unmarried or adulterous couple could be locked in alone, would be the ideal place for a discreet adulterous or otherwise illicit rendezvous. However, at this point one might note that in America throughout the 19th century women were almost never subject to harassment by males during railroad traveling. Yet, there certainly was "some flirting" on the woman's part occasionally.[101]

To return to Britain, by 1860 the English etiquette book authors had become aware of "indecent behavior" (looking and toe contact?) which women in English railroad compartments might be subject to, and who knows where even an innocent salutation might have led in such a situation: "In railway traveling you should not open a conversation with a lady unknown to you until she makes some advance towards it, but it is polite to speak to gentlemen." The author of this salutary advice, in *The Habits of Good*

Society (1859), clearly wanted to cover all bases where railroad traveling etiquette was concerned: "If you have a newspaper, and others have not, you should offer it to the person nearest to you."

If Schivelbusch thought that by the time the railroad age had arrived the English upper-classes had lost the facility for engaging in even "phatic communion," yet he seems to have overlooked the fact that by that time the English could not think for themselves, either—or so the proliferation of etiquette books full of such inanities as the above would seem to indicate. Having said that, the authors of such books were confronted with some new "philosophical" dilemmas with the advent of the railroad age, since initially there were aspects of railroad travel which existing etiquette books did not address and which meant there were certain ambiguities of conduct and attendant anxieties which had to be resolved. For instance, *The Habits of Good Society* prescribed that when riding in a horse-drawn carriage a man must take the back seat, and when it stops jump out first and offer his hand to the lady to help her off the carriage.[102] Such obviously good advice could not necessarily be generalized to the railroad compartment, since there were no "back" seats, apart from which it may not have been physically possible for the man to leave the compartment ahead of the lady—without scrambling ignominiously over her crinoline—to assist her out of it.

Indeed, one factor generally not accounted for, where the early reticence of the upper-classes is concerned, is that coach travel had always been governed by certain etiquettes of behavior. And although some matters governed by etiquette in the 19th century may seem to us incredibly trivial, yet not so for the Victorians, which is why they wrote and read "gospels" of etiquette, and why "New Testaments" had to be written from time-to-time, incorporating etiquettes of conduct specific to new developments such as railroad travel. In fact, all the etiquette books from around mid-century made some allusion to "proper" conduct during railroad travel—some even advised hapless English people how to buy tickets, what the ticket was for, and where to find the train in the station!

Before moving on to consider 19th century English railroad third-class passenger accommodation in protracted fashion, two other aspects of general passenger provision ought to be mentioned, since both relate to third-class passenger travel as well: baggage allowance and through travel.

Baggage

As opposed to the American railroad traveler, the English railroad first- and second-class passengers invariably had porterage services available to them. This was sometimes a free service or a small fee was payable. However, tipping was not permitted (but occurred anyway and was probably overlooked). The free baggage allowance varied in accordance with the class of travel, although initially some companies—such as the London and Birmingham—offered no free baggage allowance at all, an outrage that was soon put to death. And it was only with the passing of Gladstone's 1844 Act that third-class passengers could take a reasonably large amount of baggage with them while traveling by rail—up to half a hundredweight, in fact.

English railroad passengers were assisted at stations by functionaries, should they need assistance. Indeed, porters proliferated and assisted first- and second- class passengers with their baggage. But (for decades) that was not normally the case on American railroads, where passengers were pretty much left to their own devices or reliant on the assistance of fellow passengers.

Churton, in his 1851 railroad guide, remarked that "civility and cheerfulness" of English railroad servants was not always encountered "as readily as could be desired" on principal lines.[103] However, perhaps he was a little out of touch with the working conditions of many railroad servants at the time, who often did menial jobs for poor pay, were often required to work up to 12-hour days (sometimes with no extra payment for overtime worked), and who worked in cold, draughty stations. Clearly, such working conditions were much more likely to produce a stone-faced frigidity of service rather than the eternal smile and grace of the Buddha—much earlier (in 1839) I.K. Brunel had alerted his superiors "to a lack of civility" among the staff of the Great Western.[104] However, twenty years on American travelers in Britain were able to report a state of affairs rather different to that which had aroused Churton's chagrin in 1851: "The officials, in their English way, are generally models of courtesy, and the schedule time generally punctual to a dot."

Furthermore, English railroad passengers would never have encountered the rudeness from railroad servants which they encountered when they traveled in America, nor would the English companies have allowed their baggage to be handled as it was by the infamous "baggage smashers" on some American railroads. Apart from the English companies' own surveillance systems, which quickly identified "offenders," the English public—unlike the American counterpart—was very quick to complain about "offences" by railroad company servants or about railroad company service more generally, either to the company or to the news media as correspondents.

Through Travel

In England, as in America, railroad development in the early period was not necessarily conducive to the emergence of "rational" systems from the public's point of view. The proliferation of small companies and short lines, competitive rivalries, gauge differences, short-sighted management, and the absence of state "muscle" could all militate against the possibility of rational networks emerging with the public interest as their guiding rationale. In fact, "contingencies" such as amalgamations, takeovers, or new lines being built by existing companies usually effected whatever possibilities there were for through travel in the early period. So, the convenience of through travel usually emerged by default rather than by design. And it must be said that the emergence of regional consolidations (monopolies) did often serve the public interest when through travel opportunities resulted, although that may have been the only virtue of such monopolies emerging. Indeed, there was a trade-off—a monopoly, or even working arrangements which had the same effect, eliminated the competitive element and thus elevated passenger and freight rates accordingly. And, generally, all the above pertained to the American situation as well at the time.

Even by mid-century rationalizations of key routes in Britain—to better facilitate through travel—were lacking, much to the passenger's inconvenience, while some companies had, somewhat anomalously, grandiose schemes to "fast track" travel between London and Paris, for instance. We get some sense of the *dis*-articulations from the fact that although it was possible to travel by rail from London to Aberdeen (Scotland) by 1850, the journey entailed traveling on the lines of 10 companies. Furthermore, in the early period "through booking" was considered a "privilege" by the companies, and thus reserved for first-class passengers only (this seems to have prevailed until the mid–1840s). Hence, it was built into the more general discriminatory framework underlying the passenger class structure.

In America, such were the dis-articulations for decades in some states that, during the course of through travel, not only did one have to transfer from one company, one line, or one train to another; but one might have to go from a station on one side of a city to another on the other side of it to effect the transfer, and in the process be subject to extortionate "transfer" costs by taxi-type horse and carriage operators.

Third-Class Passenger Travel

While traveling in America in 1875, an American correspondent for an English newspaper recorded an amusing observation for the benefit of his English readers. He noted the progress of a "poor-looking, newly-arrived Irish emigrant girl" through the station to the train. She attached herself to some people who looked like they shared her social class background, purchased her ticket where they did, and followed them to the train. However, upon entering a car she found herself, to her consternation, in one of "what appeared to her of unusual magnificence." She took "one good, steady look at the flashing mirrors and gilded furniture, then speedily decamped," going hastily from one car to the next, apparently looking for the third-class car. She eventually sat down in the "oldest car she could discover," which was, apparently, much better than any she had traveled in previously. Her evident anxiety indicated she thought she was surely in the wrong car or on the wrong train, and that in due course she would most likely be ejected from it by the conductor. However, she was informed by an old lady that "she had paid for, and had a perfect right to," the seat she occupied; so, she "settled down among the cushions and looked as though she never had a poor relation." Indeed, our correspondent noted of America, for the benefit of his English readers: "When you obtain your ticket you have no occasion to tell the clerk you require a first-, second-, or third-class ticket—such a distinction is unknown here."[105]

I mentioned at the outset of this chapter that, viewed in historical context—that is, regarding the fact that before the advent of railroads poor people traveled on road freight wagons—the way third-class passengers were treated by the English railroad companies made some sense, even if *we* might see it as quite reprehensible. Indeed, Rogers claims that the travelers concerned did not expect to be treated any differently than they were. He notes, furthermore, that the London and Birmingham, for instance, felt obliged to make some provision for third-class passengers if only to forestall criticism, since it was expected the railroad would quickly put the road freighters out of business, and thus leave the poor with no transportation means at all apart from their legs.[106]

However, I do not think we should assume that the existence of third-class passenger accommodation necessarily meant railroad travel was accessible to all. It seems much more likely that for decades only the "aristocracy" of the working classes could afford it—lowly clerks, small business owners, prosperous costers, lowly commercial travelers, tradesmen, skilled laborers, and the like. And for members of the lower social classes not falling into those or similar socioeconomic categories, railroad travel would have been a rare treat—usually only accessible in the form of an excursion, and perhaps even then subsidized by some reform organization or a benevolent employer.

Shortly, then, we shall look more closely at the abominable and often disgusting travel arrangements—according to contemporary sources—offered to third-class passengers by many English railroad companies. However, this phenomenon was not some kind of aberration peculiar to just the first few years of begrudging third-class passenger provision. It had a certain longevity, spanning at least forty and up to fifty years in the case of some companies. Indeed, the writer of a newspaper article in 1872 remarked upon seeing: "Passengers penned in third-class carriages like overcrowded sheep, while brilliantly lighted first- and second-class carriages are practically or even wholly empty."[107]

But just to keep things in comparative context, we need to consider the fact that even after mid-century people on ships were often treated no better. In fact, in 1854 a Parliamentary committee heard that on ships between Dublin and Liverpool cattle had priority access to deck shelters—in inclement weather—ahead of the deck (railroad third-class equivalent) passengers![108] In the same connection, *Punch* declared in 1836 that the only advantage third-class railroad passengers had over cattle being herded along country roads was that they did not have to walk.[109] A 19th century American tourist was appalled by the seemingly penal and carceral treatment of third class (railroad) passengers in England, declaring: "Our policy is not to punish travelers for their poverty."[110] However, Jennings has pointed out that for the poor in England in the late 18th century, and for much of the 19th century, the school, the factory, the workhouse, and the prison were "all the same building."[111] Of course, these institutions did have intrinsic points of difference. But what they had in common was that they were all places of confinement, each with a discernible carceral quality to it, and each conducted under a disciplinary form of administration. Yet, the "inmates" of the first three institutions (school, factory, workhouse) were not detained at Her Majesty's Pleasure, even though such institutions often dominated even the most quotidian dimensions of their lives, and in extreme disciplinary fashion.

In England the experience of railroad travel by the relatively impoverished—in the early period, at least—had an institutional quality to it which makes it appear not too remarkably different from these other carceral, but non-penal, types of institution. And perhaps that is why the lot of the third-class passenger in the early period was not especially complained about by the poor travelers themselves; since it was probably more or less what they expected, and fell tidily into line with the other types of carceral experience—whether in the factory or elsewhere—and other institutionalized forms of servitude and deference they were familiar with and may have experienced personally.

Writing in 1846, Robert Ritchie described Parliamentary (third-class) carriages as "hideous and dismal," and "more adapted for the carriage of prisoners than passengers."[112] That is the more remarkable because a "Parliamentary" carriage supposedly conformed to the minimal conditions for the conveyance of third-class passengers prescribed by Gladstone's 1844 Act. Yet, even this "improved" state of affairs for third-class passengers clearly left a lot to be desired. Indeed, in the early period third-class passenger accommodation was rather like "transportation" in the penal servitude sense; although as far as we know the companies stopped short of putting the "inmates" in irons for the duration of a railroad journey.

In his 1851 railroad guide Churton suggested people consider traveling third class—presumably when the carriages were still "open," the weather fine, and the railroad company concerned not in the "incarceration" business—to better view the scenery.[113] But perhaps Churton ought to have appended a footnote advising that third-class passengers in open carriages had been known to die of exposure.[114]

Furthermore, low sides and uncovered carriages—typical of third-class carriages in the early period—were extremely dangerous in the event of accidents. On Christmas Eve 1841, eight third-class passengers were killed and seventeen injured after being thrown out of an uncovered railroad carriage (which had two-foot high sides) in an accident. In fact, the seats (when there were any in such carriages) were often elevated eighteen inches from the floor, which meant only six inches supported the passenger's back to prevent their falling out of the carriage—too bad if you dozed off! So, it would have been very easy even to fall out of those carriages. Furthermore, the "seats" were usually just planks and not held fast, since the "carriages" were quite often (temporarily) converted goods wagons. Clearly, low sides were a major hazard even without mishap, if only because trains tended to sway, jerk, and jolt a lot. And if sitting was dangerous enough, standing while the train was in motion would have been suicidal under those circumstances. Yet, spokesmen for some companies insisted, for quite some time, that low sides were not dangerous.[115]

In fact, during the 1830s/1840s it was a vexed question as to whether third-class passengers needed seats at all. In one issue of the *Railway Times* it was argued: "We do not feel disposed to attach much weight to the argument in favour of third-class carriages with seats. On a short line, little inconvenience can result from their absence."[116] Indeed, when in 1839 the London and Greenwich introduced a third class of travel those passengers were required to stand for the duration of a journey, even though they were paying 75 percent of the second-class fare.[117]

Alfred Wallace, Charles Darwin's scientific contemporary, who shared the credit for discovering the theory of evolution with Darwin, recalled later in life that his first trip on a train was in a third-class carriage, and that passengers had to stand up in an "open truck" like cattle.[118] And clearly this was not the kind of passenger experience the author of an 1899 article had in mind when ruminating somewhat romantically upon an 1838 guide to travel on the Grand Junction Railway: "The reader is able very vividly to realize the wild and novel joys experienced by his forefathers on their first railroad journey."[119]

Domingo Sarmiento remarked of French and English railroads in the late 1840s that when they did provide some seats for third-class passengers: "I do not know why they have not added thorns to the seats to make the poor suffer more"[120]—probably because they had not thought of it! But some companies compelled third-class passengers to travel virtually whole days without seats; making them on a journey which might otherwise have occupied not more than 7 ½ hours stand on their feet 16 or 17 hours. And often "the engine driver was ordered to linger on the journey"[121]—clearly the Inquisition's torture experts could have learned something from 19th century English railroad company management.

In the early period, some companies provided roofs on open third-class carriages after having been criticized for their cold-heartedness, and later Gladstone's Act of 1844 required that all passenger carriages have roofs. But in conforming to the requirements of Gladstone's Act roofs were all that some companies provided—there was no side protection, just a canopy! Yet, not all the companies were so cold-hearted. Some of the more benevolent companies which provided the meager roofed-but-sideless carriages showed just how compassionate they really were by drilling holes in the carriage floors to let the rain drain out.[122]

Third-class travelers in the late 1830s often found themselves in a wagon with no roof and no seats, "nor any other accommodation than is now (1901) given to coal, iron, and miscellaneous goods."[123] Moreover, since third-class passenger carriage usually occurred during the hours of darkness, the (enclosed third-class) passengers seem often to have been locked in pitch darkness in their little "gaols on rails"—indeed, night lamps were not normally provided for (enclosed) third-class passengers at all during the early period. And apart from the absence of a light source, these early third-class closed carriages were not always well ventilated, either—John Francis confirmed this was not at all unusual at the time.[124]

Even by 1861 things had not changed much. In a newspaper article of that year titled *A Plea for Cheap and Comfortable Traveling*, third-class passenger travel was described thus:

> The only carriage in which he (the third-class passenger) could travel would be a vehicle *purposely and ingeniously* constructed in such a manner as to be *wholly unfit for* the conveyance of a human being (he was referring to a 100-mile journey on any through line in England)...He would, moreover, have to commence his journey at some vexatiously inconvenient hour of the night or morning, and would travel at a rate, including stoppages, little greater than that of the old stage coach. In a word, he would be *imprisoned* in a Parliamentary carriage.... The magnates of the railway world have never ceased to make the means of traveling *as disagreeable, as painful, and as loathsome as possible* (for the poor).[125]

Third-class passengers were not entitled to the same services as passengers traveling in the higher passenger classes. So, although they were eventually (from 1844) entitled to a free baggage allowance of half a hundredweight, yet they usually had no claim on the services of porters; or if they did have they had the lowest priority of access to such services (after first- and second-class passengers). In fact, on some English railroads in 1844 the porters were not permitted to assist "wagon passengers, as they are contemptuously called, with their luggage, or in any other way they might require."[126] And a third-class passenger could hardly expect to be in receipt of the same deference from railroad officials that travelers in the higher passenger classes could.

In that connection, John Francis made a rather poignant observation (for the time) where the treatment of third-class passengers was concerned, when he remarked, almost casually but with great import, that railroad company directors "are men."[127] He seemed to be hinting at a lack of compassion and empathy on the directors' parts regarding the situations of (third-class) passengers who were elderly, disabled, ailing, pregnant women, and women with small children. The upshot of his remark seemed to be that if railroad company directors had women among their ranks, then perhaps company attitudes towards poor people (but especially poor women) might have been different.

The author of an 1844 newspaper article suggested some of the railroad companies had their own peculiar rationalizations for their treatment of third-class passengers:

> On no railway in the Kingdom is the system of subjecting third-class passengers to every possible discomfit, (in order) *to compel them to travel by a higher class of train*, carried out than on the Great Western. The directors of this railway clung with great pertinacity to the plan of putting third-class passengers next to the engine and tender, even after the danger of such a course of proceeding had been demonstrated to the satisfaction of everybody but themselves.[128]

Indeed, consequent upon an inquiry into the cause of a fatal accident on the Great Western in December 1842—involving a baggage train with third-class carriages attached and resulting in 8 fatalities—the jury attributed placing passenger carriages so near the engine as an aggravating factor where the fatalities were concerned. This inquiry sparked a considerable correspondence. One correspondent had long noted the "shameful and unfeeling treatment" of third-class passengers on the Great Western. Another letter, from an MP., citing other similar accidents, suggested those responsible for deaths in such circumstances should be charged with manslaughter.[129]

In fact, the Great Western was boxing its third-class passengers in "milk vans" in 1844; the lack of windows its management thought hardly a problem, since *those* people were presumed to lack sufficient sensibility to have an interest in the scenery, anyway. But the crucial factor from the company's viewpoint was that they could not fall out! But, as MacDermot[130] observed, since these "vans" had only one narrow door—on the platform side—the passengers must have had trouble "falling in," too,[131] especially given how many were usually crammed into them. Indeed, if Sydney Smith thought being locked in a first-class compartment was something to complain about, then he should have tried being locked in a Great Western milk van! But if these carriages were dungeon-like, then that made sense, too, since originally the dungeon had been a place in which to deposit somebody whom it was best to forget.[132]

MacDermot went on to note that in 1845 the Great Western, evidently experiencing worrying twitches of remorse and compassion, and presumably having discovered the odd third-class passenger possessed of a modicum of aesthetic sensibility, elevated third-class passengers from the "glorified milk van" (with ventilating venetians) to the much more glamorous "armored carriage," which was made of iron and had a small, four-pane attic window enabling a standing passenger to catch fleeting glimpses of the scenery.[133] However, this was most likely yet another spiteful response to Gladstone's 1844 Act, which required that all passenger carriages afford weather protection, adequate ventilation and light, seats with backs, and windows allowing passengers to look out. Perhaps the great I. K. Brunel designed this type of carriage for the Great Western, since he had formerly had some experience in prison architectural engineering.

William Gladstone (at the time President of the Board of Trade) largely engineered the legislation which obliged companies to make (a minimal standard of) provision for third-class passengers, though he was forcefully supported in his endeavors by Prime Minister, Sir Robert Peel, in the face of staunch, vehement, and concerted opposition from the railroad companies. Indeed, in opposition to Gladstone's 1844 Railway Bill the representatives of 29 companies tried to persuade Sir Robert Peel and Mr. Gladstone to withdraw the Bill: "They were told—by these petitioners—that the Bill would be injurious (and) contrary to the spirit of English commerce." In response, Gladstone stated (in Parliament in 1844): "Those gentlemen (railroad company directors) say, 'Oh, trust to competition.' I know of nothing more chilling than the hope which these directors hold out."[134]

Gladstone often made a point of traveling third class himself—apparently to check on the quality of such provision on the different companies' lines—although it is hard to imagine him volunteering to be locked in a Great Western milk van or armoured carriage! Indeed, I doubt he would have reclined in comfort very often, even after the passing of his Act and the adoption of its specifications by the companies, since although his 1844 Act made the enclosed carriage compulsory, yet backs on seats remained optional for third-class carriages. And although the Act prescribed minimum conditions of comfort be provided for third-class passengers, "minimum" seems often to have been the operative word where some very bitterly resentful companies were concerned.

Nevertheless, *Gladstone's Act* was revolutionary. It required the companies to operate at least one cheap train a day in each direction along its lines, charging no more than a penny a mile, with children under 12 years paying half-fare (and those under 3 years traveling free), and each adult passenger permitted half a hundredweight of baggage. Many companies failed to comply immediately, especially regarding those provisions which would have required considerable transformation of the architecture of their third-class carriages. That was understandable, since such change could not be wrought overnight and it would have been very costly. Gladstone's 1844 Act also influenced how third-class trains operated. They had to average 12 miles per hour, including stoppages; pick up and set down passengers at every station; and the carriages had to have seats and weather protection.

The incentive for the railroad companies to cooperate and comply with Gladstone's Act, albeit minimally often, was some relief of their passenger duties payable to the government. The same applied to the so-called "workmen's trains" introduced later and offered by most companies in the mid–1860s. However, the use of those trains by "workmen" was quite strictly policed by the companies—only artisans, mechanics, and daily laborers were eligible, and their shilling weekly tickets had to show the name and address of the employer, while the journey could not be varied from one day to the next. Inner-city development and the spatial expansion of cities like London had made it increasingly necessary for "workmen" to be adequately catered to, since inner-city demolition and development (quite a bit of it by railroad companies themselves) meant that the working classes were pushed out of the inner city (where many of them worked) towards its peripheral suburbs. Later, the Cheap Trains Act of 1883 also represented a response to sustained lobbying for the working classes in that regard.

It could be argued that the English Board of Trade only became proactively interested in railroad company provision for the lower social classes as a byproduct of its accident investigations; although I think some politicians, like Gladstone and Peel, had always felt very uncomfortable with the provision, or lack of it, for third-class passengers by the railroad companies. These men may have been conservatives in key respects; but their conservatism was of a kind which acknowledged that hierarchy and deference, in a highly structured society, ought not to almost entirely deprive people at the lower reaches of the "pecking order" of their dignity. And certainly not to the extent they assumed the status of "livestock" or "cotton bales." Indeed, John Francis described third-class passenger provision under Gladstone's 1844 Act as "in a kind and genial spirit."[135]

But there were still problems six years later, as an 1850 newspaper article made plain: "The least the managers could do ... would be to use glass instead of wood for the (third-class) windows." The writer of this article suggested that the expense would be "comparatively nothing"; adding (logically enough) that railroad company directors "seemed to be blind to the principles" which most other business people applied to their businesses to attract custom. The article's author also noted that on some lines even the second-class passengers were "shamefully accommodated."[136]

The Great Western seemed to come in for a lot of criticism where its accommodation of third-class passengers was concerned. But was the Great Western the worst of a bad bunch in that regard? Let us begin to answer the question by considering, based on my own research, the dimensions of the third-class (closed) passenger carriages of four companies in 1845: the Great Western, the Grand Junction, the Bristol and Gloucester, and the Colchester and Cambridge. If we focus upon how many square inches per person the carriage allowed, that gives some idea of whether passengers were crammed into the carriages like sardines.

The Colchester and Cambridge, with carriage dimensions of 20' length by 7' breadth, was the most generous in its provision of space, since its carriages accommodated just 32 people and, therefore, allowed each passenger 628 square inches of space. The Great Western, by comparison, allowed for just half that much space per passenger (320 square inches); its carriage dimensions 20'9" in length, 8'6" in breadth, and designed to accommodate 59 people! However, the Great Western carriages were 9" higher (at 6'9") than those of the Colchester and Cambridge. The Grand Junction carriages, which accommodated 40 people, allowed 411 square inches per passenger. And although the Grand Junction carriages were only 5'4" high, yet that may have been because they had seats.[137] Finally, the Bristol and Gloucester carriages, accommodating 54 people, allowed 466 square inches per passenger (although these were the highest carriages, at 8'6"). So, a declaration in 1829 to the effect that: "Men, of course, cannot be packed like bales of calico" seems to have been somewhat premature.[138] For they could, indeed, be packed like bales of calico.

In a very interesting, insightful, and illuminating newspaper editorial article (somewhat coincidentally in 1844, and perhaps for Mr. Gladstone's information as anybody else's), the strategies of various railroad companies, allegedly to coerce third-class passengers to use second-class, were discussed. The article singled out the (local) Great Western as *the* "enfant terrible," referring to that company's third-class carriages as "absolutely unfit for the reception and transmission of beasts." It went on: "Equally intolerable is that the humbler class of travelers should be subject, on all occasions, to a systematic roughness and insolence of treatment on the part of railway officials and servants, as if they were of no greater account than a herd of the lowest order of animals."

The author then proceeded to argue that class distinctions ought to be based on relative provision of luxuries, not comforts. And that all classes of passenger ought to be sent on the one train, all ought to be protected from the weather, and all ought to have "an equal chance at least of safety." He argued, moreover, that it was a misconception to think that mistreating the third-class passengers so was intended to force them into a higher passenger class. Rather, he suggested the companies feared that "if it (third-class) be made convenient or comfortable, then other (higher) classes of passenger would immediately take advantage of it." In that connection, there were numerous people who traveled third-class who probably could have afforded second-class. But some or many such people may have been traveling during their work, or to and from their workplace; so, not surprisingly, and given that their incomes were probably not that large, naturally they tried to keep their "overheads"—of which traveling expenses were one—down. This theory is supported by an assertion in an 1839 newspaper article to the effect that "the bulk of the ordinary complement of passengers" were commercial travelers.[139]

To return to our editorial article above, its author threw down a gauntlet to the directors of the Great Western Railway Company. Firstly, by asking: "If it be quite worthy of a company styling itself 'Great' thus to visit poverty with the certainty of suffering and the probability of disease and death?" And, secondly, by drawing public attention to: "The constantly distressing and frequently disgusting descriptions which reach us of the horrors of third-class railway traveling," some such descriptions "of a nature we should not like to print."[140]

When the editors of prominent regional newspapers at that time went to bat for the poor in such vehement fashion and against such a powerful corporate entity, then clearly the situation had become unconscionable for many who thought they were living in a civilized and progressive society. Indeed, Wilfred Steel (writing in 1914) suggested that around 1840 third-class passengers fared "much worse than cattle do nowadays." However, he qualified the assertion by noting that the Manchester and Birmingham, for instance, had, from the outset, been an exception to the rule; allowing third-class passengers on all its daily trains, and thus able to be moved at 25 miles per hour "and without all the other inconveniences calculatedly visited upon the poor traveler by other companies."[141]

Even in 1875 an American correspondent for English newspapers (mentioned earlier) felt impelled to declare that:

> At some future time, the English railroad kings will consent to take a lesson from their American cousins, and the poor man and woman will be enabled to travel with some degree of comfort; instead of being, as at present, compelled to sit for hours in a cold, damp, draughty carriage containing less comfort than is to be found in a well-kept pig pen.[142]

The quality of third-class accommodation did vary from one company to the next; but when any provision was made at all during the first fifty years of English railroading, then such provision was usually dismal. And, as indicated above, provision made by companies such as the Manchester and Birmingham was the all too rare exception. In that regard, Gourvish argues that from early on third-class passengers fared better in the industrial North and Scotland, and especially with smaller companies for whom third-class passenger revenues could be significant.[143]

Many companies which did provide third-class passenger conveyance also tried to resist integrating facilities in a way which would have brought the third-class passengers into even visual contact with travelers of the higher passenger classes. They often argued that the third-class passengers had to be kept well away from the higher passenger classes—because third-class travelers were offensive and might repel travelers of those higher passenger classes. An executive of the Great Northern, for instance, thought that well-to-do people should not have to "hobnob" with "working men," whom, "apart from using language, spat on the floors (in America at the time there was not much that people did not spit on!), smoked offensive pipes, cooked herrings in the waiting-rooms if they were left open, cut off the leather window straps and stole them." And if they arrived too early for work hung about the station killing time with "evil consequences for some of the young female workers."[144]

Furthermore, in the early period one of the main reasons there was resistance (by the companies) to the provision of "decent" or any third-class accommodation at all was that it was feared that those people (the lower social classes) would vandalize railroad property. And it is true there was vandalism, although it seemed to come much later (presumably not until there was something worth vandalizing in the third-class carriages, and you could actually see in the closed carriages what you were vandalizing)—apparently wooden seats were "penciled rudely and hacked" occasionally, while cushions were "cut and torn."[145] And during the 1850s station water closets were also sometimes subject to graffiti vandalism, while in 1883 the Chairman of the Northeastern complained that third-class passengers were cutting up carriage curtains and using them as handkerchiefs.[146] But these were probably isolated incidents rather than routine occurrences.

Where graffiti was concerned, it was not new, even in the early 19th century. Many centuries earlier Roman tourists were notorious for their graffiti, which was commonly found on the pyramids and other Egyptian cultural artifacts. In 16th century Europe it was commonplace for noblemen traveling in Europe to leave their escutcheons—barely one remove from the modern phenomenon of "tagging"—on the walls of the inns they stayed at. The original schoolroom at Harrow (dating to the 16th century) in 1839 had such a "splattering" of graffiti and "tags" that "scarcely a spot remained free from inscription"—famous people of the era, such as Byron and Robert Peel, were among the many who had "tagged" those hallowed walls.[147] And in colonial New England boys frequently vandalized and etched graffiti on the furnishings of the religious meeting-houses during Sunday services, something that probably occurred in England at the time, too.

But apart from some vandalism, on the English railroads there was rioting, too. Indeed, there was one occasion in the early 1860s when some passengers ran riot: "The damage to the rolling stock was frightful" and the railroad officials "driven frantic, with pandemonium let loose at the station" and railroad traffic "entirely disorganized for hours." However, those vandalistic rioters were not third-class patrons at all, but "mad freaks of inebriated (Oxford) graduates."[148] In the late 18th and first half of the 19th century riots and mutinies were not at all uncommon at English elite educational institutions. At Winchester School in 1818, for instance, two companies of troops, with bayonets fixed, had to be called out to restore order during a riot. There were also incidents at Eton and Rugby in the early 19th century; again, both serious enough for the troops to be called out—the last serious mutiny at Eton occurred in 1832, and the last important school mutiny in England was at Marlborough School in 1851.[149] And all this ought to disabuse us of the notion that the working classes during those times had a monopoly on rioting and mindless acts of vandalism. In that connection, one notes also that when Shillibeer introduced his (somewhat "classy") omnibuses to London in the 1820s and provided books and magazines for the "ladies and gentlemen" to read during transit, these "quality" customers "boned the books," so he discontinued the practice.[150]

More generally, it was thought people of the lower social classes would swear, drink alcohol, and otherwise behave offensively if permitted to use the railroads. But the fear that people of the lower social classes had an innate tendency to be disorderly and vandalize things was part and parcel of the more general perception of them as lacking both sensibility and intelligence. When parks were opened to the public around mid-century familiar voices were muttering that the lower social classes would vandalize them and copulate on the grass in full public view. And there were also fears concerning how the "shilling people" would behave at the Great Exhibition of 1851, some believing that their innate destructive urges might get the better of them and that they would want to smash things.[151] Others wondered if they would bother to use the water closets. Charlotte Bronte captured the prevailing bourgeois mood beautifully in a letter written at the time of the Great Exhibition: "The great topic of conversation was the probable behaviour of the people. Would they come sober? Will they destroy the things? Will they want to cut their initials or scratch their names on the panes?"[152] But not only did they behave themselves admirably, they often proved to be much more interested in the exhibits than those who found it all rather tedious and were simply there after a fashion.

Fourth-Class

There was, apparently, a fourth class of passenger carriage available on some English lines in the 1840s—the carriages usually had no seats.[153] In fact, during the 1840s both the (Scottish) Edinburgh and Glasgow and the Great Northern introduced a fourth passenger class. And in 1837 I.K. Brunel was contemplating a fourth passenger class for the Great Western—Brunel was a great believer in social class and privilege[154]— but he probably could not think of a way to make third-class travel any worse than it already was on the Great Western! Furthermore, some companies had two third classes (effectively creating a fourth class)—usually one of those "third" classes corresponded to the "Parliamentary" fare of one penny a mile (with manacles?), the other presumably offered "something" a bit better (roof, floor boards, and no manacles?) and had a fare of more than a penny a mile.[155]

To conclude this chapter, and in view of the preceding, perhaps we might take more seriously than would otherwise be the case the words of Friedrich Engels in *The Condition of the Working Class in England* (1845):

> Let us compare the condition of the free Englishman of 1845 with the Saxon serf under the lash of the Norman barons of 1145.... In short, the position of the two is not far from equal; and if either is at a disadvantage, it is the free working man.

Three

Nineteenth Century America: A No Less Strange Railroad System in a No Less Strange Society?

> The very insistence on the formula that "all men are equal" shows that there is something here that has to be explained away.
> —Oswald Spengler, *Man and Technics*

> Americans are less conservative than the English because they have little to conserve.
> —"Mr. George Dawson on America," *The Hull Packet*, April 23, 1875

> Few Americans shave themselves.
> —"Literary Selections," *The Preston Guardian*, March 20, 1869

Introduction

During the first few decades of railroad passenger travel there were marked differences between railroad passenger experiences from country to country. And from a comparative standpoint the differences between railroad passenger travel experience in England and America were, as I shall make plain in what follows, significant, pronounced, and more considerable than might be imagined. The differences in question, constituting as they did part and parcel of the "national style" of railroading in the respective national contexts, also, to some extent at least, tell us something about the sociocultural fabric of the respective societies at the time. In fact, I would suggest that such "incidental" gleanings provide some very useful insights into the class structure of the two societies in question in the 19th century.

We have already seen how, in the first few years consequent upon the advent of railroads, the English railroad passenger's traveling experience afforded considerable insight into the social structure of English society at the time, as well as some insight into how English commercial organizations, in the provision of their commodities (in the form of goods or services) in the 19th century, usually had to somehow negotiate the class structure in terms of both "positioning" and "packaging" their commodities. Indeed, the example of the English railroad companies, concerning their commodification of the passenger traveling experience, afforded an exemplary instance of how such a dilemma could be resolved—if only to the (railroad) companies' satisfaction, although I suggested it was not entirely inimical to some of their passengers' values, and even harmonized with some of those values to a point.

Many English tourists went to America in the second half of the 19th century loaded with preconceptions about what to expect, only to be pleasantly surprised often enough to find things different to what they had anticipated; notwithstanding that some of their preconceptions—such as those concerning American "rudeness," the railroad "baggage smashers," and the ubiquity of spitting—turned out to be real enough. In fact, many English tourists who published their (American) travel journals—this seemed to be in vogue for a few decades—made a point of mentioning how their experiences in America had undermined their preconceptions about the country. For instance, William Smith realized during his 1891 visit to America that he had much to "unlearn about the country," and that many ideas about it based on what he had read were "far from being correct."[1] Arthur Cunynghame observed in 1850 (while on a river steamboat): "In no instance did I observe that greediness at their meals of which the Americans have been accused by many travelers."[2] Likewise, Foster Zincke (traveling in 1868) was of the opinion that *middle-class* Americans did not eat any faster than their English counterparts.[3] Frances Trollope earlier had remarked upon the eating habits of Americans in her highly controversial—in America, at least—*Domestic Manners of the Americans*, although it seems the remark referred specifically to her experience on a steamboat on the Mississippi just north of New Orleans.[4] However, English travelers more generally in the late 19th century did often remark upon how fast Americans ate their meals—especially in boarding-houses and hotels, although that could have been because in such places there were often at least two meal "sittings." Furthermore, one notes that in colonial times children were not usually allowed to sit at the table at meal times, but often had to stand and were required to eat in silence, *as fast as possible, and to leave the table as speedily as possible.* Hence, there may have been many 19th century American households where vestiges of such customs were retained, thus offering one explanation as to how some American adults acquired the habit of eating fast.[5]

To return to Mrs. Trollope, Thomas Nichols, a very percipient and fair-minded man, who had lived in America forty years and been well-traveled there during that time, described Mrs. Trollope as a "self-appointed missionary of manners and civilization." And although he undoubtedly thought her a little self-righteous and myopic in outlook, yet he thought some of her criticisms of Americans, and of America, valid:

> We were dreadfully angry at Mrs. Trollope, but we read her book all the same, and profited in no small degree by its lessons. Many a time when someone in the boxes at the theatre has thoughtlessly turned his back upon the pit, or placed his foot on the cushioned front, have I heard the warning and reproaching cry go up of "Trollope! Trollope!" until the offender was brought to a sense of his transgression.[6]

Mrs. Trollope had journeyed to America with three of her five children in tow, essentially to get as far away from her husband as possible but without incurring the stigma of a formal separation. Her first impressions of America were probably not assisted by her entering the country via the mouth of the Mississippi, then heading north for a long way up the "big creek." But one thing her American critics missed was the fact her book was *intended* to be somewhat vituperative and provocative, since she wanted it to be as successful as Basil Hall's (not much less controversial in its time) *Travels in America* (1829)—in fact, Hall was kind enough to read (and commend) her manuscript for her. So, to some extent, outraging the Americans was a marketing tactic and one which certainly worked the oracle for her. Indeed, the American response was probably the main reason the book was also quickly translated into French, German, and Dutch. In fact, Harriet Martineau, whose travels in America were published not too long afterwards, was apparently annoyed that her publisher had asked her to "Trollopize" her book a little, so that it might be just as successful as Mrs. Trollope's book.[7]

In defense of Mrs. Trollope, I think it may also be said that anybody acquainted with her unfortunate, if not somewhat tragic life, could not help affording the "pocket battleship" at least a little admiration. And, for her time, she really was a female "go-getter" of very rare ilk, and perhaps as dour as any American frontierswoman or "go-ahead" man. Indeed, like American proto-feminist Margaret Fuller she presented as a rather assertive and achieving female role model for middle class women, striving to make their way independently in a male-dominated world, to look up to.

Furthermore, an American guidebook author made a very good point in the "Introduction" to his (1852) guide to Pennsylvania. He suggested that the dearth of guidebooks for the tourist in America at that time (and earlier) was one reason why foreigners "generally misunderstand and misrepresent us—they are not sufficiently informed to give a correct estimate of our resources, peculiarities, and institutions."[8] This, too, was undoubtedly fair comment. Nevertheless, I do not think we can explain away the phenomenon of Mrs. Trollope like that. After all, what did Mark Twain, for instance, say about Mrs. Trollope? He said: "She knew her subject well," set it forth "fairly and squarely," and was "merely telling the truth, and that this indignant nation knew it." But this view of Twain's is not well-known, since it was expressed in a *suppressed* passage of *Life on the Mississippi* (1883).[9] Furthermore, he thought Frances Trollope's account of America a "sort of photography."[10] And Charles Dickens, who made his own "whistle-stop" tours of America, thought Mrs. Trollope had not only "accurately" described America in many of its aspects, but that she had also worked change in many social features of American society because of her "indictment" of it.

However, Henry T. Tuckerman (a chronicler of European travelers' perceptions of America and Americans) thought the "indignant protests (about America) of travelers reached their acme in Mrs. Trollope." Indeed, he "momentarily" climbed on the "bandwagon" where "bashing" Mrs. Trollope was concerned, not the least in his assertion that she was always "on the lookout for social anomalies and personal defects, and persistent, *like her unreasoning sex*, in attributing all that was offensive or undesirable in her experience to the prejudice she cherished." Yet, he did prevaricate, and finally had several positive things to say about Mrs. Trollope's narrative: that it was "written in a confident, lively style, which made it "quite entertaining"; that her "powers of observation were *remarkable*"; and that she described "with vivacity, and often with *accurate skill*." But Tuckerman caps off his prevarication, and I suppose contradicts his earlier negative remarks about Mrs. Trollope's work, by noting that "*not a single fault is found recorded by her which our own writers, and every candid citizen, have not often admitted and complained of*!" Furthermore, he thought "the redeeming feature" of her book "the love of nature it exhibits." In summing up Mrs. Trollope's book, Tuckerman had to concede, though no doubt a little begrudgingly, since he had to appear to be objective: "With all its defects, however, *few of the class of books to which it belongs are better worth reading now* (1864)." In fact, that is very high praise given the hundreds of books in that genre Tuckerman surveyed.[11]

Englishman George Combe noted (in 1841) that in America Tocqueville's *Democracy in America* was still highly regarded "as the most correct and profound book that has been written by any foreigner on the US"; even though, as Combe noted, Tocqueville "censures American manners and institutions with nearly as much severity as many English writers, whose works have been heartily abused by the American Press."[12]

Decades after Mrs. Trollope had raised the hackles of Americans by her indictment of their manners, other English travelers in America were no less critical. Therese Yelverton remarked: "The want of good manners in all classes of Americans is unpleasantly prominent (and) you are obliged to be constantly on your guard against impertinence and intrusion." But she attributed this largely to American child-rearing practices: "Nowhere in the world, that I am aware of, is it recognized as a settled thing that no effort should be made to correct or improve unruly and vicious children."[13] But if correct this probably had as much to do with the education system as it had with parental socialization of the child. In fact, in the late 1830s George Combe thought one *defect* of the American education system and "social training" (socialization) was that: "It appears to me that they do not sufficiently cultivate habits of deference, prudence, and self-restraint."[14]

However, Thomas Nichols viewed the American education system as being powerfully underpinned by some core (*positive*) values, which he thought undoubtedly shaped personality, self-concept, and some aspects of the child's social interaction in the long term. In fact, he believed that from the early 19th century: "Our education was adapted to intensify our self-esteem and to make us believe that we were the most intelligent, most enlightened, the freest, most Christian, and the greatest people the sun ever shone on." And that: "The one perpetual incentive to study in our schools was ambition (every boy knew there was nothing to hinder him from becoming president)."[15]

English tourist, T. S. Hudson, was also critical of American manners: "The want of the most ordinary politeness everywhere was most marked—rarely was there a "please" or "thank you."[16] Anthony Trollope, too, was also perturbed by the Americans' lack of manners. But if good manners were sometimes absent, yet in some places in America—such as Boston, Philadelphia, and San Francisco—English visitors were often absolutely charmed by the *kindness and hospitality* of the people they met. Lady Hardy, who made two trips to America with her adult daughter in the early 1880s, loved San Francisco for its "genuine kindness and hospitality," the people there "disposed to open their hearts as well as their doors to their visitors from the outside world."[17] Likewise, William Ferguson found that generally, and despite the occasional incivility he encountered, the American's hospitality and friendliness were (justifiably) "proverbial."[18] However, Ferguson gauged that in America the "most erroneous ideas of English manners obtain," while also noting, interestingly: "In some points of etiquette there is greater strictness in America than at home."[19]

But if perceived rudeness was "institutionalized" in some parts of America, yet the long-established upper-classes in the north-east prided themselves on their "airs and graces." However, the "nouveau riche" in the north-east often lacked these, as did their counterparts in the West. In fact, the only New England families which married into the "new class"—which for them was "marrying down"—did so for financial reasons or because they could not marry their sons and daughters into the "old blood," for there were not enough "old families" to go around.[20] However, the subject of *perceived* American "rudeness" will be addressed more protractedly in due course.

Concerning other preconceptions or misconceptions 19th century English travelers entertained in respect of America, W. G. Marshall (visiting America 1878) "had not realized the immense distances that had to be traveled in America from state to state"[21]; a realization which probably enabled him to understand why, in certain important respects, American railroading must necessarily differ from its English counterpart—as an Illinois Central Railroad publication pointed out in 1861, Illinois alone was almost half the size of Great Britain.[22]

But these English tourists also observed some very strange propensities of the Americans which they had not even been aware of. For instance, many of them remarked upon the Americans' liking for drinking *water*. And who better to quote on this subject than the Viscountess, Therese Yelverton: "With the exception of Turkish hamals, Arabian camels, and locomotives, I never saw anything take in so much water as an American woman."[23] Foster Zincke, likewise, noted the water–drinking propensity in 1868: "Americans are a population of very thirsty souls."[24] However, the water in most cities and towns in England—even many rural streams may have been polluted by industrial discharge—was probably undrinkable, and perhaps that is one reason why the English (especially men who did hard physical work) drank so much beer and ale, and virtually no water. By comparison, safe drinking water may have been much more readily accessible in America. But it depended on the water source—once cisterns were built in Charleston, for instance, the ladies, being "extremely temperate," generally drank cistern water because the ground water was not good.[25] However, in early colonial times people had not been keen to drink the water at all—initially it seemed to the colonists a very "dangerous experiment" to drink water in the New World, Earle suggesting its "reputation of hidden malevolence" (it was believed to be permeated with minute noxious, potentially deadly, particles) as a beverage extended to its use in any form.[26] In fact, the earliest colonists imported large quantities of drinking water from England, although I doubt it was any better, and sometimes probably much worse than the local product. However, most of it may have been used for brewing and in the production of spirituous liquors, so the colonists were probably sticking with "tried and true" water. But water-drinking also became associated with those who could not afford to drink anything better. Indeed, in 1719, an eight-year-old girl wrote complainingly to her father in the Barbadoes that her (Bostonian) grandmother made her drink water with her meals. Her father advised the grandmother that: "It was not befitting children of their station to drink water; they should have wine and beer."[27]

But there was also a different language to learn, as W.F. Rae touring America in 1869 pointed out: "In the United States, as in other countries, fluency in speaking the language of the people is an art to be acquired if possible." He went on to point out some of the peculiarities of speaking "American" where railroad traveling was concerned: that they say "railroad" instead of "railway"; "track" instead of "line"; "car" instead of "carriage"; "depot" instead of "station"; "freight-train" instead of "goods train"; and "baggage car" instead of "luggage van."[28] And most English travelers noted that you take "the cars" to this or that place, not "the train."

Mrs. Trollope had also attended to some of the linguistic peculiarities of the Americans. She mentioned that the expression "getting along" was "eternally in use among them." It seemed to her to mean at the time "existing with as few of the comforts of life as possible"[29]—in chapter five I link this notion of "getting along" to the American system of railroad construction.

Arthur Cunyghame noted that Americans called a "clerk" a "clurk"[30] And John Boddam-Whetham, too, gives us a few samples of American "miscarriages" of the English language, although he said slang was heard "only among the lower classes, if the Great Republic will admit of there being such classes"—the existence of which he had no doubt. And of his time in America Boddam-Whetham said: "It is impossible to converse for five minutes without hearing a dozen times: "You don"t say so." (And) in the West that terrible word "say" (not "I say") is prefixed to every sentence"; and "the epithet "elegant" is bestowed upon the most inappropriate objects." He went on: "You meet "real (pronounced "reel") nice people wherever you go, and are constantly asked if you had a real fine time." He also recalled that "hurry up" were words that can "never be forgotten by a traveler in America."[31]

Catherine Bates also remarked at some length, but not negatively, upon American "permutations" of the English language.[32] Englishman, Foster Zincke, having been in America but a month, was surprised to be congratulated for speaking the language so well; his encouraging host saying: "I suppose you had an American tutor to teach you our language." The same gentleman informed him that the language of the English was "full of ungrammatical and vulgar expressions, from which ours is entirely free." However, Zincke suggested the gentleman's acquaintance with Englishmen was "confined to poor immigrants" and that he had thought their dialect that of all Englishmen. Zincke was also informed (in 1868 by an Englishman long resident in America) that "of all the immigrants who came to America the Englishman was the least educated."[33]

Concerning these published 19th century English narratives of travel in America, it seems the Americans were very keen to read what the English were writing about them. In fact, many of these travel narratives were published or distributed in America and today American archival sources seem to have them in stock aplenty, as if to exemplify the point. In that connection, one notes Frances Trollope's "indictment" of American values, attitudes, and behavior so got the Americans' "bristles up" that the book probably sold far better in America than it ever did in England. But her book *was* about a lot more than "manners," strictly speaking. In fact, I think it is best described as a book on "the character of America" and "the American character" at the time she was there, and perhaps it even merits a place in the history of sociology.

Even while touring America, the English chroniclers were often asked by Americans what they thought of America and Americans as if the interrogators had some deep-seated anxiety about the legitimacy or "completeness" of their national identity. In that regard, Thomas Nichols thought (1864): "America has, properly speaking, no past. Her colonial history is English."[34] And many Americans probably felt resentful about the fact that their cultural roots were essentially and ineradicably English, and that undoubtedly did have some bearing on America's sense of national identity, and quite possibly for up to a century after independence. Indeed, some of our English tourists found that many Americans were apparently so affected by perceived threats to (national) "self-esteem" they were "disposed to be very reticent towards Englishmen." And according to Englishman W.F. Rae, that was because: "A notion is prevalent that most English travelers visit America solely to accumulate materials wherewith to fill volumes with sneers and abuse."[35] William Ferguson recalled a conversation with General Cass, who referred to the obscure books written by Englishmen about America: "They come over here, he said, run over the country for three months, and think they understand it."[36] This was probably fair criticism, at least where some travel narratives penned by English travelers were concerned—but it could not be said of Therese Yelverton, for instance, who claimed to have traveled over 20,000 miles in America (she made more than one visit). Nevertheless, an 1863 American newspaper article referred to: "Sundry inflated English travelers, who have written books about America (and) filled their space with the dismal tales of the horrors of railroad traveling in America."[37]

If some Americans were reticent in the company of English people due to the perceived chauvinism of the latter, yet W.F. Rae, rather than viewing this apprehensiveness and aloofness of the Americans as bordering on the paranoid, was sympathetic (for an Englishman, that is); acknowledging that there was such a thing as "John Bullism," whereby everything in England is regarded (by the English) as superior to its American counterpart. Nevertheless, despite singing many praises of America and Americans, Rae did note an "insolent presumption of superiority" *on their part*[38]—perhaps "arrogance" was one means resorted to in defense of a fledgling sense of national identity.

But certainly not all Americans were coy when it came to conversing with the English. Indeed, Therese Yelverton remarked that the American entered into conversation easily and fluently: "Fully conscious of his superiority in this respect over the Englishman.... The greatest compliment an American can pay you is to tell you that you do not speak like an Englishman."[39] Similarly, William Ferguson remarked of Americans: "I was struck today in observing the facility with which all the speakers, whom I heard, seemed to possess of expressing themselves easily"[40]—he thought the English compared very unfavorably in that regard. But America was a large country and eventually colonized by numerous immigrant groups, so the "cultural" variations from one region to another could be remarkable—Anthony Trollope had great difficulty eliciting conversation from his fellow steamboat passengers on one occasion and rationalized that by noting: "A *Western* man is not a talking man."[41]

But where *inter*-national criticism was concerned, it was hardly all "one-way traffic." Boddam-Whetham mentioned that he had seen many letters from Americans who had traveled in England to the different New York newspapers "constantly abusing English *cookery*."[42] So the "bickering" could get both "catty" and "petty." But perhaps American nationalists had the last laugh, since in 1883 the lunatic asylum on New York's Blackwell's Island had 1,457 patients (all women), *English subjects constituting 48% of them.*[43]

When it comes to evaluating contemporary English appraisals of American *railroads* it must be borne in mind that some, or even a lot, of what the English travelers were evaluating was not simply "technological" or commodified service. In fact, it was often both enveloped in *American values*, which were themselves different—a point I draw out further in this and the chapter following. Indeed, there is still a lot to be said about American values at that time, which we need to understand so that we may in turn better understand the peculiar features which characterized America's national railroading "style" in the 19th century. And we ought always to keep in mind that all new technologies self-evidently arise within a *sociocultural context*; and that understanding that sociocultural context enables us to better understand aspects of the technology, its applications, and its sociocultural impact. Moreover, new technologies always arise (again self-evidently) within a *national* context. And in the case of railroad passenger travel, as with most commodities, both the process of commodification itself and consumption of the commodity may be imbued with, and characterized by, what we might term a *national style*. Just to highlight the latter point before explicating it further, two examples ought to suffice, one factual, the other a 19th century American joke.

Firstly, many English travelers in America—as well as both 19th century English and American commentators on railroads—referred to the "American system" of railroad construction; a concept we shall encounter manifestly here, though not usually to the accompaniment of applause for this system. This peculiar system of construction was more or less as described here: "When the rails were laid, so as to carry trains, it was not much more than half-finished.... But it began to earn money from the day the very last rail was laid, and out of its earnings, and the credit thereby acquired, it will complete itself."[44] This was not the only rationale "served up" for the seemingly "half-finished" or "bucking-bronco" lines of railroad English travelers frequently encountered and commented upon in 19th century America, but it will suffice for the moment. By comparison, English railroads were usually better "finished," and *finished before trains were run on them*. And the "way" generally was *permanent* rather than *ad hoc* (the Americans themselves conceded these differences).

Secondly, perhaps the joke concerning the "inexperienced" 19th century American railroad traveler (in reality much more likely a hapless English tourist)—who asked the conductor which end of the car he should get off, to which the reply was: "Either one: both ends stop"—highlights another conspicuous difference in national railroad (in this case passenger carriage) styles, not to mention the "well-to-do" English passenger's (more than occasionally) pathetic need to be "shepherded" in and through railroad facilities.[45]

It has been suggested railroad technology was the first technology to take on a national character.[46] That is debatable in the field of transportation technology alone, since ships and carriages probably engendered elements of national character in their design centuries earlier. More generally, tools and architecture were undoubtedly the first types of "technology" to demonstrate something approximating to "national character" and clearly many centuries, if not millennia, before the advent of railroads.

But if many of a nation's sociocultural (including economic) "practices" and material resources (technologies) reflect what we might term its "national style," yet, attempting to comprehend that national style can lead one onto "quicksand"—indeed, Charles Dickens once remarked that what a man writes of his own country or people is a picture of himself as well as what he writes about.[47] So how does he "get past" his own values when attempting to appraise—from the standpoint of the "outsider"—*another country and its peoples*? Whatever the answer, we shall venture forth near quicksand to further explicate some prominent 19th century American "values."

19th Century American Values—Materialism

Henry James remarked of America late in the 19th century that: "No impression so promptly assaults the arriving visitor to the United States as that of the overwhelming preponderance, wherever he turns and twists, of the unmitigated "business man" face ranging through its possibilities, its extraordinary actualities of intensity." And he thought America a society "serenely plundering in order to re-invest, and re-investing to plunder." He suggested, furthermore, that in late 19th century America there had emerged *a new kind of aristocracy based solely on wealth*; and these Americans he compared to the parvenus of the Napoleonic era, noting that some of them had begun to have "a Medici-like vision" and built museums, libraries and concert halls."[48]

Therese Yelverton noted of New York, although a view shared by many English travelers: "All is earnestness in New York." Thomas Nichols, writing of America in the early 1860s, remarked:

> The real work of America is to make money for the sake of making it. It is an end, not a means.... Everything, whether for sale or not, has a money value. Money is the habitual measure of all things. I believe the American husband unconsciously values his wife in the Federal currency.[49]

Even much earlier French economist, Michael Chevalier, who visited America in the 1830s, found money to be "the prime metric of everything," and that virtually everything potentially commodifiable usually was commodified.[50] During the same era Tocqueville remarked upon the "myopia" inherent to American materialism, noting that America's "ambitious men" were not very concerned about the judgement of posterity.[51] Of San Francisco in the late 1880s, Australian tourist James Hogan remarked: "Nothing is sacred enough to deter an average American from doing business.... The almighty dollar is worshipped with an ardor, a publicity, and cynical candor that most other cities endeavor to cover with a conventional veil of propriety."[52] Similarly, George Dawson, in an English newspaper column (1875), conceded that Americans did smile, but not "until business was over."[53] Peto (1866) thought that when it came to commercial relations, there was a certain "frigidity" in the American character, that Americans were impatient of delay, and that "they demand results where we (the English) look to progress." And, furthermore, that whereas "we examine and inquire carefully, and lay our foundations accordingly, the Americans lay their foundations on too great immediate expectations."[54] Henry Vincent, another English newspaper columnist, said of America (1867) that: "If a man could make people buy what they did not want, then he would get on in America."[55] Even earlier (1842) Englishman, James Buckingham perceived that the money-making mentality in America, despite its vigor, came at a price: "The code of commercial morality is growing more and more lax every year."[56] Englishman, Foster Zincke, remarked that in New York "land is a drug."[57] But it was a no less potent drug in the American West and elsewhere in America—a drug which stimulated the speculative imagination with an amphetamine "rush." However, there were times when railroad prospectuses, too, worked on the speculative imagination like a drug; although unlike the "land drug," the "railroad drug" often had the hallucinogenic qualities of opium and the nasty "withdrawal symptoms" of a nicotine addiction.

In America the railroad corridors, insofar as they facilitated both an extensive and intensive flow of people, were assimilated to the broader interests of commercial enterprise from quite early on—which is to say that the peculiar "space" which constituted the railroad corridors probably afforded the best sites available in the 19th century for advertisers of products and services. Indeed, the sensibilities of English travelers in 19th century America were often "assaulted" by the proliferation of advertising along railroad lines, which was apparently already prolific and obtrusive in the 1870s. James Burnley was quite exasperated by the American advertiser: "Wherever there is a bit of fence, a conspicuous gable end, or a surface of wood, stone, or brick *that can be seen from the railroad* and converted into a sign, there he will advertise."[58] This certainly did rankle the English. Another Englishman described such advertising as "loathsome stigmata," which "blighted the scenery" and brought "alarm and disgust to the eyes." And it is generally not realized the extent to which the presence of the railroad facilitated this "coarseness and indecency," these "portents of shameless imposture and rapacious greed" as another English traveler labeled them.[59] Indeed, English tourist W. G. Marshall noted of America (1881) that it was "daubed from one end of the country to the other" by huge advertisements:

> On both sides of the (rail) road along the shore of the Hudson, for 150 miles to Albany, you cannot look upon the beauties of the river from the train without being reminded that there are hair dyes, pills, etc. Even at Niagara, as you gaze in awe on the sublimity of the scene, you turn around and find that "Rising Sun Stove Polish" is the "Best in the World!" No one, who has not traveled in the United States, has any idea of how sadly the country is disfigured by the daubing I have referred to.[60]

However, John Boddam-Whetham observed, somewhat more pragmatically, that: "The Americans generally are far in advance of us in the art of advertising, and the Californians carry it to the utmost limit of inventive power."[61]

But this kind of intrusive advertising was hardly unknown in Britain by the 1880s, either. After all, in 1887 the Board of Trade required railroad companies to display *prominently* at each station a sign with the name of the place on it. But, as one commentator observed at the time: "As station advertising is carried to a great extent it is very difficult to recognize the station sign from the hundreds of advertisements equally conspicuous."[62] However, station advertising was in evidence in England much earlier. In 1851, W. H. Smith, a company which had a monopoly of the London and North Western's station bookstalls at that time, was also contracted—by that railroad company—to rent out space on platforms for advertising.[63] More generally in Britain railroad stations became very attractive sites for advertisers, since they were commuter concentration points. Indeed, termini, stations, ticket offices, and carriages were logical sites for advertising posters. In fact, railroad facilities afforded publicists an experimental playground where advertising was concerned. And *the fusion of engineered pedestrian traffic space with such commercialization of the same (railroad) space represented a significant—indeed, one of the first manifestations of—the cohabitation of engineering and psychology* (advertising) *in the interest of capital*.

As already alluded to, Americans were not at all reticent—and certainly not after mid-century—when it came to flaunting and spending their wealth. American magnates, instead of putting gargoyles in their gardens married them and lived the "high life" in the best hotels or palatial mansions. Englishman, James Buckingham, thought (1842): "These habits of universal extravagance and love of display, engendered by everyone *striving to be equal with those above them*, are fatal to all economical husbanding of resources."[64] But there were not as many wealthy people in America then as there were three decades later, nor were there many *extremely* wealthy people—people so wealthy that even the most reckless prodigality would have had little impact upon their wealth. In fact, many small fortunes—which were to become great fortunes—were made in the Civil War. And in the fifteen years after the Civil War many more immense fortunes were made and held onto "dynastically."

But some degree of balance is required here. If America had a "class" of restless, materialistic, rapacious people, yet as English tourist, William Ferguson, noted (1856) there was also an "inner circle"—another class altogether from the "frivolous, reckless, worldly set of rash speculators, money-worshippers, and money-getters."[65] Yet, this "class," as a coherent and conspicuous entity, was to be found only in certain cities, as Thomas Nichols noted: "No Northern city of anything like its size has so solid and what may be called as aristocratic a population as Boston." Indeed, Nichols thought the reason English people liked Boston was because its people were "cold, shy, stiff, and exclusive, but genial enough at home,"[66] while Englishman W.F. Rae noted (1876) that Bostonians, for their part, were usually gratified when told that Boston resembled an English city.[67] On the other hand, in the early 19th century the English city of Norwich was known as the "English Boston."[68]

If Americans were somewhat "grasping," yet it seems they liked to grasp at speed. Indeed, many English tourists to America remarked upon the different pace of life there, especially in cities like New York and Chicago. Thomas Nichols remarked upon the undignified haste with which Americans did a lot of things and not just constructing shoddy railroads:

> The medical profession in America bears the evil of haste and irregularity incident to so many of its institutions.... The Americans, who do everything in a hurry, educate their doctors in the usual fashion.... One can scarcely conceive of an honorable profession reduced to a lower ebb than that of medicine in the US.[69]

But flippancy and haste merged in the education of legal professionals, too—W. T. Sherman found himself admitted to the bar on the grounds of his "general intelligence"![70]

Individualism and the Myth of the Self-Made Man in 19th Century America

Ironically enough, the emergence of a stratum of exceedingly wealthy Americans, rather than denting the egalitarian ethos which underpinned American republicanism, strengthened it if anything. That was so because there developed in association with the emergence of this new class of rich people the myth of the "self-made man." The latter was supposedly a man who had seized his opportunities and made the most of them in this democratic society, this land of unbounded and equal opportunity,[71] where the possession of all the "right" values—ambition, energy, drive, innovative flair, and entrepreneurial opportunism—could make poor men rich, and allow even someone from the most humble background to become President (interestingly, Keith Thomas has suggested that *in Britain* before the 18th century "ambition" was a word used in an *exclusively pejorative* sense[72]).

This self-made man-*ism* was the cornerstone of the American Dream in the 19th century. And the existence of a newly-emerged class of rich people set it in concrete, effectively establishing, for all to see, the verity of the premises which underpinned it. Hence, excessive wealth was often admired rather than scorned by Americans, especially if its possessor had risen from humble origins. And even inherited wealth was not necessarily frowned upon if the dynastic fortune had, likewise, been "founded" by somebody who had risen from a humble background and seized his opportunities—it has been said of railroad magnate Cornelius Vanderbilt's first biographer that he presented the Commodore's story as a model for boys and young men.[73]

However, arguably, Gustavus Myers thoroughly destroyed the myth of the self-made American man of the so-called "Gilded Age"—at least where many of the richest men in the land were concerned—by exposing numerous of them as self-made cheats, thieves, swindlers, con artists, corruptors, extortionists, and other kinds of crook, and casting many of them as people not only entirely lacking any business ethics, but even devoid of anything approximating to moral sense. Myers, in *History of the Great American Fortunes*, does such a "demolition job" on the concept of the self-made American magnate it is no wonder the book is usually kept "under the carpet" in American history "butchering"—the more surprising because *all* the evidence he presented to support his case was derived from official documents. Quite simply, Myers exposes one of the great American ideals as a total myth, at least where the late 19th and early 20th centuries were concerned. In fact, his book is often described as "muck-raking," although rather than splashing muck all over the so-called Gilded Age, Myers coats it with tar and feathers—aside from which muck-raking is predicated upon the existence of muck.

Myers wrote numerous books, two at least regarded by most publishers as if they were literary counterparts to the Black Death. *History of the Great American Fortunes* was published in Chicago because no New York publisher would publish it. Myers had written the book to demonstrate that "the wealth of magnates came from forces altogether different than those represented by the crews of puffers and the staffs of adroit publicity men." Where his indictment of New York City politics (and its endemic corruption)—*The History of Tammany Hall*—was concerned, when he approached a publisher with a view to re-issuing the work in 1901, the publisher concerned declined and apologized for being "so cowardly"; while another publisher also declined to publish it, but expressed an interest in "obtaining a copy for my own library."[74]

If materialism and its sibling, conspicuous consumption, were "driving" values in 19th century America, so was *individualism*. Indeed, it was individualism which gave American capitalism an especially pernicious edge. French philosopher, J. J. Rousseau, had argued in the preceding century that a highly competitive society brings out the worst in people, even inclining some to find gratification in depriving and hurting other people.[75] And that certainly seems to have been the case where the "struggles" between

American railroad magnates such as Gould, Cornelius Vanderbilt, Drew, and others were concerned. In that connection, one notes Englishman Henry Vincent thought (1867) that New York was a city in which "all the excellences and vices of the limited liability policy" were embraced,[76] seemingly implying that "limited liability" had been extended from the corporate sphere to individual morality.

Tocqueville, much earlier, had quite insightfully linked individualism and self-interest *to American patriotism*, suggesting:

> The public spirit of the Union is ... nothing more than an abstract of the patriotic zeal of the provinces.... Every citizen transfuses his attachment to his little republic into the common store of American patriotism. In defending the Union, he defends the increasing prosperity of his own district, the right of conducting its affairs, and the hope of causing measures of improvement to be adopted, *which may be favorable to his own interests*.[77]

In his seminal essay on the American frontier, F. J. Turner interlinked American individualism, democracy, and the frontier no less insightfully. He argued that from the very beginning frontier individualism promoted a conception of democracy defined essentially as a *freedom from constraint*—however, the frontier is seen not only as fostering an antipathy for control, but also *an anti-social tendency*. Turner argued that the resulting "style" of frontier individualism ultimately contributed to the development of weak government and all the evils connected with it—such as the "spoils system"—which follow from a "highly-developed civic spirit." But Turner also linked individualism to the waning of a sense of honor in business in America.[78]

Marquis Childs more directly linked the emergence of individualism in America to government and materialism, suggesting the assumption that government exists to enable the individual to acquire wealth underlies a "primary pattern of American behavior." Furthermore, he suggested: "Every sharp practice was countenanced on the theory that the individual must advance himself by any means whatever, and that was his first duty."[79]

But individualism in 19th century America was not a value which left women behind, either. Indeed, adeptness at handling a buggy, for instance, became symbolic of female assertiveness and independence in America—the composer, Jacques Offenbach, touring America in 1877, was surprised to see "young girls of the best families" in a buggy alone and displaying "very competent mastery of a strong pair of horses."[80] Indeed, that would have been a rare sight for a European, even at that time. In fact: "Driving alone, that is a man or woman driving for pleasure alone without a driver or post-boy, is an American fashion. It was carried back to Europe by both the French and English officers who were here in revolutionary times."[81] But frontierswomen and new women settlers in the West also contributed significantly to the construction of a type of individualism which nestled comfortably enough within the ethos of the farmer-settler family, the latter "institution" itself a very important repository for the nurturing of 19th century American individualism as well as reflecting it.

In 19th century America rules and freedom were considered to be contradictory, so only the most elementary legal structure was acceptable, and even then, it was directed primarily at securing and protecting *the rights of the individual*. The absence of rules was evident even in Congress—American Parliamentary procedures were not governed by any rules at all until Henry Robert produced his *Rules of Order* in 1876.

So, it is important to realize that individualism is not only about self-assertiveness, but also (and perhaps essentially so in the American context) about limitations on constraint (of the individual.)

Another peculiarity of American individualism merits comment. In the 19th century Americans developed the tendency to highlight the (first letter) initial of either the first or second of their forenames (John T. Smith or J. Thomas Smith, for instance). This was clearly quite a new development in the 1850s, evidenced by the following extract from a court case in which an Illinois Lawyer, Abraham Lincoln, cross-examined a witness thus, presumably to discredit his testimony:

> Why J. Parker Green?—What did the "J" stand for? John? Well, why didn"t the witness call himself John P. Green? That was his name, wasn"t it? Well, what was the reason he didn"t want to be known by his right name? Did J. Parker Green have anything to conceal; and, if not, why did J. Parker Green put his name in that way?[82]

But if in 19th century America individualism was a guiding value, yet one should not assume that in such a materialistic society, driven as it was by individualism, there was no morality at all. In fact, morality, being somewhat elastic, as evidenced by its sociocultural variability alone, was pliable enough to cohere with individualism within the broader ideological framework of 19th century American republicanism. And it was only within the context of commercial values and practices, and corporate ideology, that morality in 19th century America was wanting. Indeed, Frances Trollope did have some positive things to say about Americans, one of which was: "No one dreams of fastening a door in Western America (at least not when she was there); I was told that it would be considered as an affront by the whole neighborhood."[83]

Henry James wrote of the America he had returned to (in the late 19th century) that it was characterized by a "cult of impermanence" entailing a "repudiation of the past." Furthermore, he said of America at the time that there was "much talk, but no conversation"; and that, although "the arts of life flourish, the art of living simply isn"t among them." Moreover, he thought the promise of affluence in 19th century America represented either impoverishment of values, or no values at all.[84] Indeed, if the corporation in 19th century America was commonly perceived to be a "soulless" creature, yet the values which underpinned and drove it were derived from the (often) no less soulless magnates who had preceded it, and whose accumulated wealth (and "impoverished values"?) had played some considerable part in its emergence. Indeed, one might ponder the extent to which the emergence of individual, dynastic, and corporate *philanthropy* in late 19th century America was a (cathartic) admission of guilt, or even a self-imposed form of penance for extreme selfishness and unbridled rapacity.

James McCabe, Jr., thought (1872) that men and women in New York City: "Concerned themselves with their own affairs only. Indeed, the feeling has been carried to such an extreme that it has engendered a decided indifference between man and man."[85] The Englishman, James Buckingham, thought America, even in the early 1840s: "Absorbed and overpowered by the intense love of gain and passion for display, which swallows up every minor feeling, and leaves only a concentration of selfishness, devoted exclusively to self-enrichment and self-gratification, without a thought or care for others." He went on to remark that: "One extremely unfavorable part of the American character, appears to me, to be the absence of sympathy with sufferers, unless of their own immediate family or kindred"—he probably should have said "empathy" rather than "sympathy." But was he finished? Not quite. For he referred to a "reckless indifference to the loss of life," and his own conviction that "in all the softer feelings of love, friendship, humanity, and benevolence the national character is deficient."

This was quite an indictment of American society at the time. But it was clearly intended as a generalization about a particular "class" of people, since Buckingham certainly found many Americans (as in St. Louis) extremely hospitable and helpful, and clearly not falling within the ambit of the above diatribe.[86] On the other hand, if there was at least a kernel of truth underlying some of his more pejorative assertions (above), yet one could argue Americans, compared to middle- and upper-class English people, were a more stoical, resilient, and "thick-skinned" lot. However, one Englishman visiting New York City around mid-century would have concurred with Buckingham, at least where some upper-class women were concerned, for he described the city's well-bred young spinsters as mostly "heartless worldly bitches."

However, his compatriot, Foster Zincke, thought Americans a gregarious lot, despite the evident individualism:

> Ours is a (social) system which isolates, theirs a system which brings everybody in contact with everybody. One is astonished at the number of acquaintances an American has. For one acquaintance an Englishman has, an American gentleman will probably have fifty or a hundred.[87]

But I suppose the key word here is "acquaintance." Furthermore, America was not a classless society at the time, and never has been, but nor were social class distinctions set in mortar as they were in England. So, for a start there were fewer social class barriers to conviviality. And Zincke probably did fail to appreciate the "superficiality" characterizing the bonds underlying the typical number of *acquaintances* an American apparently had. That point aside, Thomas Nichols rationalized the phenomenon in question rather credibly, to a point at least: "The settlers of new countries are forced to be more gregarious and social in their habits and customs than people of older communities."[88]

Yet, Henry James, even if he would have conceded that point, appreciated the peculiar "qualitative" dimension to the relationships formed in such unusual circumstances. Indeed, he thought the presence of an uprooted immigrant population in New York (towards the end of the century), for instance, reinforced the feeling of impermanence and alienation in the city: "A society in flux, with no settled customs and manners, confused about the old, uneasy about the new."[89] And he would have thought that to have been the case regardless of how many "acquaintances" people living in such circumstances had.

So, did this give rise, perhaps, to a "species" of individualism "by default" rather than by "design"? Indeed, as to what Henry James thought came out of the "melting pot" in America, he found nothing sufficiently coherent to give him the answer.[90] However, perhaps he missed something, since it could be argued that 19th century American individualism was often enough a "symptom" of alienation or anomie.

We should not think that because materialism and avarice were such prevalent driving values in 19th century America that Americans at the time did not have any "noble" values or virtues. Of course, they did have such values and virtues, and no less so than any other society. In fact, Foster Zincke, despite the negative things *he* had to say about America, thought the country a "nation of readers" and that they "read far more than any other nation in the world."[91] That Americans were great readers was attested to by the proliferation of newspapers, the newspapermen usually hot on the heels of the pathfinders in the penetration and settlement of the West. By 1857 Illinois, for instance, had 161 newspapers, thirteen of them in German and one in French—at that time Chicago alone had nine dailies, three of them in German.[92]

Zincke was very interested in American educational provision and might even be thought of as primarily an "education tourist." He noted of education, and the possession of superior knowledge in America:

> Though perfect equality is the first principle of *Western* life, yet the superiority of refinement and mental cultivation is fully recognized, and everybody readily defers to them. This, however, is *only done on the condition that there is no assumption on the part of the person himself.*

Indeed, to "give yourself airs" was an "unpardonable offence."[93]

More generally, education certainly was valued in 19th century America. In fact, numerous English tourists (apart from Zincke), whose travel narratives I have read, made a point of attending to educational provision during their travels in America, and the disparaging comments in that regard were few and far between. Zincke noted there were even special schools for the poor in New York—there were 16 of these so-called "industrial" schools, supplementary to the "common" schools and catering mostly to children of Irish and German immigrants (they were funded partly by the city, partly by charitable organizations).[94]

We should also note that although the Federal Government was for much of the 19th century loath to involve itself *directly* in education, yet it ceded land grants to all the states to enable them to create or bolster their education systems from the proceeds of the sales of such lands—the success of this policy varied from to state to state, aside from which some states were much more proactive in establishing educational systems on their own account regardless of what assistance they got from the Federal Government. But generally, Americans valued education, and furnishing it for the benefit of all was one of the few civic responsibilities *most* Americans acknowledged and one *not* motivated primarily by self-interest.

American Rudeness, the Concept of "Service," and Republicanism in 19th Century America

One other element of American "culture" frequently remarked upon by English travelers in 19th century America was *perceived* American "rudeness." And this perceived rudeness of the Americans is worth attending to at some length—because explicating it gives us yet more insight into American values and their ideological underpinnings in the 19th century.

Many English travelers in America in the late 19th century would have agreed with Frances Trollope writing 40 or 50 years earlier that Americans were generally very rude people. But the English were not the only critics of American society in that point of view. Domingo Sarmiento (an Argentinian intellectual and later statesman) noted that the American will take an unusual interest in the paper you are reading in the hotel lounge, the only paper that interests him because you already have possession of it; that if you are smoking quietly he will take the cigar out of your mouth to light his own, then replace it in your mouth; that if you are reading a book and put it aside for a moment, he will "seize it and read two chapters without stopping"; and that if you have interesting buttons on your coat, then he will inspect each one separately, making you turn around so he can get "a better look at the walking museum." However, the astute Sarmiento did point out that there was a degree of tacit consent underlying the taking of such liberties, and that it would be poor form to show displeasure. Indeed, we should allow the American his "forensic curiosity" and perhaps not classify the taking of such liberties as "rudeness." Sarmiento also noted (in the 1840s) that generally in public places some aspects of the American's *quest for comfort*—a concept to be addressed shortly—would undoubtedly have been frowned upon in genteel English company. He observed, in that connection, that four Americans sitting around a marble table will invariably place eight feet upon it, while lying down "seems to be the height of elegance, and that this sample of good taste seems to be reserved for when women are present."

The American's forensic curiosity and quests for comfort aside, what was often perceived to be American rudeness by European travelers in America may also be linked to the (white) American's quest to assure him- or herself that they had no social superiors nor would any be countenanced. Indeed, the percipient Sarmiento observed of Americans: "Yankees are the rudest animals under the sun wearing frock coats and overcoats; but he then qualified the assertion, suggesting this "rudeness" was "*part of liberty and the American spirit*."[95] That was insightful. But in the previous decade Tocqueville, who was a little surprised there even was such a thing as a "respectable" tavern in America, observed that even in those places "white servants see themselves as their master's equals."[96] That being the case, it was unrealistic to expect to see them genuflecting before customers.

"Service" is something the modern consumer usually expects to be in receipt of when purchasing goods or services. That was usually so in Britain and many other European countries in the 19th century. But it was not necessarily the case in America, as our English tourists invariably discovered sooner or later, and often during railroad travel. In fact, English tourists not only found "service" to be wanting in America, but often lack of service was accompanied by downright rudeness. But were Americans "congenitally" rude or were they socialized to be rude? And was, perhaps, the poor service and rudeness rooted ultimately—as Sarmiento thought—in American republicanism and individualism?[97]

Alexis de Tocqueville thought many Americans hardly civilized; something he attributed—without teasing out the filaments of this view—to *there being no aristocracy or class distinction of any sort*.[98] However, the rudeness which Tocqueville experienced was less like evidence of a classless society than it was a form of resistance to the unthinkable idea that it might be otherwise—rather less like "false" consciousness, if you like, than it was like "self-delusional consciousness" (the difference between the two is subtle, but real, nonetheless).

There is no doubt that what was often perceived by visitors to America to be rudeness could be linked to the republican "spirit." And this was especially so where persons ostensibly rendering a service were concerned. Nobody likes doing the servile and menial jobs in society, but somebody must do them. And that was no less so in 19th century America. But *white* Americans who found themselves employed in positions of service and deference absolutely resented it. And that is a principal reason why such people were often rude to consumers.

As Frances Trollope had noted: "In America the man possessed of dollars does command the services of the man possessed of no dollars; but these services are given grudgingly."[99] In the same connection, Foster Zincke (three decades later) really "cut to the nerve" when pointing out that: "The Republic could only be carried on because immigrants constituted its servile class."[100] That was absolutely so where the emergence of an urban industrial working class was concerned after the Civil War. But even much of America's railroad building—where the "spade work" was concerned—was done by recently arrived immigrants. Indeed, Foster Zincke noted that the railroads "were not made by American navvies"—immigrants did all the laboring jobs. And that was often the case—the first transcontinental railroad, for instance, was built *largely by* Irish and Chinese labor.[101]

But let us return to the relationship between "rudeness" and "servility" in 19th century America. It is important to realize this was a country in which slavery had been institutionalized and that, historically, Negroes (and white indented labor in the early period) had performed much of the servile and degrading work that had to be done in many parts of America. Consequently, that kind of (lowly and servile) work became stigmatizing (in the 19th century) for any white person who found him- or herself having to do it. In that connection, Englishman Henry Deedes noted that in Kentucky in 1868 *only Negroes* were designated household *servants*.[102] And his countryman, Foster Zincke, noted that *boy* was the new name for manservant (certainly a more palatable appellation for *white* boys than "servant"). But he also noted that generally (domestic) *service* was termed *help*, and that where *white* service was concerned the terms "service" and "servant" were avoided. Furthermore, Zincke suggested that for a white man to become a waiter "is to sink himself to the level of the black," and that "no (white) American would become a footman or hotel waiter."[103]

English tourist, George Combe, had found the servants and landlords in the inns of New England in the late 1830s cold and reserved in their manner: "The servants speak, move, and look like pieces of animated mechanism." And he noted that more generally: "Service (domestic especially) is not esteemed honorable among the Americans."[104] Englishman, Arthur Cunynghame, traveling around 1850, noted if you asked a question of a bar-keeper, steamboat clerk, or waiter they usually just stared at you contemptuously for a few seconds, then proceeded to completely ignore your inquiry—though he did not encounter that in the north-east.[105] T. S. Hudson (traveling around 1880) thought this and other types of rudeness extended to railroad "guards" as well (whom he found to be mostly of Irish descent), although he suggested their "want of civility" was "compensated for by their smartness and intelligence."[106] Lady Hardy found that rudeness in general extended to female shop assistants in large New York stores: "When they decide to attend to you it is with a sort of condescending indifference."[107]

But Frances Trollope earlier had astutely rationalized the American female attitude to *domestic* service, and her general point probably extended to female shop assistants:

"The whole class of young women are taught to believe that the most abject poverty is preferable to *domestic* service (and they) think that their equality is compromised by the latter." In fact, she referred to "the (perceived) horrors of domestic service which the reality of slavery and the fable of equality have generated." And, like others, she noted in America it was "petty treason" to call a free citizen a "servant," and that obtaining a *white* household servant was referred to as *getting help*.[108] However, the term "help" had been used in early colonial times, although it meant quite literally somebody who *helped* in the house or with outdoors work, whereas in the 19th century the term "help" had acquired the euphemistic connotation alluded to above. Indeed, that great American historian of colonial New England, Alice Earle, who had a keen eye for trivia, noted: "No gingerly nicety of regard in calling those who served by any other name than servant was shown" in colonial times. But she also noted that people who fell into the (indentured) servant category in those times "did not appear at all insulted by being termed servants."[109]

Harriet Martineau connected (correctly in my view) the prevalence of the boarding house in American society when she was there with the difficulty of obtaining domestic servants. But the latter she found a fascinating subject, which was also one of "continual amusement" for her, and noting that what she saw in that regard would "fill a volume." However, she noted in *Society in America* some of the negative aspects to domestic service in England at the time, one of which was: "It is so completely the established custom for the mistress to regulate their (servants") manners, their clothes, their intercourse with friends, and many other things which they ought to manage for themselves." But very few American women employed as "help" would have allowed themselves to be "managed" so by their employers.

Until the advent of the Pullman era, travelers in America (and not just railroad travelers) could expect to be in receipt of poor service, bad attitudes from those rendering the service, even downright rudeness from railroad functionaries during their travels. But that is not to say employees of stagecoach and railroad companies, for instance, were not subject to conditions of employment which supposedly forbade and punished rudeness to passengers. In fact, in the 1820s even the employees of stagecoach companies in the (primitive at the time) Midwest were: "Forbidden to indulge in language or conduct that was unseemly, and were instructed to treat passengers with the utmost politeness."[110] The Erie Railroad Regulations of 1854, probably typical of railroad company regulations at the time, stated that: "Rudeness or incivility to passengers will, in all cases, be met with immediate punishment." And: "The station agent must see that all servants at the stations behave respectfully and civilly to passengers of every (*social*?) class."[111] So much for the theory! Dee Brown suggests railroad servants who could get away with it delighted in being rude to people, especially "well-bred" people.[112] In the chapter following numerous instances of rudeness experienced by 19th century railroad travelers in America are documented.

But setting American rudeness aside for the moment, I want to focus now on what was perceived by many European travelers in 19th century America to be one of the most offensive and disagreeable American proclivities of the age, and one which tourists encountered ubiquitously and remarked upon no less so. This was the habit of spitting, which was closely associated with the widespread habit of tobacco chewing. But was this not the land of the free, where anybody ought to be able to spit anywhere, any time, on anything?

The American Habit of Spitting

All English tourists found American spitting objectionable and rightly so. From an English point of view spitting certainly fell into the "rudeness" category. In contrast to American society, Puckler, when touring England in the late 1820s, found spitting to be: "So pedantically forbidden that one can seek in vain through the whole of London for such an article as a spittoon." He noted, furthermore, that to spit anywhere in a room in English *upper-class society* was one of the three greatest offences that one could commit against English manners, and for which, apparently, all further entrance into "society" would be banned to one—just for the record, the other two great offences were to use a knife like a fork and to take sugar or asparagus with your hand (talk about "total institutions"!).[113]

But in America people from all walks of life commonly spat in public. First "out of the blocks" on this subject, Frances Trollope had found American spitting: "A deeply repugnant annoyance." She found that even carpets on river steamboats were often covered with spit. In fact, she and her female traveling companions found it: "Absolutely impossible to protect our dresses from the contamination of spitting."[114] Dickens thought Washington the "headquarters of tobacco tinctured saliva."[115] And American Margaret Fuller recorded that at Niagara Falls: "A man walked close up to the fall; and, after looking at it a moment, as if thinking how he could best appropriate it to his own use, he spat into it." Somewhat coincidentally, Oliver Jensen observed (of 19th century American spitting) over a century later that: "The wholesale public expectoration of our citizenry was second only, as a natural wonder, to the mighty Niagara Falls."[116] George Combe, traveling from Worcester to Boston by rail in the late 1830s, remarked: "Our journey would have been agreeable, except for the annoyance of constant showers of tobacco saliva squirted on the floor at our feet."[117] Alex Mackay, traveling in 1846–7, considered tobacco-chewing (and the associated spitting) to be a plague in American life." But he generally found the habit only south of the Hudson, where: "Carriage seats, the sides of the car, the window hangings, and sometimes the windows themselves are stained with the pestiferous decoction."[118] J. Boddam-Whetham (traveling in the early 1870s) found the ubiquitous spittoons—which were present even in Pullman cars—"nasty articles" which "intruded themselves everywhere."[119] Even around 1880, tourist W. G. Marshall found the residues of spitting in the rooms of even the best hotels in America.[120] Therese Yelverton noted that Eastern girls did not chew tobacco, though some Western girls did, but whether or not they spat all over the place as well is unclear. But Yelverton thought: "People spit more in *St. Louis* than in any other place because the women and children spit too, even though most did not chaw."[121] Thomas Nichols (writing in 1864) was unforgiving of his compatriots on this subject: "Spitting is the vice of America, pervading and all but universal. The judge chews and spits upon the bench, the lawyer at the bar, the doctor at the bedside of his patient, and the minister in his pulpit."[122]

It is not clear whether passengers were prohibited from spitting in the cars during the first four or five decades of American railroading. However, if there were such prohibitions, yet it seems spitting was such a national "institution" any such prohibitions would have been ineffectual or un-enforceable—an early colonial etiquette book, in detailing "dining etiquette at the time, advised: "Spit nowhere in the (dining) room but in the corner."

But, to be fair to the Americans, it seems the Italians at the time were not much better—an *American* newspaper article in 1867 reported that in Italian second-class railroad carriages at the time the passengers commonly spat on the floor, as well as throwing quantities of chestnut shells "underfoot or underneath the seats."[123]

Spitting was, apparently, still in vogue in America in 1889, since an etiquette book of that year advised its readers: "No gentleman should spit on the floors in cars or stations when ladies are present"[124]—presumably it was acceptable to spit in such places so long as women were not present!

Prohibitions against smoking in public places had emerged quite early in America. And at the end of the 19th century there were still New England towns which prohibited smoking on the streets, such laws traceable to colonial times[125]—such prohibitions, or the stigma attached to smoking in some places in colonial times, may explain why taking snuff, and later chewing tobacco, became popular.

It seems that eventually many tobacco chewers may have switched to smoking cigarettes, and it may have been for that reason primarily that the prevalence of spitting gradually declined. The tobacco chewing habit peaked in the 1880s, at which time tobacco cigarettes were nowhere near as popular. Having said that, the smoking habit was quite widespread in America by 1881—some 240 million cigarettes a year were being sold in America by then. However, Liggetts, the biggest chewing tobacco producer in the country at that time, did not start manufacturing cigarettes until the 1890s[126]— by 1889 over two billion cigarettes were being smoked annually in America, half the business in the hands of James Duke.[127]

In Britain in the 1840s smoking was exceptional. However, prominent people who smoked, such as Thomas Carlyle, probably served as role models for the popularization of the habit. In fact, in Britain soldiers returning from the Crimea helped spread the habit, too, which was boosted further in the 1870s with the introduction of the more pleasant Virginian tobacco cigarettes.[128]

Most English railroad companies had a complete ban on smoking until the mid–1840s; and even when it was permitted it was contained in "smoking saloons," which most English railroad companies provided by 1860.[129] And 1860 may have been a watershed for the habit in England, since prior to that time smoking had been so much the exception that many English railroad companies had not bothered to label carriages "no smoking."

In America from around 1860 most railroad companies were making some special provision for smokers in the form of the "smoking car." However, from the late 1860s the "smoking car" could be either quite splendid (as in Pullman service)—with luxurious chairs, a library, a writing desk, and a panoramic view often[130]—or quite "seedy." For instance, where the latter was concerned, John Boddam-Whetham thought the smoking cars on the Central Pacific's section of the first transcontinental railroad quite inferior, and that, effectively, they were second-class cars: "They are without carpets, the seats often without cushions, and crowded indiscriminately with whites, blacks and Chinese."[131]

The Myth of the Egalitarian Society in 19th Century America

This brings me to 19th century American republicanism and the myth of the egalitarian society. And perhaps one might begin here by noting the pun implicit in the subtitle of John Boddam-Whetham's (1874) travel narrative—*A Record of Travel in the Evening Land*. Indeed, Americans seemed to have some very odd preoccupations for a people who viewed themselves as equals in a land of equal opportunity. One such very strange preoccupation was the fascination—which Englishman George Combe and other tourists noted in America in the 1840s—with the young Queen Victoria:

> The print shops display the finest engravings of her imported from London, and an exhibition of a picture of her in Philadelphia has attracted crowds of visitors for several weeks.... All the anecdotes about her majesty are carefully copied from the English papers and circulated by the press in the US.[132]

Likewise, English tourist, James Buckingham, found that in Kentucky in 1840 young ladies: "As elsewhere, had an intense desire to know everything that could be told them respecting Queen Victoria. The idea of a female governing a great nation seemed to them to lift the whole sex in every other country."[133] Indeed, it was inconceivable in America at that time that a woman might govern a state, let alone become president.

No less curious was the obsession with honorific titles in the Republic. During my research, even before I encountered the comments of many English travelers on the phenomenon, I was struck by how many 19th century Americans had military titles—such as General, Colonel, Major, and Captain. Initially, I thought that these men must have served as officers in the Mexican or Civil Wars. But I subsequently realized that was not very often the case. That, in fact, these titles derived from the rank the people held within local militias. And so struck was I by the proliferation of "officers" in these militias, I could not but conclude that the militia officers must have outnumbered the rank-and-file by about fifty to one! Frances Trollope had even remarked upon this phenomenon. She noted that numerous of her fellow steamboat *cabin* passengers styled themselves general, colonel, and major. And she was: "Amused by the evident fondness which Americans show for titles.... The eternal recurrence of their militia titles is particularly ludicrous." She rationalized this phenomenon, rather insightfully I think, as an "aristocratic longing."[134]

But this phenomenon had a long pedigree, even though in parts of America in the early post–Revolutionary period "the temper of the time was suspicious of everything that savored of class, or caste, or rank of any kind."[135]

Every member of Virginia's governing council in early colonial times, for instance, was commissioned "colonel," which was probably where the Virginian and more general Southern custom of applying "colonel" as a complimentary title to prominent men had its roots. Furthermore, English cavalier officers emigrating to Virginia after the English Revolution often had ranks such as major and colonel, while in colonial times the commander of each Virginian county's militia was titled "colonel."[136] In Massachusetts by 1730 there were many captains and colonels, and there seemed to be a "mania" for acquiring military titles: "It holds stronger against Captain Thayer and Major Miller, than it ever did against anybody in this town (Boston), excepting Colonel Gooch and Captain Mills"—all these gentlemen were civilians![137] French noble, Count Segur, who visited America in 1783, was astonished to find men of all vocations with military titles— he was astonished because, having been a distinguished military officer himself, most of these American "officers" had never served in the military.[138]

Foster Zincke, during his travels in America, met not only a colonel, but not short of 50 generals as well.[139] Thomas Nichols, who would have known since he was resident in America, remarked that it was possible in a year or two of voluntary military service to attain the title of captain. He noted, furthermore: "In America it is safe to call any decent man (a stage driver or ostler) captain, and any gentlemanly person (a railway conductor or tavern keeper) major or colonel." He also noted that (eminent): "Republicans visiting monarchical countries naturally wish to be presented at court, and as naturally carry with them their militia uniforms, which they display with suitable magnificence on such occasions."[140] However, by 1889 it was considered "improper" to put a militia or any other "complimentary" title on one's card[141]—of course, such cards had themselves become status signifiers by then.

One might also mention the tendency, which seems to have developed in 19th century America, whereby sons had "Jr." (junior) appended to their names, while fathers appended "Sr." (senior) to theirs when these relations shared identical forenames and surnames, thus invoking a strong sense of "dynasty" in naming itself. No less significant a development, where "aristocratic longing"—as Frances Trollope so tidily described the phenomenon—was concerned was the addition of numerical referents (as in Henry *VIII*) to the American male's name, and thus to his sense of personal (*and dynastic*) identity. So, we end up with the likes of "J. Theodore Smith IV," for instance, which blends individualism with both dynastic grandiosity and aristocratic pretension. Indeed, it seems that some early American magnates began the fashion of the numerical referent appended to the surname to create a conspicuous sense of dynasty, and in emulation of that aspect to the "culture" of European aristocratic (family) identity and history. The "common" American people then began to imitate this fashion established by the magnates. Furthermore, after the Civil War it was common for women from distinguished families—especially if having a distinguished father—to stake *their* claims to (dynastic) status honor by putting their maiden (family) name before their married (family) name. For instance, if Louise Beckham had a distinguished father and she married James Shaw, then she might wish to be known as Mrs. Louise Beckham Shaw. Furthermore, in the 1860s some Americans began to append the term Esq. (esquire) to their name—at that time in England it was used as a title of courtesy, yet originally it had applied to a member of the English gentry below the rank of knight. And in America by the 1870s the term "Esq." was often appended to the names of prominent people without any other title or "office," especially professional people such as engineers. One might also note the dynastic element in corporate culture, as in publishing, for instance—G. P. Putnam's Sons, Scribner's Sons, etc.

Such phenomena were no less indicative of "aristocratic longing" than were the military titles and the fetish for uniforms among 19th century American males. But we should not lose sight of the fact that these "naming" appendages generally applied only to males and male lines of descent in families; perhaps indicating that 19th century American republicanism was not quite as divested of patriarchal elements as some might think.

The "parade," which was to become a very prominent American institution, was certainly well-established as a sociocultural phenomenon in the early 19th century. It, too, may be connected to the "aristocratic longing" Frances Trollope referred to, since it displayed a pageantry, ceremonial aspect, spectacle, and rites redolent of both monarchical and aristocratic public display and grandeur. Indeed, there was something just a little a bit peculiar about virtually the entire adult male population of towns and cities forming themselves into parades on certain occasions. There may have been a "republican" aspect to it, too, but the pageantry, grandeur, and ceremonial elements of the parade incline me to think it a more "quasi-aristocratic" than a strictly "republican" institution.

We have looked, admittedly in cursory and very selective fashion, at some values underpinning 19th century American society. For the moment, and for my purposes here, I think all that needs to be said is that the "flag-ship" values of "republicanism," "democracy," and "egalitarianism" (bearing in mind what has already been said about the myth of the self-made man) in 19th century America seem to have been somewhat "chimeric." And the argument in support of that contention is "fleshed out" in the following (brief) consideration of *real* social class distinctions in 19th century American society. But before undertaking that brief survey perhaps we might note the words of eminent American writer, R. W. Emerson, regarding railroad traveling: "It is not fit to tell Englishmen that America is like England. No, this is the paradise of the third class.... England is the paradise of the first-class; it is essentially aristocratic, and the humbler classes have made up their minds to this, and do contentedly enter into the system."[142] What Emerson has to say here is interesting, if only because *it does not deny the existence of social classes in America at the time*; but, rather, intimates that the lowest (social class) "common denominator" in America was not as "low" as it was in England.

Nineteenth century America was necessarily a society characterized by a "pyramidal" rather than a "flat earth" social structure, just as any European society at the time was. And the pyramidal nature of American social structure in the 19th century was not simply a product of some people seizing their "life chances" and "running" with them, while others were not as motivated so to do or not as enterprising; for *this was a society which practised—and glaringly so—discrimination against certain groups in society.*

From the earliest days of the Republic there was a conspicuous divide between rich and poor. The makers of the American Constitution were hardly "Levellers." And if part of the Jeffersonian vision for America was the notion of building a nation out of equal states, yet the notion of building a nation from a society of equal individuals was not part of the theory. Hence, what might seem to have been glaring anomalies in the Great Republic in the early 19th century were not necessarily so.

But the point is that 19th century America was a society in which reality did not fit very comfortably with key aspects of the national ideology; and that was especially so where egalitarianism and equality of opportunity were concerned. Indeed, as English tourist, William Ferguson, suggested (1856): "Perhaps America must learn a little more about freedom for herself before she is quite able to disperse it to all the world."[143] And Michael Chevalier, traveling in America in the 1830s, was appalled to discover murderers and arsonists could obtain bail if wealthy enough.[144]

If, in America compared to England, *visible* passenger class distinctions in the early decades of railroading were unusual, yet they were not entirely absent, as we shall evince in due course; aside from which we might take stock of Mark Twain's keen observation that being a traveler could itself confer a certain status: "I was a traveler.... A glorified condition.... I was able to look down on and pity the untraveled.... And as soon as I knew they saw me, I gaped and stretched, and gave other signs of being mightily bored with traveling."[145]

I suggested in a previous chapter it was erroneous to think 19th century English railroad *passenger classes* faithfully reflected the English social class structure; suggesting, instead, the former were not social class categories at all, strictly speaking, but status entities corresponding to stratified commodities. Similarly, if passenger class distinctions were unusual in the first few decades of *railroading* in America, yet that would not necessarily indicate that (the single class of) railroad travel mirrored a classless society at the time. Of course, the latter was the ideologically correct impression, which no doubt most *white* Americans subscribed to.

But the reality was that this was a society in which the Indians at the time, for instance, were not even considered to be American citizens, having been consigned to, or in the process of being consigned to, seemingly portable "lazarettos" euphemistically termed "reservations," while the peoples themselves were strangely dignified with the label "nations"—clearly, they were closely related to the Lost Tribes of Israel. In fact, for a time shortly after the Revolution there was a belief that the Indians were, indeed, descendants of the lost tribes of Israel! And at around the same time there was also an apparently widely-held belief that the Indians were descended from a lost tribe of Welshmen who went to America under a leader called Madoc—Indian burial mounds and ancient customs were thought to link the two cultures.[146]

The Indians aside, the Negroes were still enslaved in many parts of (mainly eastern and southern) America at the time of the advent of railroads, while later various types of immigrant were discriminated against conspicuously and unapologetically in society at large *as well as during railroad travel.*

Those considerations aside, America was no classless society. In the South there was a clear demarcation between the relatively affluent planter class and the "poor whites," many of whom lived in more abject circumstances—in terms of their standard of living—than did the average slave. Frances Kemble identified two categories of poor whites in the South (Georgia), the "buckrees" and "pine-landers," describing the latter as: "I suppose the most degraded race of human beings claiming an Anglo-Saxon origin."[147] But the "poor whites" had more "designations" than those Kemble noted. In the South, which is where they predominated, the poor whites had various names: "Tar Heels" (North Carolina), "Sand Hillers" (South Carolina)," "Crackers (Georgia), "Clay Eaters" (Alabama), "Red Necks" (Arkansas), "Hill Billies" (Mississippi), while "Mean Whites," "White Trash," and "No "Count" were used more generally in the South to describe them. Emily P. Burke, who was in America in 1850, said of the Southern poor whites: "They are not treated with half the respect by the rich people that the slaves are, and even the slaves themselves look upon them as inferiors." But Burke thought many of the poor whites of Georgia and the Carolinas were descendants of paupers brought from England centuries earlier.[148]

Tocqueville had noted that Americans never used the word "peasant,"[149] and one assumes he would not have mentioned that had he not seen quite a few (white) "peasants" in America—Washington had referred to ordinary farmers working small plots of land and living in households as "the *yeomanry* of the country."[150] In fact, in the early 19th century Stephen van Rensselaer owned 3,000 farms in Rensselear[151] and Albany Counties in New York. And Myers informs us that the "quasi-feudal conditions" prevailing on the Van Rensselaer, Livingstone, and other New York estates survived to 1846, and that they were "the prime causes" of the Anti-Renters movement of 1847–9. Furthermore, the fact that until 1800 public lands could not be purchased in tracts of less than 5,000 acres indicates that something approximating to feudal land tenure conditions necessarily prevailed in America.[152] But if by the 1880s there were supposedly no peasants in America, strictly speaking, yet at around that time Nebraska's biggest rural landlord, Englishman W. E. Scully, owned 210,000 acres in Nebraska, Kansas, Missouri, and Illinois, and much of that land was leased to tenant farmers. Indeed, an 1887 Nebraskan newspaper article impugned such foreign capitalists for introducing the "landlord system of Great Britain" into the "land of the free." But were the perceived "victims" in this case really America's first "peasants"?

But did Christianity, like a rolling pin, roll the "dough" flat in America? In Charleston church pews were being sold for up to £100 in the late 1720s.[153] In New England, even long after the advent of railroads, well-to-do families had their own exclusive pews within their churches. And one might think religion would be one area where social class differences would have been leveled in *the* egalitarian society. But the reality was that, from earliest colonial times, religion mattered in America, but it was not always in tune with republican sentiment, and was often completely out of tune with it. In fact, religious affiliation sometimes had serious implications where *equality of opportunity* was concerned in 19th century America. In fact, it was not until 1924 that a Roman Catholic (Alfred Smith, a Democrat) received serious consideration as a candidate for the presidency.

In some of the Eastern American cities in the 1830s/1840s the underlying values of the status groups constituted of the most "well-to-do" members of society may not have differed too markedly from their English counterparts. The English tourist, Lady Hardy, noted of America in the late 1870s: "Though strongly republican in principle, they do not carry their republican notions into private life: society is *more exclusive* than in the old country."[154] James Hogan, an Australian touring America in the 1880s, like most tourists to New York visited Fifth Avenue, and he remarked that its palatial abodes "may give a sharp shock to old-fashioned believers in republican simplicity." And what he saw there—"tacky" as it was—confirmed his belief that: "The passion for personal superiority in the social sphere, and the consequent extravagance and display, flourish alike under all forms of government."[155] In fact, in the 1870s, despite the conspicuous signs of affluence, there were said to be 10,000 *homeless children* in New York

City. Furthermore, by 1890 the richest 1 percent of America's population owned around 26 percent of the wealth, while the richest 10 percent owned 72 percent of it.[156]

The Englishman, John Boddam-Whetham, remarked of New York in the early 1870s that there were only two classes there—rich and poor.[157] Writing in 1872, James D. McCabe Jr., remarked that strangers visiting New York City were invariably struck by there being just two classes—rich and poor. But he did explain the absence of the "missing" middle class—a phenomenon evident in other American cities, too—as due largely to suburbanization; whereby the cost of living in the city inclined the middle classes to live up to forty miles away in suburbs or semi-rural hamlets, and to commute to the city (New York). But it was not just the cost of living that caused "well-off" people to flee the city centers.

Yet, regardless of what reasons people who could afford it had for fleeing New York, the city was left pretty much to rich and poor. In fact, McCabe Jr., took the view that there was probably no other city in the world where there were to be seen such lavish displays of wealth alongside such "hideous depths of poverty."[158] Yet, this phenomenon had been evident even 30 years earlier. Indeed, in 1845 leading newspaperman, Horace Greeley, told a Cincinnati meeting that if he seemed complacent on the issue of slavery, it was because there was so much slavery in New York—in that year one-fifth (80,000 people) of New York's population was said to need private charity or relief, while the directory of wealthy New Yorkers published that year ran to 32 pages of fine print.[159] Englishman, Samuel Peto (1866), who must have been wearing a blindfold, thought the absence of "pauperism" one of the most striking things about America when he was there. He also thought wealth was more socially diffused and that there were few millionaires.[160] However, poverty was largely a product of economic cycles, and its extent depended on the stage of a cycle. But wealth was certainly not as diffused as Peto thought it was—many fortunes were made during the Civil War.

What did the English Viscountess, Therese Yelverton, say about New York's "upper crust" in the early 1870s? She referred to them as New York's "ostentatious class," which goes to Europe: "For no better purpose than to say they have been, or to gather ideas for making the grandest display on their return home.... Ladies visit Paris with no desire beyond that of seeing the fashions, and *taking home something newer than their neighbors have got."*

She went on: "This disposition to ostentation throws an air of flimsiness over all their undertakings. Their buildings have the same showy, meretricious appearance." She suggested, furthermore, that this obsession for ostentation extended even more broadly: "Even to the naming of the most ordinary things—the Silver Palace Sleeping Car, to wit. How mellifluous that sounds, but what a horrid place of torture is the reality!"[161]

W.F. Rae also noted of New York (1871), rather perceptively for a male, that: "The ladies are dressed after the latest French mode, yet the fashion of their apparel is the only thing they have borrowed from Paris."[162] And W.G. Marshall recalled that when he traveled to America in 1878–as a *cabin* passenger—most of his fellow (cabin) passengers were, indeed, Americans (the ladies with the latest French dress patterns in hand, no doubt!) returning from Europe.[163]

Therese Yelverton, like many of her fellow English travelers, had something to say about American hotels, and especially the "upmarket" New York species, which catered as much for rich locals—many of whom lived permanently in them—as they did for travelers and tourists.[164] Indeed, Yelverton is worth quoting on this subject: "In America hotels are *institutions* for the accommodation of *wealthy inhabitants*, to enable them to display their riches to the greatest advantage, and make as much show as possible for their money." Well, the era was called the "Gilded Age" for a reason. But Yelverton was percipient enough to realize that these places (upmarket hotels) were *institutions* and very much so in the sense that a hundred years later Erving Goffman wrote about the (*total*) institution. Indeed, she observed that despite their ostensive glamor, these hotels were very much *disciplinary* institutions in certain respects: "Much as I approve of discipline, regularity, and exactitude, yet I must confess that my very soul revolts from the sound of the gong of an American hotel.... You never feel free or at home in an American hotel, for you are always under surveillance, always under discipline." So, somewhat ironically, it seems that while the English upper classes were carcerally ensconced in their railroad compartments, yet some of their American counterparts were no less institutionally (even carcerally) ensconced in American "upmarket" hotels! But Yelverton also remarked upon the *disciplinary regime* of the Pullman and Silver Palace sleeping cars (these were offered by different companies) on the first transcontinental railroad: "Everyone is obliged to retire at a certain hour." But she caps off the travesty of the grand hotel, "institutionalizing" and "disciplining" the rich in the exemplary democracy, with the observation that all the hotel's servants "repudiate the notion of being servants."[165] Indeed, English traveler Isabella Bird said no one ever summoned anyone in America, but requested their attendance, and that applied to hotel clerks, too.

America's Sense of (National) Self-Identity in the 19th Century

One claim to "status honor" which 19th century Americans had recourse to was to be, or to be a descendant of, a "pioneer" settler. W.F. Rae noted of California in 1876: "To have come here in 1849 is held to be a mark of distinction in accordance with being a descendant of somebody who arrived on the Mayflower." He thought this such a significant and conspicuous claim to status honor in California that he referred to it as "pioneer worship."[166] More generally, the pioneer settlers of some of the constituent parts of America were regarded as vitally integral to the sense of national identity, much as were the key figures of the Revolutionary generation. But was the 19th century American sense of national identity anchored as firmly as such representations of it might suggest?

If one scans the index to a comprehensive map of America it is noteworthy how many towns and cities (and other places, along with topographical features such as rivers and mountains) have names harking back to the ancient (Greco-Roman) world, are named after famous cities elsewhere in the world, or otherwise have names associated with some foreign place of historical significance. Of course, there are many place names which hark back to the "mother" country as well—even just the names of states (New York, New Jersey, New Hampshire, Pennsylvania, Georgia, and Maryland) indicate that. Does that suggest that during the early period, and perhaps for quite some time, Americans were not sure about who they were in the world?

The "mother" country aside, what is really striking where this phenomenon is concerned is the number of place names (and topographical features) harking back to the *ancient* world. For a start, we have all those place names with *–polis* or *-delphia* as a suffix. More generally, at the tip of the (nomenclature) iceberg where this phenomenon is concerned we have Alexandria (2), Athens (2), Atlanta, Augusta, Cincinnati, Corinth, Eureka, Florence, Ithaca, Memphis, Olympia, Phoenix, Spartanburg, Syracuse, Sabine (River), and Troy. A little more exotically we even have a Cairo, a Nazareth, and a Bethlehem. And, presumably just to remind themselves that the Indians had no real claim to America, there are also at least three *Columbia*s and four *Columbus*es. Moreover, apparently in accordance with some key American values and ideals we also have El Dorado, Enterprise, Independence, Providence, and the Republican River.

Indeed, I would suggest a snap-shot of American place names and topographical features affords a remarkable insight into national self-identity and key cultural values in colonial and even post-colonial times. Indeed, this peculiar naming of America tells us quite a lot about the nation's sense of self-identity and how it changed across three or four centuries. And the naming of America is a subject more than worthy of a book.

This peculiar naming of America did not go unnoticed by English tourists in the 19th century. And how could the percipient and mischievous Frances Trollope have not noticed it? Indeed, she noted on the Mississippi River north of New Orleans: "One or two clusters of wooden houses, calling themselves towns, and borrowing some pompous name, generally from Greece or Rome."[167] Likewise, John Boddam-Whetham noted on the Mississippi: "We passed a small village called Florence, whose only resemblance to its Italian namesake was that a river flowed past it."[168] James Buckingham did not miss this phenomenon, either:

> In the first reach of the stream above Cincinnati, we had Delhi, Palestine, Moscow, and Chili.... In the space from Maysville to Louisville there are found the towns of Aurora, Rising Sun, Petersburgh, Warsaw, Ghent, Vevay, Hanover, New York, and London; and below Louisville there are Rome and Troy. The ludicrous associations of such names with the insignificance of the villages which bear them do not strike the American people so forcibly as it is likely it should do those who have seen the great originals.[169]

When in 1792 New York authorities carved up a large area—acquired from the Indians—into geometrical grids for sale, the grids had such names as Hector, Ulysses, Scipio, Brutus, Junius, Cato, Cicero, Homer, Solon, and Virgil. But there were also Dryden, Milton, and Locke—all Englishmen! Furthermore, in the 19th century it was not unusual for correspondents to newspapers to sign themselves Brutus, Civis, and so on.[170] But what are we to make of this strange phenomenon? Clearly, where the Greek and Roman referents were concerned, there was a connection to (Greek and Roman) republicanism.

From Greco-Roman America to the Single Class of Railroad Travel

The single class of railroad travel generally found on American railroads before the Pullman era was somewhat anomalous when considered in broader perspective. Anthony Trollope, for one, thought the single class of railroad travel in America not just an inconvenience, but illogical and hypocritical: "If a first-class railway carriage be thought of as offensive, so should a first-class house, horse, or dinner."[171] He had a point. After all, compared to the early American *railroad* operators the American river and (eastern) seaboard shipping companies had no inhibitions at all when it came to providing extraordinary comforts and novelties for passengers, which they fully expected travelers would be prepared to pay for. Margaret Fuller recounted a riverboat journey when she was the only lady on board, and thus had the undivided attention of both the boat's chambermaids (one Dutch, one native Indian), whose praises she could not sing highly enough, and to whom she had become quite endeared by the end of her journey. And Fuller was certainly no snob—although some biographical accounts cast her as pretentious—never avoiding "rubbing shoulders" with people traveling by a lower passenger class and saying of her steamboat journeys through the Midwest: "How pleasant it was to sit and hear rough men tell pieces out of their own common lives, in place of the frippery talk of some fine circle with its conventional sentiment, and timid, second-hand criticism."[172] Of course, she was a journalist and was one of the best in 19th century America.

If Anthony Trollope thought the "classless" train anomalous, yet his compatriot, Foster Zincke, traveling in America at around the same time, was not "taken in" by the *ideology* of the "classless" railroad: "American railway trains, though they profess to put all their passengers on an equal footing of democratic equality, do in fact allow them to classify themselves." Zincke noted that at the time he was writing hotel, drawing-room, and sleeping cars were effectively first-class carriages. But, more to the point, he drew attention to the "caboose for Negroes, emigrants, and dirty people, in which the wound that is inflicted on their dignity is compensated for by a reduction in the fare."[173]

The North-east remained the wealthiest part of America for decades and affluent people there were not at all coy about indulging their wealth. This was recognized by the shipping interests early on, even if the railroad companies tended to stand aloof of passenger class discriminations. Indeed, even Mrs. Trollope had found American steamboats "greatly superior" to any she had seen in Europe. And fifty years later (1876) her compatriot, W.F. Rae, declared that no English coastal or river steamboats were on a par with the American counterparts.[174]

During the 1840s George Law's *Oregon* was quite possibly the most luxuriously appointed public passenger vessel afloat anywhere. It was 330-feet in length and could travel at 25 miles per hour. It was replete with rich curtains, carvings, and gilt-frame mirrors, while the dining-rooms had the finest French china, star-cut glasses, and silver Prince Albert Plate. The main cabin, which effectively accommodated second-class passengers, had 200 berths with a separate cabin for women traveling by this class. But for those wanting more exclusive company and style there were 60 staterooms on the top deck.[175]

The well-traveled Domingo Sarmiento was highly impressed by the steamboats on the North American rivers, describing their luxury and grandeur as "unrivalled anywhere on earth," the vessels themselves "three-storied floating palaces with promenade decks." And he thought that compared to them Mediterranean ships would look like sewers or old hulks. He mentioned one American steamboat which had "a great hall able to hold the entire Senate and House of Representatives," and which could carry 2,000 passengers, and had 750 bunks and 200 private cabins.[176]

For most people living in the Midwest before the railroad age, and in proximity to the Mississippi, Missouri, or Ohio River systems, the only glimpse of travel luxury they ever got was of a steamboat's luxurious saloons. These river steamboats provided quite luxurious accommodation for anybody able to pay for it. And it was rarely that the standard of service paid for did not measure up to the expectation of the traveler— Arthur Cunynghame was very *unimpressed* by his Mississippi steamboat in 1850, over 50 people having to use the same meagre washing facility, while the meals were "dirtily served and scantily provided." But he acknowledged the latter was a "rare fault on the Mississippi," though "scantiness" was often a source of complaint on the Ohio.[177]

Therese Yelverton noted that many of the better river steamboats had a piano and that there was dancing if somebody could be found to play dance music on it, the viscountess proving she was no snob by doing precisely that.[178]

By the 1840s American inland steamboat travel—like coastal shipping in the northeast at the time—was invariably characterized by glaring passenger class distinctions; one source suggesting such travel at the time was often two-dimensional—both glamorous *and squalid*. Cabin passengers, apart from the luxurious appointments already mentioned, might also enjoy floral carpets, inlaid woodwork, oil paintings, a gleaming bar, gaming rooms, a barber shop, even a nursery. And not uncommonly they sat down to five-course dinners accompanied by orchestral music in the grand saloons of these four-deckers. Emigrants, woodsmen, and frontier farmers, on the other hand, were crowded among cargo and livestock on the lower deck, drinking river water, cooking porridge on the boiler flues, and sleeping on bales and boxes. They were usually the first victims in the event of boiler explosion or collision, but it was cheap—one dollar for five hundred miles (one-fifth the fare *economy class* cabin passengers paid).[179]

Even on the Erie Canal there were passenger class distinctions. "Packet" passengers could expect to pay 5 cents a mile (including food)—a good deal, since it was less than the cost of coach travel (the cost of which did not include meals)—while the "line" vessels charged 1 cent a mile without food and 2 cents with it. The packet service was faster than line, the former normally hauled by three beasts as against the line vessel's two. Both packet and line boats renewed their sources of motive power—which could be horses or mules—every 15–20 miles. However, the line boats sometimes had stables on board, so one team worked while the other rested. And because canal packets kept going day and night and had right of way at locks, they could cover 100 miles a day. Packets normally carried passengers only and passenger accommodation occupied most of the vessel's space. Some of that space was allocated to the bar, and there was usually a kitchen as well, female passengers often especially well catered for—there was often a "women's cabin" as well as washing and dressing facilities for their exclusive use. Traveling on an American canal packet in 1842, Charles Dickens was impressed by both the quality and quantity of food, and thoroughly enjoyed walking 5 to 6 miles along the towpath each morning. However, he was not amused by the spectacle of "seventeen men spitting in concert" or having to wipe spit off the deck before sitting down.[180] On the Erie Canal the packets provided a very high standard of passenger accommodation and service, while the food was often of the best quality and served on silver plate. As for the line boats, they were primarily freighters, and thus not dedicated to passenger conveyance. Not only were they cheaper than the packets, they were also much slower, the accommodation not of a very high standard, the company often "rough and ready," and the passengers usually more inclined to use the shops and grog "barns" along the canal route than were their packet counterparts. Furthermore, line boats were often localized services and did not usually travel through the night.[181]

If in the 1830s and 1840s American railroad companies seldom provided two or even three passenger classes, yet some other American institutions—river and coastal steamboats aside—at that time did. In the Brooklyn and Manhattan theatres, for instance, there were effectively class divisions. Walt Whitman, at that time a regular theatre-goer, sat in the cheap third tier "along with roughs and prostitutes," though later he got to sit—by means of his Press pass—among more sophisticated types on the parquet. At that time, most American theatres did indeed have a three-class division whereby the wealthy and "respectable" gravitated towards the boxes on the second tier, with the hoi polloi above them and a mixed crowd below.[182] However, in some New York theatres in the mid–1850s there were four "theatre classes"—boxes, pit, third tier, and gallery. Negroes, when admitted, were consigned to the gallery and often railed off from the lowest class of the white population they shared it with.[183] But what is important to note here is that the lowest social classes, and even blacks, *were catered to*, whereas in England the lowest social classes would most likely have been excluded altogether. And in America this (inclusive) provision was probably typical of the consumption of many services and entertainments. Indeed, there is an interesting contrast to be drawn here. Whereas in England *stratification* of the consumption of goods and services was often designed to *exclude the lowest social classes altogether*, yet in America *stratification* of the consumption of goods and services was usually designed to *accommodate* the lowest social classes.

Given these apparent "class" distinctions in American society where the provision of goods and services was concerned, it is something of a mystery (an anomaly, in fact, as Anthony Trollope quite rightly indicated it was) that early American railroad companies failed to emulate their maritime counterparts at least, especially since they "borrowed" quite a lot else from them, by offering travelers stratified classes of travel. Instead, they usually opted for a single, leveling passenger class. Was this, perhaps, because American railroad capitalists were more powerfully imbued with the republican spirit than their maritime counterparts? I doubt it. In fact, I think the explanation has more to do with economic factors than it had to do with egalitarian ideology.

Englishman, W.F. Rae, remarked of American republicanism that it was: "A system which has its basis in the possession of brains and disregards altogether the accidents of birth."[184] That was not true in any *absolute* sense and simply reflected American nationalist ideology at the time, since to begin with emigrants and Negroes were discriminated against. But, more generally, it would be extremely tenuous to suggest that at that time (1870) *equality of opportunity* was universal in America. Having said that, Rae was probably comparing America to Britain; the latter with its nebulous social class system and all the constraints it placed upon upward social mobility, not to mention the persistence of a resilient patronage system as well. So, even if to some extent Rae was "regurgitating" a mythological element of American national self-identity at the time, yet what he had to say was fair enough comment, all considered. But the astute Thomas Nichols, writing of America in 1864, certainly did not subscribe to the egalitarian mythology which usually went together with the "celebration" of American republicanism. Indeed, he suggested that Owenism and Fourierism (and other forms of socialism) failed in America precisely because: "The Americans, holding to equality in theory, all the more resolutely reject it in practice."[185]

All of this, then, moves us in the direction of a key premise. Namely, that it would be erroneous to think that the alleged classlessness of early American railroads was reflective of a classless American society more generally. For, how could that possibly be the case if American society was "many removes" from being "classless"? Nevertheless, many (white) Americans at that time liked to believe they were all equal, or at least enjoyed equality of opportunity. But where equality of opportunity is concerned, it has hardly ever been a reality in any society in history. But there were numerous reasons why Americans might wish to delude themselves so in the matter of equality of opportunity.

This brings me to the myth of the single (social) class in America, more generally. Americans loved to believe that theirs *was* a classless society and the railroad companies willingly subscribed to the myth. Anthony Trollope noted that in the *East* one could not find a hotel which offered *different classes* of accommodation, yet, strangely enough, the hotel business itself was stratified so. However, he noted that in the West the situation was different; that often there was a common standard of hotel accommodation—which presumably tended towards the lowest rather than the highest "common denominator"—and it would have been a matter of take it or leave it.

Trollope also took the view that the single (railroad) passenger class in America was not due entirely to the "republican spirit"; rather, he thought it due to the railroad companies being aware that being "democratic" required less capital expenditure—on rolling stock and other stratified facilities. Furthermore, Trollope thought the single class (of railroad travel) was not as egalitarian as it seemed on the face of it, since the common fare was set at a level which was an imposition on the poorer travelers "exactly in proportion as it is made cheap to those who are not poor."

However, an American correspondent, reporting at around the same time (1868), thought the cost of railroad travel in England "very much greater than in the U.S."[186] So, even if Trollope thought American railroad travel exorbitant—relative to what the passenger got for his money—yet it still seems to have been "good value" when considered in (comparative) international context.[187] And it probably was much more (*economically*) accessible to the American lower social classes than was railroad travel in Britain. In fact, that may have been the reason why, even in the 1840s in America, as English tourist James Buckingham noted: "The number of children and youths who travel in this country with their parents is much greater than in England."[188]

However, if railroad travel was more accessible in America because there were ostensibly no passenger classes in the early period—whereas in Britain companies which did not offer a third class effectively excluded the lower social classes from railroad travel altogether—yet the relative standard of living in the two countries probably had something to do with it as well. Indeed, one might argue that America's lower social classes were materially better off than their English counterparts in the first half of the 19th century (wages in America were higher than in England and significantly so for much of the 19th century, despite the huge influx of emigrants across many decades—

their presence lowered wages in only some sectors of the economy, while on the West coast wages, even for unskilled workers, were generally very good, even at the close of the 19th century). In that connection, Anthony Trollope observed that proportionately twice as many Americans were likely to own a watch than was the case in England. But maybe watches were cheaper in America or Americans more time-conscious? But I doubt either was the case.

W.F. Rae suggested that in America when he was there (the late 1860s) competition between railroad companies was not usually based on fares (logically enough, if most companies provided a single class of accommodation which varied little from one company to another), but was ostensibly based on "the amount of comfort" and the "shortness of time occupied by a journey." And although Rae praised the Pullman technologies, yet he thought the *ordinary* American railroad car "very disagreeable."[189] But it really did depend on the railroad company concerned, while the grievances of English tourists in this regard were often more about their fellow (American) travelers than the quality of the car accommodation.

The Negro and the "Classless" Railroad

How the Negro was treated across the decades, where public transportation was concerned, depended on several factors, including the date, whether North or South, the state concerned, railroad company policy, and the values and attitudes of its functionaries. However, it seems that during the early period, and for many decades on some railroads, Negroes were given little consideration where passenger accommodation was concerned when they were catered for at all before abolition. In fact, they often seemed to have been treated with the same contempt (by many companies) as were third-class passengers in Britain, and for decades even after abolition. In the late 1850s the Pennsylvania Railroad, for instance, felt itself "bound to receive colored persons as passengers," but reserved the right to "dictate" where they were to be accommodated on the train.[190] However, to keep things in perspective, it would appear Negroes were not discriminated against in some of the non-slave states, where railroad travel in the early period was concerned. In fact, in the antebellum period it was not uncommon in some parts of America to find Negroes riding with whites in both stagecoaches and railroad cars—a Cambridge don traveling in Kentucky in 1834, with two Negroes as fellow stage-coach passengers, was surprised the driver refused to eject them from their seats to make way for two white ladies.[191] On the other hand, in some places Negroes were completely barred from using any form of public transportation used by whites.

However, in the South during the early period Negroes were treated in an overtly discriminatory manner when catered for at all, whether freedmen or slaves traveling with their masters and mistresses. This meant separate cars at least, which would normally have been of a remarkably different quality to those used for the conveyance of whites. Station facilities would also normally have included separate waiting-rooms for Negroes facilitating separate access to a single ticket office, while a single kitchen would serve separate station "restaurants" when Negroes were catered for.[192] And on the river steamboats around mid-century "colored" people—whether free or slave—were served their meals at a separate sitting.[193]

Dickens remarked of a Negro railroad car that it was: "A great blundering chest such as Gulliver put to sea in from the Kingdom of Brobdingnag."[194] Traveling in 1854, Charles Weld found himself on a train which had separate gentlemen's, ladies' and Negro carriages.[195] And a well-to-do Negro, Edward Blyden, noted in 1862: "In the city of Philadelphia no colored person is allowed to ride in the public conveyances, so that delicate females of education and refinement are obliged to walk immense distances in all weather."[196] And although things had changed by the late 1880s, Blyden still had cause for complaint, since on a railroad trip from Savannah to Florida he was obliged to ride in the "nigger car," as *he* called it—but he did say it was very comfortable.[197]

Ending the policy of separating black from white (railroad) passengers clearly did not follow upon the abolition of slavery. Abolition was one thing, equality another. Indeed, many of the opponents of slavery in America would not for one moment have considered black people to be equal in every respect, and many whites at the time of abolition—though supporting it—would certainly *not* have held that African Americans were entitled to what we today cast as "equal rights," or even some of what in many societies today are considered "basic human rights." Indeed, a son of freed black parents who had been *elected to Congress in 1872* complained to the House: "Here I am, the peer of the proudest, but on a steamboat or railroad car I am not equal to the most degraded. Is this not anomalous and ridiculous? Forced to share second-class carriages *with riff-raff* and refused service at inns from Montgomery to Washington?" The reference to (presumably Negro) "riff-raff" is interesting, for it indicates not all Negroes at the time saw themselves as equals, either. Indeed, sometimes even Negro house servants displayed "caste feelings," as testified to by the words of one Alabama house servant for a well-to-do (white) family: "I ain"t neber sociated with no trashy niggers an I ain't neber inten to."[198]

However, a Supreme Court ruling in 1896 possibly indicated that some progress had been made on the question of railroad travel at least where black passengers were concerned, since the ruling held that although a railroad company could legally segregate black and white travelers, yet the segregated facilities *had to be equal* in terms of their quality and services rendered.[199]

Emigrants

Let us now attend to the emigrant. At about the same time Pullman services emerged, yet another class of travel was becoming just as conspicuous in the Midwest and West. This was the class of travel which catered specifically to emigrants heading west; often under a railroad company's patronage, since in many cases the emigrant had purchased his land from the railroad company concerned. And even in the 1880s many stations or depots had separate waiting-rooms for emigrants and colored people respectively, often with separate ticketing and toilet facilities as well—in the South in the 1880s it was "very customary to have special waiting-rooms for colored people, but *often for emigrants as well.*"[200]

In fact, by 1870 one might identify at least four elementary classes of travel on the "classless" American railroads: ordinary passenger car; Negro car; emigrant car; and Pullman class[201]—in 1869 the Union Pacific was advertising three passenger classes for the transcontinental railroad journey: first-class $100 plus a $4 a day surcharge for Pullman service; second-class (ordinary car) $75; and third-class (emigrant) $40.[202] However, although the categories of "emigrant train" and "emigrant class" were firmly entrenched from the late 1860s—essentially in connection with the advent of the transcontinental railroads—yet some companies had occasionally run "emigrant trains" much earlier (the Erie Railroad, for instance, ran its first emigrant train from New York to the Midwest in 1851).[203]

But one needs to look a little more analytically at the concept of the "emigrant" here, I feel. The discriminatory aspect to the treatment of emigrants began before they left the ship. Indeed, the processing of emigrants by New York immigration authorities in 1892 allowed those who had traveled to America by first- or second-class passage (cabin passengers) to be processed on board ship, and they disembarked directly to Manhattan; whereas the steerage passengers had to pass through the newly-established Ellis Island facility and were subject to close scrutiny, both in terms of their health and their means of support.[204] But even in the preceding decades steerage passengers (which most "railroad colonists" would have been, I surmise), wherever they disembarked, would have been treated differently to "cabin" passengers. So, how the American railroad companies dealt with them was commensurate with both how the shipping companies shipped them and how the American immigration authorities processed them. Consequently, we should not be surprised to learn their transportation across America—to their new homes—entailed the experience of some indignities.

Most of the railroad companies involved in large-scale commodification of railroad grant land in the Midwest and West eventually sought to capitalize on it by "importing" European people (mostly farmers). And it was common for the land package commodity to include railroad transit for the settlers and their families to the far-flung "colonies" in the West where their land purchases were located. However, often the railroad companies concerned furnished a special type of car accommodation for the transportation of those people. And almost invariably it differed markedly from the cars furnished for ordinary passengers, *from whom the emigrants were physically separated during the journey*. Some companies even ran emigrant *trains*; but, more commonly, the emigrant cars were attached to regular passenger trains or, occasionally, to freight trains—reminiscent of the English "third-class train" described earlier. However, *by the early 1880s* the emigrant business on the transcontinental lines was so great the Northern Pacific and Santa Fe companies, for instance, were running very long trains which carried *only emigrants* and their baggage.[205] But that was a time when the commodification of railroad grant land, in association with international marketing of it, was peaking.

Emigrant trains, as opposed to *ordinary passenger trains with emigrant cars attached*, had no priority along the way, so they were shunted into sidings, even to allow freight trains to pass—this, again, was very reminiscent of the English third-class train. These delays meant that for emigrants the usual seven-day journey Omaha-California could be drawn out to ten days or more.[206] Winther claims these trains were *deliberately* run at snail's pace[207]—also reminiscent of the operation of English *third-class trains*.

The treatment of emigrants aside, in the late 1870s America clearly had train classes, although they differed somewhat from the English counterparts—the American train classes were designated "regular," "extra," and "wild" (the last-mentioned also called "irregular" or "special" trains).[208] But these train classes were usually based upon scheduling criteria, and such criteria would seem to have had nothing to do with the passengers, if any, they carried. Having said that, the Pennsylvania Railroad Company Regulations of 1875, for instance, acknowledged different classes of passenger train, although that may have simply been a distinction between express and "ordinary trains"—in the late 1870s trains that stopped at every station were known in some regions as "Huckleberry Trains."

Despite their often traveling for a week or more on the transcontinental railroad, emigrants were not usually provided with sleeping accommodation in the form of *purpose-built* sleeping cars. Indeed, families just bedded down on the floor in the (admittedly) quite generous spaces between the seats in the "tailored" (partly gutted) emigrant cars. And when some companies did introduce sleeping cars for emigrants—from the late 1870s—they became known as "Zulu cars." Whatever the "upshot" of that term, I doubt it was flattering. Sometimes the sexes were separated in these Zulu cars, although family groups normally remained together in "family cars."[209]

Emigrants were often packed ninety to a car, the car seats often hard wooden benches.[210] Emigrant cars were also often old rolling stock, and sometimes obsolete day coaches out of which the companies tried to wring a few more "drops" of service before sending them to the scrap heap. Most emigrant cars were never designed for long-haul journeys. And the attitude of some American railroad companies towards emigrants was very similar to the attitude many English railroad companies had towards third-class passengers for decades.

Tourist James MacAulay, who was traveling Pullman in 1871, made it his business to "inspect the traveling modes of the poor" out West. What he described was probably an emigrant car. He thought it large, spacious, and well-ventilated with blinds, plenty of storage space, clothes pegs, heating in winter, and filtered water. But perhaps he did not realize the passengers had to sleep in the car as well and for upwards of a week. Arthur Cunyghame, traveling much earlier (1850), had observed the emigrant car of that time to be "a sort of baggage van." And in Detroit in the mid–1850s William Fergusson observed a train of (German) emigrants start for the west: "Their accommodation is very poor—merely common box freight-cars, and with the rudest seats fitted up in them. There are no windows. I do not wonder that multitudes died from cholera in these trains last summer, or that they die still in numbers."[211]

Does this sound familiar, in view of what was said in the preceding chapter?

J. Boddam-Whetham, traveling in 1873, wondered how people who could not afford Pullman class got through the journey from New York to San Francisco (he was referring to the passengers in the "ordinary" passenger car as well as to emigrant car passengers). And he thought it must be "as near as an approach to seven days' purgatory as is possible."[212]

Another English traveler made a very astute observation, correctly noting the similarity between emigrant cars on the transcontinental railroad and "steerage class" on an emigrant ship[213]—and perhaps the only difference was that the *English* steerage passenger was protected by the English Passenger Act, whereas the Western emigrant was very much at the (American) railroad company's "mercy."

Robert L. Stevenson assumed the mantle of a sociologist undertaking a participant–observation study when he elected to travel (incognito) "emigrant class" across the Plains. He noted that even though service was generally poor at stations, yet it got worse for emigrants. He observed it was *only on emigrant trains* the conductors omitted to call out: "All aboard!" In fact, he observed that many conductors refused to communicate with emigrants. And he was disgusted at the racism directed (by railroad employees) at the Chinese in emigrant cars, although noting that its perniciousness was "typical of the feeling (towards the Chinese) in Western America" at the time. In fact, he thought the Chinese had supplanted the Irish as the popular object of "racist detestation"[214]— however, and somewhat ironically, San Francisco's Chinatown was a very popular tourist destination for the "coast to coast" tourists at that time.

The curious and percipient Stevenson noted there were three types of car constituting his emigrant train—one for women and children, a second for men traveling alone, and a third for the Chinese. He also noted that the emigrant train from Omaha to San Francisco had no right of way, "unhesitatingly sacrificed" as he put it. And although he thought emigrants were treated dismally, yet he concluded emigrants were better accommodated (more comfortably and more commodiously) on the Central Pacific's section of the transcontinental railroad than on the Union Pacific's section. Overall, he concluded because of this and other experiences in America: "Equality, though conceived very largely in America, does not extend so low down as to an emigrant."[215]

Thomas Cook also paid some attention to emigrant *cars* while touring on the transcontinental in the 1870s. He noted emigrant cars on the transcontinental route were effectively third-class cars; that often they were attached to freight trains; and that the journey from New York to San Francisco for such passengers could take up to five days longer than it did on the regular trains catering to first- (Pullman) and second-class (ordinary car) passengers. Furthermore, Cook thought the treatment of emigrants by the railroad companies reprehensible; especially since most, if not all of them on some trains, had often collectively purchased (they tended to emigrate in large groups from the same villages or towns in the European countries they had come from) large parcels of land from the company concerned, and would eventually be obliged to use the very same railroad company to send their produce to market.[216]

But emigrants were not only exploited by the railroad companies. At Omaha, where emigrants began their railroad journeys through the West, they had separate waiting-room facilities.[217] But this isolation made them vulnerable to exploitation. Indeed, one source suggested that (in the early 1850s) emigrants traveling west by rail and boat were often "fleeced by scalpers."[218] And even decades later (1893) one commentator was suggesting: "To prevent the emigrants from being swindled, the company should provide refreshment facilities run properly."[219]

Concerning the reality of "emigrant class," Dee Brown suggests that even when railroad companies such as the Union Pacific or Central Pacific had these manifest passenger "class" differences (which were specified in advertisements), yet such companies still consciously strove to sustain the myth of the "classlessness" of American railroads— by trying to keep Pullman and emigrant passengers, for instance, out of each other's view as much as possible.[220]

Furthermore, it is important to realize that Americans tended to regard the Pullman technologies as luxurious add-ons which affronted nobody, so long as the basic passenger car accommodation remained of a satisfactory standard.

Railroad Passenger Classes Beyond Special Provision for Negroes and Emigrants

Setting aside the Negro and the emigrant, the reader should not think that railroad passenger classes were completely absent in America until Pullman services arrived on the scene, which was well after mid-century. Just as the English railroad historians cherish and reproduce certain mythical aspects of English railroad history, so too did the Americans like to pretend the democratic ideal and egalitarianism suppressed the possibility of class/status discriminations on their railroads.

Louis Gottschalk, like Anthony Trollope and others, thought the perpetuation of (railroad) passenger "classlessness"—even where it did prevail in the form of the "ordinary" car—was a nonsense: "One can be a republican and not like the society of those who drink every five minutes, pick their teeth with their pen-knife, and use their fingers for handkerchiefs." Then there were the soldiers, who used "gross and profane language" and sang "obscene songs."[221]

However, the reality, even by mid-century, was that some American railroad companies were as (passenger) class-oriented as their English counterparts. The *New York State Engineer's and Surveyor's Report* for 1850 described class differentiation on the following New York railroads: the Auburn and Rochester (3 classes), the Hudson River (2 classes), and the Syracuse and Utica (3 classes).[222] These railroads may have run against the national "grain," although it seems likely that New York State was not alone where class-based railroad services were concerned.

Furthermore, the Hudson River Railroad had introduced a "parlor car" service as early as 1853. It consisted of a number of "state rooms"—intended for families or people traveling as a group—which were furnished with sofas, chairs, a small table, a mirror, and so on (and this luxury no doubt required a considerable surcharge).[223] In fact, two decades earlier (in 1832) the Philadelphia, Germantown and Norristown Rail-Road Company *allowed for the exclusive use of an entire passenger car.*[224] However, this was probably not as exclusive as it sounds, since the cars at that time were fairly primitive and quite small, so the facility was probably only suitable for a large family or a group of friends on an excursion.

Explaining the Anomalies

Since no one questioned exclusivity on canal, river, or coastal ocean-going vessels, why would anybody single out the need for railroad passenger conveyance to be radically different in that regard? That is not an easy question to answer. Nevertheless, this apparent contradiction probably derived from, and harmonized nicely with, the railroad companies' endeavors to build cheap railroads (regarding both track construction and the provision of passenger cars)—rationalization is often the cheapest option when it comes to "mass production," which is really what we are talking about here (the mass production of railroad journeys, that is). And let us not lose sight of the fact that a railroad system, conceived of as an industrial production system—to which are geared the actions of hundreds or thousands of functionaries (personnel)—is most properly recognized as the industrial "curtain-raiser" to the *modern* (mechanized) assembly line; characterized, as it is, by precisely the same kind of rhythm, synchrony, and symmetry of production, and a no less elaborate division of labor.

So, this rationalization (read "cheapness") of car manufacture and furnishing harmonized well enough, from the railroad company's point of view, with the alleged American desire for democratized travel. And recall that it may be argued, in respect of many 19th century *English* railroad companies, that often first- and second-class passenger conveyance was subsidized (effectively) by third-class passenger fares, excursion fares, and freight conveyance rates; which is to say that the first- and second-class passengers, but especially the former, did not normally pay the full cost of what their "privileged" form of conveyance amounted to. But it is important to note that such anomalies often arise only in the absence of sufficient rationalization.

However, the "democratization" of railroad travel in America did not necessarily mean a provision of service at the level of the lowest "common (consumer) denominator." It was, in fact, supposed to be the case that all passengers would share in a certain level of *comfort* rather than discomfort. But what the American railroad companies often furnished in the way of comfort often took forms English middle- and upper-class people found objectionable, even if American passengers found otherwise.

In America the advent of luxurious railroad travel, taken to a new level by George Pullman and his competitors, brought a completely new dimension to railroad passenger travel on long-haul journeys. But the adoption of the Pullman technologies had to be artful, since *it could not be seen to undermine the myths of democratic principle and egalitarianism*, which so often went together in America. This was achieved by rendering the Pullman services "appendages," which, theoretically, did not undermine the "standard" level of service offered to all-comers. Indeed, the Pullman technologies were not owned by the railroad companies; and one paid the standard fare to the railroad company for the journey in question, while the Pullman services were offered as optional "extras," by a separate company, at a surcharge in respect of each.

But the reality was that Pullman service constituted an elevated "class" of passenger travel, which catered to the well-heeled traveler. And the optional aspect had a certain fictive quality to it, especially where long-haul journeys were concerned, since Pullman class might incorporate the only sleeping class (and almost invariably did) offered to the public on a given line of railroad.

The Quest for Comfort and the Railroad in 19th Century America

Let us now look at the quest for comfort in 19th century American railroading, since that may enable some further understanding of the alleged "classless" character of 19th century American railroad travel.

Where 19th century American railroad capitalism was concerned, it seems democratic principle had to be observed, even if more than occasionally it whiffed of myth; which is to say meeting the American passenger's ostensive expectation of a "democratization" of the traveling experience had to be manifest.[225] What such observance meant, in effect, was that—with a few exceptions, as noted earlier, and notwithstanding the discriminatory treatment of negroes and emigrants—there was generally only one passenger class until the Pullman era. However, that seldom meant that car architecture was tailored to the meanest level and thus Spartan, or that passenger travel was necessarily cheap or even affordable for everybody. But since everybody paid the same fare and received for it the same standard of accommodation, that was presumed to be fair. And if the company decided to elevate the level of comfort it afforded its passengers, then (theoretically) everybody shared in such improvements.

The Americans, it should be said, became just as obsessed with car comfort and innovative gadgetry (for a while, at least) as the English were with class distinctions. But these innovations—of comfort and gimmicky gadgetry—were not "bonuses" granted compliments of the railroad companies. They had to be paid for, so their costs were built into the fares the companies set.

Nevertheless, by the early 1840s the American railroad passenger was faring very well compared to his English counterpart. Generally, he traveled at least as comfortably as the English second-class passenger and much more comfortably than the English third-class passenger. Furthermore, at that time the American car was usually a pleasant enough "room," handsomely painted, generously windowed, and furnished with curtains and floor matting (and spit!), while seats were stuffed, often reversible, and usually had arm rests. Some companies also provided "ladies carriages," which usually contained washing facilities and comfortable sofas.[226]

Many American cars were also bigger and, therefore, more spacious than the English carriages of any passenger class—until later in the century it was essentially the American broad-gauge railroads which provided such wider and more spacious cars (in 1867 the Erie was boasting it operated the best passenger cars in the country because of its 6-foot gauge).[227]

Sarmiento noted of American railroad cars in the late 1840s that they were "always large and comfortable," and: "If the cushions are not as soft as in French first-class carriages, they are not as stupidly hard as in the English second-class carriages, since there is only one class in the United States."[228]

Traveling on a North Carolina railroad in 1853, the New Yorker, Frederick Olmsted, was impressed by the car he found himself in, which he described as "full-length lounge"—the train also had a smoking room and water-closets, indicating the company was ahead of its time. A little later, an (1861) article in *The Illustrated London News* said of the "ordinary" American railroad cars at the time that they had "exceedingly plain" exteriors, but were "fitted up comfortably, even handsomely," internally.[229] However, traveling in America in 1880, Lady Hardy could not agree with this assessment:

> How we long for a lounge in one of our own easy, well-cushioned, *first-class compartments*! Here, we are forced to sit bolt upright, the back of the seats scarcely rising to our shoulder-blades; and the constant passing, to and from the cars, of the peddling community, and the banging and slamming of doors, as they come and go, is most irritating.

However, she did appreciate being able to buy all manner of fresh fruits—including strawberries and melons—from roaming vendors on the trains.[230] All considered, her assessment is probably a bit harsh, notwithstanding that the low backs of seats had by that time been a source of complaint *for nearly five decades.*

In the 1850s "comfort engineering" in America became something of an obsession with mechanical engineers and cranky inventors. This probably had a lot to do with the realization that patenting a successful invention could be as remunerative as working a rich gold claim "out West"—that is, unless a George Pullman–type came along and "pinched" your idea despite your patent! But this "craze" was not confined to engineering the comfort of railroad passengers, although the problems to be resolved in that field did attract many inventors, aside from which successful inventions in the field of engineering of railroad passenger comfort often had broader applications. In fact, the engineering of comfort in America gave rise to what became known as "patent furniture"— usually defined as furniture adjustable to accommodate various postures of the human form at rest and characterized by either, or both, multiple dimensionality of function and some mobility of the technology (we might, therefore, even view it as a remote ancestor of the mobile phone). However, Giedion defined patent furniture essentially regarding its "powers of mechanical metamorphosis."

In the early 1850s the railroad passenger seat became quite a preoccupation of the comfort engineers, whose endeavors ought properly to be considered the immediate progenitor of what became known as "ergonomics" much later (once such endeavors had become health- rather than comfort-oriented, and human posture itself problematized medically). The quest of the "seat engineers" was a search for the "Golden Fleece" in the form of the ultimate in seated comfort. Human sitting postures were studied carefully and various theories forthcoming. And it is here we might also identify, genealogically, the predecessor to what became known much later as "time and motion" studies, as well as the engineering of "work stations" on assembly lines—both critically concerned with engineering the motions of the human body to commensurate optimally with a highly rationalized industrial production technique. That aside, in the 1850s a string of inventors attempted to develop a railroad seat which could satisfactorily cushion and relax the entire body during a railroad journey. Consequently, they came up with adjustable headrests, hinged backs to seats, high back-rests, extended and swing foot-rests, swivel seats, and so on. In fact, as Giedion points out, the barber and dentist seats of the 1880s were simplified forms of the adjustable railroad seat developed years earlier.[231]

English tourist, William Ferguson, described a barber chair in the mid–1850s: "The chairs are most luxurious—great armchairs with a rest for the head, and another for the feet at an angle, the ease of which is perfect."[232] Well, strange as it may seem and as patent history would have it, this "technology" was an application of design principles used originally by those trying to design the "perfect" railroad traveler's "armchair."

By 1850 the American Railroad passenger sometimes found himself in a luxurious seat with multifunctionality and which could be swivelled 360 degrees. But these newfangled seats usually had no real longevity when they did appear in the car; evidenced by the fact that even in the 1870s and 1880s English tourists traveling on the best railroads in America almost invariably complained about the low-backed seats in American cars—presumably, from the companies' viewpoint it was as simple as the provision of half a seat back being significantly cheaper than a whole seat back!

However, reversible seats—which were very conducive to group travel—were known on American railroads decades before they were adopted by English railroad companies. But this seems to have been the only significant innovation of the seat engineers, employed in standard American cars generally, which had any longevity, most of the others probably impractical for economic reasons. However, with the advent of the Pullman era the swiveling, multifunctional armchair, developed from the earlier endeavors of the comfort engineers, had its day—many a tourist in the late 19th century enjoyed this technology in the Pullman observation car, being able to twirl this way or that to take in the scenery.

Once the comfort engineers had "done their dash" with the railroad seat they turned their attention to the problem of converting the seat into a bed, and day- into night quarters.[233] So, although even in the early 1830s some American railroad companies had put beds or bunks in cars, what we are talking about here is something much more technologically sophisticated than that. Indeed, English tourists in America, who rode in the early Pullman sleepers, were amazed at the convertibility of their day into night quarters. Anthony Trollope was spellbound by American mechanical ingenuity more generally, describing the "wondrous contrivances"—of which "railroad beds are one of the greatest"—as the "great glory" of the Americans.[234] His compatriot, Foster Zincke, suggested (in 1868) that one should walk through Washington's impressive Patent Office Building "to get an idea of the activity of the inventive faculty in America"—it contained a model or specimen of everything for which a patent had been issued in America.[235]

This American mechanical ingenuity might be thought of as the legacy of a combination of frontier resourcefulness, adaptability, versatility, and perseverance. However, it might also be considered a product of the American entrepreneurial propensity to which were harnessed the typically American materialistic drive and a competitive individualism no less typically American. Yet, perhaps we could also tie this 19th century American ingenuity and inventiveness to education and processes of socialization—and although that is an interesting subject, which probably needs to be probed further by scholars, yet it is beyond the scope of this work. However, inventive ingenuity is one thing, practicality another, as we have just seen with the "celestial railroad seat." But the Americans were also excellent at adapting existing technologies to new applications, as well as fully exploiting the inherent versatility of the un-adapted technology. A good example of the latter from the "wild" West is the bandana, which could be employed as sun protection, a bandage, a sling for a broken arm, a water strainer, a dish and pan drier, a blindfold for nervous horses, a hat tie in windy weather, a face covering for the dead, and a noose for hanging horse thieves.[236]

People who had to travel long distances for whatever reason had always tried to find a way of sleeping while traveling, if only so that journey times were considerably reduced. In the ancient world itinerant merchants traveling throughout the Roman Empire often traveled the long distances they covered in wagons fitted with beds.[237] And during the Renaissance that grand merchant and financier to royalty and the Papacy, Jacob Fugger the Elder, had a specially designed traveling set made for himself, which, apart from a bed, included a compact, efficiently organized dining service.[238] In

France in the early 17th century collapsible beds were used by the wealthy when traveling, although intended primarily for use during a sojourn somewhere or erected for visitors, rather than being used routinely during the course of travel—in early 17th century France many furniture items were collapsible.[239] Furthermore, in France in the 18th century a kind of road "sleeping car" or "mini-caravan" (the "dormouse") was used by some travelers. It was designed for long road journeys and was complete with a stove to warm its occupants—Voltaire used to travel in one.[240]

Initially in America, the provision of sleeping accommodation during railroad travel was often superfluous, since the railroad journeys concerned were not long enough to justify it, and it had more to do with the provision of comfort than slumber. In fact, a rudimentary sleeping car was available on the Baltimore and Ohio in 1836,[241] but since this was in relation to a 13-mile stretch of the road at the time it either had to do with comfort (rather than slumber) or was testimony to the unreliability of the locomotives (or even of the track) at the time. But the former was probably the case. This so-called "bunk carriage" of the Baltimore and Ohio was an ordinary passenger car which had been "gutted" and the seats replaced with bunks as permanent fixtures. Passengers were supplied with mattresses, but not sheets and blankets[242]—indicating such provision had more to do with comfort than slumber at the time. But also "touted" as the world's first sleeping car was a version of it on the (Pennsylvanian) Harrisburg-Chambersburg line in 1837, the first sleeping cars on that railroad apparently fashioned after sleeping accommodation arrangements on canal packets.[243] However, the sleeping car, once developed, may have been an architectural influence itself—tourist William Hardman remarked (in 1884) that the penitentiary cells on New York's Blackwell's Island had beds arranged "like berths in a sleeping car."[244]

Even in the thirties there were numerous attempts, more or less successful, to render the day car convertible to night quarters. In fact, Basil Hall noted that by the late 1820s some American canal companies had canal boats with day quarters convertible into night quarters—they had "lockers" which could be folded out into beds. But this preoccupation with convertibility *and comfort* sometimes had quite extraordinary outcomes—for instance, in 1843 the Erie Railroad's "Diamond Car" had seats convertible into couches even though a train could run the Erie line in three hours, aside from which there was no night passenger service on the line then, anyway.[245] Nevertheless, it required a certain degree of ingenuity to design a seat which could be converted into something approximating to a bed. But that was only half the problem. The other half was to be able to design such a contraption simple enough for anybody to be able to effect the conversion, since there was often no one whose job it was to do it for the passenger, or to show them how to do it—at least, not until the advent of the Pullman Porter.

Where railroad travel was concerned, clearly the most obvious product of the American preoccupation with comfort was the development and refinement of the sleeping car across several decades. But the sleeping car certainly was not invented by Pullman or by any of the three persons generally understood to be his patent competitors in the 1850s. Indeed, even as early as the late 1830s the convertibility of day quarters into night quarters in railroad cars had already been accomplished to some degree of technical sophistication.

The Englishman, Walter Thornbury, traveling in 1860, was very impressed with the sleeping arrangements he experienced on a railroad in what was the pre–Pullman Car era. He gushed enthusiasm for the convertibility of the carriage from day into night quarters, and he was well enough traveled in America to make some percipient comparisons: "There was no longer an aisle of double seats, but the cabin of a small steamer with curtained berths and portholes."[246] This was a car designed by Wagner, who was to become a serious rival of Pullman's for a time—two decades later, the Vanderbilts eventually acquired the Wagner Car Company, which was later merged with the Pullman Company. But as early as 1850 Woodruff, another of Pullman's main competitors, was advertising patent seats and couches for railroad cars, so it was only a short step (for Woodruff) to the production of the sleeping *car*. And some Pennsylvanian railroad companies did use the so-called "couch cars" in the 1850s, and by the end of the decade the Pennsylvania Railroad was using Woodruff's full-fledged sleeping cars.[247]

Pullman's experiments with sleeping cars did not even begin until 1858, so some of his competitors had stolen a march on him—his experiments began with his conversion of day cars into sleepers for the Chicago and Alton railroad.[248] But the following year the Baltimore and Ohio put some of E.C. Knight's sleeping cars on its roads,[249] thus indicating there were many experimenters in this field at the time apart from those mentioned hitherto.

However, even though by 1860 many patents for sleeping cars were in existence, yet the sleeping car was not commonly found on American railroads at that time. Having said that, many companies experimented with sleeping cars during the 1860s. And some had adopted other products of the "gadget-men" as well, which they used to assist the marketing of their services—for instance, in the mid–1860s both the Chicago, Burlington and Quincy and the Illinois Central were highlighting in their advertisements that their trains now had technological means for effectively dealing with heat and dust problems (in the form of Rattan's patent ventilators and dusters).

Having the convenience of a bed during railroad travel certainly did not guarantee a sound sleep or even any sleep at all. Even though impressed by his sleeping quarters in the Wagner car in 1860, Thornbury conceded that most people found it difficult to sleep, due to the train's motion, door-slamming, bells ringing, and the "general clamour and tumult" associated with railroad travel.

Although the English traveler in America was often mesmerized by the ingenuity of American car technologies, yet even with the advent of the Pullman contribution the English traveler in America still had to confront the indignity of having to share the "bedroom" (never mind having to share the English carriage compartment!) with strangers. However, this reticence was not confined to the English traveler. Anthony Trollope noted during his American travels: "Upper-class Americans were loath to travel in sleeping cars"[250] and probably for the same reasons he was. But there was a way round this dilemma for the "over-privatized" Englishman. By the 1870s the common "remedial tactic" in Pullman sleeping cars—for people who could afford it—was to purchase two seats, or half a section, to have both plenty of space during the day and to avoid having a "bunkee" at night. And some people took an entire section to themselves (not always permissible), thus virtually compartmentalizing part of the car to their exclusive use—who says the English lack ingenuity! And often ladies traveling alone, as well as "pathologically" private people, took a half-section at least.[251]

Pullman Luxury

To be fair to George Pullman, he never claimed to have invented the sleeping car or some of the other luxury types of car associated with his name.[252] Indeed, the luxury characterizing his cars was the culmination of a succession of experiments in that regard—the Erie Railroad's "Diamond Cars" of the 1840s, the "state rooms" of the Hudson River Railroad's cars of the 1850s, the Baltimore and Ohio's hanging of paintings in its plush cars during the same decade, and the Wagner experiments of the early 1860s, to name just a few of the genealogical influences. And, as indicated earlier, by the end of the 1860s Pullman was but one of four principal entrepreneurs experimenting with sleeping car technologies—Stover argues that Pullman triumphed essentially because of the simplicity of his foldaway bed.[253] Yet, in the early 1870s Theodore Woodruff sued Pullman for breach of patent; and although he won his case, yet no part of the judgement was ever collected, Pullman eventually putting him out of business.[254]

Of course, the primary influences on the Pullman-type luxury were the coastal and river steamboats—not railroad precedents—which had taken travel luxury to new heights long before Pullman and his rivals appeared on the scene; so, Pullman luxury was not *just* the culmination of successfully resolving the (railroad travel) problem of converting day into night quarters. In fact, it could be argued the problem of *converting* day into night quarters had already been resolved—to a considerable degree of sophistication—on the steamboats, rather than having been solely the product of the railroad gadget men.[255]

And let us, just for a moment, give the emergence of railroad passenger travel luxury a firmer genealogical footing. The availability of luxury accommodation during travel in America originated not on the railroads, as noted, but on steamboat services on the Northeastern seaboard, and on the Hudson and other rivers in that region. A little later, luxury travel also emerged on the major river systems of the interior—the Ohio, Missouri, and Mississippi. But arguably the railroad companies were not far behind in imitation—we have noted some railroad companies were experimenting with relatively luxurious accommodation from early on. In fact, as early as 1840 the Norwich and Worcester (in the North-east) had "parlor carriages," their "apartments" for ladies replete with washstands, dressing-tables, and sofas.[256]

Although Pullman and his competitors were clearly influenced by the luxury accommodation offered to passengers on steamboats at the time, Pullman had also been impressed by Napoleon III's luxurious private train—with its dining and reception rooms, bedroom suite, and every other luxury furnishing and convenience, as if one of the most exclusive and palatial European hotels of the time had been put on rails. Pullman sought to commodify that kind of luxury and to pedal it to those burgeoning American social classes newly possessed of an excess of disposable income and possessed, no less, of a desire to consume conspicuously in a society which now rationalized economic disparities in a way that legitimized them (the concept of the self-made man, for instance).

The Pullman technologies were, therefore, very "up-market" and intended to be so—Mencken suggests a Pullman sleeping berth cost about eight times as much as its humble predecessor. Indeed, the "classless" American railroad—despite its mythical aspects—was on its way out by 1869, at which time the Union Pacific introduced Pullman on its section of the newly-completed first transcontinental railroad (what better advertisement could George Pullman possibly have obtained for his new luxury cars?).

The first Pullman sleeping car, the *Pioneer*, cost about $20,000 to build and fully equip. It had black walnut woodwork, Brussels carpet, chandeliers, and French plate mirrors. Pullman began factory production of it in 1867 (and it was to be seen on English railroads within ten years of that date). In fact, the original *Pioneer* was used to carry Abraham Lincoln's body from Chicago to Springfield, which undoubtedly presented Pullman with yet another excellent marketing opportunity for his cars—the Union Pacific's "Head Crook," Thomas Durant, finished up with the original *Pioneer* as his private car.

Because the original Pullman sleeping cars had so much packed into them—in the way of fittings and technology—they had to be built longer, wider and higher than any standard gauge American car had ever been. This meant, invariably, the companies which used Pullman cars had to alter station platforms and sometimes bridges as well[257]—and that may well have been the main reason why some companies, such as the Central Pacific on its half of the first transcontinental railroad, did not employ the Pullman technologies initially.

It was Pullman's *hotel car* (1867) which brought the kitchen to the rails in a form which went beyond merely keeping prepared meals warm. It was a sleeping car with a kitchen at one end and private traveling "compartments" at the other. Hence, it took exclusivity to an even more elevated level than the "basic" Pullman sleeping car. But for those not quite able to afford the Pullman hotel car luxury there was the "regular" Pullman dining-car. And before its advent the nearest thing to it was often an old baggage car fitted out with a lunch counter, some stools, and Negro waiters.[258] Not unrelated Pullman also invented and patented (1886) the first working vestibule, since at the time he built his first fine dining-car there was no means of moving safely from one car to another while the train was in motion[259]; hence, the efficacy of the dining-car was questionable until this problem had been resolved. Indeed, the vestibule effectively brought the whole train under one roof and thus made it even more genuinely hotel-like. But it also made more apparent the passenger class differences *within Pullman service itself*, since they were now accommodated under one roof rather than being *dis*-articulated.

Magnates eventually acquired their own Pullman-type cars. As Giedion put it, "American industrialists were to have their private coaches that compressed into one car the luxury for which Napoleon III needed a whole train." Indeed, of the railroad magnates, Jay Gould owned several private cars, one costing $50,000; W.H. Vanderbilt spent the same amount on his private car; and Leland Stanford also had a fabulous private car—most railroad company presidents enjoyed such a facility from the early 1870s.

By the time Pullman and his competitors had begun tinkering with luxurious railroad travel possibilities the notion of one (railroad) traveling class was already being challenged in America—as one would expect to have been the case, since Pullman was responding to a market which he knew existed. But this was a very delicate issue, nonetheless, indicated by the fact that for decades Pullman-type technologies were always "add-ons" to a basic, standardized type of traveling accommodation. And on most lines the standardized traveling accommodation probably remained of a commendable standard. But there was usually a catch, and this "new order" of things did not escape the notice of the English tour organizer extraordinaire, Thomas Cook. Traveling on the transcontinental railroad in the early 1870s, he observed that second-class (ordinary car) passengers" not being permitted to purchase sleeping-car tickets was "a species of exclusiveness which does not comport with republican equality."[260]

Furthermore, one should not overlook the fact that there were multiple (commodified) discriminations, even within the Pullman class of travel; something already alluded to, but easy to overlook. Indeed, the Englishman, James McAulay, traveling in 1871, certainly did not miss this phenomenon. Apart from remarking upon the fictional quality of the "classless" American train by then, he noted not only did the Pullman services separate their passengers from other train passengers; but that *there was a stratification regime at work within the Pullman facility as well*—reclining chair, drawing-room, dining-car access, hotel- and sleeping cars, each "shot" of luxury coming with its own surcharge (it was all rather like the modern Barbie Doll with its infinitude of "add-on" accessories). But McAulay did not believe people were being short-changed, since he considered the Pullman drawing-room cars as luxurious as the cars of royalty in Europe. They had chandeliers, mirrors, exceedingly comfortable lounger chairs, bookcases, sometimes even a piano—in fact, all the fittings and furnishings were of the very highest quality.

By the early 1890s the gentleman traveler could be well and truly pampered while traveling Pullman class. He could be shaved; get his hair cut, curled and shampooed; have a bath; and do all this while traveling at up to 40 miles per hour. Moreover, by that time Pullman had a smoking car containing the barber's shop, a library, a reading room, and easy chairs and tables. At around the same time an American of some means could travel in exquisite luxury between Chicago and New York (on the Pennsylvania Railroad), the services offered on that route including: ladies' maids and men's servants; the availability of daily and weekly newspapers; a barber; a library; special telegrams of public interest were announced during the course of the journey; a stenographer was available to businessmen; and even a clergyman was provided for those wanting to avail themselves of a Sunday sermon.[261] The Chicago and North-Western, also an innovative company, put a "business car" on its lines in 1868, and it was also the first company to operate Pullman's hotel cars west of Chicago.[262]

Although it is often said that Pullman brought luxury and little else to the rails, yet, as Mencken points out, one of the key selling points of the Pullman brand was cleanliness. Pullman knew a lot of people would pay more for the guarantee of cleanliness as well as for greater comfort.[263] Lady Hardy, traveling in 1880, had a good "nose around" the kitchen in her Pullman dining-car (much to the annoyance of the chef, no doubt), finding it to be a "perfect gem of a place," and she was highly impressed by the "scrupulous cleanliness" which "reigned supreme."

Another key reason Pullman had such appeal was because it incorporated something called "service," nor was it forthcoming begrudgingly from rude and unhelpful functionaries as had often been the case on American railroads. Indeed, of the many accounts I have read of railroad traveling experiences in America penned by 19th century English travelers, yet I never came across a single complaint about Pullman porters or any other Pullman personnel—quite extraordinary, given what a bunch of "uppity" malcontents the English tourists were for the most part! Indeed, the Pullman porter turned out to be the irreproachable butler-type of menial which the English well-to-do tourist in America had been searching high and low for—until he or she found him in the Pullman car!

Pullman porters were, indeed, noted for their butler-like irreproachability. But this was probably true of all Pullman personnel, not just the porters. In fact, a "retired" train robber said (in the 1890s) of a Pullman conductor that never had he met "a finer instance of official dignity." This conductor convinced the robber (during a train robbery) in the politest possible terms not to enter the Pullman sleeper because: "It did not belong to the railway company and, besides, the passengers had already been greatly disturbed by the shouting and firing."[264]

Although the service was excellent, Englishmen like John Boddam-Whetham were, nevertheless, often surprised to discover the "chambermaid" was a "black man." Like most English travelers, William Hardman, traveling in 1883, was impressed by these "chambermaids," but thought it "a very strange sight" to see these "darkies" at their bed-making: "Their rapidity and dexterity were marvellous."

Although the first transcontinental railroad was a significant tourist attraction for years, yet the Pullman service offered by the Union Pacific on its section of the line was probably no less so. Certainly, Britain had nothing like it until the Midland Company brought the Pullman technology to Britain quite a few years later.

Pullman sleepers were an immediate "hit" when first introduced in America (in 1869). But this may have been partly because they were used on the transcontinental railroad. The Englishman, W.F. Rae, traveling on the transcontinental in 1869, found the demand for Pullman sleeper accommodation outstripped supply at that time, thus it was necessary to book well in advance by telegraph. And he was rather smug about being able to eat his delicious breakfast at 30 miles per hour, while passengers in the inferior cars had to "rush out" at the refreshment stop to "hastily swallow an ill-cooked meal." However, Therese Yelverton was not impressed by her Pullman experience on the transcontinental. And it was not only having to sleep on "shelves" that dismayed her—being confined with 30 to 60 people for seven days and nights she found absolutely "oppressive." And the principal, perhaps only, redeeming factor of the ordeal, from her viewpoint, was that bread and cake were baked twice daily on the train, and always served hot.[265]

Despite the luxury, cleanliness, and quality service of Pullman class, it did have its drawbacks. John Boddam-Whetham, like Yelverton, did not appreciate the sleeping car experience. However, Henry Williams said of the Pullman sleepers on the transcontinental railroad: "You will sleep as sweetly and refreshingly as ever upon the home-bed," when referring to his own "delightful, snug, and rejuvenating" sleeps on the Pacific Railroad.[266] However, perhaps he had "gone and got himself on the wrong train," apart from his vested interest (*as a writer of guidebooks for that railroad*!). Comparatively, W.F. Rae found his transcontinental sleeper nights "hideous," the sounds emanating from his fellow inmates "unmusical," and the general atmosphere like the "Black Hole of Calcutta." He recalled: "The horrors of that first night in a Pullman car are indelibly impressed on my mind." But he thought it worth the bother, nevertheless, remarking: "The first trip in one of these cars forms an epoch in a traveler's life."[267] Nor did Henry

Williams factor in the experience of another English tourist, who had to put up with "babies crying all through the night in Pullman cars."[268] However, the latter gentleman was much better off than Robert L. Stevenson, who, "sociological" masochist that he was, had chosen to experience emigrant class on the transcontinental railroad—he thought the washing facilities inadequate and found that after about 90 hours his car "had begun to stink abominably."[269]

The Central Pacific, which operated the Western section of the first transcontinental railroad, did not initially use Pullman services. Instead, it offered *Silver Palace* cars, which did not impress the Viscountess, Therese Yelverton: "I met with no silver whatsoever," the carriage "fitted up in the ordinary hotel style." In fact, she certainly knew her "fine metals" from the cheap "look-alikes," noting that the "silver" in the Silver Palace cars was Britannia metal—a type of pewter constituted of 92 percent tin! As a member of the English titled aristocracy and, therefore, somebody who may normally have eaten off silver plate with silver cutlery at home, she probably really did expect to find silver in the Silver Palace car—no wonder *she* was so mocking of the Silver Palace concept. But her compatriot, W.F. Rae, was no less critical. He thought the name Silver Palace flattered the accommodation concerned—he found the cars "very inferior" to the Pullman cars and "the system of management far less perfect."[270] Since English tourists on the transcontinental railroad usually ran east-west initially, they were generally disappointed with the Central Pacific's Silver Palace cars after riding in the Union Pacific's Pullman cars. William Ferguson certainly found the transition a source of disappointment and the Silver Palace Car service wanting.[271] John Boddam-Whetham said of the Silver Palace car that with its "high-sounding title" it reminded him of a palace scene in the *Arabian Nights*, but it was "simply a long railway carriage with chairs like music stools with arms"[272]—the Central Pacific did not embrace the Pullman technologies until 1883.

Silver Palace cars aside, there were other well-known "brands" of sleeping car in the 1870s—in 1876 the New York Central and Hudson River Railroad, for instance, operated Wagner sleeping cars on its lines.[273] And in the mid–1870s the Chicago and Rock Island, perhaps unusually at the time, owned its own sleeping cars, which were said to be "very good."[274] So, it is not as if George Pullman had the entire sleeping car and luxury car market to himself at the time. Nevertheless, many of the best innovations in the field of luxury railroad travel in America eventually became associated with the Pullman name—bearing in mind George was not averse to stealing other people's ideas despite their being patented, so not everything "Pullman" was original to George.

By the 1860s many of the ideas of the "patent furniture" engineers had become so widely embraced in furniture-making that enforcing patents, where they applied, would have been impossible in most cases. And, rather like innovations in military and space technology in our own time, many of the "patent furniture" innovations became adaptable to other than their original purposes, strictly speaking, and thus broadly accessible to consumers. Indeed, we get an idea of the extent to which the Pullman technologies had largely subsumed the concept of "patent furniture"—and not too long after their advent, either—from the fact that a French journalist, at the Centennial Exhibition in Philadelphia in 1876, could think of no other term to adequately describe many of the innovative exhibits of the "gadget men" exhibited than "Pullman Car Style."[275]

I suppose there is an ironic twist to the fact that, in Britain, the exclusivity characterized (in the early period) by the Duke of Wellington and his peers riding in their own carriages on flat wagons eventually yielded to the rationalizing (and economizing) bent of the companies—towards shared, but stratified carriage (compartment) accommodation. Whereas in America the tendency ran in the opposite direction—from the common denominator of ostensibly democratically-founded railroad travel in the direction of the exclusivity which the Pullman technologies typified, and which demonstrably announced the arrival of unabashed luxury and exclusivity in American railroad passenger travel.

FOUR

Traveling with the Passenger on the 19th Century "Classless" American Railroad

> A good deal of buying and selling goes on during a long railway journey.
> —Walter Marshall, *Through America*, 1881

> The Pawnees congregate at most of the railway stations and are very fond of a short trip by train. They can ride free on any car onto which they can jump when the train is in motion; the consequence is the tribe is being rapidly reduced. It has been proposed to introduce the same system at other places, wherever there are Indians.
> —John Boddam-Whetham (English tourist), 1874

Introduction

When English tourists used American railroads during the 19th century, they were often immediately struck by five aspects of them which differentiated the American from the English railroads: railroad stations; locomotive technology; passenger car architecture; the amenities and services available at American railroad stations and during a journey; and the quality of the track, and thus the comparative roughness of the ride on it. Of course, there were many other points of difference between American and English railroad travel they noted during their journeys and some of them will be alluded to here. But those mentioned above were the things which struck English tourists immediately upon entering the precincts of a railroad station, observing a passenger train at a platform, then entering a car and commencing a journey.

However, there were also the peculiar values and attitudes of American culture to be reckoned with (some of which were discussed in the previous chapter), and these were often found lurking below the surface, and thus sometimes overlooked, when English tourists critically assailed aspects of American railroading peculiar to the national style.

I want to begin this chapter, then, by addressing the five phenomena mentioned above: *stations* (and depots); *locomotives*; *passenger cars*; *amenities and service* at stations and during travel; and *track quality*. Having attended to those factors, other points of note concerning how passenger experience differed markedly between the English and Americans systems will be addressed.

Four. *Traveling with the Passenger on the "Classless" American Railroad*

When European tourists headed to America around 1870 they usually landed at one of the north-eastern seaboard ports, from where their travel plans could take them in any direction. However, sooner or later they would most likely end up in the Midwest with the intention of experiencing what was then the great "must do" for the tourist—a journey to the Californian coast on the so-called transcontinental railroad. They would usually join the train at its eastern (but in the Midwest) terminus, Omaha, from where they would ride the Union Pacific, with its optional Pullman comfort (which they almost invariably availed themselves of), for the first leg of the journey. Later, at Ogden (Utah), they would transfer to the Central Pacific, with its optional Silver Palace cars, for the final leg of the journey. Although the transcontinental was, at the time, the world's foremost touring railroad, no less a spectacle were the trains themselves, which could be up to 600 feet in length, and no less a novelty was the Pullman luxury. However, Americans of means, too, flocked to experience the rail trip to the West Coast.

We have already encountered the somewhat cynical Therese Yelverton's apprehension of the first American transcontinental railroad. However, her compatriot, W.F. Rae, viewed the transcontinental railroad in a different light. He thought Americans *justly* classed it "among the grandest and most wonderful achievements of modern times," though conceding "the line is a single one, the stations temporary structures, and the bridges built of wood."

The truth is the first of the so-called transcontinental railroads, and those similarly labeled railroads which came in its wake, never were transcontinental railroads, strictly speaking, as some English tourists discovered, having landed in America expecting to be able to hop on a train in New York and hop off it in San Francisco. Indeed, none of these "transcontinental" railroads set off west from an eastern terminus that was even within a few hundred miles of the east coast. So, there was always an element of pretence in the notion of a "transcontinental" railroad.

This element of pretence had been there from the time such railroads were first mooted. Initially, it served an ideological purpose: firstly, by generating the myth that a proposed *transcontinental* railroad was self-evidently an undertaking of national proportions, thus in the national interest, and hence a worthy object of Senate and Congressional endorsement, and of federal and state financial support; secondly, from an investment standpoint, it brought a certain grandeur and romanticism to the prospectuses of the railroad companies aspiring to build such a railroad or part of it—hence, the concept was an important tool for marketing the stock and bonds of such companies both in America and abroad. Later, once the railroad was up and running, the (mythical) concept of a transnational railroad became a marketing device for the promotion of western tourism to both Americans and foreigners. This was no less artful, since during the 19th century there never was a single railroad (let alone one operated by a single concern) which did span the continent from one coast to the other.

For the moment though, let us return to our hypothetical European tourist, who has arrived at Omaha for his mythical transcontinental railroad journey. Before reaching Omaha our tourist would no doubt already have ridden on numerous American railroads and would possibly ride on many more after the transcontinental experience. The point is, for the moment, that all this railroad traveling experience—beyond and including the transcontinental journey—would have allowed the European traveler to encounter quite a broad spectrum of American railroad station architecture.

The American Railroad Station

Poor service at railroad stations, or lack of any service at all, probably inclined European tourists to overlook the quality of some American railroad architecture, so preoccupied were they with organizing themselves and their baggage or trying to find out what the time was from a dozen clocks all showing different times. Indeed, these overwhelming perplexities perhaps indicate why a lot of European railroad tourists in America had little to say about station architecture, except to comment negatively about the station experience in general, and especially to comment disparagingly upon clearly sub-standard "depots"—even an American correspondent in England had occasion to write (in 1868) of some American railroad stations: "Such sinks of filth and abominable nastiness as are to be found at the station-houses of three-quarters of the American railroads are never seen in England."

When Tocqueville arrived in America he was surprised to see from his ship: "A considerable number of little palaces of white marble built after the models of ancient architecture." He later discovered the white marble was white-washed brick and the columns painted wood. Visiting San Francisco in 1874, English tourist, John Boddam-Whetham, noted the great variety of architectural forms in the city, characterized by "all kinds of quaint conceits and whims of form and shape," which he thought often "attractive and charming." Indeed, one architectural historian has identified 116 architectural styles in America, many of which were extant in the 19th century. And we should not be surprised to find many of those architectural styles manifest in 19th century American railroad architecture. One such style was Greek Revival, which one source has suggested was a "national style" in America from 1820 to 1860 and that it flourished in the South especially.

But we should not really be surprised at the extent of classical influences on 19th century American architecture, and there was a host of reasons why classical forms might have found their way prominently into even 19th century American railroad architecture. I have already noted the numerous American towns and cities which had names or part of their names with links to classical antiquity. And clearly that had something to do—in the popular, and perhaps more so in the "cultivated" imagination—with an alleged affinity between American republicanism and the ancient Greek and Roman republics. But there is more to it than that.

Many people among the first few generations of Americans were very "cultivated" (cultivated Englishmen, in many cases, or just one generational remove from being so), and thus immersed in the values of 17th and 18th century upper-class English culture, which identified multi-dimensionally with the Greek and Roman cultures of antiquity. Much of this classical "schooling," and the more general immersion of the people concerned in classical culture, was transplanted to America with the English colonists; where, in the early post–Revolutionary era, it was nurtured in the most English of American cities at the time, such as Philadelphia and Boston. However, the "aristocratic" planter class in the South also identified with aspects of Greco-Roman culture where its self-identity was concerned. But classical influence was more broadly evident socio-culturally—for instance, in the American preference for the grid system when it came to laying out towns and cities and commodifying land parcels (the gridiron approach exemplified in Penn's (paper) layout of Pennsylvania (1682) probably had a Greek referent, since Hippodamus had applied a grid system to the planning of Miletus and Piraeus).

In America in the first half of the 19th century "classicism" remained at the core of the educational experience for the upper classes, many aspects of the "culture" of such people more generally classically founded. And women as well as men of those classes often had an intimate knowledge of at least some of the Greek and Roman scribes. If one grafts onto that the fact the "educated" men of these classes often had some considerable knowledge of and an interest in architecture—like their English counterparts—then the classical influences on 19th century American architecture begin to make some sense. And this dual sophistication—knowledge of both classical culture and architectural styles—even found its way West in the wake of advancing the frontier. Indeed, even log structures in what was at the time the "Far West" in the 1830s (which was not very far west at all) often had classical features—for instance, dormers and porches of classical form.

In fact, where architecture was concerned, the classical influence in America was powerful enough for Handlin to identify the Greek temple as one of three primary influences on American station architecture in the Ante-Bellum period. However, such classically-inspired architecture would almost certainly have been concentrated in the northeast during that period, if for no other reason than that was where most of the professional architects practiced. But it was also where the more indulgent American railroad companies were to be found—companies not afraid to "splash out" on station architecture. Even more curiously, as we shall note protractedly in due course, until the third quarter of the 19th century American locomotives, too, often had classical motifs embedded in *their* architectural design.

Until the 1870s America did tend to import from Europe, and seldom moved far away from, the fashionable European styles of architecture—American architects were aware of the views of Pugin and Ruskin in the 19th century, for instance, and many no doubt subscribed to the English architectural journals of the time. Furthermore, some established European architects emigrated to America, not a few of whom made names for themselves there, sometimes with railroad stations beaming out of their curricula vitae. However, in the early 19th century there seems to have been an acute shortage of people in America styling themselves "architects." Nevertheless, by the 1820s there were several American *books* on architecture—Asher Benjamin's popular *The Country Builder's Assistant*, for instance, ran to 47 editions (1797–1856). And although there had been architectural "schools" much earlier, yet they seem to have stultified—Alice Earle mentions (in *Old-Time Gardens*) that in 1750 Theophilus Hardenbrook had an evening school for teaching architecture, and especially landscape architecture for gardening enthusiasts, in New York City. Benjamin La Trobe was the most important foreign architect to settle in America in the early 19th century. In fact, he could be said to have founded the architectural profession in America and to have greatly influenced

Greek Revival architecture there. But he was both architect and engineer, having worked with the engineer John Smeaton and the architect S.P. Cockerell in England previously. And in America he did more than just design buildings—he engineered Philadelphia's water supply, for instance, and was also an authority on acoustics.

Robert Mills claimed to be the first American-born person *trained for* the architectural profession—by La Trobe—whereas his predecessors had been carpenters, masons, bricklayers, or enthusiastic amateurs. And: "By the end of the thirties the profession had developed to the point that it was not uncommon for somebody calling himself an architect to oversee an entire construction project."

By the mid–19th century the profession was well-established in the northeast, offering designs for sale from portfolios, designs to specifications, or full professional service including superintendence of construction.[1] And the architectural profession in America was opened to women much earlier than it was in England—Louise Bethune, who had trained as a draughtsman, not only designed hundreds of buildings throughout New York State (in a business partnership with her husband from 1881), but was also prominent in the profession's leadership.

Cavalier argues that the early Greek Revival station in America was an adaptation of the columned facade common at the time in domestic architecture there; its commercial applications to be found commonly in the architecture of churches, banks, and other public buildings.[2] And it is reasonable to assume, I think, that such (architectural) embellishment—where railroad architecture in particular was concerned—was intended (as in the case of those other building types) both to dignify the (railroad) companies and their "business," and to establish a "cultural rapport" with the educated and classically-literate people likely to use railroad services in the eastern states, which is where such "high-minded" railroad architecture most commonly materialized initially.

But there was also a tradition of romantic rusticity in American station architecture, which John Ruskin, for one, would no doubt have approved of, and which prefigured the fin de siècle "prairie house" architecture of Frank Lloyd Wright. Henry Richardson was the pre-eminent exponent of stations in the romantic rustic style, which was most evident in the small suburban stations he designed around Boston and Albany from around 1870.[3] Gothic was no architectural outcast in America, either, and one certainly finds it in railroad architecture, notably in the East—an excellent example was the (castellated) Salem Station built in the 1840s.[4]

There was often a certain degree of eclecticism as well in the more sophisticated examples of American railroad architecture. Henry Austin's New Haven Station (1849), for instance, was one of the first architecturally sophisticated stations and certainly merited the "exotic" label. Austin was the most fashionable architect in central Connecticut for at least two decades and his New Haven Station was something of a Lewis Carroll–like fantasy, being a tincture of Italian, Moorish, Indian, Chinese, and other influences. It prefigured the Queen Anne style which emerged in the 1870s and was favored by several railroad magnates—with "Mickey Mouse" aesthetic sensibilities—for their pretentious mansions. But exotic was evident even in the 1830s, as characterized by New Bedford Station, for instance, which had been designed in a "free Egyptian manner."[5] But there were also uniquely American architectural forms—such as the

Witch's Hat Cone—which also found their way into station architecture in some regions.[6]

It is always tenuous to generalize. But Julian Cavalier has suggested the average Ante-Bellum station was quite plain and often a house, the passengers congregating in what otherwise would have been its parlor. This seems to me fair comment, since there is ample evidence to support it in the form of historical photographs and historically preserved stations in America—particularly in the east. And Handlin suggests the only features which usually marked off a "house" as a railroad station in the early period were large, sheltering, overhanging eaves, and sometimes a lofty belfry.[7]

However, during the very early period there were often no stations of any description, just "departure points," which could be hotels, taverns, general stores, crossroads, or other well-known places.[8] Indeed, some early stations were simply either eating-places or hotels with a platform at the rear[9]; an arrangement which probably suited both the hospitality interests concerned and a penny-pinching railroad company not wishing to spend any money on a station. Mount Clare Station (Baltimore), which was the first railroad station in America, was a strangely-angled, stoical brick building which afforded no clue as to its function beyond its domestic intimations.[10] And for fifteen years the Baltimore and Ohio's Washington Station was a three-storey brick house with a belfry added to the roof.[11]

Apart from the domestic influences on very early American station architecture, the inn was also influential.[12] Furthermore, European visitors to America in the Ante-Bellum period often described rural stations as being like barns. And this was probably an accurate description quite often, too, since Handlin describes the barn as one of the three principal influences on station architecture during that period. However, in Britain too some early station accommodation—for both freight and passengers—was influenced by the architecture of the barn.[13] But in American railroad architecture the barn had broader influence—for instance, there was a resemblance between the circular turntable shed and the circular barn developed by the Shakers in the mid–1820s.[14]

In the early period there were numerous American railroad companies which took a pride in their stations, although such companies were most likely to be found in the east. J. S. Buckingham, traveling in 1839, was pleasantly surprised at the quality of the ten stations between Boston and Worcester, all of them with well-furnished waiting-rooms and separate ladies' and gentlemen's precincts.[15] Later, even in the Midwest some companies went in for relatively grand station architecture. English tourist, William Ferguson, mentioned a fine station at Indianapolis in 1856, although at the time the town was a junction of eight railroads,[16] so it probably had a lot of passenger traffic passing through it. In the late 1860s the Chicago and Rock Island railroad station in Chicago was "one of the most handsome and commodious buildings of the kind in the U.S.," according to an English tourist.[17] And the Illinois Central built a "large and elegant" station costing $30,000 at South Park.[18]

However, where American railroad capitalism was concerned, architectural pretentiousness was never quite as prominent as it was within the English counterpart. And when the American railroad companies did attempt to build "expressive" architecture—following the trend set by banks and insurance companies—it was much later (in the 1860s) than in Britain. In fact, it seems that American railroad companies lagged somewhat in arrears of other American corporates in their use of architecture for the projection of a corporate image. Englishman, James Buckingham, touring America in the early 1840s, paid close attention to architecture, and he remarked of America at that time: "In no cities of Europe have there been expended so much, in proportion to the wealth of their inhabitants, on public buildings as those of the United States of America."[19] But these were seldom railroad stations at that time.

Around 1840 the U.S. bank building in Philadelphia was built with marble—in the best style of Doric architecture—after the Parthenon at Athens; the U.S. Mint, also of white marble, was fashioned after an Ionic temple on the Illysus; Girard College, also in white marble, was designed "in the richest style of the Corinthian order"; and the Exchange had a "semi-circular projecting portico of Corinthian columns, while its circular turret or tower was an exact copy of The Lantern of Demosthenes at Athens." But at the time railroad station and termini were not that majestic or built of such materials.

As for banks, Buckingham noted of Cincinnati: "The most classical and ornamental of the public buildings of Cincinnati are the banks, of which there are several of great beauty." More generally, he noted that in America the Greek temple was the favorite architectural model for banks—even in the "rising village of Shawnee town (Illinois)," he observed "a Doric edifice of stone with portico and pediment," which he assumed was intended to be a bank.[20] In that connection, perhaps it might be said that the American "materialists" of the time used architecture (especially where banks were concerned) to give their materialism a veil of seemliness; a phenomenon which, perhaps, many visitors to America overlooked when suggesting that Americans made little or no attempt to conceal or mitigate the materialistic drive.

However, America, too, had its John Ruskin types. In the mid–1840s Arthur Gilman launched a scathing attack on the appropriation of classical architecture and its applications by American commercial/industrial concerns. Viewing the phenomenon as something of a "*mis*appropriation," he saw imitation of the ancient Greeks (or Medieval Frenchmen) as a "basic absurdity," asking: "What could be more foolish than a house like a Greek temple, anyway?"[21] But Handlin suggests that in America one reason the Doric order was favored was because *it was cheap and easy to build*[22]—recall the painted, wooden "marble" edifices which had impressed Tocqueville from a distance. There again, in America Greek Revival often meant little more than the use of a "decorative vocabulary" based upon classic Greek details.[23]

Nevertheless, in America classically-inspired architecture could "pop up" in the most unlikely places. Fort Scott, Kansas, for instance, which was in 1848 an unstockaded, open-plan fort laid out like an Owenite barracks village, had wooden-frame structures mostly built with facades in the Greek Revival style.[24] Furthermore, although it might be thought only the English were silly enough to architecturally embellish tunnel entrances, yet major sections of masonry on both the Starruca Viaduct and the Hoosac Tunnel in America "had a lot in common with the pretentious tunnel entrance finery of the English engineers."[25]

Some American railroad companies were quick to try and dignify their commercial enterprises through recourse to architectural embellishment. But for the most part the early American railroad tycoons—and, indeed, the later ones—tended to signify the power of their corporations by the visible evidence of the company president's mansion and lifestyle, not through termini or station architecture (perhaps the classic examples of this were W.K. Vanderbilt's "Chateau" and Cornelius Vanderbilt II's "Castle").[26] In that connection, Talbot Hamlin has argued the emergence of the millionaire in America was "fatal" to the ideals of Greek Revival architecture, since their egoism led to a new ideal in design—ostentation. And Hamlin doubted such ostentation served its purpose, anyway—it usually failed as a "makeover" for their "philistine values and backgrounds."[27] Louis Gottschalk, regarding the arts more generally, was of similar view, seeing the nouveau riche as "a class of individuals for whom the arts are only a fashionable luxury."[28]

Monumental station architecture was not as prominent in America as it was in England. There was monumental architecture and grandeur to excess in 19th century American railroad capitalism, but as already alluded to one was more likely to find it in the form of mansions owned by the great railroad capitalist or in the architecture of the headquarters of the railroad company—the Erie Railroad's headquarters was described by the *New York Sun* in 1869 as having a "rich coup d'oeil" which few palaces would have.[29] Indeed, even if American railroad companies were not interested in spending money on lavish railroad stations, yet often a company head office could be a "flashy" piece of architecture. The Union Pacific's Durant, for instance, was well-known for his extravagance, except when it came to spending money on quality railroad construction. This Durant, who used (defective) cottonwood sleepers during construction of the first transcontinental railroad, was said to occupy offices "among the most elegant in New York in the late 1860s."[30] Collis Huntington of the Southern/Central Pacific systems said he saw no point in trying to make stations "look like Gothic cathedrals or Roman baths." But it seems he did not see much point in trying to make them look like stations, either, since Oscar Lewis describes the bulk of the Central Pacific system's stations as: "Stark sheds with rotting boards, which were periodically painted with the emblematic mustard-yellow paint."[31] As to the Roman baths concept referred to above by Huntington, it was actualized in the Pennsylvania Station's (1908) concourse, for which the tepidarium of Rome's Baths of Caracalla had been the classical inspiration—Jensen describes the concourse as a waiting-room with no seats for the waiters.[32] In the same connection, one might mention Washington's Union Station, constructed at around the same time (1907), which had a waiting-room inspired by the frigidarium of the Baths of Diocletian[33]—it had Turkish baths, a bowling alley, and, for people who chose to die there, a mortuary. Private mansions and corporate head offices aside, the ultimate in grandiosity was probably Cornelius Vanderbilt's $6 million Grand Central Terminal, one of several monuments he built to himself.

According to one commentator, many 19th century American town and city railroad stations looked like warehouses. Another source asserts that Chicago's Grand Central and other major terminals of the same era were "little more than ugly tunnels through nondescript edifices," while many smaller stations and depots were "typically barn-like."[34] However, there was often some attempt to "pretty up" such buildings, albeit cosmetically. Hence, from around mid-century commercial buildings (including station architecture) often sported facades with elaborate cast-iron ornamentation and intricate lacework, which probably did do something to offset the unattractive features of such buildings. And Americans seem to have had a more robust sensibility than their English counterparts, since in the mid–1840s, at a time when the architectural applications of cast-iron were still controversial in Britain, the material was already being employed (most conspicuously in the American South) for *domestic* porches and verandas.[35]

Many English tourists described dismal, ramshackle stations (particularly in the South and West). One such source described a station in the South in 1861 as follows:

> A log-hut, a pile of wood, and a nigger—there you have a full inventory of one of the ordinary country stations on a Georgia or Alabama railway. The traveler from Charleston to Montgomery will pass scores of these primeval Doric structures, isolated in some black swamp, where the protruding charred pine stumps alone remind him of the forest long since felled.[36]

William Ferguson, traveling in the 1850s, noted of one village—and this was probably common in some parts of America at the time, that:

> There was neither station-house nor station master; there was a signal-post, and attached to it a board with the notice "If you wish to get on the train, push up the handle" (the handle operated the signal so that the engineer, observing it, he might stop and pick up the intending passenger). This is a specimen of economic management.[37]

The English tourist, James McAuley, found country stations, even in 1871, very disappointing: "Plain wooden structures with few fittings, cheerless and ill-lit." His compatriot, James Burnley, traveling in 1879, had the utmost contempt for advertising notices along railroad routes, but remarked that such advertising could not really decorate the stations: "For the simple reason most of the stations are lost to all possibility of decoration." Indeed, he found most rural depots to be "little better than barns," usually having a "slovenly, uncared for look," and often lacking waiting-rooms, platforms, porters, or any sign to tell you exactly where in America you were. Even an American tourist, C.B. Berry, traveling in 1880, found "the general aspect of affairs" at rural stations "that of a recent reclamation from the wilderness."[38] And in Kansas in the 1870s there were numerous stations consisting of "one dwelling-house, a saloon, and a few lazy-looking Indians"[39]—the Indians probably made a bit of money by loading firewood or coal onto the tender. In fact, before the advent of the railroad depot, Indian "waifs" had tended to hang around taverns rather than depots: "Almost every community had two or three of these semi-civilized Indian residents, who performed some duties sometimes."[40]

Nevertheless, immaculately presented stations could "pop up" in the most unlikely places. There were stations in the extensive snow sheds up on the Sierra Nevada, for instance, although one doubts that regular passengers would have any cause for hopping off the train to spend a few nights at such places, but perhaps they did. Whatever the case, refreshments were taken in the sheds, which were on the transcontinental route, and people were often amazed at the quality of the fare served up in those refreshment rooms in the mountain snow shed stations. Presumably, such stations primarily serviced the railroad company employees who worked in the snow shed sections of the track—these snow shed stations were complete with switch tracks, turntables, and workmen's houses,[41] as well as being the depots for building materials and all other maintenance and operational supplies. Hence, they were not narrow corridors, but quite expansive in those spaces where the station facilities were situated.

Architectural standardization was adopted by many American railroad companies in the 19th century. But it was not the sole province of the railroad companies. Indeed, it pre-dated them. In the early 1830s New York architectural standardization was common where the construction of commercial and industrial buildings was concerned. This was more a matter of convenience than economy, since contractors and builders—rather than owners—could simply choose a building design from an architect's portfolio and get on with the job (there was also a shortage of architects). Indeed, custom-houses and post offices, produced from several standardized "moulds," were to be seen almost nationwide in the 1830s. Some of the blueprints for these public buildings were architecturally sophisticated and often made for a building pleasant to behold, embellished tastefully, as such buildings often were, with classical motifs and other ornamentation. The typical courthouse of the Midwest, for instance, was often standardized in patent classical form, usually with a colonnaded porch and cupola.[42]

Standardization certainly found its way into railroad station architecture as well quite early on. However, it is important to differentiate "standardized" from "emblematic" architecture—the latter, though not necessarily a standardized form, might, nevertheless, be immediately recognizable as typical of a company's architectural predilections. That said, often when we think of the 19th century American railroad station we think "depot," rather than "elevated" specimens of railroad architecture like some of those mentioned earlier. And although in America there was a general tendency to use the term depot instead of station, yet many railroad companies used both terms. However, when both terms were used, yet it seems that depot was more closely connected with freight conveyance and station with passenger conveyance (but generally small, insignificant stops out in the "middle of nowhere" were typically referred to as depots). Indeed, in the West the term depot was often preferred to station. And there may have been several reasons for that. However, we should not think the term depot unknown in Britain in the early period. After all, in an 1835 letter engineer I. K. Brunel referred to depots rather than stations.[43] But in America, when the term depot was used *exclusively* by a company, almost invariably the company concerned stratified its depots (1st, 2nd, 3rd class, etc.).

In America the term "station" had distinct American permutations well before the advent of *railroad* stations, which may have been at least partly why the term "depot" became more common in some parts of America, particularly in the West. In Kentucky and Tennessee, for instance, two or three log cabins arranged to form part of an enclosure—along with the stockade surrounding it—had been known as *stations*.[44] And since such places were sometimes trading centers and hostelries on transportation routes, that is another reason why they and coaching stops in America came be to be known as stations. Furthermore, commanders of wagon trains had sometimes been known (in the 1850s) as *stationmasters* and their encampments as stations, perhaps hinting at an even earlier and similar use of the terms.[45] But wagon train commanders were also known as "conductors"[46]—Twain noted that on the stagecoaches as well (and perhaps it had been the case for decades) there were conductors who sat beside the driver, the conductor the "legitimate captain of the craft," responsible for the mail, passengers, and baggage.[47]

American railroad architecture, despite the prevalence of standardized station and depot types, was remarkably diverse, sometimes highly imaginative, even extremely tasteful occasionally, and on some railroads very pleasing to the eye. Nor should one think, either, that standardized necessarily meant tasteless or "tacky" from an architectural standpoint.

As a generic concept, the term "depot," in the American railroad context, encapsulated quite a variety of types of facility. For instance, there were *combination depots*, handling both freight and passengers, and often in the sole charge of one person. Then there were *flag depots*—stations of minor importance, at which only a limited number of trains stopped, usually on "flag"—some companies called these 1st, 2nd, 3rd, or 4th class passenger depots, depending on their classification systems and what broader functions the depot served.[48] There were also what we might call *ad hoc stations*, which were easy to confuse with a depot. They were normally built near unsold railroad grant land and used as "jumping-off" points for emigrants, thus doubling as emigrant reception houses and real estate offices[49]—but they could evolve into depots once the new settlers had produce to transport. In the same connection, one notes in England during the early period some companies had created temporary wooden structures to serve as stations,[50] while after the financial disasters of the mid– to late-1840s, numerous English railroad companies tended to standardize (as an economy measure) station design (this was most evident in the Southeast), although often the standardized form was fashioned after whatever architectural style happened to be in vogue (in the locality concerned) at the time.[51]

Although in America a standardized depot might stand alone in the middle of nowhere, since it existed only to service the local farmers often, yet a (western) depot could also be but one standardized component of a standardized town. In the West it was usual practice for railroad companies to establish a depot every 10 to 15 miles in agricultural catchments; and since the companies often owned the land adjacent to the tracks—or alternate blocks of land—it was often expedient for them to create a standardized town in association with the commodification of the land parcels they offered to settlers. Companies like the Northern Pacific and the Burlington, for instance, had standard formulas for laying out such towns—Linklater states that such "paper towns" were so highly rationalized they could be laid out by a surveyor "with his eyes shut." He suggested, furthermore, hundreds of identical towns could be (and were) produced from the one blueprint—each with a railroad down the center; two parallel east-west streets on one side named Oak and Chestnut, two more on the other side named Walnut and Hickory, and both crossed by ten other streets (imaginatively) named First to Tenth.[52]

However, in the West often the depot was primarily a freight processing, receiving, shipping, and (grain) storage facility. It typified the railroad presence in the rural West. And in some places it did not coexist with a town at all, standing virtually alone in the landscape to service the local farming economy—often a windmill (and grain silos) marked its presence on the landscape from afar. Since they were in such out of the way places often and saw very little passenger traffic, it is hardly surprising that depots were often architecturally standardized to a very basic design, and often allowed to become quite rundown and ramshackle. They did not need to impress anybody, since they existed primarily as nodes on a nationwide collection and distribution system. And in the latter respect they were thus more an object of engineering than architectural

Four. Traveling with the Passenger on the "Classless" American Railroad 155

expertise, which is presumably why they were often designed by engineers rather than architects.

The engineers strove to design perfect one- or two- man depots both to economize on labor for the company and to optimize a rational movement of freight.[53] The resulting standardized designs could be used across a vast region for decades, although occasionally the standardized form had to be altered a little to meet local conditions and requirements. And when painted with the company's livery, these standardized depots no doubt stood out in the landscape—for both locals and travelers—much as the McDonalds, KFC, and many other familiar corporate motifs do today (reference was made earlier to the emblematic mustard–yellow of the Central Pacific). Indeed, one American railroad corporation superintendent remarked of depots in the early 20th century: "Since the public recognizes them as ours (because of the emblematic color schemes) we do not need to trouble ourselves by placing the railroad company name on these depots." In fact, sometimes people leasing railroad company land adjacent to depots were required—under the terms of their leases—to paint all their structures in the railroad company's emblematic colors.[54]

The expediency of, and rationality underlying, standardized depot architecture was probably missed by (English architectural commentator) Meeks, for instance, when making the tenuous generalization that many of America's 19th century railroad stations were inferior in terms of both materials and conveniences,[55] apart from which Meeks failed to appreciate the (often) functional difference between a station and a depot. And Meeks, for one, approached American station architecture with so many preconceptions derived from the English tradition that inevitably the result was a jaundiced perception of it.

Indeed, one has only to look at a book like Oliver Jensen's—probably still far and away the best "popular" history of American railroads—to get a sense of some of the brilliance of 19th century American railroad architecture. On the other hand, Cavalier's book has excellent pictorial examples of very tasteful "identical twin" and looser "sibling" standardizations in 19th century American depot architecture; and although his examples are selective, yet they certainly convince that standardization did not necessarily imply architecturally sterile, unimaginative, or insipid.[56]

While researching this book I had occasion to look at many images (photographs, engravings, and paintings) of 19th century American railroad stations. And where the Northeast and the upper Midwest were concerned, I was surprised at just how many little railroad stations were quite handsome buildings in an architectural point of view. Such stations often served villages and towns on what were in those times considered to be suburban lines, even though they were rural. Often, the external architecture gave no clue at all as to the building's commercial/industrial function, since the stations just looked like the kind of large house a well-to-do family might reside in.

America had some spectacular examples of railroad architecture—apart from the grandiose monuments to themselves erected by railroad magnates later in the 19th century—outstanding examples of which were Lake George, Trent Junction, North Conway, and Tucker stations, the latter a spectacular icon built clinging to a cliff. In fact, one has only to look at the catalogue of station architecture in the history of a company like the Pennsylvania Railroad to see 19th century American railroad architecture in a much more positive light than some English commentators and critics would have it. But such prejudice was not new. In fact, it was long-standing. In the late 1850s one English architectural critic, in comparing American railroad architecture to the English counterpart, concluded that much of the former was uninviting, ridiculous, beggarly, or pretentious.[57] Of course, it all depended on which part of the country and which companies' stations (and depots) were drawn into the critical vista. Such subjective vistas also completely overlooked the fact that, in not a few cases, railroads were built not as ends in themselves, but as means to other pecuniary ends, and often in accordance with the "American style of construction." Indeed, the American system of railroad construction, which many English tourists did not really understand, either, had different rationales and was founded upon a value system fundamentally different to those which motivated most English railroad capitalists of the same era. However, some very astute English observers (such as Therese Yelverton) fully understood the reasons why Americans built half-finished railroads, but she could not resist a sarcastic "swipe," nevertheless: "American railroads are made easily enough. Half a dozen trees are felled on either side, and thrown down somewhat at random. Half a dozen feet of earth thrown over them levels them.... Iron is laid pretty straight along the ground, and you have an American railway."[58]

But the following percipient observation—of another English traveler (in 1867)—is about as succinct and accurate as a description of the American system of construction gets, at least where the significance of the station or depot was concerned: "In the matter of railway management they got a traffic before they built a railway station."[59]

Furthermore, one cannot emphasize enough the fact that many American railroad capitalists operated as though the "public interest," if not their nemesis, was largely irrelevant to their own interests. Perhaps the following assertion, attributed to W.H. Vanderbilt, indicates that: "The public be damned!" And his father, Cornelius, a man clearly possessed of a brilliant business mind, whatever else we might think of him, is supposed to have said of the law on one occasion: "What do I care for the law? I got the powers, h'aint I?"

By way of contrast, one could argue that in 19th century Britain the railroad companies were *relatively* more "tuned in" to public opinion and more service-oriented; notwithstanding that successive governments and stentorian public complaint together ensured the public interest was served to a considerable degree (despite the enduring poor treatment of third-class passengers and ongoing safety issues).

Certainly, there were pathetically inadequate stations and depots in America, lacking both railroad officials and platforms often. But these were not normally encountered in cities or large towns. Indeed, usually they were found only in rural areas where passenger traffic volumes simply did not justify extravagant expenditure by mean, calculating companies whose owners had often never heard of something called the "public interest," even if there was such a thing to take stock of "out there" in the wilderness.

William Ferguson, traveling in South Carolina in 1854, noted: "The stations on this line are merely wooden houses or huts, generally some turpentine depot."[60] Since turpentine was produced from pine resin these no doubt were, in many cases, turpentine depots. And why would one expect to find a "flash" station in the middle of a pine forest/turpentine factory complex, anyway?[61] Of course, there were metropolitan stations which were woefully inadequate, though I would suggest that in the East that would have been the exception. Alex McKay, traveling 1846–7, would elsewhere have found some quality stations compared to the Washington, D.C., station he described thus: "A more miserable station than we were ushered into can scarcely be conceived."[62] On the other hand, one might argue the money American railroad companies *did not spend* on station architecture was spent on what was usually a good standard of comfort in the "ordinary" passenger cars—even if the depot or station and track were substandard, yet it did not follow that everything connected with the railroad was.

We have also to factor into the reckoning the frontier mentality and the concept of "getting along" (the latter explained in the previous chapter regarding Frances Trollope's encounter with it). Indeed, one should not overlook the possibility that the concept of "getting along" may have been extended from a situation of *personal* or *familial* thrift, improvisation, and forbearance into the commercial realm by railroad companies. In fact, there seems to me to have been a very close articulation between the American concepts of one's "getting along" and the "American system of railroad construction."

One notes, furthermore, that regardless of its appearance, yet in countless localities across America the station or depot was almost an institution and often a place focal for socializing—men and boys gathered at the station or depot at midday in countless towns, almost ritually, to set their timepieces "aright" when the Western Union time signal came through the telegraph. Mark Twain, evidently an avid student of railroad station "layabouts," noted "an important fact in geography," whereby at New York State stations "the loafers carry both hands in their breeches pockets," whereas elsewhere the station loafer "is universally observed to scratch one shin with the other foot."[63] But the loafers aside, Oliver Jensen, writing in 1975, noted that even at that time: "Virtually everyone over 40 who was born in a small town has something to say about the depot."[64]

American Locomotives

The 19th century English tourist in America, having entered a station, would have found that, after 1840 especially, the locomotive which was to power the train was very different to the English type. Although the Americans were designing their own locomotives from the outset, yet during the first decade of railroad enterprise in America English locomotives were often put on the tracks. They were either put on the tracks as they had been imported, adapted to meet the whims of their American owners or the experimental impulses of American mechanical engineers, or altered to accord with American conditions. Even when English locomotives were not put on American tracks in that first decade, English design principles and componentry were often incorporated into American-built locomotives. However, whatever form the technology transfer took in the early period, it was very much one-way traffic (from Britain to America) for at least a decade. In fact, from 1829 to 1841 over one-third of the 120 locomotives operational in America had been imported from Britain.[65] But no less dominant in America eventually was Mathias Baldwin, who supervised the building of some 1,500 locomotives during his working life.[66] Indeed, by the end of the 1830s the Americans were putting many American-built locomotives on their tracks; but even within the first decade of railroad capitalism in America, the locomotive technology was developing along a different path where its design and appearance were concerned.

The prominent English actress, Frances Kemble, who had been quite intimately acquainted with all the "iron horses" in George Stephenson's "stable" at the time of the opening of the Liverpool and Manchester Railway, was quite surprised at the appearance of American locomotives when she traveled through some Southern states in the late 1830s. In fact, she described them as looking like kettles[67]—not an unusual description of them at the time, Oscar Wilde also describing an American locomotive as an "ugly tin kettle."[68] On the other hand, when the English-manufactured *Stourbridge Lion* arrived in America in 1829, it was described by Americans as a "curious critter" resembling a "mammoth grasshopper."[69] But even Americans seeing one of these machines for the first time—whether it was of English or American manufacture—could be amazed at their appearance. Isabella Bird mentions a "simple country girl" going from Portland, Maine, to Kennebunk, who had apparently seen a locomotive for the first time when reporting something that had so frightened her: "A great thing, bright red, with I don"t know how many wheels, and a large black top, and bright shining things moving about all over it, and smoke and steam coming out of it!"[70] We get a later impression of American–built locomotives from Englishman, W.G. Marshall, who described an American locomotive around 1880 as "massive and clumsy-looking," with a "monster black funnel resembling a wine strainer" which was called a "smoke-stack, not a funnel," while the engine was called a "locomotive." He also thought the cow-catcher added to the locomotive's "formidable appearance," as did the large head-light and the sound of the huge bell.[71]

English tourists were often bemused by the presence of an impressive bell on the American locomotive. Around 1860 such bells could weigh up to 215 pounds and be heard from a quarter mile distant. R.L. Stevenson remarked upon "the swift beating of a sort of chapel bell from the engine," while William Hardman thought (1883) such was the racket of tolling bells before an engine was set in motion that "some religious services are about to be carried on"[72]—as for locomotive whistles, they were in evidence in America from 1836.[73]

Dunbar asserted that the unknown man who first painted the sides of his Conestoga wagon in bright colors established a decorative principle in American travel conveyances, which was speedily adapted thereafter by the owners of all other vehicles—both on land and water.[74] Such decoration extended to the stagecoaches on the National Road in the 1820s: "Ornate and spectacular operations, painted in bright colors, and occasionally even gilded." Their panels were decorated with portraits of famous men—all the early heroes of the Republic, as well as prominent personages of the times, or the coaches were named after them (every coach on the National Road had a name, which was painted on each door).[75] Other coaches were embellished with allegorical motifs or landscapes. In fact, there were companies which specialized in painting murals on stagecoaches, omnibuses, and railroad cars, and this was how some important artists made names for themselves.[76]

It was likewise with the American locomotive once it had emerged in unique national form. Apart from having a lot of highly polished brass work, all the unfinished work was painted in "showy colors," sometimes with decorative art work along the sides of the tenders as well—America tender art work included vignettes of factories, eagles, landscapes, pastoral scenes, even portraiture.[77] And color would appear to have been the most obvious decorative feature of the 19th century American locomotive, with green and red the favored colors, though color was but one of several techniques employed decoratively.[78] Indeed, in addition to the lavish use of color and polished surfaces on American locomotives, the decorative effect was heightened by the architectural design of the many fittings. Furthermore, classical and antique designs were freely borrowed and incorporated into locomotive design. In fact, American locomotive cab architecture could have Greek, Roman, Egyptian, Gothic, or Tudor designs employed, while cabs were regarded by some enginemen as if they were "offices of professional gentlemen"—often embellished with prints, photographs, and mirrors. By way of comparison, even by the late 1850s few (if any) English locomotives even had cabs, hence English enginemen were unprotected from the weather for a long time. In America the "great era" of (locomotive) "wild ornamentation" did not begin until around 1850, although by the 1890s the gay colors and most of the polished brass had disappeared[79]—when Cornelius Vanderbilt, for instance, started buying up railroads he took the cheap option of painting the locomotives black and getting rid of the polished brass.[80]

It seems that in America, especially during the early period, there was more effort made than in England to "camouflage" the locomotive—locomotive artwork was not just about aesthetics—to make it appear more "environmentally friendly," whereas in Britain locomotive decoration seems not to have progressed much beyond paintwork—often the paintwork part of the company brand and some limited refinement of the architecture of the locomotive's design to make it more pleasing to the eye. However, in America, most notably for about two decades after mid-century, locomotives (and often tenders, too) were not just painted and fashioned architecturally to appear sleek and modern; but decorated variously in what seems to have been an attempt to bridge the aesthetic gap between mechanical engineering and art,[81] as well as to mitigate the industrial aspect of the locomotive.

In America during the early period locomotive drivers were known as "engineers" because they were either the people who had built the locomotives or had the mechanical "know-how" to maintain them. Then, for several decades, they became known as "drivers" or "runners," the term engineer only coming back into vogue in the late 19th century.[82]

American Passenger Cars

Hitherto, a little has been said (in the previous chapter) about American railroad car architecture. But there is more to be said. During the earliest period there was not a lot of difference between the English and American passenger cars. In both contexts the early *unroofed* cars were of a similar basic design, as one would expect. As for the earliest *closed* cars, they were not vastly different, either, since in both contexts the stagecoach was *usually* the architectural precedent. In fact, on many of the earliest American railroads passenger cars were just ordinary stagecoach bodies mounted on flat wagons and secured to them, as had often been the case in England. Having said that, it has been suggested the first horse-drawn cars on the Baltimore and Ohio had evolved from the Conestoga wagon rather than the coach, and that contemporary engravings indicate that.[83]

Indeed, if in America in the very earliest period the coach was the major influence on car architecture, yet the design of what was to become the typical form of passenger car evolved from maritime influences, essentially. Indeed, Charles Dickens remarked upon the smallness of the car windows when he was in America (the early 1840s), describing his car as having a great deal of wall. In fact, the reason for the small windows early on was that they were in emulation of port-holes on ships.[84] Furthermore, when sleeping accommodation was provided early on by some enterprising companies the berths were arranged much as they would have been on a ship.[85] In fact, there were many other borrowings from maritime culture, including linguistic conventions, such as "All aboard," "shipping" (of freight), and even the word "freight" had a maritime origin—Alice Earle discusses some of these "adaptations" in *Stage-Coach and Tavern Days*.

When the characteristic aspects (and therefore the real points of difference) of early carriage design emerged in England and America respectively, they did so almost invariably as reflexive of the sociocultural landscapes which were their backdrops in each national context. In Britain, the rigidity, and indeed resilience, of the social class structure was such that carriage design had to "kowtow" to it; which meant that on most railroads, from the outset, two or three passenger classes (which, as argued earlier, *rationalized* social classes) evolved on most lines. Consequently, in Britain there developed gradations in carriage quality, as well as peculiar features of carriage architecture, the most important of which was the advent of the compartment.

By 1832 what was to become the standard (democratic) American passenger car had emerged on the Baltimore and Ohio. It was un-compartmentalized and had a center aisle running through it. Frances Kemble described such a car in 1833 as being "like a long greenhouse upon wheels." Indeed, even by then so accustomed was she to the English compartment carriage she found the American car quite perplexing, and was somewhat disconcerted by the fact that people could move freely around the car. However, Dee Brown notes that once English travelers habituated to the novelty of the American style of car, then they appreciated and enjoyed the freedom of movement not just within, but between cars.[86] Writing in *1872*, travel agent Thomas Cook commented that the open cars of the American lines afforded facilities for contact, and met the necessities of long journeys, far better than the sectional and boxed-up system of English carriages, and that passengers were provided with many conveniences which cannot be afforded under the English system.[87]

Yet, in America democratic principle ostensibly had to be observed despite its mythical dimension. However, it ought to be pointed out that although rare before the Pullman age, the compartment (or its equivalent) was hardly unknown on American railroads, as this 1867 account makes apparent:

> The managers of two of the favorite routes between New York and Boston have placed *compartment cars* on their respective lines within five years past, and persons who care for comparative seclusion ... *without annoyance to too many of their fellow travelers* ... could secure this by paying a small additional price for their tickets.[88]

It is interesting how this was rationalized—as catering *not to people wanting privacy or exclusivity, but so that they might not be an annoyance to fellow passengers*! But even in the earliest days of American railroading people could, for a while on some railroads, have a car to themselves—around 1834 on the Baltimore and Ohio Railroad, for instance, parties could engage an entire car for the day. Henry Deedes, traveling on the Great Western's Chicago-New York route in 1868 found that, aside from the relative exclusivity of the hotel car ($40 for two persons), yet for another $16 "a private compartment" could be secured for the duration of the 900-plus mile journey. He noted, furthermore, that two people could buy four places—a "sort of box" compartment—in a New York Central Railroad drawing-room car at around the same time.[89]

In fact, when the "compartment car" was supposedly introduced to America in 1853 its arrival was announced in *Scientific American*. However, in those new-fangled American (compartment) cars—as in the English counterpart at the time—it was impossible to move from one compartment to the next once the train was in motion. However, the compartment car was known in America much earlier than 1853. Technically, many of the earliest American cars were effectively compartmentalized, since they were just coach bodies placed on flat cars; so, there was a single (coach) compartment. In fact, one early type of car on the Baltimore and Ohio very closely resembled some of the early compartment carriages on English railroads. That (long) car type combined three coach bodies in the one car, thus the single car was effectively constituted of three "compartments, but with no center aisle running through the car." At that stage the company's board had discussed the possibility of a center aisle running through the car, with entrances at both ends of such cars. But the main reason the company did not "run with" the internal car aisle at that time was because it was thought the aisle would become "one long spittoon," which is precisely what it did become once it was introduced in the company's cars[90]—the compartments were designed to accommodate up to eight people.

The availability of compartment cars in the 1850s indicates not only that there was something approximating the compartment known in America long before the Pullman era, but also that there was an early demand for the kind of exclusivity the Pullman-type technologies ushered in more pervasively. However, Mencken suggests the compartment was never popular in America because the American was a "gregarious fellow."[91] But whether gregarious or not, most American passengers would have found the constraints on movement within the cars and between cars intolerable—indeed, compartments were sometimes known in America as "coon sentry-boxes."

The English traveler was often astonished at the *size* of American cars, too. During the decade of the 1850s some companies built extraordinarily large passenger cars, apparently to enhance company prestige as much as to cram as many people as possible into them. In fact, some American passenger cars were triple the length of the ordinary English counterpart at the time. However, as C. B. Berry discovered on one of the better railroads (the Pennsylvania) in 1880, the impressive length of the car was undermined by the niggardly supply of *two candles* to illuminate it, leaving Mr. Berry in "a dim religious light."[92]

English travelers were sometimes appalled at the dirtiness of American cars, which companies in Britain simply would not have gotten away with where first- (and possibly second-) class compartment provision were concerned. And although English tourists frequently complained about the dirtiness of American cars, that was most likely a problem only on some railroads—the parsimonious companies in question extending the American system of construction to an American system of hygiene as well. However, often American railroad journeys were much longer than they could possibly be in Britain at the time. And when passengers were traveling on the same train for days on end—as on the transcontinental lines—it may have been extremely difficult for the companies, under those circumstances, to keep the cars clean. But, given the American male's propensity to spit anywhere he pleased, the (maintenance of cleanliness) task in question was probably formidable, apart from which it seems that if people were not too particular about where they spat, then presumably littering (more generally) would also have been commonplace.

For decades train travelers in the American West had to put up with the nuisance of dust, since it was often too hot to close the windows. The dust nuisance got worse as train speeds increased. In fact, during the 1850s the dust problem was so bad passenger numbers began consequently to fall off on some railroads. And because the dust spoiled clothes, it eventually became the fashion for men to wear a duster—a long protective coat worn over the clothes (women wore "sacks"). But some enterprising companies capitalized on the dust situation—by advertising their railroads as ballasted with broken stone or gravel, and later by advertising that they employed the latest dust prevention and ventilation technologies. In the same connection, one notes that a key selling point of Pullman was the car technology—apart from the excellent suspension and minimal car oscillation, double windows were incorporated in the design, which meant windows did not rattle, other noise was prevented, and dust was kept out.[93]

But the ordinary American cars could be very cold in winter, bearing in mind the Central Pacific (on the transcontinental), for instance, went up to the summit of the Sierra Nevada. In fact, it seems there was often an undignified rush for seats in the cars in cold weather, although that did not necessarily mean the objective was to get as close as possible to the heating stove in the car. Indeed, many English travelers commented on the oppressive heat from the stoves; so, the best seats were close enough to the stove to keep warm, but not so close the heat was stifling. However, Frances Kemble did not like the car heating stoves at all: "No words can describe the foulness of the atmosphere." In fact, she thought the stoves would be unnecessary "if (American) people dressed more sensibly."[94] Similarly, Anthony Trollope viewed such heating as largely responsible for American lethargy, poor complexion, softness, general un-healthiness, and premature demise—he thought Americans had an obsession for over-heating their homes, too.[95] Another English source remarked that the stove, the "bugbear" of the English traveler on American trains, was "truly demoniacal."[96]

Trains were normally very noisy, but probably much more so on poorly constructed track. Furthermore, in hot regions the windows had to be kept open, which would have exacerbated the noise problem—both from the train noise and from rattling windows. In such circumstances people often had to shout their conversations.[97] Burning smells were also common on some American railroads. For instance, as trains cruised down the Sierra Nevada on the transcontinental railroad, brake friction caused the metal shoes to glow red, and the consequent smell of burning beneath the cars, not surprisingly, disconcerted some passengers.[98]

As to sparks emanating from the locomotive, eventually they may have been less of a fire hazard in general than were the stoves inside the cars. In fact, Mencken provides fascinating coverage—complete with patent illustrations—of some of the proposed appendages to American locomotives and cars designed to deal with dirt, dust, smoke, ventilation, and spark problems.[99] Some of those proposed innovations were quite fantastic, others decidedly wacky. Most were never employed.

In the late 1880s John Cook, son of the illustrious travel agent, Thomas, thought the "ordinary" American passenger car was little different from an English Midland Company *third-class* carriage.[100] But that is rather more flattering than it might sound, for it must be borne in mind that, by that time, the Midland was operating a Pullman service, and it had for some considerable time been using what were previously its (very good) second-class carriages as third-class carriages. That being the case, the "ordinary" American car of the 1880s was not too bad at all.

However, across the decades American car standards could vary considerably from one company to the next. Certainly, there was fault to be found with the standard American car on some, perhaps many lines. Furthermore, it would be mistaken to think that only "uppity" English travelers complained about American railroad passenger provision. Indeed, a Philadelphia merchant had this to say about *early* American railroad travel:

> If one could stop when one wanted; and if one were not locked up in a box with 50 or 60 tobacco chewers; and the engine did not burn holes in one's clothes; and the smell of the smoke, of the oil, and of the chimney did not poison one; and one were not in danger of being blown sky-high or knocked off the rail, then it *would* be the perfection of traveling.[101]

As for the English critics, one thought the "republican simplicity" of the railway car certainly placed rich and poor on a "dead level of *uncomfortableness*."[102] Another referred to (American) railroad passenger cars as being predicated upon the doctrine of the greatest unhappiness of the greatest number (of travelers). And virtually all English tourists commented upon the low-backed seats or an absence of head-rests. Indeed, the experience of the English tourist, William Ferguson, traveling in 1854, was probably exceptional at the time—he remarked upon the fact that his car, on the Hartford and Newhaven, had both headrests and footrests, while the seats themselves were "the least disagreeable I have met with in America."[103] It was a frequent complaint of railroad travelers in America, for several decades in the case of some railroads, that seat backs were too low, and hence there was nothing to relax the head and neck against. And the lack of headrests was still a problem with car seats well into the 1880s on some lines. But the entrepreneurial "gadget men" had been hard at work; and, before long, one could buy portable, attachable headrests at many stations. Of course, such wonderful enterprise did nothing to encourage the (remiss) railroad companies to spend a little more money on timber, leather, and stuffing so that the backs of their passengers" seats might be a little higher.

Having said all that, there were some railroads in America, travel upon which left English (and American) tourists highly impressed. Thomas Nichols, traveling between Cleveland and Cincinnati in 1859, found the cars to be: "Among the nicest I have seen. They are heated or ventilated in accordance with the season."[104] If the American cars had their drawbacks in certain respects, they also had enormous advantages. Indeed, one could "walk from one end of the train to the other," while the platforms between the cars were "capital" places from which to view the scenery and take the fresh air (this must have opened an entirely new dimension to English tourists).[105] Later, the introduction of the Observation Car on Pullman and similar services was a great novelty for the English traveler: "An excellent idea, and very popular with children."[106]

On American railroads, then, "through travel" had a dual meaning. And it became the norm for passengers, especially on a long journey, to wander through their cars, or from one car to another, to observe their fellow passengers, and sometimes to enquire into their business. Of course, "tripping" from one car to another was hazardous in those times (before the advent of the vestibule) and passengers were often warned of the dangers. But Americans had scant regard for authority, so they took their chances—sometimes at their peril.

Yet, the open American car, despite its advantages, still displeased many English tourists. One English traveler remarked in 1875 that one of the major advantages of English railroads was that there was less annoyance from dust and dirt, and that one person could not annoy 50 or 60 people at a time.[107] But others saw it differently, especially from a security point of view: "In these (American) cars they never feared the attack of a garrotter, as they did when passing under a tunnel boxed up in an English railway carriage (compartment)."[108] And, as another English source noted, you could usually change seats if you did not like the company.[109] But if American passengers did not have to worry about being locked in compartments with lunatics, yet there were still lunatics to be reckoned with: "A lunatic recently jumped on a locomotive on a New York railway and, turning on the steam, it ran off with him. The locomotive ran over two persons and smashed a wagon before a well-aimed billet of wood knocked the lunatic from the steam-valve."[110]

One of the reasons the English liked their own railroad passenger class system—as discussed in earlier chapters—was that it afforded an albeit limited social closure and thus exclusivity of the traveling space. This meant your chances of having to travel with somebody *remarkably different* from yourself—in terms of values, attitudes, and behaviour—were, if not decimated, certainly diminished. The compartment, which further limited the company, reinforced this sorting out process. In contrast, on an American railroad you could not normally—prior to the Pullman era—purchase an exclusive domain while traveling. You had to share an open car, possibly even a seat, with all-comers. Americans were used to this and probably quite relaxed about it. But it was certainly novel for English travelers used to first- or second-class compartment accommodation and correspondingly stratified amenities on English railroads.

But with the advent of the Pullman era some of the anxieties of English travelers in America were no doubt eased. Pullman luxury aside, English tourist, Catherine Bates, noted that in the Southwest a well-to-do Bostonian and his friends "had a railway *car* to themselves."[111] And although this facility may have been quite widely available on the long-distance lines of some companies at the time, yet that may have been a group traveling together on one of Raymonds" exclusive tours, or even a railroad company president's private car—these were often loaned to friends.

But what did go on inside the ordinary American passenger cars during a railroad journey? One English source, who was clearly not fazed by having to mix with other people during a railroad journey, noted: "In American railway carriages there were a sociality and interchange of thought which *added great freshness to travel.*"[112] But this was hardly the universal experience of an English traveler in America. J. S. Buckingham, traveling from Lancaster to Harrisburg in 1839, found the company "dirty, vulgar, clamorous, and rude."[113] And Foster Zincke was annoyed on a journey (in 1868) by two "half-breed" Indians who sang *Three Blind Mice* repeatedly. On another occasion, he was somewhat "disarmed" to learn, when the conductor entered his car and asked if anybody had a pistol with which to "finish off" a cow which had brought the train to a halt, that he was the only male in the car who was *not* armed.[114]

Although some English travelers were fazed by some of the people they encountered on American trains, especially in the West, others relaxed and took in the "sights" and "entertainment." R.L. Stevenson joked that it seemed "all the states of the North had sent out a fugitive to cross the Plains with me."[115] And one London parson was amused, rather than frightened by, the gun-slinging types strutting through his car. But he was "street-wise" enough to know that they were no problem if you did not meddle with them, and that: "They only shoot their friends and acquaintances as a rule."[116] In fact, one 19th century historian of the West estimated, based on his own experience, that the average life of the Western "rough," once he had established a reputation for himself as a "rough," was about four years.

English railroad companies would never have put up with some American passengers to be encountered out West in the pre–Pullman days. But even the "average" American male could irritate an Englishman, as Alfred Bunn made clear in 1851: "It is utterly impossible to mistake an American for anyone else. He has his feet on the seat next to him. He either sucks a piece of sweetmeat, bites a piece of wood, or chews a bit of tobacco, and invariably reads a newspaper."[117]

But there were other "human hazards" in American cars:

> To the amiable female, whose sylph-like form of 227 lbs sat its queenly bulk unceremoniously down upon my new hat, which reposed on my reserved seat (at Kingsville, SC.) while I was serenely annihilating ten minutes for refreshments.... I do most ungratefully dedicate this volume.[118]

On a long journey, such as seven or eight days on the transcontinental railroad, one was probably obliged to be gregarious. Dee Brown suggests that on that journey a sort of camaraderie reminiscent of coaching days often emerged on the second day of travel. R.L. Stevenson noted that food and the progress of the train were the main subjects of phatic communion in such circumstances (but he was traveling emigrant class) once the aforementioned camaraderie had emerged, even otherwise stoical and aloof passengers joining in *those* conversations.[119] And Boddam-Whetham noted that on long rail journeys in America, after the obligatory first day of "monastic silence" had passed, "you may learn the personal and family history of most of your fellow passengers."[120]

One guidebook for the transcontinental railroad advised travelers to form groups of four in facing seats (seats were usually reversible) at the earliest opportunity, since west of Omaha boarding passengers tended to become the more odious the more the train proceeded west. And Henry Williams advised people that to enjoy Palace Car life properly one always needed a good companion, and that they ought to take a section together—but he said it was impossible to order an entire section (like a compartmentalized space) for one person alone. Williams, traveling in 1876, found the company in the sleeping cars from the East to the mid–West mostly "quiet and refined"—until the train reached Omaha![121] But the most uncouth types of all were said to catch the train in Nevada.[122]

Female Travelers in America

In America the early railroad companies often provided some separate facilities for women, including car accommodation. The precedent had been set on both the coastal and river steamboats, on board which a ladies' cabin was often provided in addition to general cabin accommodation. The former was usually more lavishly furnished and more comfortable than the accommodation for all-comers, aside from which the latter often contained a bar, smokers, and gamblers. One Northern newspaper, which was opposed to separate ladies' cars, considered them "barbarisms," which were "ineffective in safeguarding ladies against tobacco indecencies (spitting)."[123] Mencken claims ladies' cars were not as common in the North as they were in the South and that they vanished in the North in the 1850s. They lasted a few years longer in the South, where some companies even offered a maid service to attend lady travelers and to assist them with their children—Mencken suggests that in both North and South ladies' cars were abolished for *economic* reasons. But men were not necessarily excluded from ladies' cars when they were provided, often having admittance to them if accompanying a lady on a journey. In Eastern states etiquette required that ladies be given a window seat when separate ladies' cars were unavailable.[124] However, etiquette was different out West, where ladies were encouraged to take aisle seats, since Western people were known to assume "undignified postures" in full view of the railroad.[125]

Tocqueville commented upon the good sense of American women travelers in the 1830s, observing: "They seemed to cope successfully without the personal maids and heaps of luggage that ladies in Europe found necessary when traveling."[126] However, Louis Gottschalk, later, had a different experience—he was frequently very annoyed by the "tendency of females to take incredible amounts of baggage and paraphernalia into the cars" (this may have been partly because American women carried delicate articles in their baggage, which they had no intention of placing at the mercy of the baggage smashers). And Gottschalk thought—like Anthony Trollope—that many American women were impolite, if not downright rude and pushy: "Of the thousand ladies I have given my place, lowered a window for, paid the conductor, or offered my hand to help down," seven-eighths had omitted to thank him.[127] But these were not simply the plaintiff yelps of patronizing males, who felt cheated because they were not eternally kow-towed to by the fairer sex in recognition of such magnanimous gestures. Even Therese Yelverton remarked upon this phenomenon: "If a gentleman rises and gives his seat to a lady … she drops into it as though it were her right."[128] Certainly, this "lack of civility" on the part of some American women ran counter to European etiquette at the time. For, according to *Collier's Cyclopedia of Commercial and Social Information* (1882): "Ladies traveling alone will thank gentlemen who raise or lower windows coldly but politely."[129] Likewise, an 1889 etiquette book urged: "Young ladies should avoid entering into unnecessary conversation or accepting favors from men who are strangers. Although an expression of thanks should be offered for any courtesy."[130] However, perhaps some ladies who *appeared to be rude* were governed by the rules Mrs. Olive Davenport of St. Louis was subject to: rules imposed by her tyrannical husband, which she enumerated during her divorce suit (in 1879), one of which was that she was not to speak to any person, or allow any person to speak to her, on the car, except the conductor and porter in the discharge of their duties.

Anthony Trollope had some very bad experiences at the hands of American women and he generally found the fairer sex in America to be very "unfair." If not a misogynist before arriving in America, then he probably was by the time he departed its shores. Indeed, by then he had reached the conclusion that whereas in England women become ladylike or vulgar, in America they are either "charming or odious." When traveling on the transcontinental railroad he encountered a woman in a car "who speaks as though to her the neighborhood of men was the same as that of dogs or cats." And it got worse the farther West he went: "In the West men are dirty and civil, the women dirty and uncivil," and "as sharp and as hard as nails." He also thought American women characterized by a certain "pushiness." But perhaps he put himself in the most pathetic light possible when complaining about "The indelicate manner in which American women throw their crinolines about, striking it against men's legs, and heaving it with violence over people's knees." These "violent" actions of females—on New York streetcars, actually—he referred to as "anti-feminine atrocities."[131]

It was widely asserted both by English travelers in America and in English newspapers that America was an extremely safe place for women travelers. Take, for instance, the following three assertions from different *English* newspapers published at widely different times. One noted (1867) that the American young lady could travel everywhere, not only "without meeting with insult, but she was treated with the greatest courtesy."[132] Another declared (1875): "A woman might travel in America, from Maine down to Florida, by herself, without hearing one word of rudeness."[133] The third article, likewise, noted (1879) the facility with which ladies may travel alone in safety in America.[134]

Lady Hardy said of Omaha (Omaha had 61 brothels in 1870) that, despite all the rough-looking men there: "We feel instinctively that a rude word or discourteous act in our presence is simply impossible, so we lift our unprotected heads and march on triumphant." She also noted—with regard to a pretty, young, fellow passenger traveling alone on the transcontinental—that on an American train such a female could travel from Boston to Arizona "Without running the slightest risk of annoyance or inconvenience in any way.... Indeed, to thoroughly enjoy traveling in perfect comfort and freedom from anxiety, one must be an unprotected female."[135] Therese Yelverton was of the same opinion, noting that American men were not rude to women, despite "coarse joking being one of the disagreeable features of American life."[136]

Service

It was not really until the Pullman era that passengers could expect much in the way of service on American railroads. And even then, given that the Pullman technologies were add-ons, whatever services Pullman afforded the passenger had to be paid for over and above the standard fare for the railroad journey in question. And although from an early period river and canal boats, and coastal shipping services, too, had offered more than one passenger class often, yet that did not necessarily mean that one could expect deference on the part of those employees whose jobs entailed rendering service to the passengers—well, not unless the servants happened to be Negroes! But poor service was a more general phenomenon.

The somewhat brow-beaten Anthony Trollope was disarmed to discover that in America paying for a service entitled him to no deference. He also found it "disagreeable" in Western railroad towns to be asked by hotel clerks what he meant by a "dressing room" and why he needed one. And he greatly missed the intimate pampering of the English inn: "Tea by the fire," and "to have my teacup emptied and refilled with gradual pauses."[137] But Anthony might as well have been up the Congo if he expected *that* in America! More generally, Trollope found service to be very poor in every sphere in America. And he found women in positions of service to be "the most insolent" of all. But he was "right on the mark" when he noted that in America these people were rude and unhelpful because they associated civility with subservience.[138] In fact, the only place one could expect to find the irreproachable type of servant Trollope yearned for was on the railroad in Pullman class, once it had come into existence, with its legions of poorly-paid Negro porters who were banned from virtually every other kind of railroad work by the racist brotherhoods of white workers—however, in the South some railroad companies had employed negroes as locomotive firemen from early on. The Charleston and Hamburg certainly employed negroes—both [hired] slaves and freemen—as firemen in the 1830s and beyond.

English travelers in America complained endlessly about the service at railroad stations, which was usually minimal even when there was any to speak of. And well-to-do English travelers rarely encountered the civility, helpfulness, and deference of railroad servants they had become accustomed to in Britain, not to mention the "shepherds" and "nannies" they usually needed to help them pass through railroad facilities. Traveling in 1854, the Englishman Charles Weld observed: "The passenger has to look out for himself," for "if he trusts to others he will be left behind"; while his countryman, W.F. Rae, would have included this perplexity in his generic concept of "the confusion which reigned supreme" at American stations. Henry Lucy was also dismayed, almost lost it seems, to find himself at a railroad station with nobody to shepherd him in the direction of his train. But he rather liked the way the American railroad servant rationalized a passenger's having been left behind (because there was nobody there to ensure he got on the right train): "He had gone and got himself left."

W.F. Rae believed that the absence of porters at railroad stations in America was due to the scarcity of labor and that, although the bustle and confusion at Chicago station, for instance, was in excess of what would occur at a well-managed European railway station, yet porters were dispensed with—the experienced traveler carried "no more luggage than he can move unassisted."[139] Catherine Bates certainly missed the English porter: "Whose absolute devotion can be purchased for sixpence, and whose universal civility and patient endurance seem to have no price." But she qualified that by adding of America: "I have traveled in no country where fellow passengers were so unfailingly kind and helpful to women."[140] Foster Zincke also found *middle-class* Americans "far more civil and helpful to one another, and to strangers, than Englishmen are."[141]

However, by 1878 some companies' regulations required brakemen, if so instructed by conductors, to assist ladies, children, and infirm persons to get on and off trains.[142] But why should the brakemen have had to do it? And why was the conductor apparently exempt from this "extraordinary" duty? Why did the company not employ some porters to do this? It seems the railroad companies exploited the goodwill of passengers towards fellow passengers by failing to provide porters. And what kind of strange society was this where people could be outrageously insolent in roles they were *paid* for, while others could be "unfailingly kind and helpful" when they were not obliged to be? The "independent variable" in the situation was clearly the status of paid *service*, as rationalized in this and the previous chapter. Indeed, since only desperate people were prepared to take servile and poorly-paid positions in America it is hardly surprising American railroad companies had so many rude and uncouth people working for them. Even in the late 1860s, both the Union Pacific and the Central Pacific (operating the transcontinental railroad service between them) had a lot of trouble finding suitable people to fill all kinds of roles at every level on the railroad. Charlie Crocker of the Central Pacific stated in 1868 that it was very difficult in the Midwest and Far West to find men capable of "controlling and organizing others"; but he noted there was no shortage of "first-class railroad men," it was just very difficult to entice them to work in the West.[143]

It seems that what the railroad company regulations stipulated meant very little where the service and civility of employees were concerned. One company's regulations stipulated in 1854: "Agents will observe the deportment of trainmen toward passengers, and will report to the Superintendent any rudeness or incivility that may come under their observation."[144] Most companies also required conductors to have such a (surveillance) role. However, both agents and conductors were probably often reluctant to "tell tales" on fellow employees. More generally, it seems ill-discipline among the lower ranks was at least partly due to poor management. When Snyder became Operations Superintendent of the Union Pacific in the late 1860s, he apparently went through the entire operation with a "mean broom," kicking out loafers, drunks, and crooks at every level of operations—presumably there was nobody left! He then set in place a strict disciplinary regime and an effective inspection and surveillance system. Furthermore, Snyder even came down like a ton of bricks on some of the Union Pacific's most prominent entities during the construction period of the railroad. In 1867 principal contractor (along with his brother), Jack Casement, had been (reasonably enough) permitted free transportation along the line of his construction materials; he had also operated general stores in the newly created towns and taken the liberty of transporting stock for those stores free along the line. However, in December 1867 Snyder informed him that thenceforth he would be paying the normal tariff for transportation of non-construction materials.[145]

Rudeness towards obviously well-heeled travelers was almost an institution and thus difficult to eliminate on American railroads for much of the 19th century. However, things did change where some railroads were concerned—Henry Williams could assure transcontinental passengers in his guidebook of 1875 that at Omaha they would (now) find at the station "gentlemanly attendants, ready to give you any information, and cheerfully answer your questions."[146]

Railroad Dining

In America during the 19th century refreshment facilities varied in quality from one railroad company to the next. In the early period eating places at railroad stations were known as "refreshment saloons." The companies often owned them and the food was notoriously bad. Refreshment stops conformed to the train's schedule, which sometimes gave them a certain irrational character, since three meals might be crammed into the space of a few hours, and then the passengers might have to endure an obligatory fast for an extended period.[147] There were also some fairly "exotic" dining places—William Ferguson dined at a clearing in a forest south of Wilmington during a railroad journey in 1856.[148]

An 1857 *New York Times* article described American railroad refreshment saloons as "dreary places" and "abominations of desolation," in which "painful and unhealthy performances take place." And in one of the classic American statements on the subject, the article went on to say that the consequences of such "savage and unnatural feeding" are not reported by telegraph as railroad disasters, though they ought to be[149]—in fact, American railroad companies were slow to adopt the telegraph as an administrative tool, its first use by a railroad company in that connection apparently not until 1851. (English companies were using it for administrative purposes in the mid–1840s.)

Catherine Bates found eating places bad and dining-carriages rare when she was in America: the eating stop was "hurried, degraded and miserable" and you were charged three shillings for your "revolting meal" on a dirty plate, and "that was the charm of American travel over many roads."[150] Another English tourist referred to his dining experiences, while traveling on the Kansas Pacific Railroad, as entailing some close encounters with "dangerous–looking compounds called dinner."[151] There was inconsistency, the fare ranging from the excellent to the appalling—in the late 1850s the Cleveland and Toledo was advertising its "dining rooms" as the best in the country. But on some railroads the food hardly varied from one refreshment saloon to another, and sometimes the menu hardly changed from one meal time to another as well. However, Thomas Cook, during his travels in the 1870s, found refreshment rooms on the first transcontinental railroad very good in terms of both food and service. Even at the summit of the Sierra Nevada, "We were astonished to observe the amplitude of the supplies and the smart activity of the waiter."[152] And clearly things had improved somewhat along all the trunk lines to the Pacific coast by the mid–1870s, if we can take Henry Williams at his word. He was at that time highly impressed by station eateries, which provided both snacks and full meals—he thought stops west of Ogden on the Central Pacific furnished wonderful meals served by excellent Chinese waiters. In fact, he suggested that by that time all the eating houses on the Pacific railroads were "very excellent indeed."[153]

One of the great boons to railroad dining beyond the Pullman dining-car was the advent of the Fred Harvey chain of station eateries. Harvey was an Englishman and former railroad freight agent who knew an opportunity when he saw one. He entered a contract with the Santa Fe Railroad, which enabled him to exclusively establish his dining-rooms and hotels near its stations—initially, these were on the Chicago–Los Angeles line. The railroad company asked for none of the profits, realizing that good refreshment facilities alone would draw patronage to the company's lines.[154] By 1883 Harvey had 17 dining-rooms along the Santa Fe, Dee Brown baptizing him the "Civilizer of the West." And at its peak the Harvey chain had sixty-five restaurants, sixty dining cars, a dozen large hotels, all the restaurants and retail shops in five of the nation's largest railroad stations, and so many news-stands and bookshops that its pre-publication orders (like those of W.H. Smith in England) regularly affected national best-seller lists.[155] His dining rooms were lavish, white linen and fine silverware graced the tables, the food was consistently excellent, and it was served by very pretty, immaculately groomed, and handsomely uniformed young ladies.[156] Indeed, one might even identify the Harvey chain as a progenitor of the fast food chains of the 20th century—apart from the above standardized constituent elements of the "brand," was there not a precursor to the dimensions of the Big Mac in the form of the "regulation" Harvey restaurant slice of bread, which had to be exactly 3/8ths of an inch thick? Indeed, one source has identified Harvey as the "founding father" of the American service industry and the Harvey brand as the first widely known and respected brand name in America.[157] Harvey's endeavours probably established a standard which some railroad companies felt compelled to emulate—an 1873 Baltimore and Ohio Railroad Guide claimed that the company had completed, and was further constructing, "some of the finest hotels and meal stations in the country" along its lines, where the traveler would have "ample time to enjoy a sumptuous repast."[158]

The Baltimore and Ohio Railroad, which led innovation in many respects in the early period, had introduced its first dining and buffet car in 1835.[159] But that innovation would probably not have been a rip-roaring success. And although other companies toyed with dining cars in the late 1830s, so-called "restaurant cars" did not become at all common until the early 1860s. In fact, it seems the early attempts had been quite slapdash affairs, the "restaurant" itself usually occupying just half a smoking car, while the food was not cooked on the train but taken aboard at various places and kept warm in steam boxes.[160] George Pullman took "dining on the rails" to entirely new heights, of course. One has only to look at a reproduction of a 19th century Pullman menu to realize what (multi-course) stunning fare was served up to those who could afford to pay for it.[161] But the Pullman technologies were intended to put the very best hotel luxury on rails and that extended to dining service.

W.F. Rae thought the Pullman hotel car of 1869 as luxurious as the saloon carriages constructed for the use of Queen Victoria.[162] William Smith thought the Pullman dining car exemplified the difference between "feeding and dining."[163] But if anybody is worth quoting in this regard, it is Henry James where his American travels were concerned: "I remember how often, in moving about, the observation that most remained with me appeared to be this note of the hotel, and of the hotel-like chain of Pullman cars, as the supreme social expression." He saw the Pullmans as like rushing hotels, and the hotels like stationary Pullmans.[164] But we should not lose sight of the fact that where railroad "feeding" was concerned—unlike in Britain, and from an early period—vendors of all kinds of food strolled through the "ordinary" American railroad passenger car, a facility which many English tourists greatly appreciated.

Conductors

The railroad "servant" most commonly encountered during a railroad journey was, of course, the conductor. Like many other aspects of railroad travel in 19th century America, just what kind of human being the conductor turned out to be depended on the era, the geographical location, the railroad company, and the individual concerned. The American conductor differed from his English counterpart in several respects, not the least of which was his perceived social status in the early period. And on some lines, especially in the early period, he was also noteworthy for his frequent *lack* of qualifications in the fields of civility, helpfulness, and public relations, as well as (for a few decades) his propensity to "rip off" his employer for all he could get. Concerning the latter, reference was made earlier to Cornelius Vanderbilt's role in putting an end to theft by conductors. However, even in the late 1860s theft by conductors remained a problem for some companies: "It is said ... that very large sums, in the aggregate, are annually lost by some railroad companies through the petty pilfering of the conductors, a sort of robbery there is no effective security against, except in the character of the men themselves."[165]

In the early period the conductor typically wore civilian garb, but usually with a metal strip bearing the word "conductor" on his hat—the perceptive Charles Weld noted one conductor who only displayed this badge when the train was in motion[166] (as if the badge was stigmatizing). But by the 1890s the conductor often wore a blue serge suit with gold buttons.[167] And it has been suggested the introduction of uniforms, among other things, gave American railroad company employees (including conductors) a "greater sense of responsibility and aided much in effecting a more courteous demeanor to passengers."[168]

Thomas Nichols remarked upon a "gentlemanly" conductor while traveling in Ohio in 1859.[169] And traveling in 1880, C.B. Berry admired the Pennsylvania Railroad conductors, who were "resplendent in uniforms and buttons"—the Pennsylvania was one of the best companies in America at the time. Berry also noted of conductors that they were invariably 50 inches around the girth and weighed 200–300 pounds.[170] So, clearly these conductors were not on starvation-level incomes. In fact, tourist John Boddam-Whetham remarked (1874): "Railway conductors are considered very un-businesslike if, after their first month, they have not secured sufficient means to purchase a handsome watch and chain."[171] And many of them, having acquired "gentlemanly" status, also assumed titles such as "Captain," even if they had never been in the militia. Indeed, W.G. Marshall (1881) said of the conductor: "You must treat him with great civility, for bear in mind he is a gentleman, and expects to be regarded as such."[172] In fact, in the 1850s some English travelers in America were just a little outraged by the claims to status honor made by railroad conductors: "Trying to pass themselves off as gentlemen, lounging with good company, having fashionable wives, and holding senior officer status in local militias."[173] Nevertheless, tourist Henry Deedes remarked (1869): "The conductor is a great institution in American railways. Ladies and children are without hesitation confined to his care."[174]

On the Pacific railroads in the 1870s conductors were known to make a few dollars on the side as a result of having studied the passenger lists; and if they recognized the name of some eminent person heading west, then they telegraphed the information to the Associated Press, which in turn relayed it to its Californian client newspapers.[175] In the Frank Norris novel, *McTeague*, the conductor "makes it his business to study faces," perhaps also on the look-out for villains for whom a substantial reward was on offer. However, in that novel the central character, fleeing south to Mexico to escape the law, pays the conductor of a freight train for the privilege of riding in the caboose.[176] Furthermore, one suspects that in the West trainmen were sometimes involved in various "rackets" which enabled them to plunder the company—a visitor to Julesburg in 1867 noted that many men had fine gold watches and expensive patent leather boots, although he was surprised to learn these men were not capitalists, but railroad conductors, clerks, ticket agents, and enginemen.[177]

The portly, even gentlemanly, Pennsylvania Railroad Company conductor mentioned earlier was often a far cry from his counterparts elsewhere. In fact, in the West and elsewhere the conductor could be gruff, abrasive, and unhelpful—Jensen suggests this was typical with conductors who had worked their way up the ladder from the lowly starting rung of brakeman.[178] In fact, right across the industry conductors were routinely recruited from the ranks of brakemen. However, being a conductor was pretty much a dead-end job with most companies. Having said that, conductors, if very able men, could sometimes progress a long way within a railroad company. Silas Clark, who finished up as Jay Gould's right-hand man, had started at the bottom, worked up to the position of conductor, then consistently proved himself capable of managing more than a train.[179]

The English tourist, W.G. Marshall, traveling in the West in 1878, joined the conductor and others during a stop at Wahsatch Station "taking pot-shots at one of the telegraph posts." But conductors *were* managers. They, not the enginemen, controlled the movements of the train. And Thomas Cook noted the American conductors had thorough control of trains and could meet any emergencies of passengers without difficulty,[180] despite their personality quirks and otherwise unhelpful dispositions. The *Erie Railroad Regulations of 1854* asserted that the conductor had entire control of the train and of all persons employed on it; that when a locomotive is attached to a train, then the engineman is subject to the orders of the conductor, who will direct him when to start and when to stop; that the engineman must not start his train till directed so to do by the conductor; that the conductor must not permit the sale of books, papers, or refreshments in the cars without a written license from the Superintendent of the road or division; that conductors, and other train men, must not attempt to influence passengers in favor of, or against, certain hotels or saloons, but must act impartially in this respect.[181] And these regulations—pertaining to conductors—would have been fairly typical of American railroad administration and operations at the time. However, it seems obvious to me that breach of some of the above rules explains why many conductors were able to sport all the "accoutrements" of well-heeled gentlemen.

But the conductor's being in control of the train was not always a good thing, it seems. Charles Weld, traveling in 1854, survived a terrifying event at the hands of a conductor. The conductor had resolved that the train was running very late, so he ordered the engineman to speed up considerably to make up time. Weld claimed the train was run at "excessive speed," that the conductor refused to listen to the pleas of passengers that he slow the train down, and that he "evidently attached little value to life." The passengers hung on for dear life as "lamp glasses popped out of their sockets," so violent were the motions of the hurtling train. It was obvious to the passengers that the train would surely leave the tracks sooner or later. Consequently, gentlemen were comforting frightened ladies, advising them how best to position themselves for an impact, while Weld accepted such advice from a man "experienced in railroad accidents." The train did, indeed, leave the rails, and in quite spectacular fashion, too. Fortunately, nobody was seriously injured. But what amazed Weld most about this incident was the fact hardly any of his fellow passengers shared his view that the conductor ought to be reported—most of them admired the conductor's efforts to make up lost time.[182] A very strange society, indeed!

But the buck did stop with the conductor. Indeed, since he was in charge of the train he was often held responsible for accidents in cases of alleged recklessness or negligence. When 60 people were killed in the Camp Hill collision in 1856, for instance, it was never going to be the enginemen who were the "villains." Indeed, the enquiry focused upon the culpability or otherwise of the conductors involved, since the enginemen were under their orders.[183] And an engineman would seldom be liable, *unless* he disobeyed or ignored a conductor's orders, or took an unnecessary risk.[184]

Even though in the early period many conductors were "rough and ready" characters, yet they could be zealously officious, too. Traveling in 1850, Arthur Cunyghame encountered a conductor who insisted on seeing everybody's ticket at every stop, while Lady Hardy, traveling around 1880, was amused by the conductor who "kept punching our tickets until they resemble a piece of perforated cardboard." Cunyghame found many conductors to be "particularly coarse fellows" and "petty tyrants," who sometimes treated passengers with "contemptuous insolence." Indeed, he declared: "It is scarcely possible to describe ... the style of contemptuous insolence with which they sometimes treat the passengers.... It is by far the greatest drawback to the pleasure of traveling in the United States." However, he pointed out that this never occurred in the northeast, where conductors were "more refined."[185] Yet, the regulations sometimes endorsed the "tyranny"—the regulations of one railroad company stipulated that passengers unable to produce a ticket to the conductor could be expelled, "even if the conductor knows the passenger has paid his fare!"

But Americans themselves were not uncomplaining where the rudeness of railroad conductors was concerned, as indicated by an 1856 article in a Californian newspaper, which compared the English and American conductors at the time:

> The (English) conductors are carefully selected and generally perfectly reliable men. No matter of discretion in operational procedures is left to the whim of a conductor; and in England human life is too sacredly respected, and too large an amount of capital employed in working railroads, to allow such liberties.[186]

R.L. Stevenson recalled one conductor who said that "He didn't answer any questions, since one would lead to another, and he could not afford to be eternally worried." Stevenson noted, furthermore, that "many conductors will hold no conversation with an emigrant."[187] However, in the West conductors were not universally uncouth. They certainly could be courteous, friendly, and gregarious. Abraham Lincoln often ate with conductors at refreshment stops on the Alton Railroad,[188] although he was well-known to all train personnel on the railroads which fell into the ambit of his circuit as a lawyer. Moreover, being a retained attorney for the Illinois Central he had a free pass to its roads. In fact, for over a decade Lincoln represented the Illinois Central in many cases in the lower courts of Illinois, but also won some very important cases for the company in the Supreme Court of that state.[189]

And on the matter of legal issues, Arthur Cunyghame asked a conductor why he so frequently opened the back door of the car and looked out of it, since being the last car there was nothing to look at! He was advised that escaping slaves sometimes got up onto the backs of trains; and that if they did, then they had to be forcibly removed, since the railroad company would be liable for abetting their flight if they were not[190]—around 1830 stagecoach contractors and operators, too, could be fined up to $500 for carrying any "colored person" who could not produce a county court certificate proving they were free.[191]

Escaping slaves aside, one imagines that out in the West railroad conductors had some very difficult passengers to deal with. Dee Brown mentions one Kansas Pacific conductor who always reported for duty with revolvers and a rifle.[192] Indeed, Ambrose Bierce mischievously defined a conductor as "the man who punches your ticket and your head."[193] And some conductors probably did punch a few heads, perhaps of necessity. But conductors could also be the "life of the party." Mallie Stafford, traveling on the transcontinental in the 1870s, remarked: "What fun the conductor made last evening. He is a jovial, hearty soul, and kept us awake with his jokes."[194] Indeed, despite the complaints about American train conductors by some English tourists, just as many reported encounters with friendly, jovial, gentlemanly conductors. But it all depended on the decade, the geographical location, the route, the railroad company, and the personality of the individual conductor. And perhaps there is a certain irony to the fact that, although in the early period conductors were often prepared to steal from their employers, yet by the 1890s most would have considered a tip an insult. Indeed, by that time they were often smart and dignified in appearance as well as courteous, although one English traveler thought they "rendered no great service"[195]—but at least there was *some* service by then.

That the rudeness and "tyranny" of railroad conductors had been all but institutionalized for decades is, perhaps, acknowledged by an assertion in the New York, Lake Erie and Western Railroad Company's own Summer Excursion Route Guide for 1881: "The man who said he had heard of civil engineers, but never of civil conductors, was never a patron of the great Erie Railroad." In this publication, the company described its conductors, at that time, as polite, patient, impartial *gentlemen.*

The American Train Butch

In Dickens' *Martin Chuzzlewit* (1843–44), Martin's first experience of America (like Dickens' own) was the invasion of his ship by newsboys.[196] But the newsboy also invaded the trains. In fact, the passenger on long-distance American train journeys had services available to him, while traveling, which were unavailable to the English counterpart. These services were usually provided by the train "butch" or "newsboy." Usually a teenage male, he went from car to car peddling all kinds of things. And although this "junior entrepreneur" could be a nuisance or impudent, he was often the only obliging informant as to where the train was, when and where the next stop was, and so on. R.L. Stevenson thought the newsboy the best informant (for the emigrant passengers in the West) about meals, and that he was the only employee of the railroad company who ensured nobody got left behind at refreshment stops. However, he did find some newsboys insolent or nuisances.[197]

Sometimes the butch was an employee of the railroad company, although he could also be self-employed, and thus licensed to vend on the trains by the railroad company concerned. Dee Brown suggests that an enterprising train butch could earn as much in one month as an engineman. Thomas Edison, for one, began his working life as a train butch. So did William Brady, one of the first movie producers, who used to startle the passengers by suddenly shouting words from Shakespeare as he wandered through the cars.[198]

The train butch could not have operated on English trains because of the compartmentalization of carriages, apart from which it is hard to imagine any reputable English railroad company allowing anybody to go from carriage to carriage selling anything, let alone "dodgy" novels.[199] In the latter connection, Arthur Cunynghame remarked of his fellow steamboat passengers in America that many spent their time reading "bad" novels," scores of which, he said, "issued weekly from the *libertine* press of New York," and many of which he thought "highly detrimental to the morality of the community." He suggested, furthermore, that the authors in question "pander to the democratic feelings of the multitude" by misrepresenting history, and that many such books were also "un–American."[200] The fact was that, even by 1864, three-fourths of the books printed in America were reprints (pirated editions) of English works.[201]

English travelers in America were sometimes annoyed by purveyors of anything on trains. Walter Thornbury, traveling in 1860, was surprised that "quacks" and other nuisances were allowed on board trains to hawk.[202] Louis Gottschalk, who probably spent twice as much, if not more, of his life on trains than even Lincoln did, was annoyed by evangelists who walked through the cars raining their religious tracts upon the passengers.[203] But the *train butch* was often of considerable utility to the passenger and tourists commented positively on his presence as often as they did negatively. Either way, he was almost always mentioned in the travel narratives of tourists.

R.L. Stevenson certainly appreciated his presence on his long-haul journey in the emigrant passenger cars on the transcontinental railroad—a very arduous undertaking, virtually all tourists at the time opting for the Pullman comfort or the ordinary passenger car. Stevenson noted that the "newsboy" was not merely a "newsboy," since he also purveyed much needed soap, towels, tin washing dishes, and other necessities in the emigrant cars. And on the emigrant train Stevenson found the newsboy, "who helped us with information, attention, assistance, and a kind countenance," to be "a hero of the old Greek stamp."[204]

Other travelers recalled in their narratives that the butch, with pitcher of ice water in summer, as well as vending fruit, chocolate, etc., was much appreciated: "The candy-boys have been around three times, the Negro boys with the water-can twice, the lad with the book-basket once."[205] And on some lines before mid-century urchins came on board at stations selling hot bricks as foot-warmers.[206] However, John Boddam-Whetham, for one, was not enamored of the train butch, describing him thus: "This dreadful bore on all American trains begins his persecutions, and begins on his rounds, as soon as the train starts."[207] Nor was Oscar Wilde impressed during his tour of America to find newsboys on trains: "Selling editions of my poems, vilely printed on a kind of grey blotting paper, for the low price of ten cents!"[208] But Louisa May Alcott had a rather different experience, being "most gratified" when a boy on a train to New York offered her a copy of one of her own books with the recommendation: "Bully book, Ma'am! Sell a lot, better have it!"[209]

But perhaps the comments of one English traveler afford the kind of useful comparative reference required here. He compared the American train butch, purveying his literature to passengers, to his English experience of: "The agony attendant on that hurried expedition to the book-stall in search of railway literature, which takes place at the commencement of our journey." He compared this undignified (English) ritual to the convenience of the American (train) vendor of literature, who "Makes his way from one end of the train, carrying on a tray before him a large collection of books, periodicals, and newspapers, which he offers for inspection." He went on:

> Sometimes, when space permits, this literary peddler will deposit some of his wares on one of the seats, leaving them there for a considerable time, in order that the traveler may inspect them at his leisure. There is much less risk of making a wrong choice under these circumstances than when trying to select appropriate reading material in great haste at an English station book stall.

The latter was, apparently, a harrowing experience, which he described at some length.

Many of the American train peddlers were probably *not li*censed by anybody apart from conductors and station agents to vend on the trains, another reason why some conductors seemed to make a lot of money on the side. However, the train butch was short-lived as a railroad institution—by the late 1870s most companies no longer permitted peddlers on trains.

Pullman Porters

It must have been a huge relief for upper-class English travelers to at last encounter a deferent and servile creature, in the form of the Negro Pullman porter, during their travels in America. Pullman trained his porters thoroughly, maintaining a sleeping-car for the purpose in Chicago. And, regarding the advent of Pullman *service*, Henry Williams declared: "The days of boisterous times, rough railroad men, and bullies in the Far West are gone."[210] No longer would travelers (at least where Pullman was concerned) experience what William Ferguson had in rural Ohio in the mid–1850s, when the Baggage-Master refused to put baggage in the baggage car, people having to do it themselves.[211] Indeed, Pullman introduced something apparently quite rare in America at the time—service![212]

Negroes were preferred by Pullman not only because their labor was cheaper, and they were used to subservience and deference, but also because it was thought the social divide between blacks and whites would preclude any possibility of "difficulties" arising from the "intimate association" of passengers and porters during overnight travel.[213]

Being a Pullman porter was a relatively attractive position for blacks—even if the pay was poor[214]—since it was one of the better non-agricultural or servile roles open to black men at the time. And perhaps we get a sense of the prestige associated with the position of Pullman Porter from Twain's (comparable?) Negro fireman on a Mississippi steamboat, who displayed a good many "airs" to his fellows at a Negro ball: "Who is I? Who is I? I let you know mighty quick who I is! I wont you niggers to understan' dat I fires de middle do' on der *Aleck Scott!*"[215] But the Pullman Porter, unlike our steamboat fireman, got to wear a "flash" uniform, and no doubt "upwardly mobile" (black) girls were attracted to that![216] However, the wages and general working conditions were not as flashy as the uniforms. The 1915 Commission on Industrial Relations found that Pullman porters had to provide their own shoe blacking, even though they were not permitted to charge for polishing shoes; that often they were not provided with adequate accommodation when away from their home stations; and that they were subject to an "espionage system," so that union members could be identified and sacked.[217] But twenty years earlier the United States Strike Commissioners, in their (1895) report on the great Pullman Strike, remarked that the company had continued charging the public exorbitant rates for the use of its cars, while its "consistent policy is well-known of paying its porters and conductors such poor wages that the passengers are virtually obliged to make up the deficiency by tips."[218]

Pullman porters had to be able to deal with all kinds of people. After all, not everybody who could afford to travel Pullman class in its early days was a cultivated person. One Pullman porter thought the most difficult part of the job was convincing cowboys and miners that they really ought to take their boots off before climbing into their berths. He said: "They seemed afraid to take them off."[219]

Pullman porters were, apparently, known universally as "George"—presumably after George Pullman. The Australian, F.H. James, traveling in 1887, found the Negro porters "very careful, obliging, and attentive." He also thought they were great entertainers, whom most passengers were happy to tip a quarter dollar.[220] And clearly by that time tipping was no longer stigmatized (the pretentions of gentlemanly conductors aside)—indeed, a few decades earlier Tocqueville had found himself stopped from tipping the stewards on American steamboats because "it would humiliate them."[221]

James Hogan, unlike many tourists, did not stereotype the Pullman porter: "One comes in contact with almost every type of Pullman porter—the serious and the humorous, the stately and the unassuming, the distant and the familiar, the talkative and reserved." He mentioned what good entertainers some of them were, as well as noting the "standard" passenger collection for the Pullman-porters (usual contribution a quarter-dollar) at the end of the journey[222]—something George was no doubt aware of, which probably furnished him with his rationale for paying them so poorly.

Having attended to the key personnel that travelers on 19th century American railroads were likely to encounter during a railroad journey, let us now attend to several other factors pertaining to railroad travel in 19th century America—things which an English tourist would most likely have commented upon, either favorably or otherwise.

Discipline of the Passenger on 19th Century American Railroads

For much of the 19th century on American railroads passengers were never subject to the same disciplinary regimen the English companies established and maintained to keep the passenger (and indeed the railroad company servant) in order. The company regulations governing the conduct of American railroad servants were in most cases, and certainly where those of some prominent companies whose regulations I have looked at were concerned, not much different to those of their English counterparts; nor were the company regulations pertaining to the most fundamental aspects of administering and operating railroads safely too much different from the English counterparts, either. But the difference between the two national systems seems to have been in the application of the regulations, their enforcement, or consistency regarding either or both.

Allusion has already been made to the way in which "core" values of American society and culture percolated into railroading in America, lending the national style of railroading a character which fitted comfortably with the ideological dimension to the national "self-image"—a democracy where constraints on the individual were minimal. And despite the occasional bumptious and over-officious train conductor, the tendency was for managerial imposition, during railroad travel, to be minimal and primarily safety-oriented. But even then, many Americans would have subscribed to the view that if a man wanted to take an unnecessary risk during railroad travel and injured or killed himself consequently, then that was "his business" and the railroad company ought not to be held accountable for it.

In England, by way of comparison, the railroad company would have been expected to institute a disciplinary regime governing passenger travel which made it very difficult for the passenger to injure or kill himself. As Therese Yelverton noted of the American "character": "One very prominent feature in the American character is the love of hazard, (the) love of risk."[223] But this was not just because Americans were "congenitally" reckless or speculative; rather, it clearly had a lot to with American democracy—that, within certain limits, a man ought to be able to do as he pleased. And if he chose to jump off a train traveling at 40 miles per hour, then surely he had the right so to do, and it was his business. Indeed, in 19th century America we find some remarkable inhibitions where exercising constraint (over other people), or where the concept of "not minding other people's business," were concerned. For instance, in respect of the latter, consider the following extract from a New York State Senate Committee of Inquiry (in 1890) into why the Astors (who at that time had a very substantial New York real estate portfolio) were not paying the amount of tax on rents collected which they ought to have been:

> Q: (William Irvins): Don't you think that if you are going to levy a tax properly, you ought to be vested with the power to learn what the returns and revenues of that property are?
> A: (Michael Coleman, President of the Board of Assessments and Taxes): No.
> Q. (William Irvins): Have you the power to exact from them (the Astors) a statement of their rent rolls?
> A: (Michael Coleman): No, sir, it's none of our business.[224]

Similarly, one notes the response of Andrew Carnegie's lawyer when asked by a Congressional investigating committee in 1912 why Carnegie's U.S. Steel Company underestimated its holdings—he told the committee: "It was nobody else's business."[225]

Another reason why it may have been difficult to enforce railroad company regulations, even when there was the resolve so to do by senior management, was that it was often not easy to find people (especially in the West) prepared to do the kind of work in question—people amenable both to placing themselves under discipline and willing to discipline others.

America certainly was a land of opportunity in the 19th century. But working for wages was the first option for people lacking ambition, who had no capital, or otherwise had limited options open to them in the short term. Indeed, the independence and measure of individualism which came, for instance, with being a homesteader, a business owner, or entrepreneur were magnets for materially driven, independent, ambitious types. Where the railroads were concerned, and managerial roles aside, unless an engineman, a conductor (while the work was still perceived to be high status), or later a depot or station manager or agent (and thus the first to receive news through the telegraph wires, the "controller of time" through the Western Union midday "beeps," and often the postmaster, too), then there was nothing very glamorous about working on the railroad "all the live long day." And perhaps the unattractiveness of railroad work, and the transiency of many who did such work for a while, are testified to—in the example of most companies—by the fact that anybody who was hard-working, possessed of initiative, prepared to take responsibility, and had some "sticking power" could rise from a very menial to a very senior position, and perhaps quite quickly. For instance, in the early period many men rose from the position of brakeman to become enginemen and conductors (so long as they were not too uncouth where the latter role was concerned). But for those with "clerical" and "managerial" aptitudes the career pathways within many American railroad companies opened vast vistas of opportunity, and there are countless examples of men rising from lowly positions (perhaps the outstanding example being Andrew Carnegie) to the highest echelons of railroad company management in 19th century America.

The *Erie Railroad Company Regulations of 1854* stipulated: "An Enginemen shall allow no person to ride on his engine while it is hauling a train, or on the tender thereof, other than the proper persons."[226] But some enginemen let ordinary members of the public ride with them on the locomotive occasionally, perhaps proud to demonstrate their locomotive driving expertise. And I very much doubt this was an exceptional occurrence in the first few decades of American railroading. In fact, various allusions have already been made to travelers being permitted to ride on the locomotive or even on the cow-catcher—English tourist, Benjamin Curtis, traveling on the Kansas Pacific in the *mid–1870s*, was permitted by the locomotive driver to ride both in the locomotive cab and on the cow-catcher (to better take in the scenery through canyons in the case of the latter).[227]

If the discipline ruling the passenger on American railroads was perceived to be lax from the standpoint of an English tourist, then it may have been that the regulations were, too. But generally, they were not. Nor were they usually as indecipherable as the following railroad traffic rule in the state of Kansas might suggest: "When two trains approach each other at a crossing, both shall come to a full stop, and neither shall start up until the other has gone."[228]

English tourists were at first usually amazed to discover that people could wander, pretty much as they pleased, through the car, or even between cars. Many of them appreciated it, but they were surprised at the degree of freedom passengers had and the liberties they were sometimes permitted to take, bearing in mind that moving between the cars remained a reasonably dangerous venture until the advent of the vestibule. And when, finally, the railroads began to cross the plains, passengers could amuse themselves by shooting at buffalo and other wildlife from the windows.[229]

There were very well-run railroad companies in 19th century America, yet still democratic principle necessitated that the passenger not be unduly imposed upon, besides which out in the "Wild West" the enforcer might be shot. That aside, management was often relaxed, even when not remiss.

Furthermore, rules could be openly breached to accommodate the whim of a dignitary or somebody well-known to railroad company staff. For instance, after the Republican Convention in Springfield in May 1860, Abraham Lincoln was allowed to *drive* the train for a distance.[230] But Lincoln was well-known to Illinois railroad staff, as would have been other "circuit" men, such as lawyers, judges, politicians, preachers, salesmen, and entertainers. Andrew Carnegie, when he was a railroad executive, often rode in the locomotive cab and frequently slept on the floor of freight carriages.[231] Louis Gottschalk, too, was probably able to take a few liberties: "I know with my eyes shut every one of the inextricable cross-threads that form the network of the railroads with which New England is covered."[232]

Some important people had free passes on some railroads. Lincoln had a pass for the Illinois Central in 1858, having been appointed one of its attorneys shortly after its incorporation—his free pass said on it *Hon. A. Lincoln, Attorney*. Of course, any employee seeing his free pass would have garnered that he had a connection to the company in his capacity as an attorney.[233] And people who had free passes, as Lincoln did for several railroads at least, were usually afforded other liberties over and above free travel, aside from which, often, they were probably the only travelers who might expect some deference or service beyond the minimal from railroad company employees. These "liberties," which the free pass effectively legitimized, were not formally granted, but railroad company staff knew that if somebody had a free pass, then they had a "friend" high up in the railroad company, and one did not mess with such people. Lincoln often rode in the caboose of a train rather than in a passenger car, especially if he wanted to have a sleep. And if he missed his train or needed to go somewhere in a hurry, then he was often able to ride in the caboose of a freight train. He was no stranger to the footplate, either, as we have seen.[234] And clearly the Illinois Central's regulations would not have differed from the Erie"s, which stated that: "The engineman shall allow no person to ride on his engine while it is hauling a train, or on the tender thereof, other than the proper persons."[235]

The free pass system was used in the early 1870s—if not from an earlier date—to buy influence with public officials, from the highest judges down: "To say that no return was expected from this munificence is absurd. Even if direct services were not desired, it was intended that a frame of mind should be created which would prevent unfavorable treatment by the public officials."[236] Some people thought a free pass, once granted, was a permanent privilege (bribe?) and anybody who tried to take it off them could be asking for trouble. And that is precisely what W.H. Vanderbilt got when he terminated a Mr. Lloyd's free pass after William had taken over the Vanderbilt empire following the death of his father, Cornelius. But his father had given these passes to Lloyd for years, since Lloyd was the publisher of *Lloyd's Railway Guides*. Poor William Vanderbilt did not know what hit him after revoking Lloyd's free pass, for in the very next issue of *Lloyd's Railway Guide*—on the front cover, in fact—Lloyd placed an illustration of extreme accident carnage on the (Vanderbilt's) New York Central Railroad; and, lodged beside it, was a chronology of accidents and casualty figures in recent times for that railroad, as well as a picture of the railroad's owner, a certain Mr. W. H. Vanderbilt. Mr. Lloyd got his free pass back in the next mail, apparently.[237] But it must have been very disappointing for the free pass people when a railroad changed hands and the privilege vanished, although a change of management or fiscal tightening might have had the same outcome. On the other hand, a takeover or amalgamation could extend the range of travel the free pass availed its holder of.

The free pass was, indeed, "the *most elementary unit* for persuading and influencing people," as Oliver Jensen so nicely puts it.[238] However, Gustavus Myers was rather blunter in his assessment, describing the free pass as the most "common form of *bribery*," and especially effective for silencing media criticism of railroad companies. He also pointed out that Congress did not ban the free pass "culture" until 1906.[239] Of course, if a state or Federal Government politician could collect free passes from enough companies, then he could have free railroad travel over a very large part of America for himself and his family. And often the free pass travel privilege did extend to those traveling with its holder. The classic exemplar of this "extension" (abuse?) of the free pass facility was Ulysses Grant, who was known to have as many as 18 "hangers-on" riding with him on his free pass.[240] But there were other forms of bribery—of congressmen, senators, and state governors, for instance—which did not entail cash or stock payments. For instance, such people might be afforded use of the railroad company president's (luxurious) private car for a tour with their family and friends.

The Baggage Check System

One English tourist noted of American railroads: "If the baggage system, which is in operation everywhere in the States, was in vogue on our English railways, much annoyance and confusion at our railway stations would be done away with."[241] But the transit of baggage was one thing, the people physically handling it another. The American "baggage smasher" was a railroad company functionary and the nearest thing to an American counterpart to the English porter at the time—not that this American version of a porter normally did any more than lift your baggage off or onto the train, and only if he felt inclined so to do. The baggage-smashers were not just rude, but also extremely violent with peoples" baggage. Indeed, the baggage smashers became legendary. And I doubt there would have been a single English traveler in America before the 1880s who did not have a complaint about the physical aspect to baggage handling;

and most would have wondered why such an undisciplined person as the baggage smasher would be retained by a railroad company. Even Acworth, in his *Railways of England* (1890), could not help a scornful allusion to the American baggage smasher, referring to him sarcastically as "a recognized and appreciated institution" on American railroads.[242]

George Combe, an Englishman traveling in 1839, found that even on one of the best-managed American railroads baggage and packages were "thrown about and dashed against each other on the ground most recklessly." John Boddam-Whetham was relieved to get to Omaha in 1873 "without getting my baggage knocked entirely to pieces." T.S. Hudson thought, even in the early 1880s, that a traveling trunk needed to be strongly made because of the baggage smashers. And although baggage allowances were often quite generous,[243] they were not particularly advantageous if half your baggage was of a fragile or brittle quality and it was *mis*-handled by baggage smashers.

For years Omaha was, apparently, the "Head Office" of American baggage smashing. When John Boddam-Whetham arrived at the station: "There were several boxes laying about whose owners could only recognize them by their contents."[244] Englishman, Henry Lucy, traveling in 1883, observed that the porters treated each piece of baggage as if they owed it a personal grudge. But he thought that might have been a spiteful response to the fact that tipping was prohibited.[245] However, on the transcontinental route telegraphers sometimes had to double as baggage handlers—something which may have inspired *their* contempt for baggage.[246]

Anthony Trollope, who had some harrowing and disarming encounters with pushy and insolent Americans during his travels, probably had his most disconcerting encounter of all with a baggage smasher—the villain in question had managed to smash Trollope's precious portable writing desk. When Trollope complained to the man about this state of affairs, the baggage smasher laughed at him and said: "Ha, ha, ha!" However, Trollope claimed he never had to pay for excess baggage, and he thought the baggage check system for through passengers excellent[247]—English tourists were unanimous in their acclaim for this aspect of baggage handling and many thought it marvellous. However, just very occasionally there were problems with through baggage handling. The Scottish traveler, Henry Deedes, traveling in 1868, was unable to get redress for articles stolen from his baggage. And since he had passed over three railroads during the course of his journey, each company denied responsibility for his lost baggage, and each declared that such a thing could not possibly have happened on its railroad![248] This was one of the negative consequences of company cooperation with a view to effecting an efficient flow of through traffic—at least so long as there were no sufficient means for redress in respect of missing baggage. Indeed, since some companies could not care less that baggage was smashed around, it seems unrealistic to expect them to have cared very much that it should go missing occasionally, either, despite the usual efficiency of the through baggage system. At an earlier time (the mid–1840s), one English traveler said that not only was it common for baggage to be lost because it was put in the wrong car, but the cars themselves were sometimes put on the wrong line! And apart from having their baggage smashed, losing it could be a major problem for well-to-do women, since no reputable hotel would admit a woman without baggage.

Although baggage cars had been introduced as early as 1833, yet the companies had usually refused to accept responsibility for any baggage carried. This only began to change from about 1838 and only after some very well-publicized court cases.[249] Americans were generally compliant and put up with what they had to during railroad travel, but not so Cyrus McCormick, a prominent industrialist and obsessive litigant. He sued the New York Central for $20,000 damages following an altercation over an $8.75 overcharge on his wife's baggage. With the single-mindedness and ferocity of a pit bull he pursued the matter through three Supreme Court cases over 20 years, before finally winning his case against the railroad company.

The Through Travel Facility

Although in 1843 it became possible to travel by train, rather than along the Erie Canal, when traveling Albany- Buffalo, yet the "great leap forward" (a 30 hour journey) required travel on seven different railroads.[250] And it was not until 1853 that either a through baggage facility or through ticketing were available for this journey—Erastus Corning was the driving force behind the 1853 consolidation of all those fragmented little railroads to form the New York Central System, which benefited the passenger enormously:

> The detached roads, subsequently consolidated as the New York Central, were interrupted by breaks, which compelled passengers to change cars five or six times en route, and bound by such conditions regarding payment of *canal* tolls, as amounted to a virtual prohibition of the transportation of through freight.[251]

The reference to payment of canal tolls was in respect of their being levied on the railroad companies by the State of New York—for decades, it imposed this toll to offset the impact of railroads on its Erie Canal investment, and those tolls eventually paid for the canal and its maintenance. This measure was probably the most effective such measure taken anywhere in either America or Britain to protect canals against railroad competition.

In America before railroad networks had become quite extensive it was rare to be able to travel any great distance by means of railroad alone. For instance, to travel from Charleston to New Orleans in 1849 required three railroad journeys, then a 100-mile stagecoach journey, another short railroad journey, followed by either a steamboat or stagecoach journey, the last stretch (Mobile–New Orleans) a steamboat journey.[252]

But when it *was* possible to travel the entire distance by railroad on a long journey, yet that usually entailed travel on the lines of numerous railroad companies—on a journey of 240 miles in 1852 Horace Greeley found himself on five or six different railroads. And it could be very annoying changing cars at night, as Arthur Cunyghame had to do four times on a journey in 1850. However, during the 1850s some companies did cooperate and work hard to convenience "through" passengers. During that decade, the Boston and New York Express Line emerged, which was a joint venture of four companies, and it effected a very respectable 9-hour transit time for the 236-mile journey, and priced at a reasonable five dollars. By the mid–1860s it was possible to travel from the Atlantic coast to the Mississippi by a continuous line of railroad, the junctions of three railroads forming the continuous 1,200-mile line passing through five states—

New York, Pennsylvania, Ohio, Indiana, and Illinois—in a southwest direction.[253] And in 1875 Sydney Peddlar traveled around 1,000 miles (New York–Chicago) in 36 hours.[254] But such convenient means of through travel were the exception rather than the rule. Indeed, it had been a popular saying for decades that a hog could travel cross-country through Chicago without a car change, but a person could not.[255] And Peto (1866) remarked that one of the "great deficiencies" at that time was that "Scarcely any attempts are made to render the workings of lines convenient to travellers by working the trains of one company in conjunction with another."[256] Even as late as 1876 the New York–San Francisco journey required four transfers—three of them just to get started on the transcontinental railroad at Omaha.

But there were various reasons apart from fragmented railroad company ownership for the "fracturing" of the railroad through travel experience. For instance, it was not possible to take an unbroken journey by rail from Chicago to New Orleans before 1883 because the two operating companies concerned had different gauges (they were not rationalized until 1881). But even then it was only because one of the companies (the Illinois Central) took over the other (the Chicago, St. Louis and New Orleans) that an unbroken journey became possible for that route.[257] Yet, the broken journey was not necessarily bad news *for the tourist*. Englishman W.G. Marshall noted the convenience of being able to break long journeys, even at a whim, since the conductor—unless one had a "limited" ticket—could give you an endorsement on your ticket, or a "stop-over" check.[258] Likewise, William Ferguson, traveling in the northeast in 1854, found some convenience in the coupon-like ticket which enabled him to travel on eight railroads, as did Charles Weld, traveling 680 miles on the one ticket along numerous railroads in the same year. So, tourists could hop off the train somewhere, stay for a few days, and then continue their travels without having to acquire another ticket.

One might think "takeovers" would facilitate more efficient through travel, but that did not necessarily prove to be the case. In fact, through travel conditions could deteriorate as a consequence of a takeover, depending on how customer-focused the "new" entity was. Some of these corporations grew into big, clumsy, inefficient monsters, which were too hopeless and hapless to serve the public interest, even when their owners did acknowledge the existence of such a concept. And Ambrose Bierce was probably referring to through travel, at least partly, when he said of the Southern Pacific in 1888: "Let Leland Stanford remove his dull face from the U.S. Senate, and exert some of his boasted executive ability disentangling the complexities in which his frankly brainless subordinates have involved the movements of his trains."[259] Corporate rationalizations, at the economic and managerial levels, might have no effect whatsoever on through travel, since the major impediment to improving its "rationality" was gauge discrepancies. For instance, a journey between Charleston and Philadelphia (790 miles) in 1861 required eight carriage changes for precisely that reason.[260] And the gauge discrepancy problem meant that up until the 1880s at least, one could obtain an erroneous impression of coherency when looking at a map of a state's railroad "network." For instance, a map which showed that a state was ostensibly well-served by its railroad network may have had a certain fictional quality to it where traffic flow was concerned, due to gauge discrepancies, for instance. Even one of the more progressive railroad states, Pennsylvania, despite its impressive network at one time had only two of its many railroads running on the standard 4' 8.5" gauge, most of the others running on either 4'10" or 6' gauges.[261]

Another factor which might antagonize the would-be through passenger arose from the actions of interests hostile to railroad penetration of inner-city precincts. For instance, for quite a few years on the Erie railroad local carriers and cab drivers, in some localities along the route, had been powerful enough (as a lobby) to ensure that there was a four-block break between the connecting railroads, thus preserving their own pecuniary interests.[262] However, some state legislators did not help, either—for instance, for a long time the Erie Railroad's *own charter* forbade any connection of it with Pennsylvania and New Jersey railroads.

The companies had various ruses for enticing passengers to their long-haul lines when they faced competition from other companies. Percipient Englishman, T.S. Hudson, noted, when traveling in 1882, that companies graphically represented their own routes on their timetables as running very straight, whereas their competitors' lines were represented as relatively tortuous.[263] In 1893 seven companies catered for traffic between Chicago and St. Louis, five between Chicago and Cincinnati, and six between St. Paul and Kansas City. Furthermore, there was a total of 22 routes (direct or indirect) between Chicago and New York and 106 between New York and New Orleans.[264] So, the tourist could often be bamboozled by the numerous company and route options for traveling from one place to another, unless well-informed by some disinterested party as to the best option. In that connection, it is interesting to note that the management of the Baltimore and Ohio Railroad had initially taken so seriously the public interest, that it tried to come up with a formula (in 1832) for calculating the value (in dollar terms) of traveling time, for the "average" passenger, when looking at the merits of various prospective routes.[265]

Punctuality and the Slowness of American Trains

Some railroad companies in America, as in Britain, were legend for their lack of punctuality (and high accident rates, for that matter). But let us focus on the former—the DLW (the Delaware, Lackawanna and Western) was known colloquially as the "Delay, Linger and Wait."[266] William Ferguson, traveling in 1854, noted that his train left Baltimore *about* five: "They are not particular to a quarter of an hour." Traveling in the same year, Charles Weld waited two hours for his train to show up, but enquiries as to its whereabouts were impossible, since the telegraph was not working, either. Catherine Bates remarked that in America "an unpunctual train should be estimated by days, not hours." And in 1883 Henry Lucy observed that the lateness of American trains was (still) "truly continental," and he thought railroad men were laxer where long-haul journeys were concerned, since they could make up time. Indeed, he noted that this was the attitude concerning his Ogden-San Francisco (800 miles) train, the average speed of which on such a journey was just 20 miles per hour.

But "making up time" could be quite hair-raising for the passenger, as we have already noted. W.F. Rae was quite terrified when traveling on the transcontinental in

1869, when the engineman tried to make up for lost time by running "extra risks." Rae described the speed as producing "a sensation which cannot be reproduced in words." It was night, and he looked out the window as the very long train went around a curve, observing that the axle boxes were smoking and that the "red hot" wheels glowed like "discs of flame" in the darkness.

Catherine Bates, traveling in 1886, complained incessantly about the "extreme uncertainty and unpredictability of trains." And Emily Dickinson was either exercising poetic license to excess, or had been a very fortunate railroad traveler, to be able to describe the American train in a poem as "punctual as a star"[267]—perhaps this was a poetic joke, the import of which completely missed the critics! Henry Williams insisted in the mid–1870s that "The Pennsylvania Railroad is always on time."[268] And Arthur Cunyghame, traveling from Niagara to Buffalo in 1850, experienced the "ultimate punctuality"—his train taking off a quarter of an hour early, leaving 40 passengers behind in what was, apparently, a ruse to strand people at Niagara for an extra night for the benefit of hoteliers[269] (whom, one might reasonably assume were very closely connected to enginemen, firemen, conductors, and station personnel).

Breakdowns and derailments were not at all uncommon in the first 50 years of American railroading, either. One English traveler in the late 1830s recalled all the passengers being requested to leave the cars to help push the broken-down train backwards for one-third of a mile. The English tourist in America could appreciate that misadventure might occasionally result in a train being late. But Anthony Trollope, for one, was at a loss to explain why people put up with poor service in America, observing that in England there would be an outcry if the lateness of trains, and thus the inefficient transmission of mail, was similarly all but institutionalized.[270] Indeed, what amazed English travelers, who had usually known about the unreliability of American railroads before setting foot in the country, was the stolid forbearance of American travelers— a point to be addressed shortly. Indeed, punctuality seemed hardly to be valued at all in America, at least where travel was concerned. And that was an affront to English bourgeois sensibility, since as *Martine's Hand Book of Etiquette* (1865) made clear, punctuality was one of the characteristics of politeness.[271] In fact, failing to be punctual was a "grave social offence." But Americans sometimes found that the "punctual" English railroads were mythical beings, too. Horace Greeley insisted (in the late 1850s) that English trains could not be relied upon for punctuality.[272]

American trains were notoriously slow. And what better way to begin to account for that phenomenon than with a contemporary joke:

> I said: "Conductor, what have we stopped for now?"
> He said: "There are some cattle on the track."
> We ran a little further and stopped again.
> I said: "What is the matter now?"
> He said: "We have caught up with those cattle again."

Around 1840 the average speed on all American railroads—including stops, which were often frequent—was about 15 miles per hour.[273] In 1860 a train could operate at 20 miles per hour for half the cost of being run at 30 miles per hour, while faster speed also meant more wear and tear on locomotives, rolling stock, track and bridges—in fact, it required heavier rails, stronger bridges, and a straighter line.[274] As late as 1887 the New York Central's fastest train averaged just over 40 mph, which offered almost no improvement on the schedule offered some 35 years earlier on the same run by the Hudson River Railroad.[275]

But, as in England, American trains were sometimes run slowly to calculatedly inconvenience people. Indeed, half a century after the advent of railroads in America freight trains were deliberately being delayed or run at snail's pace to force shippers to pay the exorbitant rates demanded for shipping over the Merchant's Dispatch, a fast freight line owned by the Vanderbilt family.[276]

Time Standards on 19th Century American Railroads

T.S. Hudson complained of American railroads in 1882 that "a great source of inconvenience" was "the foolish arrangement of clocks."[277] It was a problem in Britain, too, although there the Railway Clearing House was recommending the use of Greenwich Meantime to its members as early as 1847. However, in America multiple time standards persisted for decades, there being a three-hour difference from one side of the continent to the other and no attempts to rationalize all of these discrepant time standards. Even the Federal Government seemed to have no real interest in the problem, while the public, for its part, was either apathetic on the matter or defended its local time standard as if it were a holy relic. As for the railroad companies, Mencken suggests during the 1870s inter-company rivalry was probably the main factor militating against the idea of standardizing time.

In America in the early period the observance of different time standards may not have been especially problematic, at least not until scheduled long-haul railroad services came into being. However, these different time standards could be very perplexing for travelers, and especially for tourists, whom they usually managed to bamboozle. And for many travelers "transfers," often entailing fathoming different time standards in accordance with multiple station clocks, were just one more of the "punches" they received as they ran the gauntlet of a long-haul American railroad journey. But it was just a matter of time before the issue became as crucial as the gauge standardization perplexity—the possibility of an efficient *national* railroad system unrealizable until both problems had been resolved.[278] However, in America the situation must have been considerably exacerbated (for the passenger) by the fact that trains so often did not run on time.

The undisputed champion in the cause of rationalizing local time standards in America was Charles Dowd—the kind of person who pops up in every society from time to time, takes an issue by the scruff of the neck, and refuses to let go of it. He began his campaign for national time standards in 1870, promoting his ideas at railroad conventions as well as lobbying politicians, scientists, and others. He received a lot of publicity for his scheme, since the media was generally quite supportive of it. But it was not until 1883 that the American Railway Association bowed to common sense, Dowd's scheme by then also having the support of the American Society of Civil Engineers, the American Association for the Advancement of Science, and the American Meteorological Society.[279]

The American System of Railroad Construction

At this point, something more ought to be said, albeit briefly, about the "American system" of railroad construction and its implications both for passenger safety and passenger comfort. Indeed, travelers on American railroads in the 19th century often had good cause for anxiety and fear. We have noted the American obsession with "comfort engineering," which might seem ironic and anomalous when it is realized that countless railroads in 19th century America were engineered and constructed in a way inimical to the quest for comfort, not to mention safety.

Nevertheless, by 1845 American passenger cars were probably more comfortable than the English counterpart because of their architectural peculiarities. For a start, they were up to 80 feet in length by then and thus more spacious, whereas most English carriages at the time seldom exceeded 30 feet. Furthermore, the American cars were perched on six (and sometimes eight, and later as many as twelve), as against the four wheels of the smaller English carriages. The longer cars also enabled the application of wheel and spring technology which considerably reduced lateral oscillation, pitching, and hard vibrations. However, the Americans often undermined these advantages (of long-car architecture) by constructing shoddy, sub-standard lines of railroad. By 1845 the Danes and Germans, by comparison, had effectively combined long-carriage architecture *and quality track design*.[280]

I suggested earlier that the "democratization" of American railroad travel in the 19th century was a "value" which harmonized with the interests of parsimonious American railroad capitalists, and that it was so in respect of both cheap construction and the general provision of a standardized type of car. Many 19th century American railroads were hastily and poorly constructed, and notoriously unsafe—occasionally newspapers advised people against traveling on certain railroads, or advised them to avoid certain sections of a railroad. A railroad in Kentucky in 1840, for instance, was said to be so badly made that recourse to horses was necessary: "The road has fallen into such disrepute that its receipts are but barely sufficient to keep it up."[281]

Mencken argues that American railroad travelers had more cause for anxiety than their English counterparts, since they were more aware of the roadbed, which on many poorly constructed American railroads jolted and jarred them incessantly. Apart from bumpy grades, there were often sharp curves as well, which could have quite a violent effect on the motion of the carriages when combined with erratic changes in grade.[282] Thomas Nichols remarked: "Nothing in England *strikes an American with more surprise* than the smooth, solid, admirable (rail) roads over the whole island."[283]

The author of an 1873 American newspaper article concurred: "The English railroads are built with more care, solidity and finish than are the American, excepting perhaps some short lines connecting the leading cities of the New England states with New York.... The Englishman builds not only for himself and children, but for his heirs."[284] Indeed, Therese Yelverton said of American railroad construction: "They build their railroads to carry them, perhaps, as long as they live, if they do not live too long. Thus, throughout the country, wherever wooden sheds can be run up to serve for the time, not a decent station is ever made."[285] The American, Edward Dorsey, asserted

(1887): "Our system of rushing the road through, and completing it afterwards *at leisure times*, is not practised there (England)."[286]

When, in the early period in America, the railroads were built by the states, then they were generally of better quality than the privately constructed railroads, notwithstanding that numerous railroad projects arising from the "grand splurges" (the grandiose state internal development programs of the 1830s/1840s) were initially characterized by poor construction. Nevertheless, the experience of Englishman, J. S. Buckingham, accounts for a phenomenon which might have been generalizable at the time (around 1840): "The railroad from Philadelphia to Lancaster is a work of the state, well executed, and deemed perfectly safe. From Lancaster to Harrisburg it is the property of a private company, and has been so badly constructed that accidents are continually happening on it."[287]

During the 19th century Americans hardly ever (and only in the case of some outstanding exceptions) defended the relative quality of their railroad track construction against the English counterpart. In America, it was almost universally recognized that the English railroads were generally of a superior construction and "finish," and that they constituted a "permanent way" in every sense of the term. But there was method underlying the American's perceived madness where railroad construction was concerned. Indeed, Americans rationalized the difference between their own and the English style of construction on their own terms, which often made some sense, even though the "rationalizations" inevitably encapsulated the remarkable American propensity to convert vices into virtues. Indeed, "safety" was sometimes relegated or overlooked in such expedient rationalizations of the American system of construction.

Having said that, some very well-informed English people, too, fully understood why Americans built comparatively shoddy railroads. The American system was rationalized by English engineer Douglas Galton, for instance, in 1857 as follows: "A rough and ready cheap railway, although it entails increased costs for maintenance, is preferable to a more finished and expensive line. Any saving in the cost per mile of a railway adds to the means available for extension."[288] Galton, an officer of the English Board of Trade and an inspector of railroads in Britain, though acknowledging here that American railroads were not up to the standard of the English counterpart, nevertheless thought they were "sufficient," even "justified" in some cases for the purposes they served at the time of their construction.[289]

Furthermore, an article in an English newspaper the same year, written by another English engineer, asserted that a "working" American line, no matter what its condition, could command a sale of its bonds in the market. The article's author also claimed it was "only upon two or three leading lines that *permanence of construction* in bridges, stations, etc." has been "partially attempted"; that few lines were thoroughly ballasted; that rails were generally "below a fair average quality"; that dislocation of the road bed was aggravated by being worked for years without ballast and with a minimum expenditure for repairs; that on most lines rolling stock was deficient in quality; and that many companies penetrated large cities and built termini near their centers, but had failed to acquire contiguous space for expansion.[290] However, he understood the (economic) rationales underlying all these deficits.

If the Americans seldom defended their railroad construction as being comparable to an English standard, yet they did not necessarily think the English railroad superior in other respects: "In all matters relating to the construction of railroads and stationhouses, we can learn everything from Great Britain. But in all matters relating to the *operation* of railroads, absolutely nothing."[291] This (1867) appraisal was, of course, very debatable, but its argument was focused upon the relative "democratization" of American railroad travel and its implications for the passenger.

Where construction in the early period was concerned, the English spent $179,000 per mile (partly owing to the high cost of land, legal costs, and the relatively high costs for route surveying and engineering), yet few American railroad companies 1830–60 spent more than $20,000-$30,000 per mile. And by 1850 Britain was spending $200,000 per mile compared to U.S. spending of $40,769 per mile. The economy of the American railroads was effected by, apart from all the other factors alluded to, hitherto, expedient railroad surveying and engineering, which meant building along the natural contours of the land (around and over hills), thus avoiding building tunnels or expensive cuts and fills.[292]

An English newspaper article in 1879 asserted of American railroad track: "The rails would start from their socket, and the sleepers jump from their beds, were one of our express trains to go over them at its usual fifty miles per hour." The author also referred to the American passengers" "racking worry and ceaseless nervous irritation, to which they are subjected when journeying over their badly-made lines of railroad."[293] American railroad construction was sometimes appallingly bad, which could indeed make for rough journeys. But they were made even rougher in the early period by the fact the cars had no springs, and no doubt some companies kept such cars in service until they all but rattled to pieces.

Much of the "fast tracking" in the West later (especially that associated with the first transcontinental railroad) resulted in very shoddy railroads, which gave "rodeo" rides to the passengers as a bonus Western experience! And, like the bucking steer, the "bucking train" not uncommonly threw the passenger right off the "seat." The English travelers in America were clearly not used to such rough riding, which is why so many of them commented on it. But most Americans had no doubt habituated to it, perhaps many never having experienced anything different, thus thinking all railroads had the "bucking bronco" syndrome to some extent or other. Frances Kemble's little daughter had been "jolted off her seat every quarter of an hour by the uneasy motion of the carriage" in the late 1830s.[294] But even in 1871 James MacAulay found the "jumping and jolting" on many lines "terrible." And John Boddam-Whetham, traveling on the Chicago, Burlington and Quincy two years later, found the line "so rugged with ups and downs that it was a wonder how we kept on the rails at all." Catherine Bates declared of some American railroads that "You could not open your mouth without the chance of the teeth being shaken down your throat by the terrible jolting." Erastus Corning, one of the Central Pacific's executives at the time of its construction, was said to have received such a jolting ride on the railroad that it seriously injured his spine.[295] In fact, the jolting passengers received on many early American railroads was said to be "inexpressibly tiring and even distressing, to produce headaches, and to cause an incessant itching of the skin"[296]—presumably the latter had a neurological cause. And on some American railroads, almost unbelievably, rails had occasionally come loose and snaked up through the carriage floor, sometimes transfixing a passenger in the most gruesome fashion.[297]

As Peto (1866) pointed out, American railroad company directors and shareholders were deluding themselves if they thought economizing on construction costs would put more money in shareholders' pockets. Peto noted that in 1866 the cost of "working" a railroad line in America was considerably more than double what it was in England. In fact, his statistical sources, which we can rely upon, showed, when the figures were "broken down," that expenditure on maintenance of the way in America was 300 percent higher than what it was in England; that the cost of locomotive power was 250 percent greater than it was in England; and that the cost of rolling stock maintenance and replacement was almost 400 percent what it was in England. The latter was largely attributed to its quantity being insufficient and thus overworked, while track of inferior quality added to such premature wear and tear on rolling stock. Hence, an "undue and excessive proportion" of what operating profits there were had to be dedicated to putting right such deficiencies, which considerably diminished the returns that would otherwise be enjoyed by the shareholders.[298]

But some companies had always strived to be the exception where shoddy construction and shoddy service were concerned, the Pennsylvania Railroad Company being one of them. William Hardman asserted of its line between Chicago and New York: "There is no finer example of railway construction and management than that *portion* of the line between Pittsburgh and New York."[299] Lady Hardy concurred (she was there at around the same time), declaring the Pennsylvania's lines had a reputation as the smoothest, as well as the company having the best "ordinary" cars. But she thought the Chicago and North Western, which she took to Omaha, was also of a very high standard in the same respects.[300] Yet, as Mencken pointed out, even allowing for the roughest of rides on 19th century American railroads, at its worst the railroad usually made for a smoother ride than the stagecoach ever had.[301]

The Uncomplaining American

Mencken, in noting that American railroad travelers seldom complained about anything, thought this was because they so appreciated the "privilege" of speed, that discomfort, inconvenience, poor service, and risks were small prices to pay for its realization.[302]

The companies were sometimes willing to cooperate with each other when it came to economies or profit enhancement, but public convenience was another matter. In fact, it was not until the period of Federal Control (1918–20) that a federal agency with the necessary muscle went in "to bat" for the passenger and, indeed, for the railroad company employee. During that era terminals and booking offices were rationalized, so that passengers could catch different companies' trains at a single terminal and make bookings on different companies' lines from a single booking office.[303] And who knows how long the existing state of affairs might have prevailed had there not been Federal Government intervention at that point? In fact, during that brief period of Federal Control (of American railroads) the companies were "beaten up" as if vengeance was being exacted on account of their long-suffering passenger (and employee) victims of the previous eight decades!

I think many of the complaints about American railroads made by English tourists in the 19th century had some foundation; and perhaps American consumers did put up with more than they ought to have from penny-pinching railroad companies, often guided by "primitive" concepts of both the consumer and service. Yet, despite everything English travelers on American railroads had to complain about—and did, in fact, complain about in their published travel logs—perhaps what irked them most was the apathy of American railroad consumers, especially concerning sub-standard railroad construction, unsafe railroads, inadequate safety measures and procedures, reckless operation of trains; unhelpful and rude railroad servants, and poor service generally. George Combe, traveling in 1839, experienced numerous mishaps and inconveniences while traveling on railroads, and was frequently amazed at just what a stoical lot the American public were: "Not an angry or discontented voice was heard. Even people who had appointments missed bore the disappointment with good humour."[304]

However, to be fair to the Americans, if they were uncomplainingly stoic, yet perhaps by comparison the Victorian English bourgeois railroad traveler was relatively brittle, bumptious, and self-righteous. Indeed, one could argue that the well-to-do English travelers in America were, by and large, a cantankerous, conceited lot who expected too much and too unreasonably for their money. Indeed, the author of an 1879 *English* newspaper article made a very good point when addressing the Englishman's incessant and querulous complaining about English railroads at the time: "These indefatigable gentlemen, who are so constantly writing to the leading journals to complain of 'railway unpunctuality,' and what not, should pause to consider what the state of things might be here had we a Tweed or a Vanderbilt at the head of railway affairs."[305] Fair comment, indeed. Furthermore, perhaps, English critics of *American* railroads often did not allow sufficiently for the national style of American railroading; predicated, as it was, on a peculiar American value system.

Nevertheless, if American individualism was often characterized by a certain assertiveness, even aggression when harnessed to the materialistic drive or in resistance to governmental or other constraints; yet, it seemed rather reticent and enfeebled, if not pathetic, when it came to complaining about the poverty of service and amenities on American railroads. Perhaps what this tells us, aside from anything else, is that "individualism" has "multiple personalities," and that it is certainly a much more complex phenomenon than even one of its foremost "analysts," Alexis de Tocqueville, understood to be the case. There again, one might concede that the (corporate) power of the American railroad companies disparaged complaint, while the frontier hardiness and dour "getting along" mentality of the Americans—allegedly imprinted upon the national DNA—rendered them stoical "Buddhas" and thus well above the lowly realm of complaint.

Also relevant is the fact that, compared to English railroads, the American railroads were considerably under-regulated for decades. So, it was often *not* the case that the consumer could point to some rule or regulation which the railroad company might be in breach of *in law*, and thus be able to lodge a complaint with a "Board of Trade" or some similar regulatory agency, which would then investigate and impose a sanction against the company, if merited. Apart from which it was well-known that in many states the railroad companies "owned" the judicial system at every level, as well as often being able to influence media opinion. Furthermore, both the Senate and Congress were invariably crawling with leeches and toadies who served as mouthpieces for the railroad interests. Indeed, those (railroad company) interests were often inimical to the "public interest," while the public's elected representatives often could not serve both the corporations and the public—after all, the public did not pay you enough (relatively) to consistently exercise your vote on its account, whereas the railroad companies usually paid you handsomely to exercise it on theirs! That said, some sections of the media could not be bought off by the railroad companies, and served as potent gadflies against their designs.

But perhaps the final words on this matter might go to two Englishmen. Arthur Cunynghame said that Americans *did* scruple to complain, though usually to each other, and in a "secret manner," or *anonymously* in the newspapers; whereas "an Englishman will never hesitate to *openly* condemn such (poor service) practices"—an 1889 etiquette work advised its American readers to never grumble about the travel discomforts that fall to every traveler's lot, nor make comparisons. And, secondly, as English tourist, John Boddam-Whetham, remarked: "A great many improvements, both on board ship and on land, are due to a little good-natured grumbling."

Five

The Safety of Railroad Travel in 19th Century England and America

> Years ago, it was officially announced in France that people were less safe in their own houses than while traveling on the railroads; and in support of this somewhat startling proposition, statistics were produced, showing fourteen cases of death of persons remaining at home, and there falling over carpets, or, in the case of females, having their garments catch fire, to ten deaths on the rail. Even the game of cricket counted eight victims to the railroad's ten.
> —Charles Adams Jr.[1]

Introduction

In the early period railroad speed was an object of concern for many. Such concern extended from the presumed physiological and mental (cognitive, psychological, and psychiatric) disorders speed itself might facilitate to the widely-held belief (in the early period) that a "mobile boiler," speeding along a flimsy track, must inevitably result in multi-fatality disasters, at least occasionally.

The perception of railroad speed by contemporaries is an interesting subject. Indeed, if railroad speed initially perturbed many people, yet it did not take long for it to become habituated to and routinized in consciousness, or for it to become embedded "ecstatically" in the (economic) "millennialism" railroad development engendered in the 19th century. However, here I attend to numerous factors, apart from speed, pertaining to railroad traveling health and safety in the 19th century; and I consider, as well, just how safe railroad travel in the 19th century was in both England and America, but also when considered in broader historical (transportation) context.

The Railroad and Human Health

For now, let us proceed to consideration of what were anticipated, by some, to be the likely effects of railroads upon human health. In fact, the advent of railroads occasioned a raft of opinion concerning their anticipated effects on human health. Some such opinion fell into the category of reasonable conjecture, given the state of medical and scientific knowledge at the time, while other such opinion was ridiculous and proven to be so, either by contemporaries or posterity.

One medical expert predicted that sound reverberations associated with railroad travel could be seriously detrimental to human health. That, in fact, the noise of the train, when traveling under arches or through tunnels at 30 miles per hour, would be a great shock to the nerves of delicate people.[2] Indeed, the advent of railroad travel roughly coincided with certain theoretical developments concerning the human nervous system and its pathology.

In the 17th century there had developed a medical philosophy that anchored "sensation" to the spinal column and linking mind and body through the science of "neurologic." Hence, there emerged subsequently a plethora of medical diagnoses relating to "nerves" as the physiological basis for numerous ailments.[3] One such (prominent) theory in the 19th century was that encapsulated in the concept of "neurasthenia," a medical concept and theory associated with Dr. George M. Beard. The symptoms Beard associated with neurasthenia included fatigue, headaches, neuralgia, anxiety, depression, dyspepsia, poor concentration, uterine irritability, and even impotence. He thought its primary cause depletion of the energy reserves of the central nervous system in the brain or spinal cord and comparable to the way in which anemia depleted blood. And, somewhat ahead of his time, he considered it to be an affliction of "modern civilization," especially concerning the sudden increase in the tempo of life. Today, we might call this "stress." And it probably did become more widespread because of the advent of railroads. The term neurasthenia apparently took hold, one magazine editor describing it in 1888 as "almost a household word."[4] In the early 1880s railroad traveling was associated with the condition, the timetable itself viewed as a source of anxiety, ultimately giving rise to adverse neurological effects. But neurasthenia was especially associated with long-distance train travel and with people whom, through the course of their employment (not just railroad workers, but also commercial travelers and the like), spent a lot of time on trains.[5]

But even before Beard's concept of neurasthenia took hold, surgeon Alfred Smith, in an 1847 book, had suggested that "nervous disorders" had taken the place of fevers in their social prevalence; suggesting, furthermore, that quite possibly two-thirds of "civilized society" was afflicted to some extent. However, he did not view this condition (stress, effectively) as especially novel, arguing instead that whereas previously the condition had been "confined to the higher ranks" (a "symptom" of affluence, in other words), yet it had subsequently become more socially diffuse as society and most people's lifestyles were quite rapidly and dramatically transformed[6]; and he would have implicated the advent of railroads, either directly or indirectly, in its prevalence.

Another body of fears pertained to railroad *speed* itself. But we today would not consider "racing along" at 20 to 30 miles per hour very speedy. However, it was otherwise at the time of the advent of railroads, when even the fastest coaches were hard-pressed to do 15 miles per hour, let alone maintain it for any distance. And if being on the back of a galloping horse was faster, yet the horse could keep up such a pace for only a relatively short distance.

During locomotive trials near Baltimore in 1830 the newspapers were full of conjecture as to what effects traveling at a sustained speed of *13 miles per hour* might have on human physiology.[7] And no doubt this was one dimension to discussions at the

Rainhill Trials in England, too, where the locomotives were running at twice that speed. In fact, at that time some medical men predicted railroad speed could constitute such a shock for pregnant women that it might induce miscarriage. But it was not just *passengers* thought likely to be affected so by such "shocks"—miscarriages were thought also likely to be suffered by both women *by-standers* and livestock consequent upon the "sudden, formidable appearance of a locomotive."[8]

During the early period, other medical "experts" were predicting that passengers on speeding trains would be getting too much air. In fact, around 1830 a group of London scientists was seriously considering the possibility that passengers on trains exceeding 30 miles per hour might be suffocated.

But railroad speed was anticipated to have a raft of more general health consequences. Granville, an influential voice in the English medical establishment at the time of the advent of railroads, pronounced:

> A speed of 20 or 30 miles an hour must affect delicate lungs, that to such as are of a consanguineous nature, and labor under the fullness of blood in the head (read high blood pressure), the movement of railroad trains will produce apoplexy (read stroke); that the sudden plunging into darkness is of a vitiated kind, and must give rise to the worst effects; and at the bottom of cuttings, being necessarily damp, will occasion catarrh and multiply agues (fevers).[9]

But this was, of course, nonsense.

Another theorist of "railroad-induced disorders," a German doctor, anticipated that speeding trains would induce a novel *psychiatric* disorder (delirium furiosum) in some passengers.[10] One American, influential enough to have his views published (in America), predicted profound *psychological* effects as a result of people experiencing extreme railroad speed, two of which would be "mendacity" and "flightiness of intellect," since he thought people would, consciously or otherwise, generalize and exaggerate their "munificent notions of distance."[11]

But railroad conveyance *vibrations* were expected to be seriously detrimental to the brain, too, interfering with brain physiology and function, and, ultimately, resulting in brain damage in the worst cases. Hence, in the early days of railroading it was widely-recommended by some medical experts that railroad passengers use a foot cushion to offset the effects of "vibration."[12]

However, there is no evidence railroad travel itself ever directly induced any detrimental nervous condition, let alone psychological or psychiatric disorders, even if, until it was habituated to, it may have induced a certain degree of anxiety, flustered some people, and contributed something to the stress of modern life.

According to another medical expert, traveling through tunnels would make people more susceptible to common colds, inflammation of the lungs, rheumatism, lumbago, and erysipelas (a contagious infection of the skin).[13] One gentleman, who obviously took such warnings seriously, had stations built at both ends of a series of tunnels on his property, so that he did not have to ride through the tunnels.[14]

But not all medical opinion was negative. One medical man, in contrasting the therapeutic benefits of coach as against railroad travel, concluded that the latter was more salubrious. He contended that railroad travel "equalizes" the circulation, promotes digestion, tranquilizes the nerves, and facilitates sound sleep the night following. Moreover, he suggested:

> The railroads bid fair to be a powerful remedial agent in many ailments to which the civic and metropolitan inhabitants are subject; and, to thousands of valetudinarians in the metropolis, the ride to Tring (a countryside destination) and back, twice or three times a week, would prove a means of preserving health, and prolonging life, more than all the drugs in Apothecaries Hall.[15]

But that was nonsense, too. Railroad excursions were often to the seaside or into the countryside, and for many metropolitan inhabitants that would have made for a healthy outing, especially since around mid-century many large English cites—as well as large industrial cities in America, Pittsburgh being the notorious example—had extremely serious air pollution problems. And perhaps it was the case that for the inhabitants of such cities a sojourn in the sea or country air did have some short-term health benefits. But to suggest that the railroad journey en route to such destinations could itself be restorative is stretching the imagination somewhat.

For my purposes here, what is noteworthy is that in the early period the railroad was associated ideologically with health and wellbeing regardless of whether a positive or negative "spin" was put on that association. Yet, setting aside accidents—to be discussed in due course—perhaps there were only two respects in which railroad travel could directly impact upon human health. One relates to the fact that in the early period, and especially so on the narrower gauge railroads, passengers could experience something akin to seasickness, since carriages could sway incessantly and quite dramatically.[16] Secondly, and more significantly, the greater extent of personal mobility facilitated by the advent of railroads assisted the spread of epidemic and other contagious conditions (if only the common cold and influenza), though tuberculosis, for instance, "benefited greatly" from the vast increase in travel brought by trains and steamboat navigation.[17] However, during the earliest period there was the possibility that people with pre-existing respiratory problems may have had such conditions aggravated by smoke from the locomotive, while sometimes hot embers descended into open carriages, resulting in minor burns.

Railroads and Industrial Accident Shock

Another interesting conjecture concerning the relationship between the advent of railroad passenger travel and health is of somewhat more recent origin. Wolfgang Schivelbusch has argued that "shell shock" can be viewed as a successor to the railroad accident shock of the 19th century, since in both cases the victims are physically traumatized by a sudden and violent release of energy, but without being demonstrably damaged in the physical sense. Schivelbusch's is an acceptable contention as far it goes, although one might want to make a distinction here between "shock"—where often no *physical trauma is indicated at the time of the event*, although there is some evident psychological distress—and "post-traumatic stress disorder" (PTSD), where the *effects of the shock* are supposedly latent (sometimes considerably so), while significant and distressing psychological (or even psychiatric) symptoms may become manifest eventually. However, I shall not pursue that distinction here, since it is not crucial to my argument.

The argument that shell shock can be viewed as a successor to the railroad accident shock of the 19th century may be misleading. In fact, it seems to me Schivelbusch has things the wrong way around, since gunpowder, cannons, and large explosions, and, therefore, shell shock resulting from the use of such powerful technologies, had been around for centuries prior to the advent of railroads.

That point aside for the moment, Schivelbusch describes shock as "The kind of sudden and powerful event of violence that disrupts the continuity of an artificially/mechanically created motion or situation, and the subsequent state of derangement." According to Schivelbusch, the precondition for this is a highly developed general state of dominance over nature, both technically and psychically.[18] Furthermore, the degree of control over nature, and the violence of the collapse of such control in the event of "shock," are considered by Schivelbusch to be proportionate: "The more finely meshed the web of mechanization, discipline, the division of labor, etc., the more catastrophic the collapse when it is disrupted from within or without." This overlaps somewhat with another characterization of shock where railroads are concerned:

> Cultivating a capacity to react to overwhelming stimuli forces the individual to intensify awareness. This intensification arises from the need to react to stimuli perceived as "shocks"—the greater the proportion of the "shock" factor in particular impressions, the more consciousness has to be alert as a screen against stimuli.[19]

Hence, by this view the novelty of railroad travel could be viewed as entailing an overstimulation of the nervous system (stress), which might have negative physical or mental consequences.

In either characterization of shock (above) we can accept the conjecture, despite the level of generality it is cast at, and the emphasis on artificially/mechanically created motion in the situation (where Schivelbusch's theory is concerned), notwithstanding that having your leg bitten off by a shark at a supposedly safe swimming beach, for instance, might be slightly shock-inducing as well.

One of the "logical" problems with Schivelbusch's definition of "shock" is that he builds the cause (the sudden and powerful event of violence that disrupts) into the consequence or "symptom" (the subsequent state of derangement). Hence, both cause and effect are described as "shock." Nevertheless, Schivelbusch is correct in identifying the key characteristic of the (industrial) accident shock (in symptomatic terms) as the evident traumatizing of the victim in the absence (though not necessarily so) of any conspicuous signs of injury. However, not only does Schivelbusch seem to have left quite a bit out in his analysis—by implying that the "shock-inducing" railroad accident was the first type of industrial "shock" experienced by people—he also traces a logically tortuous line of descent from the industrial railroad shock to the military "shell-shock."

The truth is medical-industrial "shock" was well-known to medical men *before* the railroad age. And although Schivelbusch discusses some of the prevailing theories of shock at the time railroads emerged, yet he still wants to say there was something historically unique about the railroad accident shock. As a matter of fact, the "phenomenology" of shock became important shortly after the advent of railroads in a legal as well as a medical point of view, since seriously detrimental medical effects experienced in the event of an industrial accident, but with no conspicuous signs of physical trauma, raised legal questions concerning compensation for the victims, regardless of whether the victim was a factory operative or a railroad passenger.

Indeed, the kind of industrial shock Schivelbusch would have us believe was unique to the railroad accident victim was already a well-recognized medical condition at the time the railroads commenced operations, and had been known for at least two decades before that date. So, it is somewhat surprising that Schivelbusch's contentions, in this connection, have apparently gone unchallenged. In fact, a *Times* reporter had, well before the advent of railroads, commented upon the phenomenon, even if he lacked a word to adequately encapsulate it, when describing men who are "blown up by steam"— the victims would walk about for a few minutes, "apparently almost unhurt, though, in fact, mortally injured."[20] And it is worth pursuing this matter here—to a point, at least.

We might begin by attending to the Felling Colliery explosion in 1812, which was probably the biggest explosion in Britain attributable to a non-military cause up until that time. The explosion was heard four miles away, the tremors felt half a mile away, a cloud of dust rose into the air to form the shape of an "inverted cone," the dust eventually settling to cover the ground for up to a mile and a half away, and it fell so thick on the ground that footsteps were imprinted in it, while some places in the vicinity experienced "a darkness" from the dust cloud akin to twilight. Some of those who survived the explosion succumbed, nevertheless, though apparently not from physical injury, but from "shock."[21]

More to the point, perhaps, one of the most famous railroad accidents in history— at the opening of the Liverpool and Manchester Railway—itself establishes the fact industrial shock was already a well-known medical phenomenon at the time. William Huskisson's death, due to the accident concerned, was, it seems, the first fatality on a fully operational commercial locomotive railroad in Britain. Now let me just briefly establish some key premises to my argument here. Firstly, we ought to note that immediately after the accident (Huskisson's leg was mangled after being run over by a locomotive), at its scene, Huskisson was attended by Dr. Southey (a physician to King George IV), Dr. Hunter (a professor of anatomy at Edinburgh), and one other (no doubt eminent) doctor. Observers at the scene noted that Huskisson did not feel any pain for about a minute after the accident—clearly, he was in a state of shock. He was then removed by rail to a place called Eccles, where he was attended by four more prominent medical men, including one Dr. Whatton, whom eventually concluded that Huskisson had died not of his physical injuries, but of (industrial) *shock*. Yet, how could he reach such a conclusion if industrial accident shock was unknown at the time? His conclusion is evident in his report to the Duke of Wellington. In it he stated: "He died in consequence of loss of blood, *and from the shock sustained by the constitution.*" He went on to say: "It was not possible, under *so severe a shock* upon the nervous system, to recruit his strength." Furthermore, at a subsequent inquiry the medical team which had attended Huskisson at Eccles defended its failure to amputate the mutilated leg because, it argued, it was always "*essential to wait until the patient had recovered from the initial shock* (before amputation was attempted)."[22] Clearly, the phenomenon of industrially-caused medical shock was well-known to medical men at the time (1830). Therefore, the "railroad accident shock" was not the first instance of industrial shock known.[23]

Tunnels

There was extensive debate about the health risks of railroad tunnels in the early period. And for those traveling in open railroad carriages, no doubt passing through a long tunnel was a very unpleasant experience—the noise alone would have been bad enough. Indeed, it is also important to point out that people had a different "perceptual" experience of railroad travel then to that we have today—the trains were noisy, especially with regard to metallic, grinding, and squealing noises (exacerbated considerably in open carriages and when the train passed through cuttings and tunnels); people were exposed to smoke and smuts, the "aromas" of which even found their way into closed carriages; carriage suspension technology was crude when it existed at all; vibrations were not adequately "cushioned" and were, therefore, readily discernible; and trains jerked a lot because they could not be as smoothly accelerated or decelerated as modern trains can be.

However, the risks tunnels posed to health were hugely exaggerated by some medical "experts" at the time. And for many years this erroneous and disparaging medical opinion, along with more general fears about darkness and penetrating the earth, meant that on some lines passengers were so paranoid they were allowed to alight at the entrance to a long tunnel and meet the train at the other end of it. For instance, in England many passengers avoided the Box Tunnel in the early period—by leaving trains at Corsham or Box and posting over the hill, rather than braving the dark, sulphurous depths of the tunnel.[24]

Tunnels concentrated and amplified the mechanical sounds of the train in motion, which frightened some people. Furthermore, relatively few people—apart from miners—had ever been underground even dozens, let alone a hundred meters below the surface; hence, numerous fears attended such descents into the "bowels" of the earth. All that aside, there were long-standing fears about both darkness and the night in European society. However, some railroad companies prudently sought to allay such fears by illuminating tunnels. The London and Brighton, for instance, used gaslight in the Clayton Tunnel,[25] while in the same era (the early 1840s) the Cowlairs Tunnel on the Edinburgh and Glasgow was illuminated with 43 lamps (to allay passenger fears).[26]

But the main sources of fears about traveling through tunnels probably derived from theories about the effects of vibrations on the walls and ceilings of tunnels; the possibility of derailments in tunnels (a train could crash into the tunnel wall, causing a major collapse of the tunnel); or other accidents or breakdowns in tunnels, which might leave a train exposed to collision and the passengers pitched into darkness.

An Oxford University geology professor claimed that I.K. Brunel's tunnels would all collapse as powerful train vibrations gradually de-stabilized the surrounding earth.[27] And Dionysius Lardner no doubt fueled fears about railroad tunnels by publicizing his calculation that if a train's brakes failed in the (long) Box Tunnel, then the train would exit at the other end doing 120 miles per hour (he was apparently unfamiliar with the concept of wind resistance).[28]

But most of the irrational fears about trains in tunnels were (rationally) refuted by Dr. Neil Arnott in a book *On Warming and Ventilation* published around 1838. Of course, much of what he had to say we would today classify as common sense.[29] Furthermore, in February 1837 a study of the effects of being in the Primrose Tunnel—on the London and Birmingham Railway—was undertaken by two medical doctors, a lecturer on chemistry, and two surveyors. Their carefully considered finding was that "Judging from this experiment, we are decidedly of the opinion that the dangers incurred, in passing through well-constructed tunnels are no greater than those incurred in ordinary traveling on an open railway, or upon a turnpike road."[30]

Only very occasionally did the worst nightmares of the tunnel-*phobics* materialize. Perhaps the worst accident in England in the tunnel "genre" was the Clayton Tunnel disaster of 1861, which entailed a three-train, nose-to-tail pile-up resulting in 23 dead and 175 injured. But there was another (earlier) accident of note. In February 1839, the "dense volume of smoke and steam" in a tunnel on the London and Birmingham prevented a mail train driver from seeing some detached carriages of a baggage train, which resulted in a collision; but, apart from two guards being "precipitated" from their perches on carriage roofs (neither was seriously injured), this was not a particularly serious accident.[31]

Tunnels epitomized the way in which the railroad industrialized the landscape and passengers were "shot through" it. And in tunnels passengers directly engaged with the (concentrated) vile smells and filth of industrial production. Therefore, it is hardly surprising that in Britain there were sometimes extraordinary attempts to give a cosmetic make-over to tunnel entrances. Indeed, sometimes they were designed to appear like the entrance to a castle or palace, and I.K. Brunel went overboard in building the entrances to the Box Tunnel after the fashion of Roman triumphal arches.[32] The Freudians (see Schivelbusch[33]) attempted to link the fascination which adolescent boys have for trains and railroads to adolescent (male) sexuality. However, the English tendency to dress up man-made "orifices" (tunnels) penetrating the earth may also have had something to do—albeit subconsciously—with the culture of Victorian moral and sexual hypersensitivity. This "dressing up" of the tunnel entrance was sometimes quite extraordinary, as noted above. Indeed, our attention ought to be drawn to the Clayton Tunnel, which has been described as one of the "most ridiculous" where ornamental embellishment was concerned, and which was "made even more silly" by having a cottage perched on the "castle roof" between two castellated towers[34]—quite an impressive "fig leaf"!

Boiler Explosions

If tunnels induced anxiety and fear, no less so in the early period did the possibility of boiler explosions. In fact, steam and gas struck the same fear into the Victorians, both boilers and gasometers expected to explode at any moment.[35] Indeed, long before the "mobile boiler" in the form of the locomotive engine appeared people were extremely wary of industrial boilers because of the devastation they caused when they did explode, not to mention the somewhat sensationalized media accounts of such events, which themselves induced paranoia.

For the first half-century of steam-energy production, in both Britain and America, any industrial plant accommodating a boiler was a dangerous place to be around. Ritchie mentions a major explosion at a Barnsley (England) cotton mill which completely leveled

Five. The Safety of Railroad Travel in 19th Century England and America

the plant.[36] Also on record is a boiler explosion at a Newcastle Colliery (in 1815) which blew two people to pieces, threw a child "a great distance," and seriously injured fifty people.[37] Some other impressive boiler explosions in England are worth a mention. In December 1845, there was a boiler explosion in a Bolton factory in which "the boiler forced its way through the whole building and came down with a tremendous crash on the Bolton and Liverpool Railway," resulting in at least 10 people in the building being killed. In May 1845, there was a boiler explosion in a flour mill featuring a 3.5 ton boiler blown to a height of 200 feet and landing 100 yards away, a piece of iron from it smashing through the roof of a house 500 yards away and landing in a bedroom, just missing a woman—the mill was blown to pieces, although there had been nobody inside at the time. In April 1849, there was a boiler explosion at a London sawmill, the result of which was that "a dense mass of steam and dust ascended so high as to darken the neighborhood," and one part of the boiler, weighing almost two tons, landed in a backyard 100 feet away.[38]

But such explosions also occurred in America, and not just on steamboats (which were common enough). In February 1850, there was a boiler explosion in a printing press and machine shop in New York City:

> The whole building, which was six storeys high, was lifted from its foundation to a height of six feet, then tumbled down, crushing in its ruins a vast number. A long portion of the front wall was thrown with tremendous power into the houses opposite. All that remained of the building was a solitary piece of wall, eight or ten feet high (it seems that over 100 people died due to this explosion).[39]

I have documented these boiler explosions solely to give the incidence of *locomotive* boiler explosions, when they occurred, some context. In fact, locomotive boiler explosions, though apparently more common in America than England during the early period, were not that common even there. Nevertheless, during the early period of railroading in America such was the apparent unpredictability of locomotive boilers that there developed, for a while, the practice of placing a "buffer" car between the tender and the passenger cars on some companies' lines—sometimes the buffer (also known as the "barrier-car") car was the "nigger car," according to one cotemporary source.

During the first decade of railroading in America many of the locomotives in operation were of English origin and it may have been the case that modifications to them, or their operation by people unfamiliar with them, were causes of locomotive boiler explosions, at least occasionally, when they did occur. But, more generally in the early period of railroad operations, knowledge of boilers was hardly a "science," apart from which the people who knew most about their operation were not always in charge of them, while the technology itself was not controllable by the kind of sophisticated instrumentation most modern boiler-type technology is. An inquest into a fatal boiler explosion (which killed nine people) at Ardwick, England, in 1848 revealed that it was not uncommon for people who really did not know what they were doing to be put in charge of boilers. The inquest heard that a youth, who had previously been put in charge of the boiler in question, "had never had the care of an engine before"; had finally left his job (tending the boiler) "for his own safety, for he was afraid for his life" (the boiler leaked badly); and that he was "always afraid of it (the boiler)." Furthermore, he was never instructed as to what power to drive the boiler at, and "did it wholly by guess work." And he said that "if he had done as he was ordered, he would have blown the whole place up long ago."[40]

In the same connection, we might note the action of the fireman attending the American locomotive, *Best Friend of Charlton*, one day in June 1831. Annoyed by the hissing steam escaping from the safety valve, he decided to fasten it down, the consequence of which was that the *Best Friend of Charlton* suddenly became very unfriendly, indeed. In fact, the resulting explosion threw the boiler 25 feet and injured the engineer, the fireman and another person—the fireman later died from his injuries.[41]

In America river steamboat boiler explosions were, for several decades and compared to locomotive boiler explosions, a notoriously frequent occurrence. Such was the fear of steamboat boiler explosions—not surprising, given their regularity—passengers often positioned themselves on the boats as far from the boilers as possible. In fact, sometimes "safety barges" were resorted to, "allowing nervous passengers to ride in a raft towed behind the steamer."[42] Of river steamboats in America in the 1830s, Tocqueville remarked bravely: "You were never anxious. Yet, thirty of them blew up or were wrecked during our first six weeks in the U.S." And he thought crossing the Atlantic "harmless" by comparison.[43]

But were locomotive boiler explosions very common in England in the first decades of railroading there? In an 1839 English newspaper article, comparing the relative advantages of railroad as against coach traveling, the author posed the question: "Who ever heard of a railroad boiler bursting? No one."[44] Well, he should have heard of it, since there was quite a spectacular event the previous year. Indeed, in November 1838 a train on the Liverpool and Manchester Railway, consisting of 43 carriages propelled by four engines, two at the front and two behind, and climbing a one foot in ninety gradient, suffered a serious misadventure. The lead engine "Exploded with a noise resembling the firing of cannon, the report being heard more than a mile distant. The engine proceeded at a flying pace for three or four hundred yards along the line (the two enginemen were blown about forty yards, one to each side of the line)."[45] But locomotive boiler explosions were rare events, though they still occurred in Britain in the 1860s. One such explosion (in 1861) of a locomotive traveling at 40 miles per hour (but not attached to a passenger train) inclined one commentator to wonder "Whether any locomotive in history has ever disintegrated quite so quickly into so many small pieces." Another boiler explosion (the following year) flung a locomotive 30 feet, part of the boiler blown through the roof of a train shed to land 100 yards away.

Nevertheless, locomotive boiler explosions in Britain never presented any real threat to passengers. In fact, in the early period, in both Britain and America, the "real" risk of a passenger being killed by a locomotive boiler explosion was negligible, if, indeed—as the statistics would indicate—there was any risk at all. And this is the point I was leading to via the diversion to look briefly at other types of boiler explosion. In fact, in Britain, from 1840 to 1912, just 83 railroad employees and 9 bystanders were killed because of locomotive boiler explosions.[46] And, somewhat surprisingly, and despite passenger anxiety in the early period, no railroad *passengers* were killed in Britain by such an occurrence during that period. So, it is interesting to reflect upon that statistic relative to consideration of, for instance, the number of steamboat passenge*rs* killed as the result of boiler explosions in America across the same period. The latter figure is unknown, although I think the number of people killed—directly or indirectly (by drowning, for instance)—because of steamboat boiler explosions in America during the entire 19th century would have been in the thousands.

But the fact passengers did not die in locomotive explosions in Britain seemed to pass by those who feared perishing due to such an explosion, directly or indirectly. And no doubt media reports of locomotive boiler explosions, when they did occur and in whatever context, both increased the fear and exaggerated the risk in the passenger's mind; especially since often the media reported them in sensationalist fashion. Take the following, for instance: "Driver Legge was blown up with his boiler. His arms and legs were blown in different directions, and one of the former actually went through the windows of a private house and fell upon a breakfast table, around which the family were sitting at the time."[47] I do not believe that.

Fire

Another perceived hazard during the early period was fire. In fact, in both England and America it was not such a rare occurrence for a passenger carriage or goods wagon to be set on fire by cinders. And although the incendiary capability of railroads was one of the main arguments against proposed railroad schemes in the early period, yet the risk of that seems to have been exaggerated, too. In fact, the incendiary risk to private property was not high, either in English built-up areas or in the countryside.

Henry Mayhew documented causes of fire in London 1833–49 and locomotive sparks or cinders do not figure at all in his statistics, although he does account for 359 fires in a general category of fire-sparks during that period, some of which may have been due to locomotives. But if locomotives could have been singled out as a major cause of fires, then Mayhew would have mentioned it. And the figure of 359 spark-caused fires is not surprising in a metropolitan environment at the time, where almost every house had a fire going, at least now and then, and where many commercial premises were warmed by fires in winter, and many industries used fire (in some form) in manufacturing. Indeed, if we remain with Mayhew's statistics (1833–49), what we discover is that rather than railroads being a significant cause of fires, candles (2,876) were the worst offenders, followed by flues (1,273), gas (780), stoves (626), the drying of linen by fires (509), and manufacturing processes (440).[48]

In America, too, the phenomenon of locomotive sparks and cinders causing fires in urban areas was probably a rare occurrence. However, in rural areas, later, where the railroads often penetrated tinder-dry landscapes, there was sometimes a risk of setting off forest or prairie fires. And some cities (notably San Francisco) in some regions seemed to be especially fire-prone in the 19th century, although there seems to be little evidence that the presence of railroads significantly raised the fire risk.

Obstructions on the Tracks

Where railroad traveling safety in a narrower sense was concerned, I want to begin here not with the safety of the rail "way" itself—where issues pertaining to its construction were concerned (to be addressed in due course)—but with a hazard presented often enough to railroad travelers in both 19th century Britain and America: obstructions on the tracks. In England, this problem never reached anything like the magnitude it did in America, where both livestock and human trespassers on the tracks were concerned. In fact, cattle on the tracks was a hazard for decades in America, where track was fenced off by the railroad companies only when it was economical and practical so to do, or (not that commonly) state or local law required that the track be fenced off in certain places. But often it was more economical for the companies to pay compensation to farmers for (the frequent) cattle "strikes" than it was to construct and maintain effective fencing. However, although cattle were one of the major hazards during railroad travel in rural areas in 19th century America, not surprisingly they usually came off second-best in a collision. But a cattle strike could cause a derailment and block the line, nevertheless—cows could weigh up to 1,000 pounds and derail a locomotive.[49]

Traveling in America in 1849, Charles Casey observed that seldom did the engine even slow down, let alone stop, if a cow was on the line—he witnessed the mowing down of one cow.[50] And traveling in America in the mid–1850s, William Ferguson remarked, "The destruction of cattle on the railways in the country is immense. The Little Miami Railroad has in four years killed upwards of 1,600 head of cattle. Last night's train killed five horses and four cows."[51]

In England livestock on the tracks never posed the kind of safety issue that they did in America because the tracks were usually fenced to prevent encroachment. In fact, in England obstructions on the tracks were more likely to take the form of objects placed on them maliciously—as we shall see shortly—than wandering livestock.

The cow-catcher, apparently an American invention, was designed to scoop up the cow onto the "catcher" to prevent it going under the wheels and derailing the locomotive. The Camden and Amboy was the first company to use it in America (around 1833).[52] But the cow-catcher was invented at a time when locomotives were still a relatively light piece of machinery; the locomotives sometimes coming off second-best, and commonly derailed in a collision with a bovine creature, especially if hitting a bull. Furthermore, the cow-catcher did not always work as it was designed to, the victim sometimes having to be extricated from underneath the locomotive, and usually in quite gruesome circumstances, before the train could proceed. Foster Zincke, traveling in America in 1867, observed that cow-catchers were sometimes ineffective; the cow-catcher on his train running right over the cow, "and so did the first two or three cars."

But never mind cattle on the tracks! Traveling in America in 1840 the English tourist, Thomas Grattan, was amazed that not only did his train smash into a horse and chaise (containing two ladies) at a crossing, but the engineman never bothered to stop and the conductor was "unapologetic." Grattan learned subsequently—from the newspaper—that one of the women had been killed, the other "badly wounded."[53]

Although such figures might beggar belief, yet in America in 1919 alone 14,000 people were fatally struck by trains. In America by 1900 many wayfarers along the rails were tramps, whose sub-cultural milieu incorporated the railroad system, and many such persons killed on the railroads were not even counted in the statistics.[54]

In late 19th century America the foremost expert on the "railroad tramp" was probably Josiah Flynt. He undertook what amounted to participant-observation studies of the tramps' subcultural milieu (probably one of the first such sociological studies ever undertaken) and, subsequently, he was employed by a railroad company to report on the tramp situation on that company's lines—to determine how effective the company's policies to rid its lines of tramps were.

Flynt remarked "tongue in cheek" of the American railroads in the late 19th century: "No other country in the world transports its beggars from place to place free of charge." He explained that after the Civil War there suddenly appeared a large class of men who had become so enamored of camp life they found it impossible to return to quiet living, and so took to wandering about the country. At the time roads, particularly in the West, were usually in poor condition, and tramps found the railroad tracks a better option for a "pedestrian," from which it was only a short step for the tramp to begin "hitching" rides on trains.[55] Flynt suggested that if at that time the railroad companies had passed laws forbidding anybody but an employee to walk on railroad property—except at public crossings—and had enforced such laws, then the railroad tramp would never have become the problem he did in America.

Flynt calculated that in summer in the 1890s, when the entire tramp community was "in transit," tramps could average 50 miles a day by rail, some traveling across the continent from coast to coast, year after year, during their meandering. And in 1895 Flynt declared, based on quite well-founded knowledge and research, I surmise: "Taking this country by and large, it is no exaggeration to say that every night in the year *ten thousand* free passengers of the tramp genus travel on the different railroads... (and) ten thousand more were awaiting their opportunity to 'catch' a train."[56]

In England throughout the 19th century accident rates involving people on the tracks were nowhere near what they were in America. In fact, in England—especially in the early period—the tracks were normally under close surveillance, fenced off, or otherwise made difficult of access. However, people still trespassed and were not infrequently arrested and prosecuted for doing so. At one court sitting alone in Leeds in October 1834, for instance, 11 men were convicted for trespassing on the line of the Leeds and Selby Railway—two of them turned out to be solicitors and all of them were fined.[57] However, despite the frequency of such "transgressions," pedestrian casualties on English railroad lines in the early period were not numerous. In fact, after the first few years of railroading in England pedestrian casualties on the tracks were rare (excepting suicides).[58]

In 19th century America tramps or other wayfarers on the tracks were not the only people likely to be struck by a train. Indeed, the fact that railroad *crossings* figured so prominently in American railroad accidents should not really surprise, since by 1900 America had around 250,000 grade crossings and thousands of them posed a serious hazard—scrub, trees, tall-growing crops, and buildings could obscure the view of a railroad line for both enginemen and wayfarers. In fact, one 19th century source characterized America as "essentially a country of level crossings," while also noting that in the city "occasionally a train smashes up a street car."[59] But the latter accident types were not necessarily related to speed and often they were not—Englishman, William Ferguson was on a train which struck and killed a man at a Toledo street crossing, even though the train was traveling at just 5 mph.[60] But, as English tourist Therese Yelverton noted: "American railroads have the peculiarity of running through and over everything."[61]

Before looking at some instances of railroad vandalism in 19th century England, perhaps one might just note the tense watchfulness which characterized early railroad enterprise there. Schivelbusch suggests that on each carriage of the train we see up to three people whose task it is to scan the line ahead for hazards.[62] But why would you need three people, since they only needed to look in one direction? Although there may have been such watchfulness in the early period, I think Schivelbusch has confused "watchfulness" with the fact that, in the earliest period, there were no prohibitions against passengers riding on carriage tops. And why should there have been? Had they not been able to ride so on the stage-coach? It may also have been the case that guards, conductors, and brakemen had nowhere else to sit, given the architecture of early English (closed) railroad carriages. Having said that, in England in the early period railroad operations were, indeed, normally attended with great vigilance—though not necessarily from the tops of carriages. Railroad policemen deployed along the line and other railroad company personnel (such as semaphore signalmen, switchmen, night watchmen, and the like) were the foremost means in the early period for safeguarding the tracks.

Vandalism and Sabotage

I suppose it would be fair to say that the first instances of vandalism pertaining to railroad travel occurred at the opening of the Liverpool and Manchester Railway in 1830. On more than one occasion during that event stones were hurled at the passing passenger carriages, which were full of dignitaries. In fact, one contemporary source suggested that if the cavalry had not been conspicuous and thus a "display of military force" in evidence, then "there would certainly have been a breach of the peace, the populace having taken determined possession of many parts of the railway."[63] Yet, very seldom do accounts of the opening of that railroad mention that.

But let us look now at malicious activity connected to early railroad operations in England. And if Old Bailey records are a reliable indication, then it would seem such offences were rare before 1850. This may have been because in the early period surveillance of the line necessitated the physical presence of many people patrolling and policing it, not to mention regular watchmen and signalmen. However, the application of the telegraph to railroad administrative and operational regimes (from the mid–1840s), and some advances in the means of signaling and track switching technology by that time, meant that fewer functionaries needed to be physically deployed along the line. Consequently, it became easier for miscreants to effect acts of vandalism and sabotage against the railroad. One also notes—again assuming Old Bailey records afford a reliable indication—that many of the offenders, where placing objects on the line or throwing objects at passing trains were concerned, were quite young. And one might suggest that by mid-century merely watching trains pass had lost its fascination for young boys—it was much more fun to try and run them off the rails or bombard the passengers!

Although the number of *disturbing* cases heard at the Old Bailey across the decades was not especially large, yet we need to be mindful that it is likely only a very small number of offenders (vandals and would-be saboteurs) were ever apprehended. After all, in those times there were no surveillance cameras, systematic use of police tracker dogs, sophisticated forensic analysis of crime scenes, police cars, or police helicopters. On the other hand, there were probably countless minor incidents not pursued by the railroad companies or prosecuted by the police. And, given the youth of many offenders in this category of offending, it seems likely that often children—and some adult offenders, too—got away with a stern warning or had their ears boxed by a policeman, perhaps also their parents being advised of their conduct in the case of children. Finally, we might note that the Old Bailey was but one of hundreds of English courts which, to some extent or other, would have dealt with such offending, at least occasionally. Nevertheless, let us look at some of the cases heard at the Old Bailey, which could well have been representative of the occurrence of such offending across Britain.

Acts of vandalism along the railroad line generally fell into three categories: placing objects on the tracks with the intention of causing a derailment or just to see what would happen when the train hit the object; interfering with signals, points, or telegraph wires, all of which could cause a serious accident; and throwing objects at passing trains. Clearly the first two categories of vandalism could be serious enough for them to be considered genuine acts of sabotage. So, let us look firstly at some offenses entailing placing objects on the line.

In October 1851 a thirteen-year-old boy pleaded guilty to placing a piece of wood on a railroad line "with felonious intent" and was sentenced to a month's imprisonment.[64] In December 1856 two young men were found guilty of placing bricks on the North London Railway and sentenced to six months imprisonment.[65] In October 1866 two young men were found guilty of placing a piece of wood on a railway line, one of them sentenced to two months, the other to ten days imprisonment.[66] In August 1868 a fifteen-year-old youth was found guilty of placing three iron bolts on the London and North Western Railway and sentenced to five days imprisonment.[67]

In a more serious category of offending, in May 1872 a sixteen-year-old was found guilty of "feloniously placing a clinker and a brick on the West London Extension Railway, and *moving certain points with intent to obstruct and divert engines and carriages.*" The youth, of *"good character,"* was recommended to mercy by the jury and sentenced to eighteen months imprisonment.[68] No less dangerously, in July 1888 a youth was found guilty of placing two long poles fastened together (an obstruction measuring about 10 ft. × 8 ½ ft. and weighing half a hundredweight) on a railway line. He "received a good character" and was sentenced to six months hard labor.[69]

Other offences, entailing more serious attempts to interfere with railroad operations, included the following. In August 1851 two boys, aged thirteen and fourteen, put a stone on a railway line, placed in such a way as to prevent the points from working. Both were recommended to mercy by the jury. One was sentenced to six weeks, the other to two months imprisonment, and each was ordered to spend three days a week of his sentence in solitary confinement.[70] In November 1854 two young men were found guilty of unlawfully pulling down telegraph wires on the London, Brighton and South Coast Railway. Each was sentenced to two months imprisonment.[71] And in June 1859 a youth was found guilty of "unlawfully moving the points of a certain railway." Recommended to mercy by the jury, he was sentenced to three months imprisonment.[72]

Let us now look briefly at the throwing of objects at trains across several decades. In September 1862 a young man was found guilty of throwing a solid piece of clay at a carriage window of a passing train, smashing the window, though the train was empty. The offender was sentenced to three months imprisonment.[73] In 1867 two boys (aged ten and twelve) were found guilty of "unlawfully casting and throwing dirt and stones upon the Great Western Railway." They were sentenced to be whipped and to serve one week imprisonment.[74] In July 1868 two boys (fourteen and fifteen) were found guilty of "unlawfully throwing stones at an engine and carriages on the North Kent Railway," both strongly recommended to mercy—by both the jury and the prosecution—on account of their youth.[75] On 16 August 1869 a twelve-year-old boy was found guilty of throwing stones at the engine and carriages of a train, and although recommended to mercy by the jury he was sentenced to *three years* at a reformatory.[76] On the same date a ten-year-old boy was found guilty of throwing a brick at a passing third-class carriage, the brick hitting a passenger in the chest. Recommended to mercy by the jury, he was sentenced to two years at a reformatory.[77] And in May 1876, three young men were sentenced to twenty-one days imprisonment for "endangering the safety of passengers on the Metropolitan Railway"—by throwing cushions *out* of a carriage window![78]

One of the more unusual cases occurred in 1854. It involved two men who "unlawfully fired a certain cannon, loaded with gunpowder and wadding, at a railway train on the London, Brighton and South Coast Railway, thereby endangering the safety of persons being conveyed therein." Ultimately, the charge was reduced to one of common assault, of which they were found guilty and fined a shilling each[79] for what was evidently a harmless, if ill-conceived prank.

There were several cases heard at the Old Bailey where offences had clearly occurred, although artful lawyers sometimes managed to circumvent the charges. For instance, in July 1870 a twelve-year-old boy was charged with throwing stones at a Midland Railway train "with intent to endanger the lives of persons traveling on it." But the boy was acquitted, his lawyer arguing that the prosecution had failed to establish whether there was anybody on the train to be endangered by the boy's actions.[80]

In other cases, not guilty verdicts were returned by juries although the evidence against the defendant seemed overwhelming or the offender had even admitted his guilt. For instance, in May 1855 two boys (one aged eleven) were found not guilty of putting an iron chair on the rails of the London and South Western Railway, even though one of the defendants undoubtedly did put the chair on the line![81]

Another very interesting "not guilty" verdict was returned in the case of a twenty-five-year-old man who had "entered a room at the station without authorization" and "adjusted an instrument, the effect of which was that a signal was sent down the line indicating the line was clear, when in fact it was not." The defendant, who was not an employee of the railroad company concerned, and therefore had no good excuse whatsoever for even being in the room in question, claimed that it must have been an accident resulting from his possibly leaning on the instrument while in the room![82]

An even more questionable "not guilty" verdict was returned in the case of two men in their early twenties whom, shortly after midnight on the 18 September 1871, placed a wooden telegraph pole (at least 25 feet long) on a line of the Great Western Railway. Their lawyer argued that an engine would not have hit the pole because as the engine came around a bend about 80 yards from the pole, its driver could not have failed to see it (an irrelevant point, really). However, an engine driver testified that sometimes the engine was run pushing many wagons in front of it, and in that case an engineman may not have seen the hazard until the leading wagon was almost upon it. The defendants never denied putting the telegraph pole on the line, one of them saying they only did it "for a lark." Having received good character references, they were acquitted![83]

I surmise that in many cases (including those cited above) "not guilty" verdicts were returned, despite the evident guilt of the defendant, because of the youth or *social class backgrounds* of the offenders; the juries being aware that a verdict of "guilty" could result in terms of imprisonment (possibly with hard labor), years at a reformatory, or a good old-fashioned whipping for boys as young as ten.

We have already seen in many of the cases cited above that juries, having found a defendant guilty, had then recommended mercy be shown by the judge in sentencing the offender. And assuming the judge acted upon such recommendations normally, then the sentences meted out were still very severe in some cases, especially considering these are children we are talking about in many of the cases cited. It seems juries may also have been moved—and especially where their recommendations to mercy were concerned—by a defendant's guilty plea, so long as it was accompanied by regret and contrition. Furthermore, some defendants apparently had "glowing" character references and their actions were deemed so "out of character" that they ought to be considered an "aberration." In fact, in many of the cases cited above character references figured prominently in proceedings, and it seems that these were routinely considered by juries. But the fact that character references could figure so prominently in many of the cases concerned indicates (to me) that most of the boys and young men involved were not "vagrants" or "regular delinquents," but from good homes and well-to-do families. That was also indicated by the fact their parents (presumably) could afford very good counsel to represent them in court.

What we might conclude from all this is that although I cite just twenty cases of vandalism or attempted sabotage across a fifty-year period (1830–1880), I have absolutely no doubt whatsoever that these cases—which reached the Old Bailey—were just the very tip of the iceberg where this kind of offending was concerned. So, although the possibility of sabotage or having a rock come flying through the carriage window did not routinely figure as sources of English passenger anxiety, yet that may have been so only because English railroad passengers were largely unaware of the extent of this kind of offending. In fact, many of these cases—apart from the worst ones—probably would not have been reported in the newspapers. And my research of historical English newspapers—which covered the same period as my research of Old Bailey records—revealed few publicized cases of attempted railroad sabotage or serious railroad vandalism; which inclines me to think that the railroad companies themselves may have been instrumental in suppressing the public "airing" of such cases (that may also explain why some of them never got to court).

However, the following incidents *did* receive some media attention. In September 1830 a *fatal* accident on the Liverpool and Manchester was attributed to: "Some person, apparently with malicious design, having altered the position of a switch or junction rail" (a reward of 200 guineas was offered for the apprehension of the offender).[84] Yet, one notes that an accident on the same company's line in March 1831 was caused by workmen having "carelessly left a piece of plank lying across one of the rails."[85] A serious injury accident on the Garnkirk Railway in July 1831 was attributed to a large stone having been—most likely maliciously—placed on the track at one of the cross junctions.[86] And in October 1839 a sleeper was maliciously placed across the rails on the London and Birmingham line—the mail carriage at the end of a train was derailed and the guard thrown into a ditch, while some passengers in other carriages were thrown from their seats, but not seriously injured.[87] An 1839 newspaper article mentioned a 30-pound stone having been thrown at a train on the North Union Railway, while the previous day a sleeper had been laid across the rails on the same line. And at around the same time a wooden gate was also placed on the rails of that company. However, the article's author thought these acts of *sabotage* were most likely associated with the fact the North Union Railway was "much patronized by the noblemen from the south of England on their way to Scotland"—hence, there may have been a political motivation underlying them.[88]

But if media coverage of such incidents was neither frequent nor glowering when it occurred, yet Mark Huish, General Manager of the London and North Western Railway Company, made it clear in his 1852 paper on railroad safety issues that vandalism and sabotage *were not at all infrequent events*. In fact, his testimony is probably the most reliable source on the prevalence of malicious activity where track safety and the safe movement of English trains at that time were concerned. In his 1852 paper Huish mentioned that persons who maliciously placed obstructions on the line had become: "Unhappily, a very fertile source of danger, and one against which it is indeed very difficult to guard." He went on to state that: "Numerous instances might be given, which would excite surprise, *from the cunning design exhibited, and the care apparently exercised in selecting a spot likely to be fraught with the greatest amount of mischief.*" He also mentioned that it had become customary to offer considerable rewards for the perpetrators of such crimes.[89]

It seems that in America, by comparison, malicious attempts to derail trains were rare, except: when vested interests (such as river ferrymen or private road bridge owners) were opposed to the presence of a railroad because their livelihoods were undermined by it; during strike action by employees; and on the rare occasion when train robbers or Indians attempted to derail a train. However, an 1876 American article, which addressed the problem of trespassers on American railroad tracks, noted what happened when some railroad companies acted against railroad tramps: "The resentment of those whose wonted privileges were thus interfered with began to make itself felt. Obstructions were found placed in the way of night trains."[90]

Railroad Construction and the Comparative Safety of English and American Railroads

But how safe was railroad travel in 19th century England and America? From their inception English railroads were better engineered and better constructed—from a safety point of view—than were their American counterparts. There is nothing the least bit controversial about that assertion, since that was acknowledged almost universally in America for the first half-century of railroading there. And American railroad capitalists did often economize in ways that usually had implications for passenger safety.

At one level, the *economy* of the American railroads was often affected by building along the natural contours of the land, which meant lines were built around and over hills, thus avoiding building tunnels or expensive cuts and fills.[91] However, there were several reasons why English railroads cost more to build, not the least of which was that they were completed to a higher standard than were most American railroads. That is reflected in the fact that many American railroad companies ran their trains at relatively slow speeds, due at least in part to poor quality track construction. However, American railroad companies operated trains on their railroads at slower speeds than their English counterparts not only because the tracks were usually not of foolproof solidity, but also in the interest of economy founded on other criteria as well—to reduce "wear and tear" on both tracks *and rolling stock*, and to reduce fuel (wood or coal) consumption.

The national differences in railroad construction costs may also have been reflected in the fact that throughout the 19th century the cost of railroad passenger travel was always comparatively higher in England than it was in America—in late 1866 a report prepared for an English Royal Commission found 1st, 2nd and 3rd class fares to be greater than on any continental country's railroads at the time.[92] But they were also significantly higher, in the aggregate, than were railroad passenger fares in America, and many American commentators on railroads believed that was partly due to the fact that English companies were prepared to spend more money on track quality, *and thus on the security and safety of railroad travel*, than were their American counterparts. Indeed, as the author of an 1856 American newspaper article noted: "The comparative security from accident, which English railroads enjoy, is the result not only of the greater plenty of money there, but also of the more prudent disposition of the people"—he also noted that the more frequent use of double-tracks, the more extensive use of telegraphy, and lights along the road (for night travel) all served to make English railroads at the time safer than their American counterparts.[93]

Horace Greeley noted of an American railroad in 1859 that it had been "completed in hot haste," un-graveled and slapstick, to tap into the spring migration traffic in the locality concerned. But this slap-dash construction was typical of American railroads at the time. Another source makes the possibly extravagant, but perhaps credible, claim that 15 years after completion, *all* land grant railroads were re-built at public expense.[94] Indeed, Grenville Dodge's correspondence (April-May 1869) revealed that in Wyoming the abutments of five bridges on the Union Pacific's section of the first transcontinental railroad were "breaking and tumbling down," that bridge masonry had been known to "dissolve" occasionally, while three bridges "had collapsed before any weight had even been put on them."[95] On the other hand, what Dodge had to say about "collapsible" and "dissolving" bridges would seem to clearly indicate that the government inspectors of construction had not performed their duties to the required standard, either.

But perhaps what is most remarkable about the American system of railroad construction (already discussed in certain respects in the previous chapter) is that, although many railroads so constructed were unsafe—but not necessarily so—yet, there rarely seems to have been a universally applied, enforceable minimum safety standard in place, in contrast to many other countries at the time. In England, for instance, railroad construction, administration, and operations were more closely attended to by officialdom, even though the state agencies concerned—the Board of Trade, most notably—often had very limited powers as well as limited resources. In fact, a newspaper article in July 1866 hinted at both when noting that a line of railway could not be opened without a certificate from the Board of Trade, but after such certification had been issued the Board of Trade "took no notice of the line until an accident happened." The same article said of railroads generally in Britain at the time: "It was well known, on the authority of the Board of Trade, that in some cases the permanent way had been allowed to get into a condition dangerous to travelers."[96] However, as indicated, English railroad construction had to conform to some objectively-determined standard, even if maintenance was a different issue.

But in Britain not all devolved upon the state, since members of the public were usually quick to criticize the failings of railroad companies through the correspondence columns of the most prominent newspapers. Furthermore, one finds countless media articles and editorials criticizing various aspects of railroad administration and operations.

An 1868 American journal article asserted that:

> The rails of the past fifteen or twenty years have, in most cases, proved far inferior to those used at first. The reason of this, we suppose, is because the specifications under which the first rails were contracted for were drawn up by men *who knew something about the manufacture of iron and its application to the making of rails*; a price being made accordingly, while the more modern contracts were simply for rails at the lowest possible rates.

The author of the article went on to suggest that rails could be made—*which would stand the inspection of the authorities*—for one-third the price *good* rails would command. He suggested, furthermore, that if a foreign engineer were to walk over some American railroads—which were supposedly safe—at the time (1868) he would possibly see a "roadbed half-covered with grass, sleepers so much decayed that the rail fastenings are quite loose, joints now and then much too wide open, and shaken masonry." And he would conclude that "such railroads were unsafe unless run over slowly."[97] Based on my knowledge of 19th century American railroading, this seems to have been a fair-minded appraisal.

But were the English railroads really any safer? A February 1839 English newspaper article claimed railroad accidents in that country were *more frequent than media reports indicated*, and that *some of the companies prevented their servants talking to the media about accidents*—it was claimed there had been at least one case of an inspector being "discharged for giving information to a reporter."[98] But that was before the Board of Trade had been authorized to regulate the administration and operation of railroads, and especially so from the standpoint of public safety.

The British Act for Regulating Railways, which came into effect in October 1840, had, as key points where passenger safety was concerned, the following: (1) The Board of Trade could authorize any proper person or persons to inspect any railway; (2) It was lawful for any officer or agent of any railway company to seize and detain any engine-driver, guard, porter, or other servant found drunk on the job; or who was otherwise in violation of the by-laws, rules and regulations of a railroad company (such offenders could be imprisoned—with or without hard labor—for up to two months).

However, the state regulatory mechanism aside, English public opinion was comparatively potent in pressuring the railroad companies to move in the direction of "safety-consciousness"; and especially so the inveterate English letter-writers to newspapers, while newspaper editors and prominent people were also often prepared to speak out publicly. By way of contrast, the American public was relatively indifferent, if not apathetic, and seemingly resigned to its fate at the mercy of the railroad capitalists—it was not really until the 1870s that American journalists got "stuck into" the railroad companies where safety issues were concerned; the *North American Review* and a number of Californian newspapers especially noteworthy, from that time, for their series of critical, analytical, indeed first-rate investigative articles on various aspects of railroad administration and operations.

Perhaps the most common type of accident, for a few decades at least in both England and America—although it was all too common for longer than that on some very dubious American railroads—was derailment. In America, this was due not only to poor track construction and maintenance, but livestock on the rails frequently de-railed trains in some regions in an ongoing bovine-versus-locomotive contest, which, given the unwillingness of railroad companies to fence off their tracks in some areas, almost took on the dimensions of a national sport. However, in both England and America in the early period derailments were often not lethal, since trains were not usually going fast enough for derailments to have disastrous consequences, though obviously it depended very much upon the landscape where the train ran off the rails.

Indeed, although in America derailment was commonplace on many railroads for decades, it was not usually fatal. Tourist Alex Mackay, when taking some air on the platform between the cars on a train journey in America in 1846, was politely advised by the conductor that doing so was imprudent, since "we do sometimes run off the rails." Then there is the "legend" of the Englishman Alfred Bunn's ham. In 1853 Bunn took a Harlem Railroad train to visit some friends, but left his ham behind on the train when he got off. Met by his friends at the station, the flustered Mr. Bunn had to tell them that the train had just run off with his ham. He thought his friends crazy when they suggested they all run along the track after the train to retrieve the ham. However, they convinced him this was a very sensible course of action, since the train almost invariably derailed about a mile up the track. Sure enough, the train had derailed and the ham was retrieved. This dependability—of the Harlem Railroad—was very rare on American railroads at the time!

Another curious form of "accident" in America involved the surprising number of passengers who suffered injuries from falling or jumping out of open car windows.[99] How they managed to *fall* out of windows eludes me. However, presumably those who *jumped* out may have had good reason for doing so, but clearly, they had no appreciation of what might happen to you when you jump from a quite fast-moving train.

The Comparative Safety of Railroad Travel in 19th Century England and America

Domingo Sarmiento offered up a useful comparison of the relative safety of French and American railroads in the 1840s. Of railroad construction in France, he observed:

> Everything that makes up a railroad is carefully examined by the engineers before being turned over for use. Wooden fences guard both sides of the track, and double tracks allow the trains to go in both directions. If a highway crosses the tracks, strong gates guard the crossing; they are cleared *a quarter of an hour before the train is due* to prevent accidents (a good example of "overkill" becoming "under-kill"). Sentinels are stationed at regular intervals along the tracks to watch them and give warning, with various colored flags, of any danger or obstacle that could delay the train. It (the train) leaves the terminal four minutes after a group of guards are certain that the travelers are in their seats, the doors shut, the tracks clear, and that no one is less than a yard from the train.... Everything has been foreseen and examined, so that one can sleep without worry in this permanently sealed *prison*.

Of the American railroads, in contrast to their French counterparts, Sarmiento noted:

> Since the railway companies lack funds, the rails are made of wood with iron plates that often become unfastened, and the engineer must watch for this constantly; a single line suffices for the two-way traffic.... If an accident occurs it is not reported. The railway runs through villages and the children are at the doors of their houses, or even in the middle of the (rail) road.... The railway is also a public highway. Instead of gates where a highway crosses the tracks, there is only a notice that says *Listen for the bell as the train approaches....* As it (the train) gets under way passengers leap on board, men selling newspapers and fruit get down from the train, and all go from car to car to amuse themselves.... Cows like to rut on the roadbed.

If anything, the French were even more circumspect in their care of the passenger than the English were at the time, even though the English were very scrupulous in their attendance to safety matters. Nevertheless, Sarmiento's is a very apposite comparison for our purposes here.

In 1852 Mark Huish, General Manager of the London and North Western Railway and probably the most capable railroad company executive in Britain at the time, presented a paper entitled *On Railway Accidents* (previously alluded to) to the Institution of Civil Engineers, for which he was awarded a "Telford Medal in Silver," such were its insights.[100] Huish suggested that in Britain at the time the most important causes of accidents "result from *inattention to signals and the neglect of regulations*." He suggested, furthermore, that although both the public and the courts often blamed accidents on the lack of punctuality of trains, yet he argued that: "Under a well-regulated system of signals, and with a well-disciplined staff, the greatest irregularity ... ought not to lead to danger." In support of the argument he pointed out that his own company had transported 775,000 persons during the Great Exhibition of 1851, for whose conveyance 24,000 carriages—*over and above those attached to scheduled trains*—passed through Euston Station. And: "That such an extraordinary traffic, centering in a single focus, arriving at irregular hours in almost unlimited numbers, and from more than 30 railways, was carried on for six months without the most trifling casualty" (Huish himself had charge of these arrangements). He added that many of the incoming excursion trains (part of the Exhibition traffic) were often not even known to be en route until they reached a main line, although the telegraph was employed to track every train through its entire journey *once it was known* to be en route.

However, at the time of the Great Exhibition some railroad companies had not mastered the application of the telegraph in the cause of railroad traffic management. The Great Northern, for instance, lacked the telegraph as a traffic control technology, with a spokesman for the company offering up a rather feeble excuse for such negligence: "Unfortunately, its (the company"s) engineers *had not yet found time* to put up the electric telegraph."[101] Similarly, many American companies were slow to employ the telegraph for administrative and operational purposes. In fact, even in the early 1850s "the penny had not dropped" for some American companies, and even as late as the 1870s there were still American companies which had not employed the telegraph *administratively*.[102] But it must be conceded that it took time to train people to be able to operate the telegraph and to learn its peculiar "language."

Huish, in his paper, also drew attention to the feeling of insecurity which attached to the passengers because of their inability to stop the train in an emergency—though he suggested that at the time management was "continually reproducing a multitude of schemes for communicating between the passenger and guard, and between the guard and the driver." Huish also asserted that it was essential to adequately maintain the way, though acknowledging that could be difficult, given the increasing speed and intensification of traffic along the lines—in that connection, he noted that (as in America) many rails supplied at that time had "shown symptoms of failure at an unusually early period."[103]

But the key point in Huish's paper was that, even at that time (1852)—given the limitations of administrative (communications) technologies to assist traffic movements and traffic control—*most accidents were preventable*. Furthermore, Huish suggested (somewhat radically for the time, I think) that *securing the safety of the public ought to be the paramount and primary duty of railroad management*—what a strange notion that would have seemed to many American railroad capitalists at the time!

That point aside for the moment, it does seem some English railroads were much safer than others. Indeed, a fatal accident on the Liverpool and Birmingham Railway in September 1837 was the first time, on either the Liverpool and Manchester or the Liverpool and Birmingham, that one train had run into another.[104] But when there were serious accidents—even if they were rare on some companies' lines relative to the number of either train journeys or passenger journeys undertaken—yet, many people could be killed or seriously injured *on the one occasion*. Furthermore, serious accidents were often reported by the media in somewhat sensationalized form,[105] while injuries were often described gratuitously, in all their gruesome and gory detail:

> The most terrible railway accident that ever happened in this country took place on 20 August 1868. A passenger train ran into some wagons laden with petroleum; the inflammable oil took fire from the engine; 33 persons, unable to get out of the carriages, were burned alive; their bodies were reduced to heaps of cinders.[106]

Indeed, the media ensured the public knew trains severed heads with bonnets remaining intact[107]—nobody thought of using locomotives for public executions, despite their popularity for the commission of suicide in England. And the following detailed description of (a guard's) injuries was not uncommon at the time (1840) where graphic media accounts of (railroad accident) injuries were concerned:

> The upper part of his head was severed, the wheels of the next carriage catching him between the mouth and the nose, and his head only hung together by a bit of skin—his eyes were nearly forced out of their sockets—his right arm was cut off just below the shoulder, and the left arm between the elbow and the wrist.

The article also described the victim as being "much bruised" (as if that really mattered under the circumstances).[108]

Just to pursue the point a little further, no less graphic is the following description of a boiler explosion *on a steam packet* in June 1837:

> (One man was) blown to the height of seventy or eighty yards and fell upon the roof of the Minerva Tavern.... The body of one man, shockingly mutilated, fell into the engine room of the Yarmouth steamer.... Mrs. Farrer, a dealer in nuts and oranges, was thrown over the Thorne Packet, and her cap, and a portion of her head, were left on the masthead of the *Don*.[109]

These may have been true representations of what happened, perhaps obtained from eyewitness accounts or coroners' reports. They simply included a lot of the gory detail most modern newspaper editors would spare their readers. But the point here is that *industrial accidents* did often maim and kill people in unusually macabre fashion, and that itself heightened the fear of machinery and the industrial processes, and that applied no less to railroad travel.

There is a certain irony to the fact that for the first few decades American railroads were extremely unreliable, whereas decades later their "regular punctuality" tended to have fatal consequences more than occasionally. Indeed, many of those killed at grade crossings tended to be "locals" familiar with every scheduled train along the line; but the *occasional* early, late, or unscheduled train could kill the unwary, "who believed absolutely in railroad time-keeping accuracy."[110]

Regarding early railroad travel in both England and America, we have seen that while some of the risks were exaggerated, and sometimes extremely so, perhaps other risks were undervalued. Whatever the case, the general sense we ought to have is that railroad travel in the few decades concerned could be either very safe or very unsafe, depending upon a whole raft of variables. But can we arrive at any generalized conclusions as to how safe railroad travel was in the early period especially?

During the Victorian period, the railroads killed fewer people than did road accidents. John Francis, a notable commentator on English railroad affairs in his time, asserted in 1851 that the likelihood of death or injury to a railroad traveler was much less than to a coach traveler.[111] And writing (retrospectively) of railroad travel in America in the late 1840s, Charles Adams, Jr., said that: "In those days a very exaggerated idea was universally entertained of the great danger incident to travel by rail."[112]

Of England, Samuel Smiles noted that during the first decade of its operation the Liverpool and Manchester Railway suffered only two fatalities among the *five million* or so passenger journeys involved. But that may have been due largely to the fact that trains on early English railroads were operated at relatively low speeds, while the uncertainty associated with early railroad operations occasioned considerable vigilance, many functionaries physically deployed along the lines in that connection—for some considerable time there were no means of mechanical signaling or switching, so semaphore signaling and manual switching respectively occurred.

During a three-year period around 1840 the Great Western Railway in England

***Five.** The Safety of Railroad Travel in 19th Century England and America* 219

facilitated some *three million* passenger journeys, with only one broken leg and bruises to passengers due to accidents.[113] This may well have been a very safely administered and operated railroad during the period concerned. But it was engineered by I.K. Brunel, who capitalized on some of the engineering mistakes made in the construction of the earliest railroads, apart from the fact he was a very competent *civil* engineer, and not afraid to spend other people's money (sometimes extravagantly) on railroad construction (and on miscellaneous frivolities in connection with it). Furthermore, his broad gauge—and despite his refusal to conform to a standardized narrower gauge later— may have been more conducive to the safe operation of trains at the time than were narrower gauge railroads.

But if the Great Western was quite a safe railroad in the early 1840s, in the two years 1841 and 1842 a total of 29 passengers were killed and 85 injured on *English* railroads. However, this casualty rate needs to be contextualized. For, at that time around *18 million passenger journeys* were being made annually. And Acworth quite rightly concluded that if, at that time, accidents were not infrequent, yet serious accidents were rare.[114] On the other hand, it must be said that *national* statistics could conceal the fact that some early English railroads were better managed from a safety point of view than others, and that some companies had relatively poor safety records.

Robert Ritchie, writing in 1846, thought that English railroad traveling had become a risky business by *that* time: "Accidents are so numerous and multifarious that it would fill volumes to describe them." He listed three principal causes of accident at the time: managerial and other administrative shortcomings; construction and mechanical faults; and the niggardly tendency to employ (at low rates) persons who were often incapable of functioning efficiently and reliably in a disciplinary system. Ritchie went on to analytically discuss contemporary railroad accident causes at considerable length.[115] Yet, it seems things may have become even worse after Ritchie wrote (1846). For Altick notes that 1848 was a very bad year for railroad accidents in England; and that, at around that time, taking a train had become a "solemn occasion."[116] But it was probably rather more solemn on some railroads than others. Yet, whatever the case, and despite the accident rate by the end of the 1840s, and given the millions of passenger journeys made annually on English railroads, the *fatal* accident rate would still have been miniscule.

So, the risk was often enormously exaggerated, though largely due to people being unaware of the broader statistical contexts of accident *rates*. And hyperbole in the matter was contributed to by: the gruesome injuries to and occasional horrible deaths suffered by accident victims; media sensationalism in that connection; and safety product vendors and their advertising. Furthermore, the new-fangled travel, injury, and life insurance companies no doubt added fuel to whatever fears obtained.

But if we want to get a sense of just how safe railroad travel in Britain was in the late 1840s, then we really must have recourse to that sociological expert of his era, Henry Mayhew. Mayhew pointed out that although 106 people were killed as the result of railroad accidents in the second half of 1849, that represented a fatality rate of 1 person for every 329,476 passenger journeys undertaken. He noted, furthermore, that this compared very favorably with the chance of dying in a shipwreck during an ocean-going voyage at the time—1 chance in 203. He went on to note that in respect of the

34 million passenger journeys made during the six-month period in question, injuries (112) were hardly more numerous than fatalities. So, if we combine the fatality and injury numbers for the period in question, then the chance of somebody being either *injured or killed* as the result of a single railroad journey was 1 in 160,203.

But what is interesting about these statistics—based upon a House of Commons report—is that Mayhew failed to analytically separate the passenger fatality and injury statistics from both *trespass* (on the line) and *railroad servant* fatality and injury statistics (a rare error by Mayhew, his statistical analysis usually credible). Therefore, since the three are conflated in Mayhew's account, the fatality and injury rates *for passengers* were even much lower than his figures would indicate. In fact, only 37 of the 106 people killed in the second half of 1849 were *passengers*—and of the 106 people killed in total, 2 were suicides, 28 were trespassers on the lines, and most of the rest railroad company servants. However, Mayhew does give us a breakdown of how the *passengers* were killed or injured: 54 passengers were *injured* "from causes beyond their control," while 11 were killed and 10 injured owing to "their own misconduct or want of caution." Only one death (and one injury to passengers) resulted from derailment, the train in question "running off the rails and entering a house."

If only 37 passengers were killed as against 28 trespassers on the lines, then it seems in Britain at the time your chance of being killed while crossing or walking along the lines was almost as good—as remote as that was—as being killed as a passenger during a railroad journey. And if 11 of the 37 passengers killed did, indeed, die because of their own negligence or folly, then railroad travel looks even safer still for the period concerned.[117]

The findings of Acworth's much later reflections on early English railroad accidents seem to harmonize with Mayhew's statistical analysis. Acworth, too, remarked that during the early period quite a few passenger deaths were due to the passenger's own carelessness or foolishness—some people were killed riding on the tops of carriages[118] and thus "prone to have their heads smashed by overhead structures." Other people suffered injury or death "after jumping out of carriages to run after their hats." As for trespassers on the line, Acworth noted many of them were intoxicated or asleep![119] According to another (1868) source, in the United Kingdom in 1864 the chance of a passenger being killed during a railroad journey was 1 in 15,290,000; whereas, by way of comparison, in London alone in 1865 there were 215 persons killed by horse conveyance—something our statistician advises us indicated that traveling by railroad at the time was 150 times safer than traveling by horse conveyance on the streets of London.[120]

As the railroads spread geographically in Britain and railroad *services* increased correspondingly (as well as intensifying), self-evidently the number of passengers and passenger journeys multiplied and, not surprisingly, so too did the number of railroad casualties. For the nine months ending 30 September 1890, for instance, there were 773 railroad-related deaths and over 3,000 injuries. But the majority in both categories would have been suffered by railroad servants. However, by that time "railroad suicide" had also become fashionable—56 people successfully used the railroad as their "weapon" of choice in the nine-month period concerned.[121] In fact, an earlier (1876) American article had noted:

> In Great Britain, physical demolition by a railroad train is also a somewhat favorite method of committing suicide.... Cases have not been uncommon in which persons have been seen to coolly lay themselves down in front of an advancing train; and, placing the neck across the rail, in this way effect very neatly their own decapitation.... In England alone during the last three years there have been no less than 88 railroad suicides.[122]

The picture we are beginning to assemble of safety on the early English railroads, then, is that they were, by and large, quite safe comparatively, despite some companies having relatively poor safety records. And, all considered, the accident and injury *rates* for passengers overall (casualties relative to the number of passenger journeys undertaken) would, undoubtedly, have been reduced considerably later in the century compared to when Mayhew was mulling over such statistics.

In Britain there was often a perception that railroads would be safer if they were administered and operated under the auspices of the state; and that was probably the most common rationale advanced, in the early period at least, for nationalization of the railroads. One source (1838) reasoned that: "The high-roads belong to the public and are regulated by functionaries responsible to the public. Why should not the railroads belong to the public and be managed under the direction of government?"[123] In similar tone, the author of an 1844 newspaper article argued: "No one objects to the government assuming the sole power of the Post-Office; so why, then, to the transmission of travelers, and of all kinds of goods, as well as letters and small parcels (on the railroad)?"[124]

Where America was concerned, the *reality* was no different as to issues of railroad passenger safety, even if the statistical underpinning had its comparative permutations—train travel was *relatively* safe in America. Jensen suggests that in America serious accidents were relatively few in the 1830s and 1840s.[125] And there may have been several reasons for that. Perhaps the most obvious one was that, for both economic reasons and because of relatively poor track construction, American locomotives were seldom run as fast as the English companies ran theirs. Yet, during the 1830s/1840s there were some very well-made American railroads, most notably in those states where the state itself funded railroad development and superintended railroad construction. Furthermore, many of those railroads were built under the superintendence of very competent engineers—often graduates of West Point or one of the new schools of engineering in America. But that period was also prior to the broad acceptance of what became known as the "American System of Construction" (a euphemism for hastily and often shoddily constructed railroads, but with a rationale, nonetheless, as we have noted, hitherto). However, despite its rationale, the American System (of construction), which eventually became all but institutionalized within American railroad capitalism in the 19th century, inevitably compromised passenger safety.

Frances Kemble, who did quite a bit of railroad traveling in America (though mainly in the South) in the late 1830s, commented upon the "curious fact" that half the railroads in America were either "temporary" or "unfinished." But at that time such railroads may have been incomplete or sub-standard because of insufficient funds, rather than having been designed to be "tentative." Nevertheless, this "incompleteness" certainly had a bearing upon the safety of such railroads, but not just where passengers were concerned—Kemble suggested the principal reason so many wayfarers were killed along the tracks at that time was because most of them were railroad construction and maintenance workers.[126]

George Combe, traveling in 1838, found "incompleteness" to be a more general aspect of the American "character," and wondered: "Why many objects in America appear unfinished—the impression of newness and incompleteness is forced on the mind in this country by most of the objects surveyed."[127]

It seems American railroad travelers usually knew not only which railroads were unsafe, but also which parts of railroads were unsafe. Frances Kemble recalled crossing bridges of "a most perilous construction," which she *knew* had given way once or twice previously.[128] However, these were probably wooden trestle bridges, which were not so often encountered in Britain at the time. Such bridges usually looked more rickety than they were when competently constructed. Indeed, one has only to look at photographs of some of the spectacular bridge repair feats—especially by the Union Army Corps of Engineers—in the Civil War to appreciate *that*. Such hastily repaired or constructed bridges invariably looked like they could not take the weight of a train, but they were underpinned by very sound engineering principles regardless of what they looked like.

Domingo Sarmiento (mentioned earlier), who was to become Argentina's first civilian President (1868) and spent a lot of time in America in the late 1840s, said of the American railroads at that time: "To keep down the price it is never safe."[129] However, by "price" it is not clear whether he was referring to construction costs or passenger fares, or both. But there were certainly some very dodgy practices employed by American railroad companies in the 1840s. For instance, many companies were still using strap-iron rails, which had the remarkable tendency to come loose and rise as "snake heads" through carriage floors—Earle suggests there was a time when snake heads were as common in railroad travel as snags on the rivers.[130] And certainly shoddy (read "cheap") construction could be a factor where railroad accidents were concerned and for many decades.

In 1850 the *American Railroad Journal*, reflecting upon a coroner's report pertaining to a serious railroad accident, remarked of the company concerned that "(there was) no excuse for such frequent accidents, since the railroad companies could prevent them by use of good material."[131] And the fact that many companies were remiss when it came to track quality and track maintenance was more than hinted at, even as late as 1869, when the Chicago and Rock Island Railroad, which was in competition with two other companies for the Chicago-Omaha passenger traffic, promoted itself as having "no worn-out rails to run over."[132]

Dickens had written of the "reckless dangerousness of American trains" after his American tour in 1841. And Alfred Bunn, an Englishman traveling in America in the 1850s (the man who lost his ham), remarked that: "The occurrence of accidents is alarming in the highest degree, the casualty rate unknown, it being deemed advisable not to agitate people's nerves to fever pitch"[133]—the truth is there were many accidents, but they were mostly derailments, which were not usually catastrophic. And one of the problems stemming from sub-standard track was that apart from affecting the smoothness of the passenger ride, the jolting could result in the uncoupling of cars, or it could simply break the coupling mechanism—around mid-century it was still necessary (a duty of enginemen and firemen, in fact) to "keep a sharp look-out to see that no portion of the train becomes detached without their instantly observing it."[134]

In America in 1853 there were reportedly 100 *major* railroad accidents, resulting in 234 fatalities and 496 seriously injured persons.[135] But if we divide that number by the number of states at that time, then the per-state *major* accident rate looks a lot less spectacular. Nevertheless, at that time some companies' lines, as in England, were regarded as notoriously unsafe. In the early 1850s the Erie was one such railroad—there were 30 *serious* accidents on its lines in 1852 alone.[136] And following an accident on the Erie much later (1868), one commentator suggested: "We shall never travel safely until some pious, wealthy and much beloved railroad director has been hanged for murder.... Drew or Vanderbilt would do to begin with."[137] Dee Brown cites a contemporary source, well-traveled on both English and American railroads and styling himself a "statistical tourist," who claimed that American railroads somehow managed to kill 16 times as many passengers as their English counterparts.[138] Another source noted that, although in the 19th century American railroad company employees suffered twice as many fatal accidents as passengers, yet passengers suffered more injuries. He also noted the very high incidence of injuries and fatalities due to people "*falling out of* (*car*) *windows*."[139] Some American companies were undoubtedly very lax on the question of safety (even allowing for the American system of construction), though other companies took it more seriously. But, traveling in America in 1860, Englishman, Walter Thornbury, was impressed by the safety measures employed by one company, whereby, during an emergency, passengers could communicate with the driver and "instantly stop the train"[140]— this or a similar facility was not available on English railroads at the time, as noted earlier.

In 1861, Edmund Arnold, a surgeon living near a trunk railroad in New York State, who had been called upon to attend the injured several times consequent upon railroad accidents, published a booklet: "To suggest some means whereby more thought and efficient assistance may be rendered to the injured ... and the average fatality attending casualties greatly diminished." And he asserted of American railroads in his booklet that "There is not a day that some terrible accident may not happen."[141] However, things appeared to get worse, rather than better, across time. This seems to have been due, at least partly, to public indifference; a rather curious artifact of American culture, as already noted, which became all but institutionalized in the 19th century. One northeastern newspaper had observed much earlier (in 1837) that so regular had *steamboat* "disasters" become that "no one seems to feel any interest in the subject."[142] However, Bain suggests that in the late 1860s railroad accidents of some consequence were daily occurrences in America, providing both newspaper editors and readers with "good fodder."[143] However, it seems unlikely that railroad accidents would have merited much space in a newspaper at that time, unless they were noteworthy for the number of casualties, although during the 1860s there were some spectacular railroad accidents in America. One of the worst occurred in 1864—killing and wounding hundreds—in a collision between a coal train and a train full of Confederate prisoners. Army men from both sides of the conflict present at the scene of the accident thought the carnage worse than any they had ever seen on the battlefield. This accident occurred on the Erie Railroad and was attributed to negligence on the part of a (drunk) telegraph operator.

Another noteworthy accident occurred much later (1888) when 64 members of the Total Abstinence Union were rendered fatally abstinent when they were wiped out during an excursion mishap in Pennsylvania.[144] But even if significant railroad accidents were a "daily" occurrence in the 1860s, yet it must be remembered America had many states (and territories) at that time, and their combined mileage was considerable.

Not only did many American railroad companies experience boom times during the Civil War—especially Northern railroad companies involved in army troop movements and military logistics—some companies cheated the Federal Government for all they could get out of it. But due to all that intensive heavy traffic on those companies' lines during the War, the road-beds and equipment were seriously impacted. And it seems that many companies pocketed the profits—which were not as spectacular as they looked on paper, since inflation undermined them—without maintaining their railroads as they ought to have. And many of those companies did not get on top of those maintenance problems for a long time after the War—hence, poor track, substandard rolling stock, and the number of accidents due to either or both impacted railroad traveling for several or many years.[145]

But let us give this litany of American railroad problems and "disasters" some context. Writing in 1876, and generalizing from some very well-founded French statistics to Massachusetts experience (along with his own very astute, sophisticated, and compelling statistical analysis of the variables in the situation), Charles Adams, Jr., concluded: "There were literally more persons killed and injured each year in Massachusetts fifty years ago through accidents to stagecoaches than there are now through accidents to railroad trains." Yet, he noted: "*The first impression of nine out of ten persons, in no way connected with the operation of railroads, would probably be found to be the exact opposite to this.*" He noted that from 1861 to 1870 about 200 million passenger journeys occurred on Massachusetts railroads, but with only 135 cases of injury to passengers. He suggested that when a great railroad accident occurs the attention it receives from the Press "makes a deep and lasting impression on the minds of many people." Furthermore, citing numerous examples, he demonstrated how one serious fatality and injury accident could warp statistics within a given (narrow) time frame, thus making railroad travel seem a lot less safe that it was; whereas in a larger temporal window such statistical "bulges" level out, as well as becoming even more meaningful in a broader comparative context—as when comparing railroad transportation against other modes of transportation.[146] All considered, this was a brilliantly-conceived article for its time, logically founded and reasoned, the statistical analyses sophisticated, and the conclusions compelling.

Another (1876) American article, attempting international comparison where railroad accidents were concerned, found that in the two years 1873–74 there were 661 English railroad accidents, 492 of which could be classified as collisions of some kind, while only 63 were due to derailments. Yet, across the same period in America the statistics were "nearly reversed"—the great majority of accidents in America due to derailments. Our statistical analyst concluded, quite reasonably: "The English collisions are distinctly traceable to the constant overcrowding of their lines (he produced comparative statistics to substantiate that contention), the American derailments to the inferior construction of our road beds"[147]—perhaps he should have included maintenance and not just construction as a key variable in what was otherwise an excellent comparative analysis, the findings of which I have condensed microscopically here.

And it does seem many of the American derailments were avoidable. Peto (1866), on the basis of studying accident statistics and causes, said that three-quarters of American railroad accidents at that time were avoidable simply by using "fish joints" in construction; whereby the ends of rail joints were securely "fished" by plates bolted on each side of the ends of the rails, thus rendering them part of a permanent line.[148]

According to another American statistical "wizard," in the year 1887 a railroad passenger would have to travel 51 million miles before being killed, or 12 million miles before being injured on an American railroad; or, in another "window," would have to travel day and night on an American railroad for 194 years before being killed.[149] I have no idea if these assertions have any credible foundation. But even allowing for significant "margins of error or logical flaws in their underlying premises, yet they point in one direction—that railroad travel in 19th century America, whatever risks it did pose for the passenger, was *comparatively* safe.

Having said that, during the early period of railroading it does seem that, generally and despite what hazards there were in traveling on English railroads, American railroads were not as safe as their English counterparts. To a limited extent we get a sense of that from the comments of some English travelers on the early American railroads. Indeed, they often remarked upon poor track construction; and that factor alone (shoddy construction) would have facilitated more frequent accidents than occurred in England, although not necessarily more casualties, relative to the number of passenger journeys undertaken.

But where track construction, track maintenance, and thus track quality were concerned—as well as a range of other factors pertaining to American conditions—it depended, to some extent, on the railroad company and the state in question. It has already been mentioned that some English tourists before mid-century had thought American railroads constructed by the states themselves were usually constructed to a higher standard, and with better materials, than were many private railroads. But it depended both on the state and the (private) company—numerous English tourists in the 19th century remarked upon how good some (privately-owned) Pennsylvanian and New York railroads were, for instance, but how incompetently managed and unsafe private railroads *elsewhere* were.

English tourist W.F. Rae, traveling in the mid–1870s, thought it "a wonder" that more accidents did not happen on American railroads.[150] On the other hand, some English tourists traveled thousands of miles by rail in America and never experienced a mishap. Foster Zincke, for instance, although he traveled 8,000 miles by train in the U.S. (1867–8) was never involved in a railroad accident.[151] Nor, it seems, was Therese Yelverton, who claimed to have traveled around 20,000 miles while touring America (but not all of it by railroad, of course). One notes, furthermore, that in America some people whose vocations necessitated their frequent use of railroads—Abraham Lincoln in his lawyer days or Louis Gottschalk (the composer and pianist), both of whom would have traveled tens of thousands of miles by rail—seem not to have been caught up in any serious railroad mishaps.

Perhaps one other reason why railroad travel in both Britain and America in the early decades was regarded as being much more dangerous than it was could relate to the number of *prominent people*, or those closely connected to such people, either killed or injured in railroad mishaps. Some of those people may have had occasion to travel more often than most people; therefore, the chance of their being involved in a railroad accident would have been considerably greater than for the population at large, although still very low. First up, on such a casualty list of notables was, of course, William Huskisson, fatally injured during events surrounding the opening of the Liverpool and Manchester Railway in England—he had been a President of the Board of Trade, Secretary for the Colonies, Leader of the House of Commons, and an enthusiastic supporter of railroads. Remaining with Britain, Joseph Paxton—prominent as a landscape gardener, architect, and for his role in the design of the Crystal Palace—was left lame after a train accident. And it is quite well-known that Charles Dickens was injured in, and seriously traumatized by, a major railroad accident in 1865, after which he declared: "No imagination can conceive the ruin of the carriages. I don't want to be examined at the inquest and I don't want to write about it."[152] Later (1876), a son of the English "Railway King," George Hudson, was hit and killed by a train.[153]

Moving across the Atlantic, of the American Presidents, John Q. Adams had been involved in the first fatal railroad accident in 1833 on the Camden and Amboy. Franklin Pierce's son, Benjamin, was killed in a railroad accident in 1853—ten weeks before Pierce was inaugurated as President.[154] And Ulysses Grant's aide, Theodore Bowers, was also killed in a gruesome railroad accident.[155]

Of people connected prominently with American railroads, Cornelius Vanderbilt, a foremost railroad magnate of his time, was involved in the same accident as John Q. Adams; but, unlike Adams, he did not escape serious injury, and nearly everybody else in his carriage was killed.[156] And, interestingly, of the original four prominent American sleeping-car designers (Woodruff, Wagner, Mann and Pullman), two of them (Woodruff and Wagner) were killed in railroad accidents—Wagner burned to death in a carriage of his own design![157]

One factor which no doubt contributed significantly to railroad accidents in the early period was the very limited and ineffective train braking systems. In fact, they were inefficient until Westinghouse patented his air brake in 1869 and it became widely used, automatic features incorporated in its design. In America in the 1860s there had been ongoing trials of various kinds of braking system. In fact, in 1866 some 15 railroad companies co-operatively funded a trial of a brake supposedly able to stop a train running at 45 miles per hour in 10 seconds—the trials were held on the New Jersey Central Railroad, "a great many railroad men were present, and great interest taken in the experiments."[158] The Westinghouse was by 1889 the highest development of the automatic air-brake in America, and by that time most of the rolling stock used in passenger conveyance there was equipped with the Westinghouse automatic braking system, although a few companies did use the Eames Vacuum-brake instead. And in America "air" or "vacuum" brakes were made compulsory on all trains in 1893.[159]

In England in June 1875 trials were conducted on the Midland Railway—with the cooperation of five other companies—to ascertain which of the various braking systems available at the time was the most effective. Those trials, under the watchful eye of a Royal Commission on Railway Accidents, determined that the Westinghouse was the best system. However, it was not until 1889 that automatic, continuous braking systems (applying the locomotive brakes automatically applied the brakes throughout the entire train) were made compulsory on English railroads.[160]

In America, the railroad accident problem escalated quite dramatically as the 19th century progressed, such that in 1900 to 1905 around 10,000 people were being killed and four times that number injured annually.[161] And by then it would have been a moot point to suggest, relative to the number of passenger journeys undertaken, that this was not such a terrible thing, but inevitable and thus acceptable. In fact, most fatalities at that time were the result of crossing accidents, although collisions still accounted for around 30 percent of the fatalities during that period.

As we have seen, America had a very high fatality rate in respect of both wayfarers on the tracks and crossing accidents, and in the early period many of the former were probably working in some connection with railroad construction, maintenance, or operations. But even decades later many track maintenance men were killed up in the Sierra Nevada by coasting (downhill and thus noiseless) trains.[162] But if this kind of work was dangerous, it was probably par for the course where American work safety more generally was concerned—indeed, in 1904 alone *27,000* Americans lost their lives at work, while around half a million were injured seriously enough for the injury to figure in accident statistics.[163] Those workplace fatalities, according to my calculations, amounted, on average, to around ten fatal workplace accidents, per week, per state (48 states) at the time. But obviously some states had more railroads and far more intensive railroad activity than other states. Furthermore, some states may have had more effective work safety legislation in place—pertaining both to railroads and to work more generally—than other states. But in America there was no statutory requirement that fatal accidents be investigated—let alone anybody whose job it was to investigate them—until 1887, when such "forensic" capability was instituted at the federal level under the auspices of the Interstate Commerce Commission.

Another important factor, which may have impacted passenger safety in the early period, which is probably not well-known today, was the color blindness of some railroad company employees. In fact, it did not begin to be realized that color blindness could be a safety issue in the operation of railroads until the early 1860s. The first developments in that area came in France, where one company took the initiative, testing 1,050 men aged 18–50 years between July 1863 and October 1876. The railroad workers were shown objects colored violet, green, blue, yellow, and red. Nearly 10 percent (98) of the men tested mistook at least one of those colors and another 37 men gave correct answers only after repeated hesitations, or otherwise with some difficulty.

This research (reported in America in 1878) made it apparent that it was necessary to first test the eyesight of any man before he was employed in a role which included observation of railroad signals or otherwise required the ability to discriminate colors. Further experimentation with the phenomenon of color blindness was undertaken in America in the early 1880s and its findings publicized. Consequently, the Pennsylvania Railroad Company, taking the lead as it often did at that time, began to employ a consulting ophthalmologist from 1882, both to supervise its color blindness testing program for employees and to decide all doubtful cases.

The employees of the Reading Railroad Company, five years later, were not especially willing to submit themselves for such eye examinations and threatened industrial action in response to that company's proposed eye testing regime. However, the testing of one engineman employed by the Reading Railroad Company found that he declared a red danger signal to be a green light at a distance of two feet, as well as being unable to distinguish a red from a green flag at six feet; and he was also unable to discriminate white, red, green, and blue flags, even with them in his own hands! This research was conducted before representatives of the employees of the company, which served to silence their opposition to such testing, since clearly public safety was at issue. And it also made it apparent that enginemen or people otherwise employed by railroad companies, whose duties included the monitoring of signals during their work, ought not to be employed in such capacities should they have any problem with color discrimination.

Of America, it must be said that it was always the railroad company employees who took the clear majority of "hits" where company safety issues and policies were concerned. Even from 1888 to 1907 over 53,000 American railroad company employees were killed and over 800,000 maimed or crippled on the job—the death statistics cited account only for those who died within 24 hours of the accident. Furthermore, in that 19-year period (1888–1907) the percentage of the U.S. railroad workforce either killed or injured at work *increased* by 3.1 percent.[164]

There are three other factors worth mentioning in this chapter, *which might be thought* to have marked off 19th century American from English railroad travel where the question of *passenger safety* was concerned: the use of stoves for heating in passenger cars, which significantly increased the risk of fire in the event of a mishap; train robberies; and Indians.

Stoves, Train Robbery, Indians and American Railroad Passenger Safety

An 1889 American magazine article noted that even by that time stoves were still being used in railroad cars and presented an especial hazard:

> The number of passengers burned in wrecks is greatly exaggerated in the public mind; but that fate is so horrible (that not surprisingly) the deadly car stove (has been) the object of persistent and energetic attacks by the Press and in State legislatures. The result has been the development in the last three years ... of heating by steam or hot water, and even by electricity. In fact, the manufacture of such apparatus has already become an industry of some importance...[165]

However, the article went on to point out that fires in train accidents were probably just as often started by kerosene lamps as by stoves; its author noting, furthermore, that America lagged way behind other countries, such as Germany, in that few American railroads had adopted compressed gas for car illumination—which was described as safe, inexpensive, and a very good source of illumination.[166]

How safe were 19th century American railroad passengers in the event of train robbery? Perhaps 19th century America's foremost detective affords the authoritative statement on the subject. Writing in November 1893, William Pinkerton referred to a "recent epidemic" of train robberies in different sections of the country at the time. He pointed out that at the time, although train robbing had been "practiced pretty steadily in the South and West during the last twenty years," yet "during the last few months outrages have increased at an alarming rate." He noted, furthermore, that of this recent spate of robberies the greater proportion occurred south and west of the Missouri River, with Texas being the most seriously afflicted state—apparently, the first train robbery occurred in 1866, but the robbers netted only $3,000, rather than the $100,000 they had anticipated, because they got their train schedules mixed up!

Armed robberies of *coaches* had been common enough and had been most likely to occur in the goldmining states—Nevada, Colorado, Montana, and California—where coaches were known to carry large gold and cash consignments. And one reason train robbery became increasingly prevalent related to the fact that as railroads penetrated those mining regions, the express companies switched from using coaches to railroad cars for moving cash and precious metals. In fact, in earlier times there had been very little highway robbery in America because people tended to use drafts and bills of exchange instead of carrying large cash sums with them. But there was the occasional "highway robbery"—just as a stage was to start off from a tavern door, "a woman jumped on the step, seized the bonnet of a woman, tore it from her head, and made off with it!"[167]

Coach robberies had not usually resulted in fatalities. Between 1870 and 1884 Wells Fargo coaches, for instance, were robbed on 313 occasions. However, only ten fatalities resulted from those robberies (4 passengers and 6 Wells Fargo employees). But Wells Fargo was very successful in bringing to justice those who robbed its coaches—it achieved 206 convictions in that regard. However, the low fatality rate in respect of robberies of its coaches meant that only 7 of the 206 convicted robbers were sentenced to hang. Yet, in Montana the Plummer Gang killed over 100 people during its coach robbery career before its members were all hunted down and killed.[168] But the deterrent to killing people during a robbery was that the killer faced hanging if caught.

Pinkerton suggested there had been "no train robberies of any importance before the (Civil) War." And he attributed the phenomenon's emergence partly to the "general business depression" and partly to "the reading of yellow-covered novels." In respect of the latter, he suggested "country lads get their lives inflamed with this class of literature." Although we might think this a laughable (causal) attribution where the motivation of train robbers was concerned, yet there are many people today who attribute violence and crime to media influence; so, Pinkerton may have been both correct and ahead of his time (with his criminologist's cap on), rather than off the mark. In fact, he suggested impressionable, wayward boys reading such literature were easy targets for professional thieves recruiting would-be train robbers. And Pinkerton mentioned, in that connection, a seventeen-year-old boy who had participated in a train robbery in Arkansas in 1882 "Who had seen a railway train for the first time to hold it up."[169]

Sometimes one gang alone had been responsible for robberies within a state. Indeed, Pinkerton remarked, "I do not recall a single case of train robbing in Southern Indiana since the execution of the Renos, whereas before that a train was usually robbed there about every sixty days." Indeed, one thing Pinkerton had noticed about train robbers was that "they generally go in families," there usually being two or three members of one family in the same gang.

But the robbers were not always considered to be the villains. Christopher Evans and John Sontag, for instance, who robbed Southern Pacific trains in the San Joaquin Valley until taken by a 3,000-strong posse were regarded popularly as folk heroes—because they were engaged in "robbing the biggest robbers ever known (the Southern Pacific was widely hated in California and beyond)."

Pinkerton suggested it was a myth that many train robbers got away with large sums of money; suggesting, to the contrary, that *in every case* capture and punishment are "*almost certain*." And this was not mere bravado on the part of a law enforcement officer promoting his own business. Pinkerton attributed robbery crime resolution rates not to state law enforcement agencies, but to "The *prompt and energetic action of the express companies* (*they* were the victims of robbery, not the railroad companies) in persistently following up train robbing gangs, and never giving up the search until all the robbers are landed in prison or killed." But clearly Pinkerton's agency did a lot of that kind of work.

In the decade of the 1890s there were 261 train robberies in America resulting in 88 fatalities. However, the robbers often came off second-best ultimately, as Pinkerton suggested they did; since a remarkable *two-thirds* of train robbers during that period were either killed in attempted robberies, or subsequently apprehended and executed. That was impressive, since very few police forces anywhere in the world today—given the investigation techniques and technologies they have at their disposal—would be able to boast of such a resolution rate in respect of armed robbery crimes, fatal or otherwise.

Pinkerton also made it clear that *railroad passengers were not usually in any danger during train robberies*, since it was only very rarely *they* were robbed; the express car, which usually carried large amounts of cash, was invariably the target, and the clerks or security guards inside it the people most likely to be killed. In fact, passengers were unlikely to be harmed unless they confronted the robbers during a robbery.[170] But even if the chance of a passenger being killed during a train robbery was remote, yet it seems sometimes fear in that regard was disproportionate to the risk—the English traveler, T. S. Hudson, noted in 1881 that recent train robberies near Tucson, Arizona had made the (railroad) route in question "temporarily unpopular."[171]

If the railroad companies were not, strictly speaking, the victims of train robberies, yet they sometimes could capitalize on the notoriety of those who robbed their trains. In Alabama there was a legendary negro train robber in the 1880s, "Railroad Bill" (Morris Slater), who had commenced his "career" by breaking into boxcars to steal food and other items, which he sold, or, Robin Hood–like, gave away to poor blacks. He progressed to armed robbery, once terrorizing the entire crew and passengers of a night train with his "gang"—which turned out to be a gang of scarecrows, each holding a lantern or torch. But when he was finally killed, the Louisville and Nashville Railroad capitalized on his folk hero status by exhibiting his body in every colored waiting-room along its Atmore-Grenville line, and charging people twenty-five cents to view it![172]

Indian attacks on trains—even if good fodder for moviemakers later—were rare in the West, but did happen occasionally. There were instances of Indians derailing trains, for instance, their primary intention being not to kill whites, but to loot freight wagons since the extermination of the buffalo had left many Plains Indians near starvation (steamboats on the Missouri River were occasionally attacked by Indians from 1860 to 1876 as well).

In the late 1860s the Kansas Pacific, whose trains were attacked occasionally, was arming passengers on some of its trains.[173] But generally after the Civil War railroad passengers in the West had little to fear from Indians. In fact, railroad passengers in the West passing through some Western towns probably had more to fear from drunken cowboys taking pot-shots at the lights of passing trains at night!

During the 1870s (railroad) tourists in the West often had their closest encounters with Indians at railroad stations, where the women and children were often to be seen begging or selling trinkets, while the men made a few cents loading wood onto the tenders. R.L. Stevenson was shocked at the degraded state of the "noble" Indian, confiding that he was "ashamed for the thing we call civilization."[174] But all tourists to the West recoiled so when encountering the state of the Indians. William Hardman, for instance, touring in 1883, thought the Indians he encountered along the railroad "hideous, dirty, sly-looking imbeciles."[175] Australian tourist, James Hogan, thought the Indians he saw at Reno "unkempt, sly-looking," and that "most seemed to be sadly in need of a good sleep."[176] Englishman, W.F. Rae's first sight of Indians (Pawnee) was at Jackson, 100 miles west of Omaha, and he thought the Pawnee probably considered themselves civilized because "each carries a revolver in a belt strapped round his waist."[177] And of the Indian women hanging around stations, Boddam-Whetham noted: "The women will inform you that they are good squaws, and sometimes produce a dirty scrap of paper on which is written a certificate of good character, and the information that they can wash well. (But) from their appearance unfortunately never do!"[178]

Tourist William Hardman encountered Chief Sitting Bull at Mandan station, where the Chief was selling his autograph for $1.50.[179] And at some Union Pacific depots around 1870 railroad tourists could buy scalps from Pawnee[180]—at Elm Creek Station Boddam-Whetham was offered a "most disgusting-looking scalp" for one dollar. But the ever-candid Therese Yelverton remarked of Indians she encountered in the West (Wyoming): "Certainly the picture of civilization set before them was not calculated to raise them in the scale of humanity."

At Laramie station in 1876 Henry Williams found a platform with a collection of fossils, minerals, animal heads, and "other interesting curiosities" (no doubt many pertaining to Indian culture) on display and for sale; though Williams noted that that such collections were to be found "at all stations on this part of the route"[181]—presumably all of this paraphernalia was intended for sale to tourists as souvenirs of the West, but it probably had little to do with the railroad company concerned, being a stationmaster's or company agent's business "on the side."

Capitalizing on the Fears of 19th Century Railroad Travelers

In England entrepreneurs were quick to capitalize on public fears concerning the perceived risk of railroad accidents—there were even hats said to eliminate all risk of concussion from railroad travel,[182] though it is not clear how many people acquired one and used it. And in his superb little book Mencken considers some of the very strange, though occasionally sensible and quite practical, contrivances patented in America in the early railroading period—some intended to pacify and reassure passengers, or even physically protect them from harm.

If there were risks involved in early railroad travel, and such risks were either exaggerated or their extent misunderstood in a broader comparative (statistical) context, yet there were vested interests (and not just sellers of hard hats) able to capitalize on the (often misguided) anxieties and fears of the early railroad travelers—enter the travel insurance companies.

In America a passenger injured in a railroad accident had only a reasonable chance of getting any compensation from a railroad company, just as taking a railroad company to court for anything was unlikely to be successful. Twain "milks" this fact in *The Gilded Age*, where a J.P. advises a passenger: "But suin's no use. The railroad company *owns* all these people along here, and the judges on the bench, too.... You hain't no chance with the company."[183]

Likewise, in Britain for several decades railroad companies attempted to evade responsibility for railroad accident fatalities or injuries. However, people could prosecute a case before a jury in a civil court *if* the railroad company was not forthcoming with a realistic offer of compensation. Occasionally, and rather cynically, English railroad companies attempted to prove passengers had been negligent in the matter of their own safety—as in one case (in 1836), when the railroad company claimed the injured party had jumped from, rather than having been thrown out of, an open carriage in a derailment accident. The passenger, who had been traveling in an open third-class carriage on the Leeds and Selby Railway, suffered serious leg and foot injuries, which left him partly disabled. The jury found for the victim and awarded him £400 damages![184]

If, in the early period, the English railroad companies had often failed to be "proactive" when it came to compensating railroad accident victims, yet it seems that later they tended to concede liability often. In fact, during the five years 1867 to 1871 the English railroad companies paid out a sum equivalent to U.S. $11 million in compensation for injuries occasioned by accidents.[185] But, as a Royal Commission was told in 1877, *it was more economical for the companies to pay compensation to injured passengers (by that time) than to put adequate safety measures in place.*[186] Furthermore, it may also have been more economical than allowing compensation cases to go to court, and thus having legal expenses to pay as well; ultimately the company paying more in compensation and legal expenses than would have been the case had a reasonably realistic offer of compensation to the victim been made in the first instance. Furthermore, well-publicized court cases involving wrangles over accident victim compensation could harm the company's image, and especially so regarding safety matters, more generally; so that was another reason for the companies to opt for out of court settlements.

The advent of railroad travel insurance in Britain around mid-century took a lot of pressure off the railroad companies in the matter of compensation, which is probably why, from the outset, most railroad companies cooperated closely with the early travel insurance companies.

The first of the English railroad travel insurers, the Railway Passengers Assurance

Company, was incorporated in England in 1849. And it did its efforts at self-promotion no harm by asserting at its first general meeting (in 1850): "There were great numbers (of casualties) which never found their way into the newspapers, especially in the provincial districts." By early 1850 the company—with the cooperation of numerous railroad companies—was offering single-journey and "time-period" insurance tickets on 27 companies' lines. In fact, only a few companies had by March 1850 chosen *not* to cooperate with that insurance company or any other.[187] Such insurance schemes enabled passengers, for a small surcharge on their tickets, to purchase insurance for the duration of any journey, or to cover travel across a short timespan, but there were also comprehensive annual insurance packages covering all railroad travel for an entire year.

In its first six months, the Railway Passengers Assurance Company issued over 11,000 single-journey insurance tickets—most (4903) were issued to third-class passengers, 4,063 to second-class passengers, and 2,516 to first-class passengers. And two things are of especial note here—one is that so many third-class passengers *could afford* travel insurance, although they apparently could not afford to travel second-class (which was arguably safer); and, secondly, that these third-class passengers (who could afford to pay for travel insurance) evidently perceived an elevated risk associated with traveling third-class.

The Railway Passengers Assurance Company also offered insurance to those railroad company servants who traveled on trains during their work—a premium of £1 per annum was payable for insurance against fatal accidents, and 10 shillings per annum for insurance against personal injury. But surely the employer should have been insuring those people, or adequately compensating them when work-related injuries occurred?[188]

Arguably, such insurance schemes were popular with the railroad companies because they enabled them to limit their own financial liability (and moral responsibility) in the event of serious accidents or disasters—effectively, by shifting financial liability for injuries and death onto the passenger (or railroad company servant). It was probably assumed (and no doubt correctly) by the railroad companies that passengers would be less likely to sue for negligence (often hard to prove) if they were insured.[189] On the other hand, perhaps the enthusiasm with which English railroad companies endorsed such insurance schemes indicated, if nothing else, their wont of faith in their own ability to safely administer and operate their railroads!

Travel insurance was commonly offered to rail and steamboat passengers in America from the early 1860s. In fact, the first travel insurance company in America was chartered in 1863 (James G. Batterson's Traveler's Insurance Company) and eleven other companies had entered the field by 1866—in that year seven accident insurance companies consolidated to form the Railway Passengers Assurance Company, and for a long time it and the Travelers' Insurance Company (both under the Presidency of Batterson) commanded the field.[190]

When the Englishman, Robert Ferguson, was touring America in the 1860s, he was approached by an insurance agent while traveling on a steamboat from Washington to Richmond, the insurance agent providing him with a copy of the *Railway Accident Gazette* as part of his "sales pitch"—the *Gazette* detailed "all the most frightful cases of smashing to pieces, scalding to death, drownings, blowing up into the air...."[191] English tourist, W.F. Rae, found, when departing Omaha west-bound on the transcontinental railroad in 1876, that many passengers took out passenger insurance—in fact, an insurance company agent walked through the train before its departure. And Rae remarked of this phenomenon: "Americans are too shrewd a people to omit making arrangements in view of the consequences of a railway accident."[192]

However, taking out travel insurance fitted rather comfortably, I think, with the prevailing American ideology of individual responsibility. But it also indicates, in respect of earlier arguments here, that if the American railroad traveler was more (cheerfully?) "risk-prone" than the English counterpart, for whatever reasons, yet there was, at least occasionally, some "method" to his perceived "madness."

Risk-Taker Versus Inmate

We have considered a raft of factors concerning the relative safety of English and American railroads in the 19th century. But perhaps the last word on *that* subject ought to go to Domingo Sarmiento, who, in astutely summing up the two different railroad systems that prevailed in Europe and America in his time, suggested that the "European (railroad traveler) *is a minor under the tutelage of the state*; his instinct for self-preservation is not considered sufficient protection: bars, gates, fences, watchers, warning signals, and inspection are required to save his life."

By comparison:

> The Yankee looks after himself, and if he wants to be killed no one stands in his way.... *This is how the character of a nation is formed and how liberty is used.* Perhaps there are a few more victims of accidents; but, on the other hand, *there are free men, instead of disciplined prisoners leading regulated lives.*[193]

However, perhaps this needs a bit of unravelling.

In America the persistence of "frontier" and "early settler" mentalities, not to mention the stoical, driven, self-made man-*ism* mentality, all helped to inure people against the exigencies and adversities of life. And it might be argued that, relative to the English upper and middle-classes, for instance, Americans were more likely habituated to, and steeled against, discomfiture and risk, and thus in no need (or so they liked to think) of the "indignity" of being coddled by the state, or by a railroad company for that matter. And as Sarmiento pointed out, these were also people who liked their liberty unconditionally and accepted the relatively higher degree of risk entailed in exercising it. Perhaps this aspect of the American "mentality" was indicated by the fact that in America by the 1890s collisions between speeding trains were being staged as fund-raising stunts—one such stunt, attended by 30,000 paying spectators, involved a head-on collision between two trains running at 60 miles per hour (one spectator was killed and others injured by flying debris).[194] But surely the dead and injured had the right to place their lives at risk as spectators of such a mindless undertaking (one assumes there was no research rationale underlying this stunt?).

In 19th-century England and America railroad passenger safety also had a lot to do with the extent to which central government assumed the role of regulating railroads. In England, for at least the first couple of decades of railroading, Parliament scrutinized each company's Bill of incorporation and safety issues were certainly given due consideration, even if they were not to the fore. The problem was that as the railroad industry developed—speeds increased, traffic intensified, and the railroads extended—there was no sufficient ongoing regulation of railroad administration and operations. The Board of Trade ostensibly had a role to play in regulating railroad administration and operations from quite early on, but it lacked both the muscle and resources to be able to adequately regulate railroad operations in a safety point of view. However, the state did introduce legislation, from time to time, *which applied to all railroad companies.*

The situation was quite different in America. From the outset, the Federal Government stood very much aloof of regulating railroad company activities, including in a safety point of view. To a point, the states assumed that role, although generally their (regulatory) agencies—where they existed—were even feebler than England's Board of Trade was for a long time. Another problem was that for decades every railroad company chartered by the states had its own unique charter; and, whereas in England a degree of central government oversight and regulation of railroad companies tended to rationalize the regulatory framework all companies were eventually subject to, in America that kind of rationalization was largely absent for a long time—because neither the federal or state governments would or could (railroad corporations became much more politically powerful in America than they ever did in Britain) step into rationalize railroad administrative and operational regimes. In fact, for decades each company continued to operate under its original charter, despite radically and rapidly changing circumstances. Passenger safety was one of the "casualties" of that.

Six

The "Railroading" of Consciousness in the 19th Century

Few buildings are vast enough
To hold the sound of time,
And now it seemed to him
That there was a superb fitness in the fact
That the one that held it better than all others
Should be a railroad station.
For here, as nowhere else on earth,
Men were brought together for a moment
At the beginning or end
Of their innumerable journeys.
Here one saw their greetings and farewells.
Here, in a single instant,
One got the entire picture of the human destiny.
Men came and went, they passed and vanished,
And all were moving through the moments of their lives,
To death,
All made small tickings in the sound of time—
But the voice of time remained aloof and unperturbed,
A drowsy and eternal murmur
Below the immense and distant roof.
—T. Wolfe, *The Railroad Station*

Introduction

It has been said that every means of transportation, once adopted, imposes itself on society and exacts a "price" that nobody ever bargained for; and, furthermore, that as it becomes dominant it compels the society that uses it to conform to its own special demands.[1] That was undoubtedly true of the advent of railroads in some respects. However, as argued here, the "national style" of a technology is *shaped by* sociocultural (and economic) factors, rather than the technology having something inherent to it which gives it a powerful (sociocultural) determining dynamism of its own. To some extent, this chapter further explores such considerations as they apply to the advent of railroads in the 19th century.

The advent of railroads was a major element both underlying and precipitating many of the seismic shockwaves which washed over society, culture, and consciousness in the 19th century; instituting, and effectively defining (or *re*-defining) many aspects of life and experience which we today may recognize as quintessentially modern. Indeed, it has been said that the railroad ushered in America's modern age and that no aspect of American life remained unaffected by the railroad in the post–Civil War period.[2] But the same could be said of Britain and, indeed, of every society in which the railroad arrived, sooner or later.

In this chapter I want to focus not so much on the social and cultural impact of railroads; but upon how, in a broad conceptualization, their advent impacted upon *consciousness*. This "psychological" dimension to the impact of the advent of railroads has had little attention in the literature, although Wolfgang Schivelbusch probed it somewhat tentatively in *The Railway Journey*. And although the psychological dimension to the advent and impact of railroads is thematically central here, yet that theme is not conspicuously signposted on every page; nevertheless, it is always lurking somewhere beneath the surface. Furthermore, to some extent the "railroading of consciousness" in the 19th century was impacted by the peculiar national styles of railroading that developed; so, it was not necessarily a phenomenon experienced in the same way by early railroad travelers everywhere.

Even as early as 1829—well before the commercial viability of railroads had been established *indubitably* or their likely impact fully theorized and rationalized—the *Mechanic's Magazine* had declared of the railroad: "We think it will produce an entire change in the face of English society."[3] Almost seventy years on the American *Commercial and Financial Chronicle* could look back to the advent of railroads and declare: "The fact is the railroad revolutionized everything."[4] Walt Whitman certainly had no doubts about the historical significance of the railroad, describing it as: "Type of the modern—emblem of motion and power—pulse of the continent."[5] And in attempting to give the advent of railroads some broader historical context, Thomas C. Clarke (1889) stated: "The world today differs from that of Napoleon more than his world differed from that of Julius Caesar; and this change has chiefly been made by railways."[6]

The railroads did, indeed, revolutionize society, overturning long-standing traditions, conventions, and institutions—the railroads impacted powerfully, both directly and indirectly, upon the social structure of Victorian society in Britain, as I hope I managed to evince in earlier chapters. But everywhere they gave rise directly, or contributed to, the emergence of new institutions and structures. Furthermore, they absolutely gave the pace of life, in both its economic and sociocultural aspects, an adrenaline-like infusion. And they profoundly altered the everyday experiences of people, especially so regarding broadly-conceived "lifestyle" factors. Indeed, in America the railroad was described in 1877 as:

> The agent teaching order, punctuality, and business promptness to the whole country.... Local prices no longer exist, but are all regulated by reference to those of the cities, quoted in the daily papers. Agriculture has been infused with a spirit of business, and the farmer ... now looks to the distant market.... It is the same with the small interior towns. The freight of the railroad enters as a factor in *every exchange* performed all over the country, and its rise or decrease is a subject of importance to everyone.[7]

The advent of railroads had a profound, and one might even say "severe" impact upon society, culture, *and consciousness* in the 19th century. Indeed, the severity of the impact was not just material and visual, as in its impact upon the landscape and the built environment; but also, directly or indirectly, regarding the undermining of local traditions, communities (and the "sense of community" as well, often), subcultures, and symbolic forms, meanings, and values—all of which serve to give people a relatively fixed sense of personal identity.

Indeed, there were aspects to the advent of railroads which did not impact differently—well, not remarkably so—in the two national contexts under consideration here, England and America. On the other hand, there were significant points of departure—notably where the construction, administration, and operation of railroads (as well as passenger traveling experience) in England and America respectively were concerned. Yet, the points of convergence are no less interesting and ought to be accounted for.

So, although a lot of what follows is cast in general terms, the reader ought always to be cognizant of the fact that the national styles of railroading—English and American—may have influenced the phenomena I generalize about here; but, arguably, not to the extent that the tenor of what I have to say here is undermined.

From Horse Power to Mechanical "Horsepower"

The advent of the (rail) "way" itself, regardless of what it gave rise to eventually, portended the demise, or significant transformation of, some other modes of transportation, and the ancillary industries and institutions associated with them. Such change, albeit over an extended period, had a subjective dimension to it, insofar as it impacted upon many people's experience of day-to-day reality—hence, it engendered and necessitated some *psychological* adjustment to the new order of things.

That such change penetrated consciousness to the extent it did was one reason why some people declaimed against the advent of this new mode of transportation so vehemently. On the other hand, romanticizing that which is in demise, or already "bygone," is a phenomenon which often has a deep psychological mooring. So, moving to that level of analysis, let us momentarily reflect upon how the transition from a world in which *horse power* ruled, to one in which *mechanical* power was to become transcendent, impacted upon people at the level of "consciousness."

The horse had always been a favored emblem of speed (and strength) wherever its powers were familiar. Its applications also related to considerations of status and dignity in many societies, as memorialized in the colloquialism of somebody said to be "riding a high horse." In a similar (linguistic) connection, we also have the "dark horse"—a concept applied to people who, like the unpredictable (possibly fractious or intractable) horse, represented uncertainty, an unknown quantity, or an enigma. Such colloquialisms indicate the horse had weaved its way into popular consciousness (via language) over many centuries in much the same way that the locomotive and the railroad did in the 19th century—think of all the railroad metaphors which came to infuse language (off the rails, getting up steam, letting off steam, fast track, etc.).

The significance of the horse was also weaved into the religious tapestry of the pre-modern era. St. George, the patron saint of England, was also the "special protector" and patron saint of horses, and recognized as such more widely throughout Europe. St. Stephen was also a patron saint of horses. Even further back historically, St. Anthony, too, an Egyptian Christian (3rd/4th centuries CE.), had been a patron saint of horses. And one notes Saint's Day (December 26th) had formerly been considered an auspicious day for bleeding horses.[8] So, we see the horse was even implicated in Christian religious culture. And that, too, probably helped to consolidate its "cultural" and "psychological" significance more broadly across the centuries.

For those experiencing the speed and power of the locomotive for the first time there was nothing comparable to it. Previously the fastest and most powerful transportation means had, indeed, been the horse. And, logically, mechanical force or power came to be calculated in terms of "horse power"—a measure which, somewhat anachronistically, survived the Industrial Revolution and is still applied.

But its strength or power aside, the horse posed problems as a motive power—the horse had a head of its own, it was costly, it was exhaustible, it could have a very limited working life, and its industrial applications were also limited (the use of stationary steam engines was much more feasible in factories). True, the early steam engines—both stationary and mobile—were unreliable, they were sometimes dangerous (due to boiler explosions), they were expensive, there were few people who knew how to operate them safely and maintain them, and they consumed vast quantities of water and fuel (coal, coke, or wood). But as the technology was refined across the decades such problems were ironed out.

The boiler, when incorporated into rolling stock and *placed on rails* to effect mechanically-induced vehicular mobility, was a technology (more correctly an amalgam of technologies) which took many decades to master. Indeed, even after the early railroads appeared to have proved their utility, doubts remained for many years concerning both their economic viability and mechanical reliability. The Stockton and Darlington, for instance, used horse-drawn carriages on and off until April 1834—primarily because the cost of using horse power was about one-third the cost of operating locomotives.[9] And the directors of other English companies were still debating *in the mid–1830s* whether horses might turn out to be the more reliable motive power option for railroads.

Initially, many people simply could not comprehend the new technology or its effect upon sensibility, except in terms of equine concepts and metaphors. English actress Frances Kemble's encounter with the new technology—the "mares" in George Stephenson's stable (the horse analogy was apparently Stephenson's own)[10]—is quite illuminating in that connection. Indeed, Kemble's quite comprehensive description of the locomotive gives us a wonderful sense of exactly the kind of incomprehensibility I refer to above, despite her having been acquainted with (and understanding perfectly) the niceties of the locomotive's (mechanical) "workings":

> The *reins*, *bits* and *bridle* of this wonderful beast is a small steel handle, which applies or withdraws the steam from the *legs* or pistons…. The coals, which are its *oats*, were under the bench, and there was a small glass tube affixed to the boiler, with water in it, which indicates, by its fullness or emptiness, when the *creature* wants water, which is immediately conveyed to it from its reservoirs…. This *snorting little animal*, which I felt rather inclined to pat, was then harnessed to our carriage.[11]

Similarly, as late as 1839 the author of a newspaper article described an English locomotive thus: "The *bones* here are iron and brass," the "tireless *tendons* rods of steel," and he thought it did *"pant and snort* in grand style."[12]

The use of equine metaphors to describe the new technology reflected the fact that a monumental transition was occurring—both objectively and subjectively. Objectively, it was in the form of a transition from the organic to the mechanical; subjectively, it went deeper—from the experience of natural rhythms, to mechanical, artificially-induced, "rational" rhythms and processes.

This transition, from the organic to the mechanical, the natural to the artificial rhythm, was encapsulated in the equine metaphor variously in the 19th century. Thoreau, for instance, wrote: "I hear the iron horse make the hills echo with his snort like thunder, shaking the earth with his feet, and breathing fire and smoke from his nostrils." And, again: "The fire steed flies over the country.... He will reach his stalls only with the morning star.... At evening I hear him in his stable, blowing off the superfluous energy of the day, that he may calm his nerves, and cool his liver and brain for a few hours of iron slumber."[13]

Apart from being called the "iron" horse (and sometimes the "steam" horse[14]), there was also the iron *steed*—the title, in fact, of a poem by R.L. Stevenson, in which he describes the "iron horses" in an "iron stable":

> In our black stable by the sea,
> Five and twenty stalls you see—
> Five and twenty strong are we....[15]

A German visitor used similar terms to describe the locomotive depot at Derby (England) in 1844: "Not less than sixteen engines were standing in this immense rotunda, and I compared the whole to a colossal stable for the reception of these snorting and roaring railway horses."[16]

Leo Marx has suggested that the term "iron horse" supports the notion that mechanization under North American conditions had a peculiarly intense impact upon consciousness[17]; notwithstanding that, although the term "iron horse" may not have been used as prevalently in Europe as in America, yet it was used there, along with similar metaphors.

But in North America the horse (or mule) had been *one* form of (animal) motive power prominently implicated in the "opening" of the West—*bovine*, not equine, beasts usually hauled the Conestoga wagons and prairie schooners in the West. The railroad eventually replaced the horse as the transportation lifeline linking remote regions with towns and cities. But in America it certainly was an *iron* horse that was needed to help fully conquer the most "rugged" parts of the West.

Wolfgang Schivelbusch has argued that the relatively uniform motion of the steam engine and the ride on rails very quickly became accepted as "natural" compared to the motion generated by animal power; hence, mechanical uniformity became the "natural" state of affairs, while the nature of draught animals, comparatively, came to be viewed as dangerous and chaotic[18]—he might have stream-lined this view, had he ridden on one of the 19th century "bucking bronco" American railroads! But we can accept his point, albeit with the qualification that it took several decades for the "iron horse" to become "tractable" enough for it to be considered fully "domesticated."

Indeed, there was also the concept of the iron *pet*, as used by Max Maria von Weber, for instance: "The iron pet must conform its entire being so precisely to circumstances of place and time, that its construction must ... be as carefully acclimated as the nature of the live pet." This invocation of *pet* is interesting and perhaps has a different connotation to that of "iron "horse." After all, a horse needs to be "broken in" and tamed; and even after it has been, the horse may remain fractious and unreliable, unwilling, sometimes intractable. By way of contrast, the concept of "pet" implies domestication, tameness, and human mastery; so that the pet is not "unruly" and does not pose any sort of threat. Furthermore, early locomotives, in both Britain and America, were given names, which could also be interpreted as a pet-like regard for them (although this was consistent with the naming of coaches in both national contexts)— in America, the Galena and Chicago, for instance, continued naming its locomotives until 1857.

However, the concept of "iron" in the term "iron horse" has its own peculiar imputations. Indeed, the concept of iron, employed metaphorically, has been used to describe, among other things, the laws of nature, political rule (of Bismarck, for instance), and bureaucracy (Max Weber). Furthermore, the concept of "iron" in the term "iron horse" did not necessarily refer only to iron as a material used in the construction of locomotives or rails. Rather: "The attribute iron, about the natural as well as the human and historical, pops up *wherever irrefutable, utmost energy and necessity have to be made evident.*"[19]

In 19th century America *railroads* were commonly described in terms of iron metaphors, such as "veins of iron," "arms of iron," "iron bands," and the peculiarly Mississippian "iron stream." In the 1840s railroads were also referred to as "iron bonds," since they had the potential to bind the states indissolubly, or so some thought. And in the American West the train brakeman, whose job incorporated "rounding up" and coupling cars, was often known as an "iron horse *wrangler*" (a "wrangler" on a ranch rounded up or herded stock).[20]

The Railroad and the "Nomad"

In what is one of the sillier attributions to the advent of railroads I have come across, it has been suggested the "gift of mobility," which the advent of railroads in Britain engendered (as if the wheel was only discovered with the advent of railroads!), was bestowed upon "a race that retained a strong nomadic instinct," and thus it "touched deep and ancient human feelings."[21] Although, as I argue here, the advent of railroads had a powerful impact upon consciousness, I doubt it ever took the form of awakening atavistic or primal urges such as those underpinning prehistoric nomadism. But what of all the transportation technologies which preceded the advent of railroads? Why had they not touched "deep and ancient human feelings" and aroused the same "strong nomadic instinct?"

As is often the case with new technology, it is only accessible, in the first instance, to the wealthier people in society. The advent of railroads *in England* was no different. The poorer English "nomads" sometimes had to wait a long time (decades) before they could satisfy their "primal nomadic urges" by means of a railroad journey. But in England after mid-century, consequent upon the advent of railroads, aristocratic and wealthy types could own numerous country houses, easily access them from London, and be hunting in the morning or even the early afternoon, and yet be in the debating chamber of the Commons or Lords for an evening debate. And the poor, although unable to participate in such esoteric forms of "nomadism," could, nevertheless, enjoy a richer diet—fresh milk, fish, fruit, and vegetables, and often at cheaper prices than hitherto, as the railroads played their part in re-configuring the capitalist system (the production, distribution, and consumption of commodities).

The Railroad as an Industrial Production System

How we conceive of a railroad is fundamental to our understanding of precisely what railroad passenger travel entails. In an earlier chapter I discussed the sense in which a railroad ought to be conceived of—essentially as entailing a factory-like, industrial production system. Indeed, a railroad has many of the characteristics of a factory production process. In fact, in England the commodification of railroad travel was wedged between the rationalizing imperatives of the bureaucratically administered, factory-like, industrial production process on the one hand; and some observance of the existing social class boundaries on the other, which gave rise to the peculiar English passenger class system *and* the compartmentalization of carriages.

However, what essentially makes modern mass production, mechanical assembly line techniques models of efficiency is the way in which the interlocking rhythm, synchrony, and symmetry of the production process underpins them. Yet, arguably, the railroad production system has these interlocking attributes as finely-tuned (when all is going well) as any other (factory) production system. In fact, one might argue that the railroad is the exemplar of such a process. Indeed, in the early period the railroad industrial production system came to epitomize—and arguably served as a microcosm for and exemplar of—the rhythm, symmetry, and synchrony *typical of* a capitalist industrial production system. And one might go further—to argue that it was the production of a railroad journey that first suggested the idea of a unified *production line* in many other industries, though I know there are historians who would take issue with that contention. However, the production of a railroad journey was a much more complex process and characterized by a much more elaborate division of labor than making pins or nails in a factory at the time.

Although the entire technique of production incorporating a railroad—with all its ancillary institutions—has seldom been understood in the literature as "factory," yet it has often been described as machine-like. Benjamin Burt, an early 20th century American railroad executive, conceptualized the railroad so. He noted the "quasi-military character" of railroad organization, as well as how the small-town depot, the railroad agent, and the station were all simply cogs in a vast machine and operating in accordance with imperatives emphasizing hierarchy, precision, and obedience[22]—if American railroad functionaries lacked discipline, yet that had no bearing on the overall disciplinary aspects, systemic rationality, and machine-like character of railroad *systems* themselves. Indeed, the railroad has been described as an expensive, complex *machine*, spread out over vaster distances than one mind can comprehend at a single moment, and programmed to do many things, in many different places, at the direction of many different people. It either works right or it hardly works at all; and when it does not, it can be disastrous for both human life and property.[23] If nothing else, this conception of a railroad, too, highlights its similarity to a complex factory production-line system.

But an *1874* American magazine article makes that equally apparent in describing the Erie Railroad at the time as:

> One of the longest lines of railroad in the world, employing fifteen thousand persons *in various occupations*. It is estimated that there is scarcely an hour of the day or night when there are not one hundred trains running along its line. The *administration of such a force of men*, the *management of such a system* of railroad trains, without clashing or collision, requires executive ability of the very highest order.[24]

True. But what was it that really marked off the railroad from any other *industrial, factory-type, assembly-line production system* working "around the clock"? Nothing. It was no different. It simply produced railroad journeys or freight transit instead of cigarettes, screws, bonnets, or pork sausages! And I know many railroad romantics out there are going to hate me for asserting that, but it is a simple fact.

System and Network

It is often said of railroads, and more so of communications developments more generally today, that they annihilate space and time; and more especially is it said that such developments "shrink" space, compressing us all into an ever tautening "global village"—as if we are all now wired up to each other through our Internet connectivity and mobile telecommunications systems. Thinking about that enables us to get a sense of how, in the same regard, the advent of railroads may have appeared somewhat ominous to contemporaries. But the apprehensiveness concerned began with the gas system, not the railroads. Schivelbusch has noted of the early 19th century gas networks:

> To contemporaries, it seemed that industries were expanding, sending out tentacles, octopus-like, into every house. Being connected to them, as consumers, made people uneasy. They clearly felt a loss of personal freedom.... Once a house was connected to a central gas supply, its autonomy was over.... No longer self-sufficiently producing its own heat and light, each house was inextricably tied to an industrial energy producer.[25]

Some people were no less apprehensive about the development of the telegraph system later (in the 1840s). By 1848 Britain's telegraph systems extended some 3,500 miles, half that mileage associated with railroads.[26] But the railroad systems appeared on the landscape just as ominously as the gas and telegraph systems did. And just as the domestic gas user was pulled into a network, a system, so, too, were towns, cities, regions, *and people* drawn into a network, a system, by the railroads. And as this railroad network grew and intensified, so too did all its little sinews constrict correspondingly and, consequently, *people became increasingly aware of their subjection to, reliance upon, and being part of, indeed integral to, a (railroad) network.*

An American Congressman addressing the House in 1846 enthused of the railroad and telegraph that "With the social influence of these two great inventions, all the peoples of the continent may be molded to one mind."[27] Similarly, one notes the celebrations in San Francisco attending the opening of the first transcontinental railroad and a notion expressed on that occasion that railroads somehow dynamically impact upon the "collective consciousness" of society: "Causing the sentiments, thoughts, ideas, feelings, and wishes of each section (of society) to intermingle with, and become assimilated to, the thoughts, sentiments, ideas, and feelings and wishes of every other section."[28] Yet, at the time this was thought by most people to be a benign, if not a desirable end. In fact, one might well search in vain to find a thoroughgoing "George Orwell type" in America at that time—somebody who thought the intensification of communication and transportation systems was an *inherently bad* thing (in America critics of the advent of railroads tended to focus on selected presumed negative *consequences* of it and often from the standpoint of a sectional *economic* interest). In fact, the railroads" presumed contribution to the intensification of "collective consciousness" was a premise invoked *in support of railroads generally* in the 19th century. Indeed, one (American) writer described railroads (in 1838) as: "The strong clamps which are destined to bind together, with ribs of steel, the whole of this great country."[29] In the same connection, railroad systems were also described as "iron nets."[30] And in more recent times John Stilgoe has invoked the concept of the "metropolitan corridor" to characterize the radiating nature of modern railroads (as well as what they convey)[31]—a concept which seems to harmonize very well with sociologist Georg Simmel's concept of the railroad radiating the "tumult" of the metropolis.

In America during the early period railroads were almost invariably promoted—at least in part—for their presumed regional, or even national, significance; and how, in the latter case, they would ultimately contribute to effecting "national unity." In fact, that was a *central* argument in support of the first transcontinental railroad, while across the decades the same argument was invoked to support the notion that railroads would prevent secession by some states.

An underlying assumption to that kind of thinking was that a national railroad network would "shrink" the nation; consequently, social relations would become more compact, and thus more intimate and solidary.[32] In the 1850s Walt Whitman, for instance, was somewhat intoxicated by the notion that railroads (along with telegraphy) would have an undeniable *unifying* impact upon society.[33] And this was, for decades, generally thought to be an inevitable and most desirable consequence of global railroad development. Yet, the reality was that, arguably, *society*—especially in America—did *not* become more coherent and solidary. But, rather, and paradoxically enough, increasing individualism, apparent demographic instability, loss of a sense of "community," and the anomic and alienated person were to emerge as *conspicuous bi-products of the advent of railroads*, and of modernity, more generally.

The Railroad and the "Aura" of Place

We have already seen how the railroad *system* gave people the sense of being drawn into a *network*, resulting in a perceived loss of autonomy. We also considered (earlier) some of the ways in which railroad companies attempted to impose their presence, such that their stations seemed like "gateways" to towns and cities, while their aesthetic embellishments of environs gave the presence of the railroad a friendly visage. Furthermore, in the early period the popular notion, that the presence of a railroad might somehow augment or enhance the "aura" of towns and cities, was highlighted by the "millennial" fervor which often preceded and attended the railroad's appearance in a locality. Indeed, in Britain, but much more so in America for decades, cities and towns were often tripping over each other in their bids to attract a railroad to their vicinity. Clearly, that was because the presence of the railroad was thought to variously *enhance* the "aura" of the locality. However, in *The Railway Journey* Schivelbusch describes the impact of railroads on "local identity" in terms of a *loss* of aura. But the railroad *could* variously enhance the aura of a place, and especially so, for instance, if the "place" happened to be: a rundown fishing village converted into a seaside resort; an obscure, depressed rural town or "place" converted into a rustic retreat or spa; or a village or town suburbanized and embellished by an impressive railroad station, with landscaped and "prettied up" environs.

That said, the tentacle-like expansion of railroad systems—along with all their economic, social, cultural and psychological consequences—went some way towards undermining the distinction between city and country, urban and rural. In fact, Leo Marx has cast the railroad's erosion of the traditional distinction between rural and urban in terms of a "centrifugal force that threatens to break down ... the conventional contrast between these two styles of life."[34] And John Stilgoe's concept of the "metropolitan corridor" (already alluded to) has no less force in that regard. However, we should not lose sight of the fact that in major English and American cities, even before the advent of railroads and for decades after they appeared, intensive dairying and other types of farming (even market gardening) were to be found in the very hearts of such cities. Furthermore, the "countryside" could be considerably less than two hours walk from the center of such cities as London. Therefore, it is possible to overestimate the extent to which the advent of railroads contributed to a narrowing or "etherealizing" of the urban/rural divide, at least in the short term.

The "Industrialized" Railroad Traveler

In an earlier chapter I discussed the bureaucratic form of managerial administration which emerged within 19th century English railroad capitalism, as well as attempting to explain the reasons for its emergence. I drew attention to how the institutionalization of various disciplinary regimes within English railroad capitalism highlighted the nature of its administrative and operational form and "culture." And I noted how that impacted upon the different passenger classes and, ultimately, upon the class structure at large. But I emphasized that such "bureaucratic domination" of the English railroad passenger was necessary, due to the nature of the industrial process which the production of the commodity (travel) entailed. Indeed, in England the passenger neither stood beyond these disciplinary regimes nor could be unaffected by them, since they were necessary for the establishment and maintenance of fundamental (safety) boundaries.

In America, comparatively, although similar boundaries governed the operation of railroads, yet certain American values (as described earlier) effected some peculiar "forms of resistance" to the imposition of a factory-type *discipline* upon the American traveler. However, such forms of resistance had no significant impact upon the factory *system* which governed the production of a railroad journey; and that factory system of production progressively strengthened as corporate power increasingly came to govern the production system in question, regardless of the forms passenger accommodation took.

It has been remarked that transportation systems are, "strictly speaking, neither structures nor machines."[35] However, they have some of the characteristics of both, though neither, nor both together, adequately portray what a railroad is. A railroad is, in fact, *a factory-type production system, characterized essentially by industrial process and an attendant system of bureaucratic administration (of the processes of production, commodification, and consumption); conducted in accordance with imperatives pertaining to surveillance and (time-) discipline, and all of this within an over-arching corporate structure.*

Indeed, as one source has noted, on a railroad every movement of the traveler, suitcase, mailbag, locomotive, and employee is somehow channeled, somehow *engineered*.[36] From another angle, we might note how the railroad station—before the electronic age, which changed things a little—was incomplete without its crop of notices to inform, exhort, or order passengers about[37]; not to mention the horns (in the earliest period), whistles, bells, gongs, shouted orders, and (in England especially) functionaries to shepherd, superintend, and discipline passengers.

In the 19th century there was nothing necessarily "mindless" about railroad constraint of passenger movements—even allowing for the national differences where this phenomenon was concerned—since it was often in the interest of safety that passengers were, to a point, "herded," streamed, disciplined, and variously processed. In fact, as we have seen, it did not take long for some people to start complaining about the "coddling" of (English) railroad passengers—treating them as if they had no "common sense" at all and, therefore, that they needed to be treated like sheep or cattle. On the other hand, and as already alluded to, many English railroad passengers wanted, or needed to be herded, guided, directed, and shunted by railroad officials, and eventually many of them associated this (disciplinary) "coddling" with safety and security of railroad travel.

The railroad terminals were eventually of an architectural form highly conducive to the rational engineering which moving masses of people (and freight) through space necessitated. But, conceived of correctly, *the station or terminal was an extension of the train* because both were integral to the over-arching factory-like, industrial process which "produced" a railroad journey. Hence, the terminal or station engendered an engineering of space for the purposes of separating, otherwise ordering, conveying, channeling, and controlling people, as well as optimizing the administration, discipline, and surveillance of them (*and* of railroad servants). Certainly, the elements of *engineering* and *discipline* were conspicuous, in that passengers: had to timetable their movements in conformity with the railroad companies' schedules; had to queue for tickets and to gain access to platforms; had to present tickets on demand; often had to sit (or even stand in the early period in Britain) where directed so to do; and, more generally, they had to follow and conform to the procedures laid down by the railroad companies.

In that connection, Schivelbusch has noted that before 1860 there was generally no direct access between reception area and station platforms:

> The latter could be reached only by moving through the waiting-rooms. In these, the passengers (like air travelers in our day) had to congregate and wait until the doors were opened shortly before the train's departure.... This regulation prevented the travelers from reaching their trains in an uncontrollably individual fashion.... There were doubts as to the general public's ability to deal with industrial machinery in the absence of precise regulations.

This processing of people in large numbers insinuated itself powerfully upon the sensibility of some people. Louis Gottschalk was, in his time, as well-traveled (by train) as anybody in America, yet he never really accommodated to the "alienating" aspects of railroad travel. He remarked of his railroad traveling experience: "To be alone and find yourself surrounded ... by the multitude and feel that, aside from the indirect relations of the ticket office, no other tie attaches you to those who surround you—*is it not worse than ostracism or the desert?*"

Yet, perhaps such experiences of "alienation" or "anomie" were symptomatic of what was happening in society at large at the time—the "microcosm" of the railroad journey simply making the experience rather more stark. In fact, if in the early period the industrial dimension to the passenger traveling experience disarmed people, yet in England the *administrative and operational constraints* (which were part and parcel of the industrial process) exercised over passengers were, perhaps, even *shock-inducing* initially *for most middle-class people*, and certainly novel (and quite possibly traumatizing initially) *for the upper-classes*. Indeed, we, habituated as we are to industrial process, probably underestimate the extent of that, and certainly many railroad historians seem to. But the latter is indicative of the fact that railroad historians have never really taken a philosophical approach to the phenomenon of the railroad; hence, its true nature has never really been fathomed. And Wolfgang Schivelbusch seems to me to be the only railroad historian who has not "missed the train" in that regard.

Mitigating the Industrial Dimension to Railroad Travel

In the 19th century the rapid industrialization of the objective world and of corresponding everyday subjective experience were evidently "shock-inducing" to some extent. Hence, it was sometimes necessary to attempt to cushion the impact of such shocks and various strategies were employed by *railroad companies* to that end. What I want to suggest is that much station architecture—and other aesthetic embellishment of railroad systems, for instance—had to do with the fact that railroad traveling entailed the passenger's "processing" within a factory-like, industrial production system. Hence, the architecture and other aesthetic embellishments of the railroad system were often designed essentially to mitigate the impact of the industrialization of the railroad traveling experience. On the other hand, railroad systems both engineered space and industrialized the landscape wherever they went. And these industrial "corridors," as well as their nodes and terminal points—which could themselves industrialize large areas in towns and cities—also needed to be aesthetically varnished by various means to mitigate the sometimes woeful impact of the railroad on the landscape.

Indeed, the inclination to camouflage, and thus mitigate the industrial aspect to such impact on the landscape and the lived environment, was reflexive from the earliest times of industrialization. This tendency is identifiable initially regarding relatively innocuous technologies with *domestic* associations, such as the chimney—an architectural appendage which the domestic dwelling shared with the first industrial establishments proper. In the 16th century a house emitting smoke was, apparently, as disagreeable as the body's discharge of "matter," presumably one reason why chimneys atop the grand houses of the wealthy began to be elaborately decorated with carvings, or otherwise tastefully ornamented. In Italy, at around the same time, fireplaces, too, in the houses of the wealthy, were embellished quite extraordinarily, often with columns, pilasters and entablatures. Were such developments essentially aesthetically-inspired? Were they primarily symbolic of status and affluence, and thus forms of conspicuous waste? Undoubtedly, these would often have figured as rationales. After all, the hearth could be something of a "shrine" in such households, just as it was in poorer households (as a source of heat and light). But why elaborately ornament a *chimney*, the detail work of which could not be seen from the ground, anyway?

In the early 19th century attempts to mitigate or camouflage the glaringly industrial character of railroads by means of architectural embellishment were hardly unique within industrial "culture." This was, in fact, a more general symptomatic response to early industrialization and its impact upon consciousness and the environment. When gas lighting was first introduced, for instance, its novelty and presumed hazards led to the use of architectural forms intended to present such new technology to the public in a "secure and familiar image."[38] In fact, gas tanks had become ubiquitous in public places by around mid-century and they had to be made "agreeable" to the eye—however, they were embellished not just to be aesthetically pleasing, but also to offset public anxiety about the likelihood of their exploding. Hence, they were embedded in architectural forms which both reassured the public and "softened" the technology's industrial character. There was similar embellishment of (gas-lit) sidewalk candelabra and consoles, both of which could be eyesores during the day—they were often given an ornamental character, both to mitigate their industrialization of the landscape and to dignify them.[39]

The physical transformation of the world by humans may necessitate some corresponding manipulation of symbols and imagery, both for aesthetic purposes and to accommodate the needs of human sensibility. One fundamental impact of the railroad on the landscape was to industrialize it simply by running the rails and locomotives through it, let alone whatever else appeared on the landscape relating to the railroad. This industrialization of the landscape was mitigated not just by architectural means, but by recourse to numerous other strategies as well. One such strategy related to the naming of stations and other structures associated with railroad administration and operations. Sometimes this "naming" (in England) was calculated to conjure up images of rustic torpor and beauty:

> Many bailiwicks illustrated the flora and fauna of their regions. Signal boxes reveled in such names as Thrustle Nest Junction, Sutton Oak, Etruria, and Bo-Peep. Smoke- and dust-laden engine sheds were designated Belle Vue, Botanic Gardens, and Dairycoates. Dusty, draughty marshalling yards had names like Daisyfield, Freshfield, and Mayfield, conjuring up images of pastoral serenity.[40]

Six. The "Railroading" of Consciousness in the 19th Century 249

But the cosmetic dimension to mitigating the industrial, factory-like quality of the railroad and railroad travel extended beyond the manipulation of language. It began with landscaping and planting railroad embankments—the latter effectively "dumps" for earth excavated when making cuttings, which could be deep and extend for miles. That was followed by the aesthetic embellishment of tunnel entrances, the "prettying up" of the "mobile boiler," the use of railroad architecture to "soften" the industrial "processing" of the passenger, and, indeed, *dignifying one type of freight by calling it a "passenger."*

In Britain, the hanging flower basket became a common sight at rural and some suburban stations. And in the 1880s some companies also encouraged the creation of gardens on station platforms.[41] However, the railroad gardening movement had its origins on the Continent—most notably in France, Germany, and Switzerland. And it was also evident in North America before long, where shrubbery, ornamental trees, and especially depot and right-of-way lawns "represented the first fruits of a spatial aesthetic, which came to be peculiar to suburbs, and dear to the hearts of commuters torn between urban and rural aesthetic values." But in Canada railroad companies went further, sometimes responsible for the laying out of station gardens which covered entire city blocks (complete with bandstands and fountains).[42]

We should not underestimate the significance of these horticultural embellishments of railroad property in England; where it was still being debated, around mid-century, whether there should even be such things as *public* parks and whether there should be floral displays in such parks. English railroad company involvement in horticultural display, apart from being used to enhance a railroad company's public image or even an image of itself as being "environmentally friendly," was also conducive to a perception of it as "progressive." Indeed, flower gardens in public parks gave most people without gardens the opportunity to see flowers. Arguably, those railroad companies which went in for "floral prettiness" were aligning themselves with the forces of progress by endorsing the concept of the "democratization" of aesthetic experience—even if they did not extend it to third-class passengers locked in windowless carriages![43] In Britain, the Jacobean and Tudor villa styles of country and suburban stations—with their trellised gables and pretty flower gardens—certainly did the corporate images of the railroad companies no harm at all, either. After all, such quaint, rustic-flavored railroad stations even found their way into Loudon's 1842 edition of his *Encyclopedia of Cottage, Farm and Villa Architecture*![44] But there was another dimension to this "prettying up" of railroad stations (and of railroad property, more generally).

The station or terminal often served effectively as a "gateway" to a town or city. Some railroad companies wanted their stations—both their architecture and the broader aesthetic embellishments of them—to be either the most prominent or the most aesthetically pleasing of local landmarks. Hence, their stations and termini were vying with the town hall, cathedral, churches, and other public buildings for, quite literally, "pride of place" (this was more evident in Britain than in America). Indeed, a persistent idea around mid-century was that the station was to the modern city what the gate had been to the ancient city; the railroad companies went in for great "gates," too— for the first decade of its existence the great gate at Euston Station led anticlimactically to a ridiculously small building. And although the grand entrance to Euston Station cost over £30,000 to construct, the company thought it money well spent from a publicity point of view—probably true, since for quite some time it attracted visitors as a spectacle. However, it was suggested, a few years later, that a good *station* could have been built at King's Cross for less than the cost of the ornamental archway at Euston.[45]

Schivelbusch takes this point further, suggesting that the station functioned as a gateway which had to connect two different kinds of traffic space (and traffic) with one another—the traffic space of the city and that of the railroad. One part of it—the neoclassical stone building—belonged to the city, while the other part, the iron (or steel) and glass construct was a pure function of the railroad's industrial side.[46] The station entrance, which in Britain (in the case of city stations) was often not unlike entrances to museums and art galleries, could be grandiose; and insofar as it demarcated two different kinds of space, as Schivelbusch suggests, it served effectively as a threshold, and one like that of a church—the church entrance separates two different types of space, the sacred and the profane (or secular). But within the context of this analogy the church entrance is not just an entrance and a boundary, but a "limit"—even a "frontier"—separating two distinct dimensions to reality, *psychologically* as well as materially (spatially and architecturally). Likewise, the threshold of the railroad station entrance separated the (relatively) non-industrial experience of everyday life beyond the station from the industrialized, factory production space, which the inside of the station engendered.

On the other hand, it seems the railroad companies often intended—by using architecture and architectural ornamentation—to collapse that very distinction between (industrial) "railroad space" and what lay beyond it. Indeed, it has been suggested that mid–19th century (European) termini were characterized by such architectural grandeur and majesty that they might be "More fitted for the performance of an oratorio on a gigantic scale than for the wanderings of bewildered travelers."

As noted earlier, John Ruskin believed that the use of classical architectural styles in railroad buildings resulted in travesty, serving to demean more appropriate applications of such styles in the construction of art galleries and museums, for instance.[47] However, there were many grand mansions of the aristocracy built with classical architectural features during the period concerned—if not earlier—which Ruskin, no doubt, would have thought *did not* make a mockery of such architectural styles. Was that inconsistent? After all, what was the difference between embellishing a *mansion* chimney and a *factory* chimney with classical architectural motifs?

If the railroad company's "front-door" was immaculately swept, so to speak, by being aesthetically decorated architecturally, yet often its back-door—in the form of warehouses, marshalling yards, and workshops—was usually more or less a dirty blot on the landscape. So, the (immaculate, grandiose, or otherwise embellished and aesthetically pleasing) front-door did often serve a conspicuously cosmetic function for the railroad company and its operations. But it is important to understand that *what the railroad passenger was subject to—within the industrial process of producing a railroad journey—was simply a "makeover" of (parts of) the very same industrial process which gave rise to the nasty back-door areas of railroad operations.*

The Railroad and Time Consciousness in the 19th Century

Time is necessarily bound up with rhythm, synchrony, and symmetry: "The symmetrical-rhythmic formation emerges as the first and simplest structure through which, as it were, reason stylizes the material of life, and makes it controllable and assimilable. It is the first framework, by means of which reason is able to penetrate things."[48] Moreover, in modern society time is inextricably bound up with social structure, and especially so in its connection with authority, power, knowledge, and status. Indeed, time has been described as a "veritable social institution" and as one of the key categories bound up with the moral conformity which makes society possible.[49]

People undoubtedly became more time-conscious as the 19th century proceeded. The advent of railroads played a part in that development. But countless other factors were of consequence, not the least of which was the time-discipline which became increasingly institutionalized within industrial capitalism from the late 18th century. But time consciousness was fetishized in Victorian Britain more generally. Indeed, Davidoff has attended closely to the Victorians' strict ordering of time—diurnal, weekly, and seasonal—suggesting that previously only monastic and religious orders had ever controlled behavior through the day with the same minute exactitude as the Victorians. But she also suggests that it was the introduction of train travel, at fixed times and to fixed destinations, that did so much to create boundaries of time units in people's minds.[50]

However, arguably that was a development in motion well before the advent of railroads. Indeed, even in the pre-railroad era a socially expansive time-consciousness was in evidence, the growth of the clock- and watch-making industries themselves (which were already "gearing up" for mass production by the mid–19th century) indicating that. In fact, pocket watches had started to become popular around 1700, and upward of 150,000 were being manufactured annually in Britain by the end of the century.[51] In America, even by 1814, there was one manufacturer (Eli Terry) of wooden clocks—with interchangeable parts—made by mechanical techniques, the mass production of which could produce 12,000 such clocks a year. And from the late 1830s Terry's compatriot, Jerome Chauncey, was producing cheap brass clocks which flooded both the European and American markets. So, it seems that, even in the early 19th century, increasingly people thought they needed to know the time, but not so that they could catch a train!

The clock has been described as the most important *machine* of the industrial age; and especially so for its contribution to the need for exact measurement and for synchronizing human activity.[52] Yet, by the time the railroad age arrived there was already a socially pervasive time-consciousness in both England and America, and a corresponding remarkable demand for both watches and clocks, as noted above. This demand was met by the development of mass production techniques. Consequently, clocks and watches became cheap enough to be accessible to a broad cross-section of society. And the phenomenon of timepiece possession was rather like the way in which today mobile phones—which for many years were quite expensive and not widely accessible—have become broadly accessible because they are so cheap (virtually given away, in fact, by some companies). And people became more time-conscious than they had ever been simply because personal timepieces became more accessible to them, However, these timepieces were initially "novelties" and (the more expensive of them) also fashion accessories and status symbols, regardless of the extent to which their pervasive presence in society indicated the emergence of a new time consciousness. So, it is not as if *before the railroad era* people did not care very much for knowing the time or had no need for precision time-keeping. However, no doubt once the railroads appeared on the scene and regular, scheduled services commenced everybody who used them regularly, and could afford to buy a *portable* timepiece, rushed off to buy one—certainly, we can say that the advent and increasing use of the railroads *boosted* the sale and use of timepieces.

In fact, we know a bit about just how accessible timepieces had become in Britain by the mid–19th century because Henry Mayhew tells us something about that. Mayhew estimated that at that time there were around 25 people vending *cheap* watches on London streets alone and that German-made *children*'s gilt watches were being sold on London streets from 1850 at the remarkably accessible price of a penny each—the supply of these watches was not equal to the demand, one street vendor of them telling Mayhew he had sold *24 dozen* during one Saturday night/Sunday morning sales stint. In the mid–1850s better quality French-made watches were being sold on London streets; initially for a shilling before the price dropped to sixpence—they were said to be "delicate."[53] Mayhew also noted that *the best venues for street-sellers of watches were railroad station precincts*—who would have guessed that? Of course, there were also the much more expensive gentlemen's timepieces, which were not sold by street vendors; and people who traveled first- or second-class on the English railroad would most likely have bought their timepieces from a specialist watch-maker or a watch retailer of some distinction.

As for domestic clocks, American Thomas Nichols remarked in 1864: "Clocks are made in great factories, and so entirely by machinery, that almost the only hand-work is in putting them together; they are made so cheap as to be brought to England in immense quantities, and from England exported to every part of the world.[54]

But it is important to emphasize timepiece ownership did not necessarily equate with "elevated" time consciousness, since watches became status symbols, too[55]— indeed, as watches became broadly accessible, finely crafted silver, gold, bejeweled, elaborately chained, or multifunctional watches became status symbols by means of which the wealthy and "superior" marked themselves off from the rest. In America for a time the "Engineer's Special," characterized by gold chains and loud ticking, became popular with the well-heeled. And no doubt many connected with the railroads owned one (railroad entrepreneur Jim Fisk had one).[56] But they were also in demand by members of the public who could afford one.

The advent of railroads could only *raise* further the level of time consciousness in society, a certain marked degree of which was already in evidence in both England and America at the time of the advent of railroads.

Railroads and Timetables

The late Jack Simmons informs us that the word "timetable" was invented by the railroads. And that the mail-coach time bill was "not a schedule, but a device" for "checking the punctuality of coaches over each stage of their journey."[57] Well, how could one check their punctuality unless the time bills were, effectively, schedules?

It seems to be a common misconception among transportation historians that the railroad companies were the first agencies to popularize the notion of timetables. The advent of railroads may have made people *more time-conscious*. But *timetables* are a different matter. And surely even in the 18th century people—especially factory operatives and those otherwise engaged in time-critical types of work (mail coaches, for instance)—were already subject to an objectively imposed time discipline. They were, therefore, already relatively time-conscious and their daily lives governed by timetabled routines. But the key point here (and one many railroad historians seem to overlook) is that *timetables do not have to be written down for people to conform to them*, nor do people need access to the time to conform to them. Indeed, people can and do conform to timetables, even though such timetables may not be in print or general circulation—so what did Rousseau really achieve by (famously and somewhat melodramatically) throwing away his watch? Not much!

The simple fact of the matter is that timetables have long been extant in Western culture, perhaps for at least fifteen hundred years, first in monastic culture and, later, when they became more generally embedded in Christian liturgy. Indeed, beyond monastic culture, consciousness timetabling became firmly and more broadly nestled in Western culture with the advent of *The Book of Hours* and, later, due to the Reformation and the influence of Calvinism. Was not the Calvinist a very time-conscious man, who ordered his time on some rational basis and, therefore, structured his day in accordance with that timetable? But did he need a clock and a timetable to do it? Later, the self-imposed disciplinary regimen of the Puritan added another layer of time-consciousness to the time-discipline of the "Protestant Ethic."

Where *secular society* was concerned, it seems that from around the 15th century time consciousness became increasingly embedded in the cultures of *etiquette* which the European upper classes identified with. And from that time etiquette incorporated "timetables of decorum."

But it is really within Christian religious culture that we ought to locate the genealogical roots of the Victorian (middle- and upper-class) preoccupations with eating, dressing, visiting, and quite possibly even breeding in conformity with a rigid time schedule. And even if, relatively, the lives of the upper classes of society were not governed by the same "cast-iron" time-frames as the lives of factory operatives in the late 18th/early 19th centuries, yet dinner was usually served at a regular time and "morning calls" could only be made between certain hours (in the afternoon!).

As for agriculturalists, fishermen, and the like, they too were governed by timetables, and always had been, but timetables of the kind which derived their impetus from the rhythms of nature.

Industrial capitalism, and especially the factory system of production—which is precisely the institutional setting I have argued the production of a railroad journey occurred within—imposed a *new kind of time discipline* on the lower social classes subject to it. But this preceded the advent of the railroad. So, the advent of the railroad was not such a monumentally significant event as might be thought where time consciousness and timetables were concerned—at least not for *some* social classes.

Nevertheless, the railroads made their own peculiar contribution to time *consciousness* and time *discipline* in the 19th century. And *the timetabling of consciousness*, which *regular* railroad travel required, was not necessarily unproblematic for people. Indeed, it no doubt required a considerable psychological adjustment for the *bourgeois* traveler not accustomed to the temporal disciplines of factory culture or to the exactitude of imposing timetables. And the railroad's contribution to the *precision* timetabling of consciousness, first impressed upon the English (middle- and upper-class) public *on a grand scale* with the advent of railroads, may be considered a significant factor in the emergence of modernity.

The advent of the *precision, printed* railroad timetable in the 19th century, given its novelty for some social classes in both Britain and America, was significant enough. But it was even more significant for capitalists, whose business interests were predicated upon a capitalist system which entailed the rapid, reliable, regular circulation of raw materials and consumables, and thus a rapid and "rational" circulation of capital.

However, we should not overestimate the relationship between a new, railroad-impacted *time consciousness* and the advent of railroad *timetables*, since the early 19th century railroad companies, in both England and America, operated in accordance with printed timetables which often had the same fictive quality as a novel. In fact, in the 1830s the unreliability of the locomotives on some companies' lines in both countries was such that timetables were suspended altogether or they became the objects of popular jokes. Again, this is something many railroad historians are either unaware of, or they obscure it because it does not fit with the thesis they are advancing.

Indeed, on one English company's lines in 1838 trains left each station "as soon as ready," not necessarily at the time stated in the timetable.[58] And even in the early 1840s the advertised departure times of trains probably turned out to be fictional rather than iron-cast quite often (and perhaps that had not changed much on some lines by the late 1850s, indicated by the number of complaints to English MPs from their constituents about late trains during that decade).

The Great Western conceded its timetables were works of fiction in 1840—in that year it abandoned timetables altogether for about four months, so unreliable were its locomotives. (I.K. Brunel seems to have had some influence on their specifications and design.) And during that period the company was often only prepared to announce at what times trains would leave termini, *not venturing to prophesy when they would arrive at any particular station*.[59] Of course, the company had only a limited number of locomotives, so there was no guarantee one would even come out of the "starting-blocks," let alone on time![60]

However, in Britain these "teething" problems had been ironed out by the mid–1840s on most lines; had they not been, then Bradshaw's monthly national timetable guide, which first appeared in 1841, would have seemed as if it belonged in the literary black humor genre. In fact, Bradshaw's had first appeared in pamphlet form in 1839, then in booklet form the following year. However, somewhat surprisingly, the advent of the monthly national timetable guide was, apparently, viewed unfavorably by the railroad companies themselves, which feared that such timetables would make punctuality "a sort of obligation."[61]

But timetables were one thing, station clocks another. A letter to an English newspaper in 1845 pointed out that the two public clocks at Edmonton Station—within 100 yards of each other—differed by four minutes![62]

In America there were no such things as timetables on the early railroads. Starting times were usually governed by the arrival of stage coaches or steamboats from other places—many early American railroads were seen by their proponents as "feeders" to canal or river systems. The passenger on an early train, therefore, often never knew beforehand when he might reach his destination, while a person who was waiting for a train at some station along the line never knew when it would arrive. Dunbar put this in rather attractively quaint terms, though what he had to say was no doubt accurate: "After a brigade of cars disappeared in the distance, nothing could be known of its adventures until it came back again the next day." And the "enigmatic" train did not endure for just a year or two in America, for it was not until about 1847 that the principal railroad companies began to issue regular printed schedules—up until that time most companies advertised the "hoped-for movements" of their trains.[63] So, again, we need to realize that the timetable, where early railroads were concerned, was seldom made of the same "stuff" as the rails.

Having said that, B.F. Skinner noted a phenomenon from his younger days (in the early 20th century), which would have been extant many decades earlier in most outlying American towns and country villages. He recalled that a remark like "I came back last night on the twenty-six" needed no further explanation. And if the local paper reported that "the happy couple departed on train seven for points in the West" everyone knew exactly when they had left.[64] Well, perhaps not exactly. But even if the train was late, and even considerably so, yet people still had some sense of approximately what time the (train) event had occurred.

Likewise, we might attend to some lines of a poem by S. Sassoon:

> I hear a local train along the Valley, and "There
> Goes the one-fifty," think I to myself; aware
> That somehow its habitual traveling comforts me,
> Making my world seem safer, homelier, sure to be
> The same tomorrow; and the same, one hopes, next year.[65]

Of course, it did not matter much if the "one-fifty" turned out to be the two o'clock, since, again, the *approximate* time was sufficient to reflect the predictability and reliability of the "one-fifty" from the local standpoint.

The Creation and Imposition of Railroad Time

During the 19th century English railroad capitalism effected some monumental time rationalizations. That development was first and foremost a response to railroad administrative and operational imperatives, insofar as they related to considerations of safety, efficiency, and profitability. But, essentially, it entailed a more "rational" production of railroad capitalism's basic commodity—motion at speed. Indeed, the rationalization of temporal structures within railroad capitalism was part and parcel of the broader development of capitalism, and of industrial capitalism, especially. Hence, railroad capitalism's "engineerings" of time were more broadly functional to the capitalist system.

The time standard eventually embraced by English railroad capitalism in the 19th century was derived from the time standard "invented" at the Royal Observatory, Greenwich in 1675 and known as "Greenwich Meantime." This time standard had originally been invented for the benefit of maritime interests and in consideration of military/strategic factors. So, it was by no means widely recognized in England at the time of the advent of railroads. In fact, it did not make its first metropolitan appearance as a standard until 1829, when a new Post Office was opened in London, and Greenwich Meantime was the time shown on its turret clock. This "London Time" was not officially recognized at the time as a national time standard, but arguably it was a national time standard, since it became the time standard for the mail coaches. However, one might qualify that by noting that although the mail coaches were regular along some routes and operated on an extensive network, yet their relevance to the everyday lives of most people was not such that London Time was widely embraced as a time standard at the parochial level. And some people realized a national time standard was desirable—as early as 1828 scientist Sir John Herschel, for instance, had pressed for a standardization of time in England.[66]

In 1840 the Great Western Railway Company adopted London Time as a standard for its operations and displayed it on its station clocks. In the same year the Board of Trade recommended all railroad companies use London Time as a standard, while in 1845 Henry Booth, Secretary of the Liverpool and Manchester Railway, petitioned Parliament to establish one standard time for railroad operations throughout the country.[67] Most English railroad companies were not averse to observance of a universal time standard, since they recognized its utility as their operations extended geographically and something like a national railroad network began to emerge. Furthermore, as the intensification of traffic (especially through traffic) increased the possibility of human error as a cause of accidents also increased—due to miscalculations in reconciling regional or company time discrepancies.[68] Furthermore, regional time standards were not at all conducive to the degree of calculative rationality which the railroad companies' individual and intersecting operations across geographic space necessitated. Yet, it seems that for many years neither the politicians nor the railroad company administrators collectively saw it as their responsibility to attempt to effect a formal time standardization. Finally, in 1847 member companies of the Railway Clearing House resolved to adopt Greenwich Meantime at all stations on their lines. And eventually all companies came into the fold—not all companies had been members of the Railway Clearing House. The Post Office, which was by then largely dependent upon the railroads for national mail circulation, also saw advantages in a national time standard where its interests were concerned.

The new-fangled telegraph technology (adopted by railroad companies in the 1840s) was recognized almost immediately as an indispensable tool for establishing a national time standard; and an agreement was reached in 1852 between the Electric Telegraph Company, the Astronomer Royal, and the South Eastern Railway Company to enable time signals to be sent by telegraph, every hour on the hour, from Greenwich to railroad stations throughout the country.

If railroad companies throughout Britain were to share a time standard, then that necessarily obliged many other vested interests—whose economic activities were closely tied to railroad operations—to follow suit. Consequently, the public was also obliged to embrace the national "railroad time" standard, although initially there was resistance to the imposition of Greenwich Meantime, especially in outlying regions where the imperatives of the metropolis were not recognized. Local time standards were, just like other local traditions—history, folklore, dialects—unique to the local identity and considered by some to be sacrosanct. Indeed, opposition to "railway time" was variously manifest in the provinces for a while—some communities had public clocks with two minute hands, thus acknowledging the imposition of railway time but without genuflecting before it. In fact, in 1858 the highest court in the land was called to rule upon *the legitimacy* of railroad time. It ruled that "Ten o'clock is ten o'clock according to *the time of the place*, and a town council cannot say that it is not, but that it is ten o'clock by Greenwich Time. *Nor can the time be altered by a railway company*, whose railway passes through the place, nor by any person who regulates the clock in the town hall."[69] This "quaint" ruling remained in force until 1880 (the passing of the Definition of Time Act supplanted it). But the ruling was largely irrelevant, anyway, since the railroad companies did not have to impose "railroad time" on any community. Rather, communities had no choice but to conform to the imperatives of railroad time or find themselves completely out of kilter with just about everything going on in the rest of the nation. But this resistance to the imposition of a *standard time* was hardly a unique phenomenon in English history.[70]

In Britain railroad operations were so bound up with the imperatives and interests of the capitalist system and its rhythms that resistance to the imposition of railroad time could be little more than token, except in places that were so isolated and economically insignificant they could be left to their quaintness. But Charles Dickens, for one, could not resist a swipe at the advent of railroad time, wryly observing: "There was even railway time observed in clocks, as if the sun itself had given in."[71]

In America, local time was commonly called "sun time," which was based on the transit of the sun across the meridian. Initially, each railroad company adopted the time standard of its home city or of some other important city on its lines. For instance, in 1854 the Erie Railroad used the chronometer in the Superintendent's office in New York as the time standard for the railroad, and telegraphed *the* time daily to all principal railroad stations on its lines.[72] And some cities and towns adopted the time standard of a railroad company from quite early on.

But local time standards persisted in America, too. Generally, railroad companies observed them, sometimes to the extent that passengers on long journeys certainly needed at least some rudimentary mathematical ability to complete a journey. The Union Pacific, for instance, for a while (from 1869) operated its railroads in accordance with at least six different time standards. But if six time standards might be thought confusing for travelers, the *Chicago Tribune* on one occasion listed 27 local times observed in Michigan, 38 in Wisconsin, and 27 in Illinois! And nationwide at various times there were from 68 to 80 different time standards used by railroad companies—by the end of the 1860s some *49 to 50* time zones were still recognized by railroad companies.

On November 18, 1883, public clocks all over America were altered in accordance with a new standard time which had been agreed upon by the railroad companies, other corporate interests, scientific bodies, and the Federal Government. Hence, the 54 regional time zones in existence at that time were rationalized to just four time zones covering the entire country.

As in Britain, some localities tried to resist the imposition of standard time—Pittsburgh banned standard time until 1887, while Augusta and Savannah held out until 1888.[73] But in America railroad time came to rule supreme. Indeed, there developed the ritual, in countless lazy Western towns, where at noon on Thursday businessmen and boys drifted over to the railroad depot to assess the accuracy of their watches by the Western Union time signal, which was flashed through the telegraph wires: "The electric time signal and the station clock governed small-town time everywhere in the nation. The clock in the drug store or on the church steeple told time, but only the station clock provided the standard time of the metropolitan corridor."[74]

If the whistle of the train was reassuring for "yokels" and the Western Union time signal a mantra for rustic students of time, yet those who previously had traveled long distances—hopping from one train to another, perhaps onto a different company's train operating from a different state and in accordance with a differently set clock—must have heaved a huge sigh of relief when American time standards were formally rationalized. In fact, before the advent of standard time zones in America a traveler going from Maine to California, for instance, if anxious to have correct railroad time throughout the journey (which was necessary to make connections), was obliged at one time to change his watch some twenty times during that journey.[75]

The Speeding Up of Everything and the Railroad Traveling "Frenzy"

Charles Sallandrouze, a member of the French Council of Manufacturers, said when he arrived at Euston Square, London, in 1840: "I cannot describe to you the apparent tumult and hurry."[76] Thirty years later, the author of an English article entitled *The Pace That Kills* wrote:

> It must surely be that heart disease and nervous complaints are largely engendered by what we go through when we travel. Are not the circumstances attending the *starting of a train alone* enough to give any man a heart complaint? We look at our watches and run; we hear a bell ring, and run faster; a sudden steam whistle sounds, and with alarm in our souls we run faster yet.[77]

If anything, the advent of railroads, with their timetables and deadlines, *added to an already escalating pace of life in the 19th century.* Indeed, it seems things were speeding up even before the advent of railroads and with other transportation technologies to the fore in that regard, notably steamboats. Nevertheless, the railroads introduced a new degree of "bustle."

In the late 1850s Charles Darwin probably typified the anxiety experienced by railroad travelers when remarking upon his tendency to get to railroad stations long before the train was due to leave. But that may have had as much to do with the unreliability of the means of transportation used to get to the station and traffic holdups on the way there as it had to do with the (alleged) punctuality of the train. Whatever the case, an 1866 article captured the perplexity associated with railroad travel at that time quite nicely:

> Surely it is not too much to say that the two conditions of hurrying and waiting may have their part in throwing our nervous machinery out of gear. Consider for a moment the harassment that belongs to railway traveling.... To begin with, a punctuality, which is a thing of half seconds is indispensable. You cannot hail a train which has just started, as you could a coach. You cannot run after it, or overtake it in a swifter vehicle.... You refer to your watch incessantly; you compare the public clocks that lie along your line of route.... You have bags to carry, your hands are full—there are whistlings, screamings, bells—where is the luggage? Who knows? A door bangs and you are off. What sort of work for the nerves is that?[78]

Indeed, catching the train seemed to fluster people and hurry them up. Oscar Wilde was certainly flustered by train travel: "Everybody seems in a hurry to catch a train. This is a state of things which is not favorable to poetry or romance."[79]

The more rapid circulation of people, letters, raw materials, and consumables meant, in theory at least, that time was "saved." However, *rather than saving time people tended to, or were somehow obliged to, cram more activity into their everyday lives.* Contemporaries in both Europe and America were fully conscious of this speeding up of the pace of life and accommodating themselves to it was not necessarily unproblematic. But, in comparative national context, this "speeding up" of everything certainly was relative. And, if anything, the new pace of life was more hectic in America than it was in Britain.

Much earlier I recounted the experiences of English travelers in America in the 19th century, not the least concerning their perceptions of the relative bustle and pace of life there. In the same connection, Louisa May Alcott remarked of her travels in England in 1865 that "what impressed her most profoundly" was the *lack of urgency* she saw in all directions, "nobody in a hurry, and nowhere did you see the desperately *go-ahead* style of life that we have"[80]—perhaps just as well, since (in England) "the eroticism of hesitation was a vital component of protracted Victorian engagements."[81]

Nevertheless, if Americans thought the pace of life in Britain slower than it was in America, the English would have thought their pace of life in 1865 much faster than it had been three or four decades earlier. But it all depended, of course, on geographical location in both national contexts—the pace of life would have been perceived to be much faster in large cities than in small towns, and faster in small towns than in rural hamlets.

The individualism, materialism, and greed may not have been as crass in 19th century Britain as they were in America—possibly accounting for the differences in the perceived "pace of life" in the two national contexts—but those traits were certainly apparent in Britain. On the other hand, it is not as if everybody in America wholeheartedly embraced the new pace of life—Philip Hone recorded in his diary in the 1850s that the growing mania for speed (and for speculation and ostentation as well) was destroying the *"old gracious dignity* of New York life."[82]

This remarkable increase in the pace of life in the 19th century, which was significantly determined by the advent of railroads directly or indirectly, is peculiarly "modern." And, just as the early railroad travelers eventually habituated to railroad speed and its impact on perception, so, too, eventually did everyone who had to accommodate themselves to the increased pace of life. But, as most of us are aware today, the pace and bustle of modern life are stress-inducing, stress a causal factor in numerous medical conditions, some of them potentially fatal.

Two early 20th century sociologists, Georg Simmel and Emile Durkheim, drew their reflections upon the effects of increasingly intensive and rapid communications systems into their more general theories of modernity. Simmel, in noting how improvements in communications systems impacted upon the rural-urban divide, also suggested that *the metropolis extracts a different amount of consciousness from the individual* than does rural life, which is relatively sedate, and where the rhythms of life and sensory-mental imagery flow more slowly, more habitually, and more evenly. Consequently, because the urbanite receives (relatively) an excess of different stimuli in a relatively short time span, a permanent state of nervous tension prevails.[83]

Like Simmel, Durkheim thought this over-stimulation of the nervous system had to be compensated for: "It is because this hyperactivity of general life is wearisome, tensing up our nervous system, that it finds itself needing compensation, proportionate to the effort that has been expended, in more complex satisfactions."[84]

Obviously, the advent of railroads played a significant role in such developments. But Simmel and Durkheim also draw our attention to one of the paradoxes of modernity—that the production and consumption of commodities (in whatever form, including railroad travel) ultimately makes our lives more stressful, yet we attempt to offset that by consuming even more (most obviously during our leisure activities). Indeed, perhaps a stark manifestation of this paradox resided in the fact that the very railroad system at the heart of this stress-inducing new order of things in the 19th century was at the same time—by means of the railroad excursion and rapid access to spas and resorts—no less implicated in the "remedy."

The "Art" of Railroad Reading

I want to conclude this book in somewhat more lighthearted fashion by putting "under the microscope" the phenomenon of reading on trains in the 19th century. Wolfgang Schivelbusch has argued that the development of reading on trains can be related significantly to the anxieties and fears of early railroad travelers: "The traveler who sat reading his newspaper or novel, instead of worrying about the ever-present possibility of derailment or collision, no doubt felt secure. His attention was diverted from the technological situation to an entirely independent object." However, Schivelbusch does invoke some other factors—speed, the associated "dissolution" of the landscape, and avoidance behavior—to assist the explanation of the development of reading on trains. In fact, Schivelbusch, in noting that the view from the (train) window was conditioned by velocity (which resulted in both distortion of the perceived landscape and its "ephemerality"), suggested that the compartment/carriage passenger therefore needed some "compensatory" preoccupation. However, not only does he suggest that *reading* fulfilled this need of the passenger, but, "To adapt to the condition of rail travel, a process of de-concentration, or dispersal of attention, took place in reading as well as in the traveler's perception of the landscape outside; Hatchette's rising sales of newspapers and falling sales of books attest to that."[85] That is interesting because *today*, increasingly it seems, people want their information and entertainment in the form of "snippets," much as Schivelbusch suggests the 19th century railroad traveler did.

Certainly, the advent of railroads *coincided with* the proliferation and increasing popularity of newspapers, magazines, and the "bytes" of serialized novels. And the advertising such publications often carried (especially the two former) meant they could be sold at less than the cost of production, which assisted their accessibility. And such media certainly were very amenable to reading during railroad traveling, as opposed to genres which required more serious and sustained attention. However, the logical connection Schivelbusch makes between the rising sales of newspapers and processes of "de-concentration" or "dispersal of attention" during railroad travel is tenuous to say the least.

In fact, newspapers alone were becoming very cheap, so one would expect their sales to be increasing for that fact alone, apart from which at a railroad station news stand people would be more likely to buy a newspaper than a book for reading matter during a railroad journey simply because they would have to pay considerably more for a (hardback) book. But in the early period especially, railroad journeys were not of such a duration that one had time to read an entire book, anyway.

However, there is support for Schivelbusch's general argument: "Perhaps no other single element (as the Victorian railroads) in the evolving pattern of Victorian life was so responsible for the spread of reading."[86] However, that assertion, too, would be hard to prove *indubitably*. For, as we shall see shortly, the proliferation of literature; the increasing affordability and, therefore, accessibility of reading material; rapidly increasing literacy levels; and a burgeoning middle-class "bent" on self-improvement and "rational" recreation, all were developments which *paralleled* the advent of railroads *without the latter necessarily having a causal relationship* to the growth in the popularity of reading or the consumption rates of literature.

There was also a proliferation of (widely-circulated) journals, many of which targeted "niche" reader interest, while others, such as Dickens" *Household Words* and *All the Year Round*, had broad appeal. And such journals may have had more appeal as reading matter for railroad travelers than newspapers solely because they were not as unwieldy to manage in a compartment as a newspaper was, while, like the newspaper, their content consisted of "bits and pieces" rather than the single narrative of a novel or work of nonfiction.

But if the advent of railroads roughly coincided with the rise of the novel (serialized or otherwise) and the proliferation of newspapers and magazines, yet during the Victorian period there was a discernible shift away from reading primarily for "improvement" to reading as an acceptable, indeed respectable form of "entertainment" and leisure—itself evidenced by the increasing popularity of the novel across the period in question (bearing in mind the novel had always been regarded somewhat suspiciously, and especially so when the *romantic* novel fell into the hands of presumed "flighty" young women).

But the advent of "railroad reading" also coincided with the rise to prominence of a generation of great fiction writers. Charles Dickens was the outstanding figure, and the popular journals he owned or edited often contained serializations of his novels, which was part of their appeal. And perhaps the real significance of Dickens is that his literature, for the first time in history, enabled an entire society to reflect upon itself sociologically by means of the fiction genre. Indeed, collectively Dickens' works afforded a snapshot of Victorian society no less compelling than, for instance, Henry Mayhew's four-volume sociological study of London around mid-century. Even that most famous of revolutionaries, Karl Marx, paid homage to the rise of the Victorian novel: "The splendid brotherhood of fiction writers in England had issued to the world more political and social truths than have been uttered by all the professional politicians, publicists, and moralists put together"[87]—he forgot to mention ideologues like himself.

The period was also noteworthy for a remarkable growth in publishing capitalism and (related) developments in printing technology (increasingly books, magazines, and newspapers were illustrated), as well as for the abolition of certain taxes in respect of both developments. There was also a burgeoning middle-class with increased disposable income and an appetite for literature which fitted tidily with its aspirations to gentility. But literacy was increasing generally, too—a basic education becoming increasingly accessible to working class children, even if, for some, it was only the "third-rate" education of the so-called "ragged schools."

But to return to the railroad itself, there was also the fact that, compared to the coach, the train afforded a relatively smooth passage and usually better illumination, thus making reading more practicable as a carriage activity (but not necessarily so on rough American railroads!). And once the novelty of railroad travel wore off, then *boredom* itself may have been sufficient motivation for people to read during a railroad journey—rather than their being compelled to do something to compensate for the "perceptual chaos" experienced when looking out the window of a train moving at speed. Of course, that aspect of Schivelbusch's argument holds very little water, too, where the early decades of railroad travel were concerned, since trains did not go fast enough to make looking out the window at the scenery as perceptually chaotic as he would have it.

Furthermore, railroad stations became excellent places for selling print media. Indeed, for a while in the early period the railroad station bookstall was a place where one might even obtain a cheap translation of a seedy French novel. However, Altick suggests the latter reflected poorly on the English railroad companies—the main reason, he suggests, many of them eventually leased their bookstalls to established reputable concerns such as W.H. Smith,[88] rather than granting such leases (as had often been the case) as concessions to injured or retired railroad company servants.

However, it seems the railroad traveler usually paid "through the nose" for a newspaper at an English railroad station bookstall. Henry Mayhew, who was an expert on such trivia, noted that newspapers sold at railroad stations cost more than elsewhere (sixpence as against five pence)[89]—however, the railroad station bookstalls were usually among the first outlets to the get the earliest editions of daily newspapers, which was yet another incentive to buy a newspaper before hopping on a train.

But the key point here is that *there was no necessary connection between dispersal of attention—due to "perceptual chaos"—and the railroad traveler's assumed predilection for snippet-like forms of literature.* And let us retrace some (historical) steps here for a moment.

Reading had always been difficult for coach travelers—due both to the motion of the coach and to poor illumination inside it. Coach travel was also much noisier than we might think and people were often stuffed inside coaches like sardines in a can.

Canal travel, by way of comparison, was much more conducive to reading, as was steamboat travel on American inland waterways. But because canal boat and river steamboat passengers were normally able to be "outside" and thus to have a good view of the scenery, perhaps they would have had less inclination to read than had coach or train passengers.

But if it was difficult for coach and carriage passengers to read during travel, it could be done. Samuel Pepys recalled that when traveling by coach in 1688 he had a lady read her book aloud during the journey.[90] And in the mid–17th century Queen Christina of Sweden had a fellow passenger read the classics to her during a long carriage ride.[91] Some people were even able to write under such testing circumstances.

Reading did become a favored activity of the 19th century railroad traveler and it was not as difficult to read on the train as it had been in the coach. In fact, people could write while traveling by train, too. Anthony Trollope, who spent many hours on Irish trains on Post Office business in 1850, could write while traveling using a sort of portable desk he had made for himself (and which an American baggage smasher put paid to, as described earlier). And he boasted: "I could write as quickly in a railway carriage as I could at my desk."[92]

The truth is there could be any number of reasons why people read on trains. Altick has suggested railroad reading was so common because railroad compartment travel afforded Victorians *a rare peace and quiet*, which was very conducive to being able to read undistracted.[93] This may have been so to a point, but 19th century trains were much noisier than Altick thought, and certainly much noisier than modern trains. So, that, too, is hardly an adequate explanation as to why reading during a railroad journey became popular in the 19th century.

Schivelbusch has suggested that reading involved an avoidance behavior often; arguing, furthermore, that railroad passengers had lost the ability to interact in the way early travel novels suggested they had in coaches.[94] But perhaps Schivelbusch over-romanticizes coach travel in that regard. Writing in 1658, Edward Phillips recorded that conversation was difficult inside coaches of that period due to the noise (of wheels and horses) and the motion of the coach.[95] But coaches had always been quite noisy vehicles and remained so, especially on cobbled streets in cities. Nor in the early period were railroad carriage compartments insulated against noise, while olfactory "distractions" were also apparent: "Early trains were not only bumpy, noisy, and uncomfortable, but they also smelt strongly; not only from their human cargo, but also because vegetable oil or animal fat was used as lubricating fluid until mineral oil was introduced in the third quarter of the century."[96] So, if reading was not that difficult during railroad traveling, yet clearly it had its distractions in the above forms alone. But other passengers could also be distractions.

If guidebooks and etiquette books contributed something towards knowing how to conduct oneself with propriety during a railroad journey, as well as which engineering feats to gasp and gape at on cue, yet there were still "perplexities" which the well-to-do European railroad compartment "inmate" had to confront. Again, the English etiquette books were of some didactic utility on the question of maintaining one's dignity inside this moving "inglenook" (compartment), regarding whom one might talk to, under what circumstances, and what about. But such advice books—both etiquette and guidebooks—did not normally address such matters as how to alleviate boredom (although there did develop a genre of so-called "railroad literature") during the railroad journey, or how to overcome fears and anxieties pertaining to the technology itself. And how would Europeans—used to compartment accommodation during railroad travel—fare when cast into an "open" car on an American railroad? Would this have been tantamount to throwing overboard from a boat people who could not swim, such were the limitations of the (well-to-do) English passenger's capacity for conviviality in any company, not to mention his ineffable bewilderment at having nobody to tell him what to do next at a railroad station.

But let us focus now on the argument that reading on trains developed partly or largely as an "avoidance" strategy. And certainly, even today commuters have strategies to avoid engaging with fellow passengers, the modern tendency being a preoccupation with pressing matters arising from their mobile phones or other portable communications technologies. But sociologist Erving Goffman is worth quoting at length concerning such *dis*-engagement:

> When a few persons find themselves in a small space, as in a European railway compartment ... civil inattention is hard to manage tactfully. To not stare requires looking very pointedly in other directions; which may make the whole issue more of a matter of consciousness than it was meant to be, and may also express, too vividly, an incapacity or distaste for engagement with those present.... If the individual decides against contact, *he may well have to find some activity for himself in which he can become visibly immersed to provide the others present with a face-saving excuse for being unattended to.* Here again we see the situational function that newspapers and magazines play in our society, allowing us to carry around a screen that can be raised at any time, to give ourselves or others an excuse for not initiating contact.[97]

This is very percipient and I think we can all identify with it. And if the (literary) avoidance "device" is like a screen, often it is a screen as effective as a burkha. But does Goffman's analysis go far enough? I would suggest not. We are talking about Victorian times here, so the variables in the situation had some historical specificity attending them. And one factor Goffman overlooks in the passage above is class or status differences, another is gender.

Where the latter is concerned, if people did communicate more in the coaches earlier, then that may have been because coaches were used much more by men than women—men had to travel regarding their "business affairs" much more then than they need to today. But when genteel women did travel in coaches, with or without their husbands or chaperones, would they have been prepared to be drawn into conversations with men they did not know? Would that have been proper? And could not the same question be asked in respect of the railroad carriage compartment, bearing in mind that both before and after the advent of railroads etiquette books usually had something to say on the matter of how women ought to conduct themselves in such social situations? Indeed, sometimes, and perhaps often, female silence and withdrawal were recommended in such situations by the authors of such books, so long as that was practicable.

But if, where considerations of gender were concerned, reading material allowed for "escape" from the situation, then perhaps in some circumstances the possibility of seduction, and considerations of romance and sexuality, may have been factors in the situation, too. We know little about the role the railroad compartment played in romance and love, seduction, and lust in Victorian times. And perhaps, all considered, in Britain romance was much more likely to be found evolving in the "open" (non-compartmentalized) carriages occupied by third class passengers than inside the cloister which the compartment was. Perhaps, therefore, given that in America before the advent of Pullman "class" virtually all passenger cars were "open," the possibility of (consensual) fraternization occurring between male and female passengers was greater relatively than in the European compartment.

But let us now focus on other sociocultural and psychological factors in the situation. The English railroad compartment forced upon those members of the upper classes who wished to use it an intimacy with strangers they had seldom encountered previously. This was one of the major threats which the advent of railroad travel posed to those classes—it threatened to undermine the class structure of society by, on the one hand, compressing social class distinctions into compartment classes (first- and second-class); on the other hand, it undermined the degree of physical intimacy and personal spatial proximity which had traditionally been inherent to social class distinctions. True enough, in the early period aristocrats could have their own carriages lashed onto flat wagons, and thus remain aloof entirely of other passengers. But that nonsense could not persist for long. And it was simply impractical to give somebody *an entire carriage* to themselves, even if they were prepared to pay an extraordinary price for the service.

But do "avoidance" and the "dissolution" of the landscape, or even anxiety, fear, or conformity to etiquette adequately explain why people might have found reading an appropriate preoccupation during railroad travel? Perhaps reading on trains had simply become a fashion or even a fad—bearing in mind that fashions and fads may be quite "mindless" and not necessarily amenable to rational explanation. There again, perhaps reading on a train, an activity conducted in public, fitted rather tidily with the Victorian "value" of "rational recreation"—*to be seen* reading in public demonstrated not only that one was ostensibly literate, but also "rational," as well as being "up with" *that* fashion (reading on trains). Indeed, what better way could there be to conspicuously demonstrate one's literacy, "seriousness," and "rationality" than to be such an avid reader one even read on trains!

But did it matter what one was reading? Of course, it did! Because what one was reading—the Bible or a "dirty" French novel, for instance—was also a statement about the "self." In fact, in England *in the early period* cheap, "seedy" French novels, accessible at railroad stations, eventually led to the concept of "railway literature" becoming one of "abuse and disapprobation."[98] However, according to Mayhew, literature sold at English railroad stations *in the Mid-Victorian period* had become pretty much restricted to "light" reading and novels, monthly parts of works issued in weekly numbers, and books of poetry, but rarely political literature or controversial pamphlets. As to price, nothing usually cost more than one shilling.[99] And by that time the railroad companies were able to exercise some degree of control (indirectly) over what was sold within termini and station precincts, since by then they tended to lease bookstall rights to "safe" parties, such as W.H. Smith, whose name in England eventually became synonymous with "railroad bookstall"—but *people did not read only literature they had bought at railroad station bookstalls* when railroad traveling.

Yet, it was important that other people know what you were reading, so that you could create the right impression and project the kind of image of yourself that you wanted people to perceive. You wanted to impress upon people not just your rationality, but also to announce publicly your *taste* in literature, notably in respect of your choice of newspaper or journal (many new magazine titles aimed at niche readerships came onto the market from the late 1830s, and reading some such titles no doubt became *the fashion*). Indeed, perhaps you felt the need to conspicuously display your "savoir-faire" or fashion-consciousness, your broad-mindedness, your religious orientation if any, your "progressive" way of seeing the world, your good moral sense, your "style," or even your "modernity"—and you could do any of these through the symbol of the book and its cover.

John Gibson, editor of the *Quarterly Review* in the 1830s, thought that some of his readers would be reluctant to be found with a *sporting newspaper* in their hands[100] (such publications provided coverage of horse racing, prize-fighting, and ratting–dog contests, all of which were activities usually associated with gambling). So, you certainly would *not* want to be seen reading that kind of newspaper in public. But for "decent" people who wanted to project the right kind of impression, there were some very safe bets for railroad travelers. For instance, in England there was *Murray's Railway Reading*—advertised as containing works of "sound information and innocent amusement," and described by the *Athenaeum* as "healthy" reading.[101] And Lord McAulay encouraged Longmans to introduce a cheap and popular series called *The Travelers Library*, which included a range of "improving" literature.[102]

But, strangely enough, there developed a notion of what *appropriate* railroad reading material was, newspaper literary review articles after mid-century often commending books *as suitable for railroad reading*. In fact, during my research for this book I just happened to notice a "Literary Selection" alongside the (1860) newspaper article I was reading—it reviewed eight books, three of which were recommended as *suitable for railway reading* (they were all collections of short stories or articles).[103]

What one read in public certainly did matter. In fact, in Britain there were organizations such as the Pure Literature Society (founded 1854) which were self-appointed censoring agencies, and which set themselves the formidable task of identifying—from the flood of literature on the market—periodicals, books, and authors which they could endorse as "pure" enough for "decent" people to read.[104]

When traveling by train on one occasion in 1840, Charles Darwin noted the reading matter of those sharing his compartment. There was an elegant female "who pulled out of her pocket a religious tract ... and commenced reading with great earnestness and marking the best passages." The other person was an elderly gentleman, "who was studying a number of the *Christian Herald*."[105] Ostensibly, these people were making statements about their religious orientation or rectitude. But, without knowing for certain, I should not be surprised to discover this was *Sunday* travel and that these "decent" Christian folk were excusing themselves for traveling on the Sabbath by reading, penance-like, appropriate literature to expiate their "sin."

Manguel, in *A History of Reading*, mentions that: "A cousin of mine ... always chose a book to take on her travels with the same care with which she chose her handbag.... So important is the symbol of the book, that its presence or absence can, in the eyes of the viewer, lend or deprive a character of intellectual power."[106] Absolutely so! But it can also lend or deprive a character of much more than *intellectual power*, as already indicated.

During the Victorian period there were perceived "good" and "bad" novels, and "good" and "bad" novelists—those anybody "up with the times" must read, those everybody read, those no "decent" person would be seen reading, and what about that strange Mr. Dickens who wrote about "low" people?

Hence, within the confines of the railroad compartment or carriage the "text" was never just an avoidance mechanism, a compensatory recourse for the dissolution of the landscape, or a panacea for anxieties and fears. It was usually symbolic, and often articulated to claims to "status honor," rectitude, and fashionability, even a "declaration" of one's "modernity." But, more generally, the text served admirably as *a multi-purpose technology of the self*, and no less so for railroad travelers.

Conclusion

I began this book with a "phenomenology" of railroads, which led us in the direction of casting the railroad as a factory-like, institutional, industrial production system. We then attended to the observation that railroad travel necessarily implicated the traveler in this industrial production system, noting also some of the engineering applications that arose within this peculiar industrial production system (which *produced* passenger journeys and freight conveyance) both to offset the "industrialization" of the traveler, and to deal with the unprecedented volumes of traffic—developments which led ultimately to the framing of new concepts of "traffic," "traffic engineering," and the "mass transit" of persons.

The various engineerings of railroad space and movement through it, which production of the passenger travel commodity entailed, also necessitated the emergence of an administrative and operational infrastructure to, among other things, oversee the safe and efficient transit of passengers. These developments encapsulated a surveillance and discipline of the passenger, a phenomenon which highlighted both the institutional and factory-like aspects of the production system concerned.

But in the two national contexts under scrutiny here—England and America—this "administration" of the passenger was configured differentially, albeit in both cases relative to the key values of national self-identity, and to the respective prevailing forms of social class structure, not overlooking the "mythical" elements incorporated ideologically within both, and especially so where America was concerned.

In the case of England, we found not only that the administrative and operational dimension to railroad passenger travel entailed closer surveillance and more severe discipline of the passenger than was the case in America, but, in certain respects, the discipline of the English railroad passenger bordered on the "carceral." And explaining this relative carceral dimension to English railroad passenger traveling experience required some penetration of the "ether" constituting English middle- and upper-class values at the time; but it was also necessary to penetrate the nebulous contemporary English social class structure to understand why the English railroad companies stratified passenger travel as they did. But we also had try to understand why middle- and upper-class English people *preferred* to travel in little "boxes" called compartments in their carriages; a mode of traveling for such people which was a far cry from the "open" American car typical of the period in question.

Where the stratification of railroad passenger travel (and associated amenities) in England was concerned, it was found that this was unexceptional, given that England was a highly structured (hierarchical) society, and that discriminatory practices routinely characterized the commodification (of goods and services) and consumption at the time. However, the dilemma for the English railroad companies was that they could not reproduce the complexity of the social class structure itself in their *passenger class* provision. This observation led me into a brief analytical discussion whereby the concepts of "social class" and "passenger class" were explained and differentiated. What I argued was that the English railroad companies, in their provision of the basic commodity (motion at relative speed), *effectively rationalized social classes in their provision of passenger classes*, which normally numbered just two or three.

But this did not necessarily make railroad passenger travel palatable for the English middle- and upper-classes, since the "first" and "second" passenger class categories were themselves not sufficiently exclusive to satisfy the "hierarchical mentality" in question. And that is one of the reasons why we find multiple gradations (classes of train, four- or six-seater compartments, aristocrats being able to ride in their own carriages lashed to flat wagons in the early period, and so on) within and beyond the basic gradations (the passenger classes) provided by English railroad companies. And this hierarchy of *gradations within gradations*, which characterized passenger provision in the first half-century of English railroading, was the nearest the railroad companies could get to reproducing the "niceties" of the English social class structure.

The English middle- and upper-class preference for the compartment, as an architectural form within the carriage, was not easily explained, either. Various explanations were proffered—the well-to-do Englishman's "fetish" for privacy, his demand for exclusivity, and the maladjusted personality of the upper-class Englishmen, all were to the fore in that regard. However, the "well-heeled" Englishman's preference for the compartment was also a preference, or so it seems, for a carceral railroad traveling experience. In fact, I went on to suggest that the English *middle- and upper-classes* liked to be coddled during railroad travel and that, generally, they identified the close surveillance and "imprisonment" which prevailed on English railroads with safety, security, order, and discipline—the last two of which were values their relatively privileged positions in society were predicated upon.

Indeed, any society which is highly stratified necessarily has protocols of order, discipline, and deference integral to its "culture." And that is why English middle- and upper-class railroad passengers were comfortable with an over-arching form of railroad company surveillance and discipline—it was a normal element of sociocultural reality for the people concerned. And it is also why, when they went to America, they often had considerable difficulty adapting to the American "open" car. In fact, English tourists in America were often entirely hapless, due to having nobody to organize and supervise them as they moved through American railroad systems; while the relative laxity of discipline, which characterized American railroad administration and operations, also disconcerted many an English traveler in America.

The next task was to try to explain some of the peculiarities of the American railroad system. As in the case of England, I believed the key to understanding the national style of railroading resided in the values encapsulated in the ideology of national self-identity and in the form of social structure which prevailed in America at the time.

Having mused upon some of the key American values of the age (democracy, egalitarianism, equality of opportunity, self-made man-*ism*, materialism, and individualism, essentially), and having noted their respective significance for national self-identity, it was discovered that these values (enshrined in national self-identity) did not necessarily fit very comfortably with social structure or with social reality more generally. Nevertheless, notwithstanding the discriminatory practices of most American railroad companies in respect of Negroes and some categories of emigrant, yet we identified a tendency of American railroad companies to offer a single passenger class, which materialized in the form of the "open" or "democratic" car. Certainly, such provision harmonized well enough with key aspects of the *ideology* of national self-imagery, and especially so where the concepts of "democracy" and "equal opportunity" were concerned.

But such provision (of a single passenger class) by the American railroad companies seemed anomalous in one important respect—it seemed to be out of kilter with the differentiated forms of commodification which were evident in society at large, and most notably in respect of the "passenger class" stratification regimes routine on river and coastal steamboats at the time. It was necessary, therefore, to explain the anomaly? Were American railroad company owners and managers more in tune with the republican spirit than their maritime counterparts?

Although the single class of railroad travel in America did, indeed, fit very comfortably with republican *ideology*, it fitted no less comfortably with the values and interests of parsimonious railroad company owners and managers. American railroad companies generally spent less on railroad system infrastructure than did their English counterparts at the time, and we might expect that frugality to have extended to passenger cars and other passenger amenities. Indeed, my suggestion was that "rationalization," where commodification and consumption are concerned, is often the cheapest option from a capitalist's standpoint—which is precisely why we have so many "standardized" goods and services available to us today. And the American single "railroad car" class represented a rationalized commodity form.

In support of that contention, it was noted English railroad travel was generally, and for the duration of the 19th century at least, more expensive than American railroad travel. That was partly because the "American system" of railroad construction was characterized by relative frugality, too. But it also related to the fact the class-based system of English passenger travel provision was inherently more expensive *because it was not rationalized sufficiently*. In fact, it was not necessarily (and often probably was not) remunerative where the "higher" classes of passenger travel were concerned—which is to suggest that, often, they were effectively subsidized by third-class passenger conveyance (provision for which was, as noted, often scant), excursion traffic revenue, and freight revenue.

But, setting aside the relative "cheapness" of the American single passenger class provision, and despite the various shortcomings of American railroad systems at the time (notably with respect to safety), the "open," single class of car provided by American railroad companies usually afforded: quite comfortable accommodation; a more than adequate *sense* of personal safety and security for the traveler (as many English travelers in America noted); a more gregarious experience for the traveler; and a freedom of movement within and between cars which was impossible on English trains with compartmentalized carriages. From a passenger-traveling standpoint these were, indeed, the key differences marking off the American from the English national style of railroading in the 19th century. But there were numerous other differences, many of which we encountered as I drew upon the travel narratives of English (and other foreign) tourists recounting their railroad traveling experiences in 19th century America.

We next attended to the comparative safety of railroad travel in 19th century England and America, focusing upon some of the anxieties and fears which most troubled the early railroad travelers in both countries, as well as considering some significant factors (such as railroad vandalism and sabotage) which posed real enough threats (certainly so in England), yet seemed neither to be well-publicized nor sources of passenger anxiety. On the other hand, there seemed to be (in England) unrealistic and inflated fears concerning the safety of women traveling in railroad carriage compartments, while English women travelers in America perceived absolutely no threats at all to themselves from other people during railroad traveling there. The other major concern of that chapter was the "de-mystification" of the "American system" of railroad construction, which was rationalized essentially regarding some key American values.

But more generally, where railroad travel safety was concerned in the two national contexts, recall how the astute Domingo Sarmiento had summed up the difference between European and American railroad travel before mid-century. The European railroad traveler was subject to a much more severe disciplinary regimen than the American counterpart, which made European railroad travel safer. But Sarmiento suggested that the American traveler preferred to be less constrained during railroad travel, even if that meant being less safe and secure. And these *differences of attitude*, Sarmiento believed, reflected a difference in the core values of the societies in question—the constraining social structure and the relative degree of discipline integral to it, which characterized many European societies at the time, as against the unbridled individualism which characterized American republicanism at the time.

Everything considered, and in view of what was said in the final chapter, we might appreciate that, where the advent of the railroad in the 19th century was concerned there were many facets to it which were not experienced differently (or not remarkably so) in the English and American national contexts. And perhaps the two most significant points of departure related to: *the forms of commodification and consumption of passenger travel* and *the American system* of railroad construction, the latter along with all its implications for the passenger. These *key* differences, along with an infinitude of less significant points of divergence, highlighted the existence of two distinct national styles of railroading in 19th century England and America.

Even journeys on the most decrepit of 19th century American railroad lines thankfully always came to an end, and so has this one. I hope I have managed to enhance the reader's understanding of railroad travel in 19th century England and America respectively, satisfactorily drawn out and highlighted the signal features distinguishing those two national styles of railroading, and disabused the reader of any misconceptions they had entertained in respect of those and other aspects of 19th century railroad travel.

Chapter Notes

Chapter One

1. *The Preston Guardian*, March 20, 1869. An 1852 American newspaper article thought it probable that "English obstinacy and prejudice would yield to American progress" because of the introduction of sleeping- and dining-cars in England; but these innovations seem to have had negligible impact in that regard. See *The Charleston Daily News*, February 28, 1852.
2. William Hardman, *A Trip to America* (London: T.V. Wood, 1884), 191.
3. "Winter Traveling in America," *Northern Echo*, March 18, 1875.
4. cf. Susan Cheever, *American Bloomsbury* (New York: Simon & Schuster, 2006), 102.
5. Thorstein Veblen, *The Theory of Business Enterprise* (New York: Charles Scribner and Sons, 1935), 13.
6. Robin Evans, *The Fabrication of Virtue: English Prison Architecture 1750–1840* (Cambridge: Cambridge University Press, 1982), 266.
7. *The Illustrated London News*, May 10, 1862.
8. John Clapham, *An Economic History of Modern Britain* (Cambridge: Cambridge University, 1926), vol. 1, 400; vol. 2, 182.
9. Jack Simmons, *The Victorian Railway* (London: Thames and Hudson, 1991), 272.
10. Judith Flanders, *Consuming Passions* (London: Harper Perennial, 2007), 241–2.
11. Henry Mayhew, *London Labour and the London Poor* (New York: Dover, 1968), vol. 3, 323.
12. Philip S. Bagwell *The Transport Revolution from 1770* (London: B.T. Batsford, 1974), 43.
13. As against coach travel, railroad passengers usually saved money on accommodation, meals, and tips; and that is another reason why the railroad may have been more affordable and attractive relatively as a transportation option.
14. "German and Danish Railway Carriages," *The Illustrated London News*, March 8, 1845. In America, the Baltimore and Ohio originated and perfected the eight-wheel car.
15. The commercial opportunities railroad company engineering of pedestrian traffic opened ought not to be underestimated—part of Dickens' massive publicity campaign to launch *All the Year Round* in 1859, for instance, involved distributing 250,000 handbills through W.H. Smith, which had many retail outlets at stations. See Michael Slater, *Charles Dickens* (New Haven, CT: Yale University Press, 2009).
16. "The English Railways," *The Lancaster Gazette and General Advertiser*, March 1, 1879.
17. There was also an "old world" belief that narrow streets were healthier than wide ones because they excluded the sun—this belief is traceable as far back as the Romans, who thought the sun maleficent and dangerous. Mrs. St. Julian Ravenal *Charleston: The Place and the People* (New York: The Macmillan Company, 1912), 350
18. Moncure D. Conway, *Republican Superstitions* (London: Henry S. King, 1872), 85, 89.
19. Esther Moir, *The Discovery of Britain: The English Tourists 1540–1840* (London: Routledge and Kegan Paul, 1964), 85.
20. See Sigfried Giedion, *Space, Time and Architecture* (Cambridge: Harvard University Press, 1971), 746.
21. See T.J. Stiles, *The First Tycoon: The Epic Life of Cornelius Vanderbilt* (New York: Alfred A. Knopf, 2009), 516.
22. Wilfred L. Steel, *The History of the London and North Western Railway* (London: The Railway and Travel Monthly, 1914), 69.
23. August Mencken, *The Railroad Passenger Car* (Baltimore: The Johns Hopkins University Press, 2000), 141.
24. See *ibid.*, 174.
25. Dee Brown, *Hear That Lonesome Whistle Blow* (London: Chatto and Windus, 1978), 145–6.
26. Mencken, *The Railroad Passenger Car*, 32.
27. Robert Ritchie, *Railways: Their Rise, Progress and Construction* (London: Longman, Brown, Green, 1846), 566.
28. William M. Acworth, *The Railways of England* (London: John Murray, 1890), 70.
29. Edward Churton, *The Railroad Book of England 1851* (London: Sidgwick and Jackson, 1851), 110.
30. See Henry Parris, *Government and the Railways* (London: Routledge, Kegan, Paul, 1965), 44.
31. Acworth, *The Railways of England*, 50–1.
32. "Railway Traveling," *Illustrated London News*, May 10, 1862.
33. Mayhew, *London Labour and the London Poor*, vol. 3, 339.
34. Brown, *Hear That Lonesome Whistle Blow*, 180.
35. Seymour Dunbar, *A History of Travel in America* (New York: Greenwood, 1968), vol.3, 1039.
36. David H. Bain, *Empire Express: Building the Transcontinental Railroad* (New York: Viking, 1999), 441.
37. George B. Ayres, *New Descriptive Handbook of the Pennsylvania Railroad, and Traveler's Guide to the Great West* (Pittsburgh: W.S. Haven, 1859).
38. See Edwin P. Hoyt, *The Vanderbilts and Their Fortunes* (London: Frederick Muller, 1963), 179–80.

39. See Markman Ellis, *The Coffee House: A Cultural History* (London: Phoenix, 2005), 59.
40. Keith Thomas, *The Ends of Life: Roads to Fulfilment in Early Modern England* (Oxford: Oxford University Press, 2009), 151.
41. Catherine E. Bates, *A Year in the Great Republic* (London: Ward and Downey, 1887), vol. 2, 312, 314, 317.
42. Norman Nicholson, *The Lakers: The Adventures of the First Tourists* (London: Robert Hale, 1955), 184.
43. Gertrude Himmelfarb, *The De-Moralization of Society: From Victorian Virtues to Modern Values* (New York: Alfred A. Knopf, 1995), 7.
44. Christopher Hibbert, *Charles Dickens: The Making of a Literary Giant* (Basingstoke: Palgrave Macmillan, 2009), 271.
45. According to English historian Keith Thomas the word "respectable" did not come into common usage until the late 18th century—until then people were said to be of "good name" or similar terms were used to refer to them. Thomas, *The Ends of Life*, 32, 163.
46. Richard D. Altick, *Victorian People and Ideas* (London: J.M. Dent and Sons, 1974), 174–5.
47. Leonore Davidoff, *The Best Circles* (London: Croom Helm, 1973), 36.
48. Joseph Tatlow, *Fifty Years of Railway Life in England, Scotland and Ireland* (London: The Railway Gazette, 1920), 18–9.
49. Quoted in Henry T. Tuckerman, *America and Her Commentators, with a Critical Sketch of Travel in the United States* (New York: Charles Scribner, 1864), 255
50. See Hugh Barty-King, *New Flame* (Tavistock: Graphmitre, 1984), 83.
51. Altick, *Victorian People and Ideas*, 187.
52. Alice Morse Earle, *Old-Time Gardens* (New York: Macmillan, 1896), 66.
53. See Jacqueline L. Tobin, Raymond G. Dobard, and Maude S. Wahlman, *Hidden in Plain View* (New York: Anchor, 2000), 107.
54. See Alice Morse Earle, *Two Centuries of Costume in America 1620–1820* (New York: Macmillan, 1910), 576; Alice Morse Earle, *The Sabbath in Puritan New England* (New York: Charles Scribner's Sons, 1898), 71.
55. In the 1860s many Americans used the word "proud" to describe the English. Samuel Morton Peto, *The Resources and Prospects of America* (London: Alexander Strahan, 1866), 281–3.
56. Hugh Brogan, *Alexis de Tocqueville: A Life* (London: Yale University Press, 2006), 252.
57. David Sinclair, *Dynasty: The Astors and Their Times* (London: J. M. Dent and Sons, 1983), 5.
58. Raymond Carr, *English Fox Hunting* (London: Weidenfeld and Nicolson, 1976).
59. See John Stilgoe, *Metropolitan Corridor* (New Haven, CT: Yale University Press, 1983), 170.
60. Arguably, individualism in England had the concept of privacy integral to it more pointedly than was the case in America at the time; and, along with the fact that English social structure also shaped it, English individualism was not as dynamic, and not as crucially definable by materialism as the American counterpart.
61. Nicholas T. Parsons, *Worth the Detour: A History of the Guidebook* (Stroud: Sutton, 2007), 3.
62. See David Blackbourn, *The Conquest of Nature: Water, Landscape and the Making of Modern Germany* (New York: W.W. Norton, 2006), 168.
63. E.W. Bovill, *The England of Nimrod and Surtees 1815–1854* (London: Oxford University Press, 1959), 165.
64. Cole is also linked to the advent of the *adhesive* postage stamp and the Christmas card. John E. Vaughan, *The English Guidebook c.1780–1870: An Illustrated History* (Newton Abbot: David and Charles, 1974), 117.
65. See Elizabeth Bonython and Anthony Burton, *The Great Exhibitor: The Life and Work of Henry Cole* (London: V and A Publications, 2003), 71.
66. "Literature," *The Bristol Mercury*, July 12, 1862.
67. Brown, *Hear That Lonesome Whistle Blow*, 154–8.
68. "An Orange Railway?" *Freeman's Journal*, February 21, 1850.
69. Mentioned in Christopher Hill, *Society and Puritanism in Pre-Revolutionary England* (London: Secker and Warburg, 1964), 408–9.
70. Alfred Cobban, *The Social Interpretation of the French Revolution* (Cambridge: Cambridge University Press, 1961), 140.
71. Earle, *The Sabbath in Puritan New England*, 33–4.
72. "Pews in Parish Churches," *Liverpool Mercury* May 3, 1839.
73. In the early 19th century some industrial companies, which had their own "self-contained" communities, even charged their operative-inhabitants pew rents. O'Neal, J. 214
74. Dorothy Davis, *A History of Shopping* (London: Routledge Kegan Paul, 1967), 173–4.
75. Anthony Burton, *The Railway Builders* (London: John Murray, 1982), 2.
76. Nicholson, *The Lakers*, 122.
77. Lazlo Tarr, *The History of the Carriage* (London: Vision Press, 1969), 274.
78. See Nicholson, *The Lakers*, 122.
79. See Roger Dixon and Stefan Malthesius, *Victorian Architecture* (London: Thames and Hudson, 1985), 85–7.
80. *The Sheffield and Rotherham Independent*, September 19, 1840.
81. Flanders, *Consuming Passions*, 366.
82. Dixon and Malthesius, *Victorian Architecture*, 116, 118.
83. Ronald Hayman, *Nietzsche: A Critical Life* (London: Quartet, 1981), 339.
84. Robert Gutman, *Mozart: A Cultural Biography* (New York: Harcourt, 2000), 745.
85. See Flanders, *Consuming Passions*, 229–30.
86. *Ibid.*, 4, 5, 421.
87. *Ibid.*, 194.
88. *Ibid.*, 404.
89. Francis D. Klingender, *Art and the Industrial Revolution* (Chatham: Evelyn, Adams and Mackay, 1968), 142.
90. Gordon Biddle, *Victorian Stations* (Newton Abbot: David and Charles, 1973), 19.
91. "Railways," *The Belfast News-letter*, February 12, 1836. Nevertheless, during its early period the Stockton and Darlington derived only about 3 percent of its revenue from passenger conveyance.
92. Simon Garfield, *The Last Journey of William Huskisson* (London: Faber and Faber, 2002), 25, 199;

93. Acworth, *The Railways of England*, 27.
94. Thomas C. Cochran, *Pennsylvania: A History* (New York: W.W. Norton and Co., 1978), 97.
95. Ritchie, *Railways*, 494, 551.
96. Simmons, *The Victorian Railway*, 254.
97. I may be a little unkind to, and ruthless with, the late Jack Simmons here; but he was a university history *professor*, so I see no justification for donning "kid gloves."
98. Samuel Smiles, *The Life of George Stephenson, and His Son Robert Stephenson* (New York: Harper and Brothers, 1868), 389.
99. See Jack Simmons and Gordon Biddle, *The Oxford Companion to English Railway History* (Oxford: Oxford University Press, 1997), 84; Simmons, *The Victorian Railway*, 359.
100. H.C. Rogers, *Turnpike to Iron Road* (London: Seeley, Service and Co., 1961), 36.
101. *The Leicester Chronicle*, March 23, 1833.
102. Steel, *The History of the London and North Western Railway*, 46.
103. "Opening of the Bolton and Leigh Railway," *The Newcastle Courant*, August 9, 1828. The Liverpool and Manchester loaned some of *those* coaches to the Bolton and Leigh for its opening.
104. "Eastern Counties Railway Investigation," *Daily News*, April 28, 1849. Roof-riding was certainly known in America in the early period—Marryat was able to ride on the roof of the car on a journey to Niagara.
105. On the Baltimore and Ohio in America baggage was carried on car rooftops until 1834—it was found to be labor-intensive and otherwise inconvenient, so purpose-built baggage cars came into use.
106. Jeffrey Richards and John M. McKenzie, *The Railway Station: A Social History* (Oxford: Oxford University, 1986), 137.
107. Hoyt, *The Vanderbilts and their Fortunes*, 84
108. See Georg Simmel, *The Philosophy of Money* (London: Routledge, Kegan and Paul, 1990).
109. See Rogers, *Turnpike to Iron Road*, 80–1.
110. It has been argued that the *early motor car* differed from the horse-drawn *coupe* only in that it did not need the horses—a steering-wheel rose high in the box and the wheels had tires. Tarr, *History of the Carriage*, 295. This analogy strips the motor car to its essentials, yet it is a fair assessment of the facts, where the earliest motor vehicles were concerned.
111. Acworth, *The Railways of England*, 58.
112. Olinthus Vignoles, *Life of Charles Blacker Vignoles* (New York: Longmans, Green and Co., 1889), 146.
113. The horn was also used on some of the earliest American railroads.
114. Smiles, *The Life of George Stephenson*, vii.
115. See Garfield, *The Last Journey of William Huskisson*, 141.
116. Charles Lee, *Passenger Class Distinctions* (London: The Railway Gazette, 1946), 14.
117. Parris, *Government and the Railways*, 97.
118. The "Experiment" ended its life as a railroad "cabin" near Shildon, England. William H. Brown, *The History of the First Locomotives in America* (New York: D. Appleton and Company, 1874), 58
119. Tony Hall-Patch, *The Great English Railway: A Living History* (Newton Abbot: David and Charles, 1992), 19.
120. C. Hamilton Ellis, *Nineteenth Century Railway Carriages in the British Isles* (London: Modern Transport Publishing, 1949), 24.
121. Wolfgang Schivelbusch, *The Railway Journey* (Berkeley: University of California, 1986), 85.
122. Ellis, *Nineteenth Century Railway Carriages*, 26–7.
123. Schivelbusch, *The Railway Journey*, 72.
124. Alfred Williams, *Life in a Railway Factory* (Gloucester: Allan Sutton, 1986), 113.
125. Harold J. Perkin, *The Age of the Railway* (Newton Abbot: David and Charles, 1971), 246.
126. Flanders, *Consuming Passions*, 97.

Chapter Two

1. Mentioned by Garfield in respect of the Liverpool and Manchester Railway. See Garfield, *The Last Journey of William Huskisson*, 97.
2. Terry Gourvish, *Mark Huish and the London and North Western Railway* (Leicester: Leicester University Press, 1972), 36.
3. "Letter from Dr. England," *Sacramento Daily Union*, August 29, 1868.
4. Abbott P. Usher, *An Introduction to the Industrial History of England* (London: Harrap, 1921), 457.
5. Gourvish, *Mark Huish and the London and North Western Railway*, 37.
6. Lee, *Passenger Class Distinctions*, 16.
7. Ellis, *Nineteenth Century Railway Carriages*, 15.
8. See John R. Kellett, *The Impact of Railways on Victorian Cities* (London: Routledge, Kegan and Paul, 1969), 99.
9. Jack Simmons, *Railways: An Anthology* (London: Collins, 1910), 130.
10. *Ibid.*
11. Acworth, *The Railways of England*, 38.
12. "Third Class Carriages," *The Sheffield and Rotherham Independent*, August 22, 1840.
13. Rogers, *Turnpike to Iron Road*, 114.
14. "Third-Class Railway Traffic," *The Pall Mall Gazette*, December 24, 1873. The usual discount for first- and second-class was for the passenger to pay a fare-and-a-half on return tickets.
15. Lewis Mumford, *Sticks and Stones: A Study of American Architecture and Civilization* (New York: Dover, 1955), 163.
16. *Ibid.*, 166.
17. Michel de Montaigne, *The Complete Works* (New York: Alfred A. Knopf, 2003), 156.
18. Vignoles, *Life of Charles Blacker Vignoles*, 146.
19. Mary Cowling, *The Artist as Anthropologist: The Representation of Type and Character in Victorian Art* (Cambridge: Cambridge University Press, 1989), 263, 271.
20. Davidoff, *The Best Circles*, 50.
21. Clement Eaton, *The Growth of Southern Civilization 1790–1860* (New York: Harper Torchbooks, 1963), 199.
22. See Jill Hamilton, *Thomas Cook: The Holiday Maker* (Thrupp: Sutton, 2005), 78.
23. See Aileen Ribeiro, *Dress and Morality* (Oxford: Berg, 2003), 97.
24. Elizabeth Wilson, *Adorned in Dreams: Fashion and Modernity* (London: Taurus, 2003), 229.
25. See Ribeiro, *Dress and Morality*, 130.
26. Samuel Florman, *The Existential Pleasures of*

Engineering (New York: St. Martin's Press, 1976), 126. This is a book that merits greater recognition than it appears to have had beyond the field of engineering.

27. Lewis Mumford, *Art and Technics* (New York: Columbia University Press, 1952), 110, 113.

28. David L. Lloyd and Donald W. Insall, *Railway Station Architecture* (Newton Abbot: David and Charles, 1978), 19.

29. Edgar Jones, *Industrial Architecture in Britain 1750–1939* (London: B.T. Batsford, 1985), 13.

30. Although the classical influences on American architecture during the 19th century were no less powerful than they were in Britain, yet they may have had a different rationale or ideological underpinning. Early in the 19th century it was quite common for "cultured" Americans to identify an affinity between the American and the ancient Greek republics, while Handlin suggests the Greek-Turkish War of 1821 reinforced the already emerging tendency to use a Greek temple front in architecture as a symbol of republicanism. However, Handlin also notes the Doric order was favored in America because it was cheap and easy to build. David P. Handlin, *American Architecture* (London: Thames and Hudson, London, 2004), 64.

31. Lloyd and Insall, *Railway Station Architecture*, 47.

32. John Ruskin, *The Seven Lamps of Architecture* (London: George Allen, 1911), 13, 128, 22.

33. See John W. Robertson-Scott, *The Day before Yesterday* (London: Methuen, 1951), 257.

34. See Bryan Morgan (ed.), *The Railway Lover's Companion* (London: Eyre and Spottiswoode, 1963), 228.

35. George Hersey, *The Lost Meaning of Classical Architecture* (Cambridge: MIT Press, 1988), 1, 152.

36. Dixon and Malthesius, *Victorian Architecture*, 17.

37. Jones, *Industrial Architecture in Britain*, 13, 20, 24, 40–1.

38. Ibid., 62, 71, 74; Dixon and Malthesius, *Victorian Architecture*, 11, 86–7, 116.

39. Talbot Hamlin, *Greek Revival Architecture in America* (New York: Dover, 1944), 201, 270.

40. Kathryn Hughes, *The Short Life and Long Times of Mrs. Beeton* (London: Fourth Estate, 2005), 23, 50.

41. Simon Schama, *Landscape and Memory* (London: Fontana, 1996), 563.

42. "Railway Stations," *The Essex Standard*, October 26, 1838.

43. "Railroads," *The Morning Post* July 13, 1837.

44. Rodney Symes and David Cole, *Railway Architecture of the South-East* (Reading: Osprey, 1972), 8.

45. See Dixon and Malthesius, *Victorian Architecture*, 36, 81.

46. See Churton, *The Railroad Book*, 20, 158, 174.

47. See George Dow, *Railway Heraldry* (Newton Abbot: David and Charles, 1973), 83.

48. Rogers, *Turnpike to Iron Road*, 24.

49. Edward T. MacDermot, *History of the Great Western Railway* (London: Great Western Railway Co., 1927), vol. 1, 699.

50. Charles Babbage, *Passages from the Life of a Philosopher* (New Brunswick: Rutgers University Press, 1994), 137.

51. However, in colonial America traveling "post" had an entirely different connotation. To travel "post" in 18th century New England, for instance, was to travel in the company of the "post man," who could be either a colonial government employee or a private post rider—the latter were supposed to carry only merchandise, but carried private mail anyway. And women on horseback usually traveled by "post" (in this way) for safety reasons (Alice Earle discusses this in *Stage-Coach and Tavern Days*).

52. See Alfred R. Wallace, *The Wonderful Century: Its Successes and Its Failures* (New York: Swan Sonnenschein, 1901), 4.

53. Steel, *The History of the London and North Western Railway*, 120.

54. Janet Browne, *Charles Darwin* (New York: Alfred A. Knopf, 1995/2002), vol. 2, 476.

55. See Morgan, *The Railway Lover's Companion*, 227.

56. Michael White and John Gribben, *Darwin: A Life in Science* (New York: Dutton, 1995), 275.

57. Carr, *English Fox Hunting*, 110.

58. "High Court of Justiciary," *Glasgow Herald*, November 7, 1845.

59. John V. Beckett, *The Aristocracy in England 1160–1914* (Oxford: Basil Blackwell, 1986), 240.

60. Lloyd and Insall, *Railway Station Architecture*, 17.

61. Rogers, *Turnpike to Iron Road*, 81, 112.

62. Terence R. Nevett, *Advertising in Britain: A History* (London: Heinemann, 1982), 64.

63. Simmons, *The Victorian Railway*, 86.

64. Robertson Scott, *The Day Before Yesterday*, 75.

65. Alice Morse Earle, *Colonial days in Old New York* (New York: Charles Scribner's Sons, 1896), 275.

66. "The English Railway."

67. *Daily Alta* (California), January 12, 1868.

68. See Mencken, *The Railroad Passenger Car*.

69. Edward B. Dorsey, *English and American Railroads Compared* (New York: John Wiley and Sons, 1887), 11.

70. John Francis, *A History of the English Railway: Its Social Relations and Revelations 1820–1845* (Newton Abbot: David and Charles, undated facsimile of the 1851 edition), 10.

71. Mayhew, *London Labour and London Poor*, vol. 3, 324.

72. Steel, *The History of the London and North Western Railway*, 45.

73. Ritchie, *Railways*, 19–21.

74. See Bovill, *The England of Nimrod and Surtees*, 37; Hermione Hobhouse, *The Crystal Palace and the Great Exhibition* (London: The Athlone Press, 2002), 110.

75. Acworth, *The Railways of England*, 183–4.

76. "American and English Railways," *The Preston Guardian*, March 20, 1869.

77. Foster Zincke, *Last Winter in the United States* (London: J. Murray, 1868), 2.

78. Smith was known in America. In fact, Sydney Tuckerman (1864) said of him: "Notwithstanding the rebuke to our State delinquency in his American letters…no writer has better appreciated the institutions and destiny of the United States." Tuckerman, *America and Her Commentators*, 262.

79. "Frightful Accidents on the London and Birmingham Railway," *The Operative* February 24, 1839.

80. Quoted from Philip S. Bagwell, *The Railway Clearing House in the English Economy 1842–1922* (London: George Allen and Unwin, 1968), 191–2.

Notes—Chapter Two

81. "Railroad Management," *The North American Review*, January, 1868.
82. Simmons, *Railways: An Anthology*, 149–50.
83. Schivelbusch, *The Railway Journey*, 196.
84. Therese Yelverton, *Teresina in America* (London: Richard Bentley and Sons, 1875), vol. 2, 306.
85. (Lady) Duffus Hardy, *Through Cities and Prairie Lands: Sketches of an American Tour* (New York: R. Worthington, 1881), 59.
86. "Letter to the Editor," *Glasgow Herald*, August 12, 1875.
87. "Letter from Dr. England."
88. "Outrages on Women," *The Era*, July 24, 1864.
89. *Old Bailey Records*: t18591128–79, t18600227–287, and t18640711–730.
90. Simmons, *Railways: An Anthology*, 102.
91. See C. Willett Cunnington and Phillis Cunnington, *Handbook of English Costume in the 19th Century* (London: Faber and Faber, 1959), 461.
92. When there was little circulation of coins there was no need of purses; but once (coin) purses became necessary, so too did pockets to hold them. Earle, *Two Centuries of Costume in America*, 583, 585, 590.
93. Schivelbusch, *The Railway Journey*.
94. Emily Cockayne, *Hubbub: Filth, Noise and Stench in England* (New Haven, CT: Yale University Press, 2007), 179.
95. Maria Fairweather, *Madame de Stael* (New York: Carroll and Graf, 2005), 427.
96. Browne, *Charles Darwin*, vol. 1, 427.
97. See Arthur Arschavir, "The Inception of the English Railway Station," *Architectural History* 4, no. 39 (1961): 73–76.
98. See Tarr, *The History of the Carriage*, 257.
99. Montaigne, *The Complete Works*, 963.
100. Victoria Glendinning, *Trollope* (London: Hutchinson, 1992), 60, 452.
101. The railroad alluded to was the New York Central. See "American Railway Carriages," *The Penny Illustrated Paper*, July 23, 1864.
102. See Rosemary Hawthorne, *Do's and Don'ts: An Anthology of Forgotten Manners* (London: Pavilion, 1977), 74.
103. Churton, *The Railroad Book of England*, 110.
104. Adrian Vaughan, *The Intemperate Engineer* (Hersham: Ian Allen, 2010), 77.
105. "Winter Traveling in America."
106. Rogers, *From Turnpike to Iron Road*, 112.
107. "Third Class Railway Traveling," *The Huddersfield Chronicle*, January 20, 1872.
108. See Terry Coleman *Passage to America: A History of Emigrants from Great Britain and Ireland to America in the Mid-19th Century* (London: Hutchinson, 1972), 58.
109. See Richard D. Altick, *Punch: The Lively Youth of an English Institution, 1841–1851* (Columbus: Ohio State University Press, 1997), 543.
110. See James A. Ward, *Railroads and the Character of America 1820–1887* (Knoxville: University of Tennessee, 1986), 69.
111. Humphrey Jennings, *Pandaemonium: The Coming of the Machine as Seen by Contemporary Observers 1660–1886* (London: Andre Deutsch, 1985), 48.
112. Ritchie, *Railways*, 418.
113. Churton, *The Railroad Book of England*, 176.
114. See Wallace, *The Wonderful Century*, 4–5.
115. See Parris, *Government and the Railways*, 45–6.
116. See Stuart Legg (ed.), *The Railway Book: An Anthology* (London: Rupert Hart-Davis, 1952), 42.
117. Lee, *Passenger Class Distinctions*, 12.
118. Browne, *Charles Darwin*, vol. 2, 25.
119. "An Ancient Railway Guide Book," *Northern Echo*, March 6, 1899.
120. Domingo Sarmiento, *Travels: A Selection* (Washington, D.C.: Pan American Union, 1963), 142.
121. *Ibid.*, 98, 103.
122. See Ellis, *19th Century Railway Carriages*, 16, 31.
123. See Wallace, *The Wonderful Century*, 4.
124. See Francis, *A History of the English Railway*.
125. "A Plea for Cheap and Comfortable Traveling," *Dundee Courier and Daily Argus*, August 29, 1861.
126. "Railway Reform," *The Bradford Observer*, April 11, 1844.
127. Francis, *A History of the English Railway*, 104.
128. "Railway Reform," *The Bradford Observer*, April 11, 1844.
129. "The Late Frightful Accident on the Great Western Railway," *The Observer*, January 2, 1842.
130. It is important to note that although I draw heavily upon McDermott's somewhat critical history here, his history of the Great Western Railway (the first edition, that is) was published by the Great Western Railway Company itself; clearly, the latter, to its credit, made no attempt to "sanitize" it.
131. MacDermott, *History of the Great Western Railway*, vol. 1, 828–9.
132. Evans, *The Fabrication of Virtue*, 76–7.
133. MacDermott, *History of the Great Western Railway*, vol. 1, 834.
134. See Francis, *A History of the English Railway*, vol. 2, 109, 112–3.
135. *Ibid.*, 122.
136. "Third Class Railway Trains," *Daily News*, June 28, 1850.
137. See the greater number of companies compared in this way in an article that appeared in: "Third-Class Railway Carriages," *The Morning Chronicle*, August 19, 1845.
138. "Advantages of Locomotive Carriage on a General Rail-Road," *The Leicester Chronicle*, November 7, 1829.
139. "Railroad versus Stage Coach Traveling," *The Derby Mercury*, November 13, 1839.
140. "Railway Reform." This newspaper, the *Bradford Observer*, was consistently critical of the railroad companies' treatment of third-class passengers over many years.
141. Steel, "The History of the London and North Western Railway," 121.
142. "Winter Traveling in America."
143. Gourvish, *Mark Huish and the London and North Western Railway*, 37.
144. See Kellett, *The Impact of Railways on Victorian Cities*, 98.
145. Robertson Scott, *The Day Before Yesterday*, 69.
146. David N. Smith, *The Railway and Its Passengers: A Social History* (Newton Abbot: David and Charles, 1988), 19.
147. See Joseph Thomas, *Railroad Guide from London to Birmingham* (London: Willoughby & Co., 1839), 16.

148. See Michael Brander, *The Victorian Gentleman* (London: Gordon Cremonesi, 1975), 80.
149. Philippe Aries, *Centuries of Childhood: A Social History of Family Life* (New York: Vintage Books, 1967), 318–9.
150. Mayhew, *London Labour and the London Poor*, vol. 3, 339.
151. The Duke of Wellington thought that at least 15,000 soldiers would be needed to keep order due to the lower social classes flocking to London for the event. See Flanders, *Consuming Passions*, 30.
152. See her letter of June 7, 1851, as well as similar comments by Henry Mayhew and George Cruickshank in Jennings, *Pandaemonium*, 258–9, 261–2.
153. See Acworth, *The Railways of England*, 40.
154. See Vaughan, *The Intemperate Engineer*, 81.
155. Steel, *The History of the London and North Western Railway*, 337.

Chapter Three

1. William Smith, *A Yorkshireman's Trip to the United States and Canada* (London: Longmans Green and Co, 1892).
2. Arthur Cunynghame, *A Glimpse of the Great Western Republic* (London: Richard Bentley, 1851), 186.
3. Zincke, *Last Winter in the United States*, 62.
4. Frances Kemble had vehemently criticized another dimension of American "feeding": "The ignorant and fatal practice of the women of stuffing their children, from morning till night, with every species of trash which comes to hand." Frances Kemble, *Journal of a Residence on a Georgian Plantation in 1838–9* (New York: Harper and Brothers, 1864), 14.
5. See Alice Morse Earle, *Home Life in Colonial Days* (New York: The Macmillan Press, 1899), 101.
6. Nichols, *Forty Years of American Life*, vol. 2, 150; vol. 1, 150–1.
7. See Pamela Neville-Sington, *Fanny Trollope: The Life and Adventures of a Clever Woman* (London: Viking, 1997).
8. See Eli Bowen, *Pictorial Sketch-Book of Pennsylvania* (Philadelphia: Willis P. Hazard, 1852).
9. See Neville-Sington, *Fanny Trollope*, 176, 383.
10. Quoted in Henry Hitchings, *Sorry! The English and their Manners* (London: John Murray, 2013), 227
11. See Tuckerman, *America and Her Commentators*, 215, 225, 228.
12. George Combe, *Notes on the United States of America* (Philadelphia: Carey and Hart, 1841), vol. 2, 103.
13. Yelverton, *Teresina in America*, vol. 1, 271; vol. 2, 263. Yelverton devoted an entire chapter of her work to American child-rearing.
14. Combe, *Notes on the United States of America*, vol. 1, 146.
15. Nichols, *Forty Years of American Life*, vol. 1, 61, 63.
16. T.S. Hudson, *A Scamper Through America* (New York: E.P. Dutton and Co., 1882), 12.
17. Duffus Hardy, *Through Cities and Prairie Lands*, 166. Despite that, in San Francisco in the 1870s few of the city's prominent men were known for their good manners or modesty. Oscar Lewis, *The Big Four*, 288.

18. William Ferguson, *America by River and Rail* (London: J. Nisbet and Co., 1856), 58.
19. *Ibid.*, 91, 432.
20. Charles Beard, *The Rise of American Civilization* (London: Jonathan Cape, 1927), vol. 1, 388.
21. Walter Marshall, *Through America* (London: Sampson, Low, Marston, Searle and Rivington, 1881), 2.
22. Illinois Central Railroad Company, *A Guide to the Illinois Central Railroad Lands* (Chicago: Illinois Central Railroad Office, 1861), 4.
23. Yelverton, *Teresina in America*, vol. 1, 31.
24. Zincke, *Last Winter in the United States*, 36.
25. Mrs. Ravenal, *Charleston*, 131.
26. Alice Morse Earle, *Child Life in Colonial Days* (New York: Macmillan, 1915), 28.
27. *Ibid.*, 102–3
28. W. Fraser Rae, *Westward by Rail: The New Route to the East* (New York: D. Appleton and Co., 1871), 54.
29. Frances Trollope, *Domestic Manners of the Americans* (New York: Dodd-Mead, 1901 [1832]), vol. 1, 33.
30. Cunynghame, *A Glimpse of the Great Western Republic*, 209.
31. John W. Boddam-Whetham, *Western Wanderings: A Record of Travel in the Evening Land* (London: R. Bentley, 1874), 87.
32. See Bates, *A Year in the Great Republic*, vol. 2, 313.
33. Zincke, *Last Winter in the United States*, 14, 34.
34. Nichols, *Forty Years of American Life*, vol. 1, 49.
35. Rae, *Westward by Rail*, 56.
36. Ferguson, *America by River and Rail*, 431. This General Cass was later (1874) President of the Northern Pacific Railroad Company.
37. "Perils of English Railway Traveling," *Cleveland Morning Leader*, August 6, 1863.
38. Rae, *Westward by Rail*, 374.
39. Yelverton, *Teresina in America*, vol. 2, 114.
40. Ferguson, *America by River and Rail*, 90.
41. Anthony Trollope, *North America* (Harmondsworth: Penguin, 1968), 41.
42. Boddam-Whetham, *Western Wanderings*, 10.
43. Hardman, *A Trip to America*, 57.
44. T.C. Clarke quoted in Thomas M. Cooley (ed.), *The American Railway: Its Construction, Development, Management and Appliances* (New York: C. Scribner's Sons, 1889), 45.
45. For other 19th century jokes pertaining to American railroad travel, see Thomas Jackson, *On a Slow Train Through Arkansas* (Chicago: T.W. Jackson, 1903).
46. Colleen Dunlavy, *Politics and Industrialization: Early Railroads in the U.S. and Prussia* (Princeton, NJ: Princeton University Press, 1994), 202.
47. See Nichols, *Forty years of American Life*, vol. 1, 290.
48. Henry James, *The American Scene* (London: Rupert Haret-Davis, 1968), xi–xii, 64.
49. Nichols, *Forty Years of American Life*, vol. 1, 403–4.
50. Bernstein, *Wedding of the Waters*, 346.
51. Tocqueville, *Democracy in America*.
52. James Hogan, *The Australian in London and America* (London: Ward and Downey, 1889), 38.

53. "Mr. George Dawson on America," *The Hull Packet*, April 23, 1875.
54. Peto, *Resources and Prospects*, 395–6. At the time Peto visited America (1866) he was the Chairman of the London Board of Control of the American Atlantic and Great Western Railroad Company.
55. "Mr. Henry Vincent on America," *Liverpool Mercury*, July 31, 1867.
56. James Buckingham, *The Eastern and Western States of America* (London: Fisher, Son and Co., 1842), vol. 2, 4.
57. Zincke, *Last Winter in the United States*, 16.
58. See Mencken, *The Railroad Passenger Car*, 171–2.
59. See Brown, *Hear That Lonesome Whistle Blow*, 234.
60. Marshall, *Through America*, 111–2.
61. Boddam-Whetham, *Western Wanderings*, 183.
62. Dorsey, *English and American Railroads Compared*, 16.
63. Flanders, *Consuming Passions*, 38, 290.
64. Buckingham, *The Eastern and Western States of America*, vol. 2, 6.
65. Ferguson, *America by River and Rail*, IV.
66. Nichols, *Forty Years of American Life*, vol. 1, 98.
67. Rae, *Westward by Rail*, 341.
68. Nicholson, *The Lakers*, 196.
69. Nichols, *Forty years of American Life*, vol. 1, 363–6.
70. H.W. Brands, *The Age of Gold* (London: Random House, 2002), 406.
71. Mrs. Trollope thought the only real form of equality in America (relative to England) was equality of opportunity.
72. Thomas, *The Ends of Life*, 18.
73. Fraser, *Every Man a Speculator*, 98.
74. Gustavus Myers, *The History of Tammany Hall* (New York: Boni and Liveright, 1917), Preface.
75. Lester Crocker, *Jean Jacques Rousseau* (New York: Macmillan, 1968), vol. 1, 239.
76. "Mr. Henry Vincent on America."
77. Alexis de Tocqueville, *Democracy in America* (London: Saunders and Otley, 1838), vol. 1, 193.
78. Frederick J. Turner, *The Frontier in American History* (New York: Holt, Rinehart and Winston, 1962), 30, 32.
79. Marquis Childs, *Mighty Mississippi: Biography of a River* (New Haven: Ticknor and Fields, 1982), 70.
80. See Tarr, *The History of the Carriage*, 272.
81. Earle, *Stage-Coach and Tavern Days*, 227.
82. Carl Sandburg, *Abraham Lincoln: The Prairie Years* (London: Jonathan Cape, 1976), 44.
83. Trollope, *Domestic Manners of the Americans*, vol. 1, 141.
84. James, *The American Scene*, xvii–xix.
85. James D. McCabe, *Lights and Shadows of New York Life* (London: Andre Deutsch, 1971 facsimile of the 1872 edition), 57.
86. Buckingham, *The Eastern and Western States of America*, vol. 3, 38–9, 90; vol. 2, 407.
87. Zincke, *Last Winter in the United States*, 263.
88. Nichols, *Forty Years of American Life*, vol. 1, 24.
89. James, *The American Scene*, xviii.
90. *Ibid.*, xix
91. In America in 1861 the enthusiasm for reading was attested to by the existence of some 450 daily newspapers, over 4,000 weeklies, and 356 monthlies and semi-monthlies. Nichols, *Forty Years of American Life*, vol. 1, 319.
92. See Frederick Gerhard, *Illinois as It Is* (Chicago: Keen and Lee, 1857).
93. Zincke, *Last Winter in the United States*, 188, 230.
94. Zincke thought they were an American counterpart to the English "ragged schools," and that the "rags and habits" of the children rendered them inadmissible to the "common" schools. Zincke, *Last Winter in America*, 14.
95. Sarmiento, *Travels*, 132, 134
96. See Brogan, *Alexis de Tocqueville*, 183.
97. Salmon suggested in her book, *Domestic Service* (1901), that "service" was called the "great American question." However, based on my research, I think "divorce" deserves that sobriquet, since the subject seemed to be a preoccupation of sociologists and the like at that time. That said, Salmon's study of "service" was probably one of the best sociological studies of the era—it entailed a "phenomenology" of "service"; a history of "service" in America; attended assiduously to the perceived problematical and positive aspects to "service" in America at the time; and the study was quite sophisticated, and methodologically possibly a first of its kind—it entailed an extensive mail survey of both "servants" and employers. See Lucy Maynard Salmon, *Domestic Service* (New York: The Macmillan Company, 1901)
98. Mark Pachter and Frances S. Wein, *Abroad in America* Washington DC: Smithsonian Institution, 1976, 55.
99. Trollope, *Domestic Manners of the Americans*, vol. 1, 261.
100. Zincke, *Last Winter in the United States*, 290.
101. After the Civil War, many ex–Union soldiers worked for a while on the Union Pacific's section of the first transcontinental railroad. But it seems that, generally, such labor did not have to perform the *most menial* work—former Union Army Generals Dodge, Sherman, and Grant, all of whom were associated with construction of the railroad, directly or otherwise, made sure these former soldiers were "looked after."
102. Henry Deedes, *Sketches of the South and West* (London: W. Blackwood and Sons, 1869), 40.
103. Zincke, *Last Winter in the United States*, 57, 214, 224, 290.
104. Combe, *Notes on the United States of America*, vol. 1, 38, 93.
105. Cunynghame, *A Glimpse of the Great Western Republic*, 21.
106. Hudson, *A Scamper Through America*, 39.
107. Hardy, *Through Cities and Prairie Lands*, 64
108. Trollope, *Domestic Manners of the Americans*, vol. 1, 74, 165
109. Alice Morse Earle, *Customs and Fashions in Old New England* (New York: Charles Scribner's Sons, 1893), 86, 106.
110. Dunbar, *A History of Travel in America*, vol. 3, 761.
111. Erie Railroad Regulations 1854, rules 8, 116, quoted in H.R. Romans (ed.) *American Locomotive Engineers: Erie Railroad Edition* (Chicago: Crawford-Adsit, 1899).
112. Brown, *Hear That Lonesome Whistle Blow*, 232.

113. Prince Puckler-Muskau, *Puckler's Progress* (London: Collins, 1987), 45. However, this may have applied only to very select company. And it would be mistaken to think people, including first- and second-class railroad passengers, did not spit on trains in Britain, at least occasionally. In fact, early to mid–Victorian Britain was an age "much given to spitting"; spittoons were normally provided in first- and second-class compartments and carriages, while "thirds spat on the floor." See Tom Quinn, *Tales of the Old Railwaymen* (Newton Abbot: David and Charles, 1998), 73.

114. Trollope, *Domestic Manners of the Americans*, vol. 1, 20, 25.

115. Charles Dickens, *American Notes* (London: Chapman and Hall, 1907), 16.

116. Oliver Jensen, *The American Heritage History of Railroads in America* (New York: American Heritage Publishing, 1975), 32.

117. Combe, *Notes on the United States of America*, vol. 1, 46.

118. See Mencken, *The Railroad Passenger Car*, 104–5.

119. Boddam-Whetham, *Western Wanderings*, 27.

120. Marshall, *Through America*, 99.

121. Yelverton, *Teresina in America*, vol. 2, 109.

122. Nichols, *Forty Years of American Life*, 16.

123. "Railroad Travel in Italy," *Sacramento Daily Union*, February 23, 1867.

124. John A. Logan et al., *The Home Manual: Everybody's Guide in Social, Domestic, and Business Life* (Washington, D.C.: The Brodix Publishing Company, 1889), 26.

125. See Alice Morse Earle, *Stage-Coach and Tavern Days*, 13.

126. Chewing *gum* became widely available in the early 1890s, and it, too, may have become a substitute for chewing tobacco.

127. Ray Ginger, *The Age of Excess: The United States from 1877 to 1914* (New York: Macmillan, 1975), 29.

128. Robertson Scott, *The Day Before Yesterday*, 64–5.

129. Rogers, *Turnpike to Iron Road*, 125.

130. Smith, *A Yorkshireman's Trip to the United States*, 192.

131. Boddam-Whetham, *Western Wanderings*, 101.

132. Combe, *Notes on the United States of America*, vol. 2, 17.

133. Buckingham, *The Eastern and Western States of America*, vol. 3, 67.

134. Trollope, *Domestic Manners of the Americans*, vol. 1, 24, 255.

135. Mrs. Ravenal, *Charleston*, 359.

136. Philip Alexander Bruce, *Social Life of Virginia in the Seventeenth Century* (Richmond, VA: Whittet and Shepperson, 1907), 76; Sydney George Fisher, *Men, Women and Manners in Colonial Times* (Philadelphia: J.B. Lippincott Company, 1913), volume 1, 40.

137. See Albert Bushnell Hart (ed.), *American History Told by Contemporaries* (New York: Macmillan), 1901, vol. 2, 217–20.

138. See Tuckerman, *America and Her Commentators*, 116.

139. Zincke, *Last Winter in the United States*, 224.

140. Nichols, *Forty Years of American Life*, vol. 1, 38.

141. Logan et al., *The Home Manual*, 10.

142. William H. Gilman, *Selected Writings of Ralph Waldo Emerson* (New York: Signet Classics, 2011), 126.

143. Ferguson, *America by River and Rail*, 9.

144. See Bernstein, *Wedding of the Waters*, 346–7.

145. Mark Twain, *Life on the Mississippi* (New York: Harper and Brothers, 1917), 39.

146. See Sydney George Fisher, *The Evolution of the Constitution of the United States* (Philadelphia: J.B. Lippincott and Company, 1897), 14.

147. Kemble, *Journal of a Residence on a Georgian Plantation*, 148. Peto (1866) thought the poor whites he encountered in the South "disgustingly filthy in their persons," and that they appeared like "corpses." Peto, *Resources and Prospects*, 320.

148. The "crackers" were so-called because of their long, "cracking" stock whips; and the "clay eaters" did eat dirt, which had some dire consequences for their health, although they seemed to think it was good for them. The "sand-hillers" were named so for the barren, sandy, and hilly land they often occupied. See James O'Neal, *The Workers in American History* (St. Louis: Rip-Saw, 1912), 205; Mrs. Ravenal, *Charleston*, 138, Emily P. Burke in Hart, *American History Told by Contemporaries*, volume 4, 59–60.

149. Alexis de Tocqueville, *Journeys to England and Ireland* (London: Faber and Faber, 1957), vol. 2, 161.

150. Joseph Ellis, *Founding Brothers: The Revolutionary Generation* (New York: Alfred A. Knopf, 2001), 157.

151. Stephen Van Rensselear was one of the commissioners of the Erie Canal.

152. Gustavus Myers, *History of the Supreme Court of the United States* (Chicago: Charles H. Kerr, 1912), 149–50, 306.

153. Mrs. Ravenal, *Charleston*, 99

154. Hardy, *Through Cities and Prairie Lands*, 69.

155. Hogan, *The Australian in London and America*, 74.

156. Jack Beatty, *Age of Betrayal* (New York: Alfred A. Knopf, 2007), 432.

157. Boddam-Whetham, *Western Wanderings*, 38.

158. McCabe Jr., *Lights and Shadows of New York Life*, 14, 57.

159. Hale, *Horace Greeley*, 106.

160. Peto, 386

161. Yelverton, *Teresina in America*, vol. 1, 14, 16.

162. Rae, *Westward by Rail*, 21.

163. Marshall, *Through America*, 2.

164. There had been many famous hotels in America long before the advent of railroads, which is why even the best of them had developed very institutional forms and bureaucratic styles of administration later in the 19th century.

165. Yelverton, *Teresina in America*, vol. 1, 278, 290, 294; vol. 2, 6.

166. Rae, *Westward by Rail*, 311.

167. Trollope, *Domestic Manners of the Americans*, vol. 1, 28.

168. Boddam-Whetham, *Western Wanderings*, 48.

169. Buckingham, *The Eastern and Western States of America*, vol. 2, 435.

170. See David Andress, *1789: The Threshold of the Modern Age* (London: Little, Brown, 2008), 129; Hamlin, *Greek Revival Architecture in America*, 5.

171. Glendinning, *Trollope*, 311.

172. Jeffrey Steel (ed.), *The Essential Margaret*

Fuller (New Brunswick, NJ: Rutgers University Press, 1992), 214, 220.

173. Zincke, *Last Winter in the United States*, 258–9.

174. Trollope, *Domestic Manners of the Americans*, vol. 1, 18; also Rae, *Westward by Rail*, 246.

175. Hoyt, *The Vanderbilts and their Fortunes*, 106.

176. Sarmiento, *Travels*, 120–1.

177. Cunynghame, *A Glimpse of the Great Western Republic*, 139.

178. Yelverton, *Teresina in America*, vol. 2, 97.

179. Walter Havighurst, *Ohio: A Bicentennial Portrait* (New York: W.W. Norton, 1976), 43–4. Often, people traveling upstream this way were flatboat men returning north, having taken a flatboat full of produce down a river; and they were often able to get "extra cheap" fares by fetching firewood along the route as required.

180. Alan Nevins, *America Through English Eyes* (New York: Oxford University Press, 1948), 191.

181. Bernstein, *Wedding of the Waters*, 327–8, 333; and Robert E. Riegel and Robert G. Athearn, *America Moves West* (New York, Holt, Rinehart and Winston, 1971), 227.

182. David S. Reynolds, *Walt Whitman's America: A Cultural Biography* (New York: Alfred A. Knopf, 1996), 156–7.

183. Nichols, *Forty Years of American Life*, vol. 2, 229.

184. Rae, *Westward by Rail*, 372.

185. Nichols, *Forty Years of American Life*, vol. 1, 407.

186. "Letter from Dr. England," *Sacramento Daily Union*, August 29, 1868.

187. Many commentators remarked upon how expensive railroad travel in Britain was compared to elsewhere in Europe and America—but there were reasons for it, other than explaining it simply in terms of the comparative greed of English railroad companies. Nevertheless, during my research I never found one source that took issue with the contention that English railroad travel was relatively expensive, or even over-priced.

188. Buckingham, *The Western and Eastern States of America*, vol. 3, 27.

189. Rae, *Westward by Rail*, 31, 376–7.

190. Ayres, *New Descriptive Handbook of the Pennsylvania Railroad*.

191. Eaton, *The Growth of Southern Civilization*, 57.

192. See Julian Cavalier, *North American Railroad Stations* (Cranbury, NJ: A.S. Barnes and Co., 1979), 8.

193. Cunynghame, *A Glimpse of the Great Western Republic*, 185.

194. Dickens, *American Notes*, 6.

195. However, the ladies' carriage was, apparently, primarily to spare the ladies the sight of "spitters." See Mencken, *The Railroad Passenger Car*, 119.

196. Pachter and Wein, *Abroad in America*, 157.

197. *Ibid.*, 164.

198. Virginia V. Hamilton, *Alabama: A History* (New York: W.W. Norton, 1977), 66, 76.

199. Howard Zinn, *A People's History of the United States* (New York: HarperCollins, 1999), 205.

200. Walter C. Berg, *Buildings and Structures of American Railroads* (New York: John Wiley and Sons, 1893), 340, 347.

201. An article in an English newspaper in 1875 suggested that at that time American emigrant cars amounted to a third class; palace, drawing-room, and parlor cars to a first-class; while the ordinary car effectively constituted a second-class.

202. Brown, *Hear That Lonesome Whistle Blow*, 140.

203. E. Andrews, *Railroads and Farming* (Washington, D.C.: Department of Agriculture, 1912), 18.

204. Edwin G. Burrows and Mike Wallace, *Gotham: A History of New York City to 1898* (New York: Oxford University Press, 1999), 1110.

205. Brown, *Hear That Lonesome Whistle Blow*, 241.

206. *Ibid.*, 236.

207. Oscar O. Winther, *The Transportation Frontier: Trans-Mississippi West 1865–1890* (New York: Holt, Rinehart and Winston, 1964), 125.

208. Marshall M. Kirkman, *Railway Service: Trains and Stations* (New York: The Railroad Gazette, 1878). This work contains a very interesting glossary of the 19th century railroad terminology employed in both Britain and America, apart from also describing work roles on the railroads of both countries at that time.

209. See Brown, *Hear That Lonesome Whistle Blow*, 242–3.

210. Interesting is Rufus Zogbaum's sketch of the interior of an emigrant car (1886), reproduced in Jensen, *The American Heritage History of Railroads in America*, 130.

211. Ferguson, *America by River and Rail*, 434.

212. See Mencken, *The Railroad Passenger Car*, 160.

213. See Winther, *The Transportation Frontier*, 24.

214. Robert L. Stevenson, *The Amateur Emigrant: Across the Plains* (New York: Scribner, 1895), 35–6, 62–4, 139–40.

215. *Ibid.*, 115–6, 121, 134.

216. See Hamilton, *Thomas Cook*, 237.

217. Brown, *Hear That Lonesome Whistle Blow*, 239.

218. Henry G. Pearson, *An American Railroad Builder: John Murray Forbes* (Boston: Houghton Mifflin, 1911), 67.

219. Berg, *Buildings and Structures of American Railroads*, 347.

220. Brown, *Hear That Lonesome Whistle Blow*, 236.

221. In fact, after the Civil War railroad companies contracted to transport federal troops often used emigrant cars for the purpose. And by that time such cars had become known colloquially as "Jim Crow" cars. See Louis Gottschalk, *Notes of a Pianist* (New York: Alfred A. Knopf, 1964), 142, and Edward M. Coffman, *The Old Army: A Portrait of the American Army in Peacetime 1784–1898* (New York: Oxford University Press, 1986), 160.

222. Ritchie, *Railways*, 554–5.

223. See Mencken, *The Railroad Passenger Car*, 17.

224. J. Lippincott, *History of the Baldwin Locomotive Works from 1831 to 1897* (Philadelphia: J. Lippincott, 1897), 13.

225. Peto (1866) thought American railroads would be more profitable, and better serve the public, if there were two passenger classes instead of one— he thought the poorer people would rather pay less for more modest car accommodation if there was such a "second" passenger class. However, some com-

panies' charters precluded their providing more than one passenger class. Peto, *Resources and Prospects*, 287.
  226. *Ibid.*, 16.
  227. Henry T. Williams, *Suburban Homes for City Business Men* (New York: Press of the Erie Railway Company, 1867).
  228. Sarmiento, *Travels*, 120, 133.
  229. "Railway-Cars in America," *Illustrated London News*, April, 1861.
  230. Hardy, *Through Cities and Prairie Lands*, 59.
  231. Sigfried Giedion, *Mechanization Takes Command* (New York: Oxford University Press, 1955), 446.
  232. Ferguson, *America by River and Rail*, 68.
  233. Giedion, *Mechanization Takes Command*, 458.
  234. Trollope, *North America*, 73.
  235. Zincke, *Last Winter in the United States*, 65.
  236. Dee Brown, *The American West* (New York: Charles Scribner's Sons, 1994), 69.
  237. Eve D'Ambra, *Roman Women* (New York: Cambridge University Press, 2007), 133.
  238. Lewis Mumford, *The City in History* (New York: Secker and Warburg, 1961), 364.
  239. Aries, *Centuries of Childhood*, 394.
  240. Roger Pearson, *Voltaire Almighty: A Life in Pursuit of Freedom* (New York: Bloomsbury, 2005), 335.
  241. The idea of conveying passengers had been very much an afterthought for the Baltimore and Ohio management.
  242. Mencken, *The Railroad Passenger Car*, 33.
  243. Dunbar, *A History of Travel in America*, vol. 3, 1044.
  244. Hardman, *A Trip to America*, 53.
  245. Mencken, *The Railroad Passenger Car*, 17.
  246. *Ibid.*, 56, 138.
  247. See Ayres, *New Descriptive Handbook of the Pennsylvania Railroad*.
  248. Railroad Historical Company, *History of the Illinois Central Railroad and Representative Employees* (Chicago: Railroad Historical Company, 1900), 724.
  249. J.S. Murray, *History of the Baltimore and Ohio Railroad Company* (Washington DC; Interstate Commerce Commission, 1922; 8.
  250. Trollope, *North America*, 100.
  251. "Mr. Sydney Pedlar's American Notes," *The Ipswich Journal*, January 12, 1875.
  252. Mencken, *The Railroad Passenger Car*, 78.
  253. John Stover, *American Railroads* (Chicago: University of Chicago Press, 1961), 47.
  254. Giedion, *Mechanization Takes Command*, 461–2.
  255. See Riegel and Athearn, *America Moves West*, 227.
  256. Jensen, *The American Heritage History of Railroads in America*, 22.
  257. Mencken, *The Railroad Passenger Car*, 68.
  258. Giedion, *Mechanization Takes Command*, 458, 463.
  259. Fried, *Appetite for America* (New York: Bantam Books, 2010), 41, 120.
  260. Hamilton, *Thomas Cook*, 236.
  261. David Nasaw, *Andrew Carnegie* (New York: Penguin, 2006), 338.
  262. Stennett, A. *Yesterday and Today: A History of the Chicago and North Western Railway System* (Chicago: Chicago and North Western Railway Company, 1910), 71
  263. Mencken, *The Railroad Passenger Car*, 79.
  264. See Jensen, *The American Heritage History of Railroads in America*, 127.
  265. See Mencken, *The Railroad Passenger Car*, 161–2.
  266. Henry T. Williams, *The Pacific Tourist* (New York: Henry T. Williams, 1876), 9.
  267. See Mencken, *The Railroad Passenger Car*, 149, 158.
  268. Benjamin Curtis, *Dottings Round the Circle* (Boston: J.R. Osgood and Co., 1876), 9.
  269. Stevenson, *The Amateur Emigrant*, 54
  270. Rae, *Westward by Rail*, 190.
  271. *Ibid.*, 153.
  272. Boddam-Whetham, *Western Wanderings* 16.
  273. One knowledgeable source described the Wagner sleeping cars in the 1870s as "the finest sleeping-cars ever run upon a road." Brown, *History of the First Locomotives*, 234.
  274. See Williams, *The Pacific Tourist*. Gilbert, Bush and Company was also a prominent manufacturer of sleeping and other luxury cars in the 1870s. Brown, *History of the First Locomotives*, 34.
  275. Giedion, *Mechanization Takes Command*, 439. In the same connection, one notes 1850–1900 a style of domestic architecture known as "Steamboat Gothic" emerged—named after the luxuriously appointed furnishings of river steamboats.

Chapter Four

  1. Hamlin, *Greek Revival Architecture in America*, 143–5
  2. Cavalier, *North America Railroad Stations*, 8.
  3. See Milton W. Brown, *American Art to 1900* (New York: Harry N. Abrams, 1977), 38.
  4. Hamlin, *Greek Revival Architecture in America*, 117.
  5. *Ibid.*, 168. Perhaps also in the "exotic" category were some of the American Army's open plan forts, most notably those in the West influenced by Californian mission station architecture. See Harris, *American Architecture*, 213.
  6. See Cavalier, *North American Railroad Stations*.
  7. Handlin, *American Architecture*, 74.
  8. Cavalier, *North American Railroad Stations*, 8, 15; and Jensen, *The American Heritage History of Railroads in America*, 206.
  9. *Ibid.*, 7.
  10. *Ibid.*, 35.
  11. Jensen, *The American Heritage History of Railroads in America*, 207.
  12. Two vestiges of the inn which sometimes found their way into American station architectural accommodation were the saloon and the boot-black, both eventually finding their way into Pullman service as well.
  13. See Biddle, *Victorian Stations*, 20.
  14. See Harris, America Architecture, 61.
  15. See Mencken, *The Railroad Passenger Car*, 101.
  16. Ferguson, *America by River and Rail*, 333.
  17. Rae, *Westward by Rail*, 50.

18. William K. Ackerman, *Origins of the Names of Stations on the Line of the Illinois Central Railroad* (Chicago: Illinois Central Railroad Company, 1884).
19. Buckingham *The Eastern and Western States of America*, vol. 2, 2. Therese Yelverton said of Philadelphia: "For good taste in architecture, Philadelphia stands unique on the American continent." Yelverton, *Teresina in America*, vol. 2, 132.
20. *Ibid.*, vol. 2, 1, 391; vol. 3, 57.
21. See Hamlin, *Greek Revival Architecture in America*, 335.
22. Handlin, *American Architecture*, 64.
23. Hamlin, *Greek Revival Architecture in America*, xviii.
24. See Ron Field and Adam Hook, *Forts of the American Frontier 1820–91* (Botley: Osprey Publishing, 2005), 34.
25. See Handlin, *American Architecture*.
26. John E. Burchard, *The Architecture of America: A Social and Cultural History* (Boston: Little, Brown and Co., 1961), 166–7. Jensen reproduces good photos of the Vanderbilt dynasty mansions.
27. Hamlin, *Greek Revival Architecture in America*, 334–5.
28. Gottschalk, *Notes of a Pianist*, 705.
29. Donald Porter, *Jubilee Jim and the Wizard of Wall Street* (New York: Dutton, 1990), 263.
30. Bain, *Empire Express*, 28.
31. Oscar Lewis, *The Big Four* (New York: Alfred A. Knopf, 1938).
32. Jensen, *The American Heritage History of Railroads in America*, 211.
33. Nigel Rodgers and Hazel Dodge, *The Illustrated Encyclopedia of the Roman Empire* (London: Lorenz Books, 2008), 312.
34. Burchard, *The Architecture of America*, 166–7.
35. Hamlin, *Greek Revival Architecture in America*, 354.
36. "A Railway Station in the Southern States of America," *The Illustrated London News*, March, 1861.
37. Ferguson, *America by River and Rail*, 465.
38. Mencken, *The Railroad Passenger Car*, 157, 171–3.
39. Curtis, *Dottings Round the Circle*, 9.
40. Alice Morse Earle, *Stage-Coach and Tavern Days* (New York: The Macmillan Company, 1911), 92–3.
41. Brown, *Hear That Lonesome Whistle Blow*, 168.
42. Hamlin, *Greek Revival Architecture in America*, 108, 133, 309.
43. Vaughan, *The Intemperate Engineer*, 52.
44. Lewis C. Gray, *History of Agriculture in the Southern U.S. to 1860* (Washington, D.C.: Carnegie Institution, 1933), 867.
45. Horace Greeley, *An Overland Journey from New York to San Francisco in the Summer of 1859* (London: MacDonald, 1965), 75.
46. Winther, *The Transportation Frontier*, 18.
47. Mark Twain, *Roughing It* (London: Penguin, 1985), 54.
48. Berg, *Buildings and Structures of American Railroads*, 246, 264.
49. Brown, *Hear That Lonesome Whistle Blow*, 244.
50. F.R. Conder, *The Men Who Built Railways* (London: Telford, 1983), 97.
51. Symes and Cole, *Railway Architecture of the South-East*, 9.
52. Andro Linklater, *Measuring America* (New York: Walker and Co., 2002), 183–5.
53. See Stilgoe, *Metropolitan Corridor*, 199.
54. *Ibid.*, 203.
55. Carroll Meeks, *The Railway Station: An Architectural History* (London: The Architectural Press, 1957), 49.
56. See Cavalier, *North American Railroad Stations*, 126–7.
57. See Jensen, *The American Heritage History of Railroads in America*, 207.
58. Yelverton, *Teresina in America*.
59. "Mr. Henry Vincent on America."
60. See Mencken, *The Railroad Passenger Car*, 126.
61. There was a time when North Carolina was known as the "Turpentine State." J. Logan, et al., *The Home Manual*, 328.
62. Mencken, *The Railroad Passenger Car*, 111.
63. Twain, *Life on the Mississippi*, 187.
64. Jensen, *The American Heritage History of Railroads in America*, 221.
65. John H. White, *American Locomotives: An Engineering History, 1830–1880* (Baltimore: The Johns Hopkins University Press, 1968), 13, 27. The first locomotive exported from the U.S. (to Europe) by its relatively fledgling locomotive building industry was shipped in 1836 or 1837.
66. Brown, *Hear That Lonesome Whistle Blow*, 25.
67. Kemble, *Journal of a Residence on a Georgian Plantation*, 18.
68. See Brown, *Hear That Lonesome Whistle Blow*, 222.
69. *Ibid.*, 20–1. It was ordered, along with two other locomotives, by the Hudson and Delaware Canal Company; but trials with the *Stourbridge Lion* showed the track was not robust enough to sustain such locomotives in regular use—the other two locomotives were, therefore, never commissioned.
70. Isabella Bird, *The Englishwoman in America* (London: John Murray, 1856), 104.
71. Marshall, *Through America*, 61.
72. *Ibid.*, 213. See also Stevenson, *The Amateur Emigrant*, 104; Hardman, *A Trip to America*, 75.
73. But the origin of the steam whistle was English—it was first used on English locomotives in 1835 (although invented two or three years earlier). See White, *American Locomotives*, 214–5.
74. Dunbar, *A History of Travel in America*, vol. 3, 852.
75. *Ibid.*, vol. 2, 722, 726.
76. See F.F. Dunwell, F.F. *The Hudson: America's River.* (New York: Columbia University, Press 2008), 122.
77. White, *American Locomotives*, 218–20, 223.
78. Stephenson's *Rocket* was itself brightly painted—yellow and black with a white chimney—when it appeared at the Rainhill Trials. See Vignoles, *Life of Charles Blacker Vignoles*, 129.
79. *Ibid.*, 221. In the 1870s the "ornamentation" of locomotives could cost up to $2,500 per locomotive.
80. Jensen, *The American Heritage History of Railroads in America*, 45.
81. Jensen discusses this. *Ibid.*, 45–6.
82. See B.A. Botkin (ed.), *A Treasury of American Folklore* (New York: Crown, 1944), 241–4; Brown, *Hear That Lonesome Whistle Blow*, 171.
83. See M.N. Forney quoted in Cooley, *The American Railway*, 101.

84. See the illustration in Giedion, *Mechanization Takes Command*, 441.
85. Sometimes the bunks were so narrow passengers had to strap themselves to them so that they did not fall off; a very real possibility given the jolting they would have received on some of the poorly-constructed roads. And while those on the bottom of these multi-tiered bunks were virtually at floor level, those on the top were often so close to the ceiling they could not sit up.
86. Brown, *Hear That Lonesome Whistle Blow*, 141.
87. Hamilton, *Thomas Cook*, 235.
88. This was 1867. "Railway Management."
89. Deedes, *Sketches of the South and West*, 160–1.
90. See Brown, 103
91. Mencken, *The Railroad Passenger Car*, 11, 14, 17.
92. Ibid., 173.
93. Rae, *Westward by Rail*, 51–2; Marshall, *Through America*, 28.
94. Kemble, *Journal of a Residence on a Georgian Plantation*, 14.
95. Trollope, *North America*, 23.
96. "The English Railways."
97. See Lewis, *The Big Four*, 325.
98. Ibid., 347.
99. See Mencken, *The Railroad Passenger Car*, chapter five.
100. See Acworth, *The Railways of England*, 189.
101. See Stover, *American Railroads*, 17–8.
102. "Traveling in the Federal States," *The Derby Mercury*, February 26, 1862.
103. See Mencken, *The Railroad Passenger Car*, 123.
104. Ibid., 131.
105. This was the verdict of an English tourist traveling on the New York Central en route to Chicago via Niagara Falls.
106. Smith, *A Yorkshireman's Trip to the United States and Canada*, 192.
107. "English and American Railways," *Freeman's Journal*, August 23, 1875.
108. "Mr. Henry Vincent on America."
109. "The English Railways."
110. *Illustrated London News*," January 9, 1869.
111. Bates, *A Year in the Great Republic*, vol. 2, 77.
112. "Mr. Henry Vincent on America."
113. See Mencken, *The Railroad Passenger Car*, 102.
114. Ibid., 144; Zincke, *Last Winter in the United States*, 173.
115. Stevenson, *The Amateur Emigrant*, 59.
116. See Brown, *Hear That Lonesome Whistle Blow*, 159.
117. See Mencken, *The Railroad Passenger Car*, 115–6.
118. Anon., *The Travellers' Grab Bag: For Utilizing Fragments of Time in Way-Stations, etc.* (New York: The Authors Publishing Co., 1876), "Dedication."
119. Stevenson, *The Amateur Emigrant*, 58.
120. Boddam-Whetham, *Western Wanderings*, 40.
121. See Mencken, *The Railroad Passenger Car*, 165. Henry Williams was a travel guide author, and claimed to have spent almost $20,000 on the production of his impressive enough guide, *The Pacific Tourist* (1876).
122. Lewis, *The Big Four*, 342.
123. See Mencken, *The Railroad Passenger Car*, 15.
124. Brown, *Hear That Lonesome Whistle Blow*, 157.
125. Lewis, *The Big Four*, 326.
126. Brogan, *Alexis de Tocqueville*, 184.
127. Gottschalk, *Notes of a Pianist*, 103–4, 235–6.
128. Yelverton, *Teresina in America*, vol. 2, 139.
129. Hawthorne, *Do's and Don'ts*, 76.
130. Logan et al., *The Home Manual*, 25
131. Trollope, *North America*, 38, 114, 117–8, 198.
132. "Mr. Henry Vincent on America."
133. "Mr. George Dawson on America."
134. "The English Railways."
135. Hardy, *Through Cities and Prairie Lands*, 88, 92.
136. Yelverton, *Teresina in America*, vol. 2, 97.
137. Trollope, *North America*, 309, 311, 319.
138. Ibid., 9–10, 182.
139. Rae, *Westward by Rail*, 53.
140. Bates, *A Year in the Great republic*, vol. 2, 281.
141. Zincke, *Last Winter in the United States*, 62.
142. Kirkman, *Railway Service*, 157–8.
143. See Bain, *Empire Express*, 539.
144. Kirkman, *Railway Service*, 157–8.
145. See Bain, *Empire Express*, 424.
146. Williams, *The Pacific Tourist*, 18.
147. See Mencken, *The Railroad Passenger Car*, 26.
148. Ferguson, *America by River and Rail*, 105.
149. See Mencken, *The Railroad Passenger Car*, 27.
150. Bates, *A Year in the Great Republic*, vol. 2, 65.
151. Curtis, *Dottings Round the Circle*, 10.
152. Hamilton, *Thomas Cook*, 241.
153. See Mencken, *The Railroad Passenger Car*, 165; Williams, *The Pacific Tourist*, 10–11.
154. In India in the days of the Raj *the children of princes* considered it a great treat not to have to eat off gold plate; but, instead, to occasionally dine on *railroad curry* in a railroad dining-room! The Rajmata of Jaipur, quoted in Ann Morrow, *Highness: The Maharajahs of India* (London: Grafton Books, 1986), 47.
155. Fried, *Appetite for America*, xvii–xviii.
156. See Brown, *Hear That Lonesome Whistle Blow*, 223.
157. Fried, *Appetite for America*, xvii, 93.
158. Advertisement in John T. King, *Guide to the Baltimore and Ohio Railroad 1873* (no publication details furnished).
159. Murray, *History of the Baltimore and Ohio Railroad Company*, 9.
160. Mencken, *The Railroad Passenger Car*, 28.
161. See, for instance, the menus reproduced in Marshall, *Through America*, 109.
162. Rae, *Westward by Rail*, 21.
163. Smith, *A Yorkshireman's Trip to the United States and Canada*, 225.
164. James, *The American Scene*, 406, 408.
165. "Railroad Management."
166. See Mencken, *The Railroad Passenger Car*, 119.
167. Jensen, *The American Heritage History of Railroads in America*, 144.
168. H. Porter quoted in Cooley, *The American Railway*, 259.
169. See Mencken, *The Railroad Passenger Car*, 131.

170. *Ibid.*, 174.
171. Boddam-Whetham, *Western Wanderings*, 355.
172. Marshall, *Through America*, 62.
173. See Coleman, *Passage to America*, 50.
174. Deedes, *Sketches of the South and West*, 67.
175. Brown, *Hear That Lonesome Whistle Blow*, 226. In the early 1880s "celebrities" traveling on the transcontinental to California were often interviewed by a newsagent (on the train) a few days before getting to San Francisco; and their arrival times were telegraphed ahead to the newspapers, which routinely published such "news" at the time.
176. Frank Norris, *McTeague* (New York: Holt, Rinehart and Winston, 1965).
177. Brown, *Hear That Lonesome Whistle Blow*, 94.
178. Jensen, *The American Heritage History of Railroads in America*, 194.
179. See Maury Klein, *The Life and Legend of Jay Gould* (Baltimore: The Johns Hopkins University Press, 1986), 148.
180. Hamilton, *Thomas Cook*, 235.
181. Erie Railroad Company Regulations 1854: Regulation nos. 60, 68, 86, 90, 141, in Romans, *American Locomotive Engineers*.
182. See Mencken, *The Railroad Passenger Car*, 120.
183. See Jensen, *The American Heritage History of Railroads in America*, 180.
184. Erie Railroad Regulations 1854 quoted in Romans, *American Locomotive Engineers*.
185. See Cunynghame, *A Glimpse of the Great Western Republic*, 20; Mencken, *The Railroad Passenger Car*, 112–15, 176.
186. It was also suggested in this article that fares were higher in England because safety and security cost money. *Sacramento Daily Union*, September 26, 1856.
187. Stevenson, *The Amateur Emigrant*, 36, 122.
188. Sandburg, *Abraham Lincoln*, 302.
189. When Lincoln remarked to his traveling companion during a train journey: "I guess my hat hain't chalked on this road," he was alluding to the fact that if he had a free pass, then the conductor would chalk a mark on his hat so that he was exempt from the frequent ticket checks. *Ibid.*, 15.
190. See Mencken, *The Railroad Passenger Car*, 115.
191. Columbia Correspondence College, *A History of the Railway Mail Service* (Washington, D.C.: Columbia Correspondence College, 1903), 30.
192. Brown, *Hear That Lonesome Whistle Blow*, 180.
193. Ambrose Bierce, *The Devil's Dictionary* (Ware, MA: Wordsworth Reference, 1996), 47.
194. Mallie Stafford, *The March of Empire Through Three Decades* (San Francisco: George Spaulding and Co., 1884), 145.
195. See Mencken, *The Railroad Passenger Journey*, 190.
196. Pachter and Wein, *Abroad in America*, 87.
197. Stevenson, *The Amateur Emigrant*, 37–8.
198. *Ibid.*, 176–7.
199. Reynolds suggests that in the 1840s there was an underground pornography industry in America, such material not uncommonly peddled at railroad stations. Reynolds, *Walt Whitman's America*, 196.
200. Cunynghame, *A Glimpse of the Great Western Republic*, 187–8.
201. Nichols, *Forty Years of American Life*, vol. 1, 340.
202. See Mencken, *The Railroad Passenger Car*, 137.
203. Gottschalk, *Notes of a Pianist*, 122.
204. Stevenson, *The Amateur Emigrant*, 120–1.
205. "Winter Traveling in America"; and "American Railway-Carriages."
206. See Jensen, *The American Heritage History of Railroads in America*, 22.
207. Boddam-Whetham, *Western Wanderings*, 100.
208. See Brown, *Hear That Lonesome Whistle Blow*, 227.
209. John Matteson, *Eden's Outcasts: The Story of Louisa May Alcott and Her Father* (New York: W.W. Norton, 2007), 366.
210. Williams, *The Pacific Tourist*, 12.
211. Ferguson, *America by River and Rail*, 506.
212. Pullman became a joint stock company in 1867.
213. See Liston E. Leyendecker, *Palace Car Prince: A Biography of George Mortimer Pullman* (Niwot: University of Colorado Press, 1992), 203.
214. W.F. Rae thought Pullman porters well-paid, but noted they "hold office on the condition that no complaint is preferred against them." Rae, *Westward by Rail*, 80–1. However, they were not very well paid, although the tips they received more than compensated for that.
215. Twain, *Life on the Mississippi*.
216. Before abolition, negro slaves (and "free" negro servants, too) no doubt had their own structures and systems by means of which social status, within their ranks, was established hierarchically; and perhaps that is a phenomenon which, hitherto, has been under-researched. Indeed, slaves and servants certainly ranked themselves within their own broader communities according to the perceived status (within the *white* community) of the household they served, or the eminence of the lady or gentleman whose household it was. Indeed, based on my reading, negro slaves and servants were always very aware of where the household and its members they served ranked in the broader white community, and thus aligned themselves (in status terms) with that perceived status of the (white) family concerned. Furthermore, on many occasions during my reading I noted slaves or servants who enjoyed some relative (delegated) authority or responsibility on a plantation, would, for instance, refer pejoratively to their fellows in such a way as to demean the latter. I recall reading of a white visitor to a plantation, who was being shown around it by a slave who had some authority; and the latter, pointing to another slave, referred to him as "that there nigger"—although, according to my source, "that there nigger" was no "darker" than his overseer.
217. Myers, *History of the Great American Fortunes* (New York: The Modern Library, 1909), 208.
218. *Ibid.*, volume 1, 285
219. Brown, *Hear That Lonesome Whistle Blow*, 178.
220. See Mencken, *The Railroad Passenger Car*, 188.
221. Brogan, *Alexis de Tocqueville*, 183.
222. Hogan, *The Australian in London and America*, 45–6.

223. Yelverton, *Teresina in America*, vol. 1, 37.
224. Quoted from Gustavus Myers, *History of the Great American Fortunes*. Part of the Astor fortune found its way into railroad capitalism, with J.J. Astor taking a huge holding in the New York Central. But that sort of investment may well have been more broadly strategic, since it would have harmonized with the dynasty's New York real estate interests—they owned around 700 commercial premises and tenements in New York at the time (bearing in mind also that property speculation and railroad investment often went together).
225. Nasaw, *Andrew Carnegie*, 288.
226. Erie Railroad Regulations 1854 quoted in Romans, *American Locomotive Engineers*.
227. Curtis, *Dottings Round the Circle*, 9.
228. See Jensen, *The American Heritage History of Railroads in America*, 178.
229. Frederick S. Dellenbaugh, *Breaking the Wilderness* (New York: G.P. Putnam's Sons, 1905), 44.
230. Stephen Ambrose, *Nothing Like It in the World: The Men Who Built the Transcontinental Railroad 1863–1869* (New York: Simon & Schuster, 2000), 41.
231. Burton J. Hendrick, *The Life of Andrew Carnegie* (New York: Doubleday, Doran and Co., 1932), 88.
232. Gottschalk, *Notes of a Pianist*, 116.
233. Elmer E. Smith, *Abraham Lincoln as Attorney for the Illinois Central Railroad Company* (Chicago: Ginthorp Warren, 1905).
234. See Sandburg, *Abraham Lincoln*, for a good account of Lincoln's association with railroads during his years as an Illinois circuit lawyer.
235. Romans, *American Locomotive Engineers*.
236. Solon Buck, *The Granger Movement* (Cambridge, MA: Harvard University Press, 1913), 13.
237. See Hoyt, *The Vanderbilts and their Fortunes*, 228–9.
238. Jensen, *The American Heritage History of Railroads in America*, 240.
239. Myers, *History of the Great American Fortunes*, 323.
240. Jensen, *The American Heritage History of Railroads in America*, 240.
241. Smith, *A Yorkshireman's Trip to the United States and Canada*, 62.
242. Acworth, *The Railways of England*, 116.
243. In the 1880s the Union Pacific was offering long-haul passengers a free baggage allowance of 150 pounds.
244. Boddam-Whetham, *Western Wanderings*, 50
245. See Mencken, *The Railroad Passenger Car*, 182–3.
246. See Brown, *Hear That Lonesome Whistle Blow*, 179.
247. Trollope, *North America*, 9–10, 74–5.
248. See Mencken, *The Railroad Passenger Car*, 146.
249. Hawthorne, *Do's and Don'ts*, 22, 80.
250. See Kurt C. Schlicting, *Grand Central Terminal* (Baltimore: The Johns Hopkins University Press, 2001), 19–20.
251. "The Railroads and the Farms," *The Atlantic Monthly* 32, no. 193 (1873).
252. Wellington Williams, *Appleton's Railroad and Steamboat Companion* (New York: D. Appleton and Co., 1849).
253. "American Railways," *The Morning Post*, October 2, 1865.

254. "Mr. Sydney Peddlar's American Notes," *The Ipswich Journal*, January 12, 1875."
255. Brown, *Hear That Lonesome Whistle Blow*, 137.
256. Peto, *Resources and Prospects*, 277.
257. Andrews, *Railroads and Farming*, 21.
258. Marshall, *Through America*, 65.
259. See Lewis, *The Big Four*, 350–1.
260. Stover, *American Railroads*; Ferguson, *America by River and Rail*, 97.
261. Cochran, *Pennsylvania*, 123.
262. See Jensen, *The American Heritage History of Railroads in America*, 36.
263. See Mencken, *The Railroad Passenger Car*, 180.
264. Saloman F. Van Oss, *American Railroads and English Investors* (London: Effingham Wilson and Co., 1893), 15.
265. Baltimore and Ohio Railroad Company, *Annual Report of the President and Directors to the Shareholders* (Baltimore: William Wooddy, 1832).
266. Botkin, *A Treasury of American Folklore*, 488.
267. See Seth Lerer, *Inventing English* (New York: Columbia University Press, 2007), 187.
268. Williams, *The Pacific Tourist*, 12.
269. See Mencken, *The Railroad Passenger Car*, 114.
270. Trollope, *North America*.
271. See Hawthorne, *Do's and Don'ts*, 9.
272. He also thought English long-haul trains both unimpressive and overpriced.
273. White, *American Locomotives*, 73–4.
274. D. Jervis quoted in White, *American Locomotives*, 73.
275. White, *American Locomotives*, 74.
276. See Myers, *History of the Great American Fortunes*, volume 2, 318.
277. Hudson, *A Scamper Through America*, 78.
278. Jensen, *The American Heritage History of Railroads in America*, 144.
279. Mencken, *The Railroad Passenger Car*, 90.
280. "German and Danish Railway Carriages."
281. Buckingham, *The Eastern and Western States of America*, vol. 3, 2.
282. Mencken, *The Railroad Passenger Car*, 5–6.
283. Nichols, *Forty Years of American Life*, vol. 1, 32.
284. "English and American Railroads," *Memphis Appeal*, October 7, 1873.
285. Yelverton, *Teresina in America*, vol. 1, 19.
286. Dorsey, *English and American Railroads Compared*, 5,
287. He spent around three years traveling in America. Buckingham, *The Eastern and Western States of America*, vol. 1, 471.
288. White, *American Locomotives*, 4.
289. "An Interesting Paper Has Recently Been Printed," *The Morning Post*, May 4, 1857.
290. "Railways in the United States," *Daily News*, December 2, 1857.
291. "Letter from Dr. England."
292. White, *American Locomotives*, 3.
293. "The English Railways."
294. Kemble, *Journal of a Residence on a Georgian Plantation*, 33.
295. See Bain, *Empire Express*, 539.
296. Alice Morse Earle, *Stage-Coach and Tavern Days*, 288.
297. See Mencken, *The Railroad Passenger Car*, 7.

Snaking rails are mentioned in various contemporary sources, so they were a real hazard.

298. See Peto, *Resources and Prospects*, 281–3.
299. Hardman, *A Trip to America*, 188.
300. Hardy, *Through Cities and Prairie Lands*, 81.
301. Mencken, *The Railroad Passenger Car*.
302. *Ibid.*, xv and chapter eight.
303. Walter D. Hines, *War History of American Railroads* (New Haven, CT: Yale University Press, 1928), 61–2.
304. See Mencken, *The Railroad Passenger Car*, 97–100.
305. "The English Railways."

Chapter Five

1. Charles Adams, Jr., "The Railroad Death-Rate," *The Atlantic Monthly* 37, no. 220 (1876)
2. Gosta E. Sandstrom, *The History of Tunneling* (London: Borrie and Rockliff, 1963), 91.
3. See Brian Dolan, *Ladies of the Grand Tour* (New York: HarperCollins, 2001), 142.
4. Jack Beatty, *Age of Betrayal* (New York: Alfred A. Knopf, 2007), 5.
5. Albert Fried and Richard Elman (eds.), *Charles Booth's London* (London: Hutchinson, 1969), 28, 107.
6. Vaughan, *The English Guidebook*, 128.
7. See Mencken, *The Railroad Passenger Car*, xi.
8. See Edwin A. Pratt, *A History of Inland Transit and Communication in England* (London: Kegan, Paul, Trench, Trubner, 1912), 249.
9. See John A. Pimlott, *The Englishman's Holiday: A Social History* (Hassocks, UK: Harvester, 1976), 89.
10. Schivelbusch, *The Railway Journey*, 113. See also Ellis L. Armstrong, *History of Public Works in the United States 1776–1996* (Chicago: American Public Works Association, 1976), 33.
11. See Simon Garfield, *The Last Journey of William Huskisson*, 57.
12. Maxine Feifer, *Going Places: The Ways of the Tourist from Imperial Rome to the Present Day* (London: Macmillan, 1985), 166.
13. Sandstrom, *The History of Tunneling*, 91.
14. See James Lees-Milne, *The Bachelor Duke* (London: John Murray, 1991), 171.
15. Legg, *The Railway Book*, 62.
16. See Pratt, *A History of Inland Transit and Communication*, 245–6.
17. See Julie M. Fenster, *Mavericks, Miracles and Medicine* (New York: Carroll and Graf, 2003), 100. In America after the Civil War the river steamboats greatly assisted the spread of yellow fever the length of the Mississippi.
18. Schivelbusch, *The Railway Journey*, 148.
19. A theory of Georg Simmel's, quoted by Paolo Jedlowski in M. Kaern, B.S. Phillips, and Robert S. Cohen (eds.), *Georg Simmel and Contemporary Sociology* (Dordrecht: Kluiver Academic, 1990), 137.
20. See Deborah Cadbury, *Dreams of Iron and Steel* (New York: Fourth Estate, 2003), 27.
21. See Jennings, *Pandaemonium*, 132–3.
22. See Garfield, *The Last Journey of William Huskisson*, 158, 163, 173, 192; "Mr. Huskisson's Death," *Caledonian Mercury*, September 20, 1830.
23. In his 1861 booklet on American railroad accidents, Dr. Edmund Arnold asserted many people died at railroad accident scenes from "shock"; and he attributed the death of a woman in an 1859 accident, which he had attended, "mainly to the shock of the accident." This indicates that by that time the medical diagnosis of shock was neither controversial nor unusual in America, either. See Edmund S. Arnold, *On Medical Provision for Railroad Accidents* (Yonkers, NY: Examiner Print, 1861), 4.
24. L.T.C. Rolt, *Isambard Kingdom Brunel: A Biography* (London: Longmans, Green and Co., 1957), 138.
25. See Barty-King, *New Flame*, 96
26. See Acworth, *The Railways of England*, 32.
27. See Sally Duggan, *Men of Iron* (London: Pan, 2003), 51.
28. *Ibid.*, 50. An 1836 newspaper article described Lardner as a "leading man in the scientific world." He illustrated his lectures "with a model of a steam engine and train of carriages, which he put in motion." "Dr. Lardner's Lectures," *The Hull Packet*, December 30, 1836.
29. "Ventilation of Tunnels in Railways," *The Bristol Mercury*, March 24, 1838.
30. See Steel, *The History of the London and North Western Railway*, 60–1.
31. "Frightful Accidents on the London and Birmingham Railway," *The Operative*, February 24, 1839.
32. See John Gloag, *Victorian Taste* (Newton Abbot: David and Charles, 1972), 110, 113.
33. See Schivelbusch, *The Railway Journey*.
34. Symes and Cole, *Railway Architecture of the South-East*, 17.
35. See Wolfgang Schivelbusch, *Disenchanted Night: The Industrialization of Light in the Nineteenth Century* (Berkeley: University of California Press, 1988), 34.
36. Ritchie, *Railways*, 291–2.
37. John F. Layson, *Famous Engineers of the Nineteenth Century* (London: J.G. Murdoch, 1880), 19–20.
38. "The Fatal Boiler Explosion," *Freeman's Journal*, December 19, 1845; "Terrific Boiler Explosion and Destruction of Steam Mills," *The Standard* May 22, 1845; "Terrific Boiler Explosion," *The Derby Mercury* May 2, 1849.
39. "Dreadful Steam Boiler Explosion," *Manchester Times*, 20 February, 1850
40. "The Dreadful Boiler Explosion at Ardwick," *The Manchester Times and Gazette*, February 15, 1848.
41. This was the first locomotive boiler explosion in America, the locomotive had been the first built in America *for commercial service* and the "rebuilt" *Best Friend* was renamed the *Phoenix*.
42. *Ibid.*, 84.
43. Brogan, *Alexis De Tocqueville*, 213.
44. "Railroad Versus Stage Coach Traveling."
45. "Accidents on Railroads," *The Champion and Weekly Herald*, November 18, 1838.
46. Simmons, *The Victorian Railway*, 379.
47. See Legg, *The Railway Book*, 52.
48. Mayhew, *London Labour and the London Poor*, vol. 2, 379.
49. White, *American Locomotives*, 212.
50. See Mencken, *The Railroad Passenger Car*, 111–2.
51. According to Ferguson, normally a company had to pay half the value of stock killed, unless the stock had broken through fenced parts of the line. Ferguson, *America by River and Mail*, 321. But it

would have depended on the state the accident occurred in.

52. White, *American Locomotives*, 211. The cowcatcher was possibly first mentioned in England in a letter to a newspaper in November, 1838: "Safety Guards on Railways," *Caledonian Mercury*, 10 November, 1838.

53. See Mencken, *The Railroad Passenger Car*, 103–4.

54. See Stilgoe, *American Railroads*, 167–9.

55. Flynt also associated the emergence of the "railroad tramp" in the decades after the Civil War with the decline of apprenticeships, the tramp lifestyle said to hold some attraction for restless youth. He also remarked upon the fact that most railroad tramps were alcoholics.

56. *The Manufacturer and Builder* 12, no.1 (1880); "The Tramp and the Railroads," *The Century*, 58 (1899); "How Men Become Tramps," *The Century*, 50, no.6 (1895).

57. "Convictions for Trespassing on the Leeds and Selby Railway," *The Leeds Mercury*, October 4, 1834.

58. This is still a major problem today in some countries—about 15,000 people are killed annually trying to cross the tracks on India's huge railroad network (India has 64,000 km of track, many lines penetrating densely populated cities and running through or near shanty towns).

59. Hardman, *A Trip to America*, 74–5.

60. Ferguson, *America by River and Rail*, 360.

61. Yelverton, *Teresina in America*, vol. 2, 123.

62. Schivelbusch, *The Railway Journey*, 30.

63. The "trouble" was attributed to radicals stirring up the locals. "Mr. Huskisson's Death," *Caledonian Mercury*, September 20, 1830.

64. Old Bailey Records (www.oldbaileyonline.org.), t18511027–1966.

65. *Ibid.*, t18561215–129.
66. *Ibid.*, t18661022–963
67. *Ibid.*, t18680817–710
68. *Ibid.*, t18720506–416.
69. *Ibid.*, t18800702–679.
70. *Ibid.*, t18510818–1660.
71. *Ibid.*, t18541121–109.
72. *Ibid.*, t18590613–605.
73. *Ibid.*, t18620922–983.
74. *Ibid.*, t18670923–854.
75. *Ibid.*, t18680706–637.
76. *Ibid.*, t18690816–733.
77. *Ibid.*, t18690816–746.
78. *Ibid.*, t18760529–377.
79. *Ibid.*, t18540814–960.
80. *Ibid.*, t18700919–742.
81. *Ibid.*, t18550507–530.
82. *Ibid.*, t18580104–208.
83. *Ibid.*, t18710816–690.

84. "Births, Deaths, Marriages and Obituaries," *The Lancashire Gazette*, September 11, 1830.

85. "Shocking Accidents on the Railway," *The Standard*, March 31, 1831.

86. "Accident on the Garnkirk Railway," *The Standard*, July 23, 1831.

87. "Railway Accidents," *The Champion and Weekly Herald*, October 13, 1839.

88. "Railroad versus Stage Coach Traveling," *The Derby Mercury*, November 13, 1839.

89. "Railway Accidents," *Daily News*, October 21, 1852.

90. "The Railroad Death Rate," *The Atlantic Monthly* 37, no. 220 (1876).

91. White, *American Locomotives*, 3.

92. *Daily Alta California*, January 15, 1867.

93. *Sacramento Daily Union*, September 26, 1856.

94. Steve Fraser, *Every Man a Speculator: A History of Wall Street in American Life* (New York: HarperCollins, 2005), 119.

95. See Bain, *Empire Express*, 642. Where the first transcontinental railroad was concerned, government inspectors did occasionally refuse to certify some construction, which held up access to subsidies for the companies concerned. Brown, *Hear That Lonesome Whistle Blow*, 191.

96. "Royal Commission on Railways," *The Standard*, July 27, 1866.

97. "Railroad Management."

98. "Frightful Accidents on the London and Birmingham Railway," *The Operative*, February 24, 1839.

99. Brown, *Hear That Lonesome Whistle Blow*, 153.

100. But Huish was an exceptionally talented manager, indicated early on (1837) when he was elected—ahead of 59 other applicants—to the position of Secretary of the Glasgow, Paisley and Greenock Railway.

101. Charles H. Grinling, *The History of the Great Northern Railway* 1845–1895 (London: Methuen, 1898), 104.

102. See Jensen, *The American Heritage History of Railroads in America*, 52.

103. On Huish, see "Railway Accidents," *Daily News* October 21, 1852; "Institution of Civil Engineers," *The Morning Post* August 10, 1852; "Municipal Elections," *Caledonian Mercury* November 9, 1837; Gourvish, *Mark Huish*.

104. "Fatal Accident on the Liverpool and Birmingham Railway," *The Morning Chronicle* September 12, 1837.

105. Flanders mentions a number of English newspapers around mid-century which seemed to specialize in "sensationalist" content. Flanders, *Consuming Passions*, 140.

106. Simmons, *Railways: An Anthology*, 75

107. See Legg, *The Railway Book*, 52.

108. "Appalling Railway Accident," *The Northern Liberator* May 23, 1840.

109. "Explosion of the Gainsbro' Packet," *The Sheffield Independent*, June 10, 1837.

110. See Stilgoe, Metropolitan Corridor, 173.

111. Simmons, *The Victorian Railway*, 17.

112. Charles Adams, Jr. "The Railroad Death-Rate," *The Atlantic Monthly* 37, no. 220 (1876).

113. Acworth, *The Railways of England*, 38.

114. *Ibid.*, 35.

115. Ritchie, *Railways*, 361–416.

116. Altick, *Punch: The Lively Youth of a English Institution,1841–1851*, 33.

117. Mayhew, *London Labour and the London Poor*, vol. 3, especially 326.

118. One of the early Baltimore and Ohio cars (described below) offered car-top accommodation: "On the top of the car is placed a double sofa (along with "plank" seats)...A wire netting rises from two sides to the top of the car to a height which renders the top seats perfectly secure." There was also a top-awning to protect the passengers from the elements. Brown, *History of the First Locomotives*, 101–2.

119. Acworth, *The Railways of England*, 36.

120. "Railroad Management."

121. Garfield, *The Last Journey of William Huskisson*, 208.
122. The article noted that in America such suicides were not "returned in a class by themselves," but bundled together under the general head of "accidents to trespassers." "The Railroad Death-Rate." So, there may have been more "railroad suicides" in America than was thought to be the case at the time.
123. "An Ancient Railway Guide Book."
124. "Railway Reform," *The Bradford Observer*, April 11, 1844.
125. Jensen, *The American Heritage History of Railroads in America*, 178.
126. Kemble, *Journal of a Residence on a Georgian Plantation*, 12.
127. Combe, *Notes on the United States of America*, vol. 1, 32.
128. Kemble, *Journal of A Residence on a Georgian Plantation*, 15.
129. Sarmiento, *Travels*, 120.
130. Earle, *Stage-Coach and Tavern Days*, 286.
131. Ritchie, *Railways*, 355.
132. Rae, *Westward by Rail*, 50.
133. See Mencken, *The Railroad Passenger Car*.
134. Kirkman, *Railway Service*, 175.
135. Stover, *American Railroads*, 50.
136. See Klein, *The Life and Legend of Jay Gould*, 17.
137. Jensen, *The American Heritage History of Railroads in America*, 187.
138. Brown, *Hear That Lonesome Whistle Blow*, 233.
139. Winther, *The Transportation Frontier*, 132.
140. See Mencken, *The Railroad Passenger Car*, 137.
141. Arnold, *On Medical Provision for Railroad Accidents*.
142. See Stiles, *The First Tycoon*, 126. Buckingham noted that legislation in 1840 had improved safety on Western steamboats (on the Mississippi and its tributaries)—such legislation had been forced by public pressure. By then steamboats required a certificate of inspection and their engineers had to be licensed after examination of their "competency, skill, sobriety, and good moral character." Furthermore, steamboat employees found guilty of negligence or misconduct concerning a passenger fatality were to be "considered guilty of manslaughter and punished by imprisonment" (there were a good many other stringent regulations, essentially pertaining to inspection and testing of machinery, contained within the legislation). Buckingham, *The Eastern and Western States of America*, vol. 3, 63. But this legislation seems not to have had much impact and may have been unenforceable.
143. Bain, *Empire Express*, 635.
144. Jensen, *The American Heritage History of Railroads in America*, 186, 188.
145. This matter gets some coverage in Railroad Historical Company, *History of the Illinois Central Railroad and Representative Employees*, 1900.
146. "The Railroad Death-Rate."
147. *Ibid*.
148. See Peto, *Resources and Prospects*, 275
149. E.P. Alexander quoted in Cooley, *The American Railway*, 191.
150. Rae, *Westward by Rail*, 31.
151. Zincke, *Last Winter in the United States*, 147.

152. Letter of June 1865. See Morgan, *The Railway Lover's Companion*, 337. Ten people were killed in this accident and Dickens assisted at the scene for two hours. Subsequently, he was always nervous when traveling by rail. See Slater, *Charles Dickens*, 535, 537, 551, 556, and 613.
153. Robert Beaumont, *The Railway King: A Biography of George Hudson* (London: Review, 2002), 211.
154. Brenda Wineapple, *Hawthorne: A Life* (New York: Alfred A. Knopf, 2003), 258.
155. William S. McFeeley, *Grant: A Biography* (New York: Norton, 1981), 244.
156. Stiles, *The First Tycoon*, 90; Hoyt, *The Vanderbilts and Their Fortunes*, 94–5; Jensen, *The American Heritage History of Railroads in America*, 186.
157. Stanley Jackson, *J.P. Morgan* (New York: Stein and Day, 1984), 152.
158. *Sacramento Daily Union*, February 19, 1867.
159. "Safety in Railroad Travel," *Scribner's Magazine* 6, no. 3 (1889). This is a very good article, which traces the history of braking systems—and other safety appliances—until 1889.
160. By 1889 the Westinghouse system was widely used not only in England and North America, but also on the European continent, India, Australia, and South America.
161. Stilgoe, *Metropolitan Corridor*, 153.
162. Brown, *Hear That Lonesome Whistle Blow*, 167.
163. Ronald Wright, *What Is America?* (Philadelphia: De Capo Press, 2008), 179.
164. Furthermore, late in the 19th century numerous American railroad companies adopted a policy of requiring new employees to sign employment contracts releasing the company from liability in the event of an accident. See Myers, *History of the Supreme Court of the United States*, 655, 657.
165. "Safety in Railroad Travel."
166. *Ibid*.
167. Earle, *Stage-Coach and Tavern Days*, 374.
168. See Winther, *The Transportation Frontier*, 141, 143.
169. In this connection, one notes that the first Western movie was Edwin Porter's *The Great Train Robbery* (1903).
170. William A. Pinkerton, "Highwaymen of the Railroad," *The North American Review* 157, no. 444 (1893)
171. Hudson, *A Scamper Through America*, 188.
172. See Hamilton, *Alabama*.
173. Brown, *Hear That Lonesome Whistle Blow*, 89.
174. Stevenson, *The Amateur Emigrant*, 67.
175. See Mencken, *The Railroad Passenger Car*, 183–5.
176. Hogan, *The Australian in London and America*, 38, 48.
177. Rae, *Westward by Rail*, 81.
178. Boddam-Whetham, *Western Wanderings*, 54, 64, 68.
179. Hardman, *A Trip to America*, 179.
180. Winther, *The Transportation*, 140.
181. Mencken, *The Railroad Passenger Car*, 168.
182. Alison Adburgham, *Shops and Shopping, 1800–1914* (London: Allen and Unwin, 1964), 92.
183. Mark Twain and Charles D. Warner, *The Gilded Age* (London: Cassells, 1985), 195.

184. "Important to Railway Companies," *The Leeds Mercury*, July 21, 1838. Another key factor impinging upon the issue was whether the company had been negligent as to the cause of the accident. But something I found curious about this case was that although the complainant had been traveling *third-class*, still he could afford three counsel.
185. "The Railroad Death-Rate." *The Atlantic Monthly* 37, no.220 (1876).
186. Philip S. Bagwell, *The Railwaymen* (London: George Allen and Unwin, 1963), 115.
187. Including the South Eastern; North Kent; London, Brighton and South Coast; and the London and South Western.
188. "Railway Passengers Assurance Company' *The Morning Post*, March 7, 1850.
189. "Important to Railway Companies," *The Leeds Mercury* July 21, 1838.
190. Albert S. Bolles, *Industrial History of the United States* (Norwich, CT: The Henry Bill Publishing Co., 1878), 848–9.
191. See Mencken, *The Railroad Passenger Car*, 142–3.
192. Rae, *Westward by Rail*, 78.
193. Sarmiento, *Travels*, 139–40.
194. Jensen, *The American Heritage History of Railroads in America*, 186.

Chapter Six

1. Bruce Catton, *Michigan* (New York: W.W. Norton, 1976), 95.
2. Schlicting, *Grand Central Terminal*, 40.
3. See Garfield, *The Last Journey of William Huskisson*, 117.
4. See Schlicting, *Grand Central Terminal*, 40.
5. See J.H. Schaub in James H. Schaub, Sheila K. Dickison and M.D. Morris, *Engineering and Humanities* (New York: John Wiley and Sons, 1982), 49.
6. See Stephen Ambrose, *Nothing Like It in the World*, 25.
7. "A Railway Study," *Harper's New Monthly Magazine* 55, no. 328 (1877).
8. M. Oldfield, *The Horse in Magic and Myth* (Mineola, NY: Dover, 2002), 180, 183.
9. Pratt, *A History of Inland Transit and Communication in England*, 227.
10. Garfield, *The Last Journey of William Huskisson*, 20.
11. See Legg, *The Railway Book*, 19.
12. "Railroad versus Stage Coach Traveling."
13. Henri Thoreau, *Walden or, Life in the Woods* (New York: Signet, 1949), 82–3.
14. See Dolf Sternberger, *Panorama of the Nineteenth Century* (New York: Urizen, 1977), 29.
15. See Hopkins, *The Poetry of Railways*, 19.
16. cf. Barry Trinder, *The Making of the Industrial Landscape* (London: Dent, 1982), 158.
17. cf. Bruce Mazlish (ed.), *The Railroad and the Space Programme: An Exploration in Historical Analogy* (Cambridge, MA: MIT Press, 1965), 207.
18. Schivelbusch, *The Railway Journey*, 23.
19. Sternberger, *Panorama of the Nineteenth Century*, 25.
20. See Brown, *Hear That Lonesome Whistle Blow*, 174.
21. David Ross, *The Willing Servant: A History of the Steam Locomotive* (Stroud: Tempus, 2004), Preface.
22. See Stilgoe, *Metropolitan Corridor*, 198.
23. Albro Martin, *Railroads Triumphant* (Oxford: Oxford University Press, 1992), 244.
24. "The American Railroad" *Harper's New Monthly Magazine* 49, no. 291 (1874).
25. Schivelbusch, *Disenchanted Night*, 29.
26. Simmons, *The Victorian Railway*, 240.
27. Brown, *Hear That Lonesome Whistle Blow*, 26.
28. "The Railroad Celebration in San Francisco," *Sacramento Daily Union*, May 10, 1865.
29. See James A. Ward, *Railroads and the Character of America 1820–1887* (Knoxville: University of Tennessee Press, 1986), 19, 24–6.
30. See Conder, *The Men Who Built Railways*, 2.
31. See Stilgoe, *Metropolitan Corridor*.
32. See Ward, *Railroads and the Character of America*, 13–15.
33. See Reynolds, *Walt Whitman's America*, 374.
34. Leo Marx, *The Machine in the Garden: Technology and the Pastoral Ideal in America* (New York: Oxford University Press, 1964), 31.
35. Tom F. Peters, *Building the Nineteenth Century* (Cambridge, MA: MIT Press, 1996), 354.
36. Stilgoe, *Metropolitan Corridor*, 43.
37. Biddle, *Victorian Stations*, 218–9.
38. See Jones, *Industrial Architecture in Britain*, 71–2.
39. See Sternberger, *Panorama of the Nineteenth Century*, 178–9.
40. Frank McKenna, *The Railway Workers 1840–1970* (London: Faber and Faber, 1980), 234.
41. Simmons, *The Victorian Railway*, 260.
42. See Stilgoe, *Metropolitan Corridor*, 238, 242.
43. In America in 1867 agricultural reformer and landscape architect, D.G. Mitchell, wrote chapters on railway gardening and landscape treatment of railways in the journal *Rural History*. The idea was to turn unpleasant railroad property into aesthetically pleasing gardens and landscapes. See also Stilgoe, *Metropolitan Corridor*, 229.
44. Dixon and Malthesius, *Victorian Architecture*, 98.
45. Meeks, *The Railway Station*, 40.
46. Schivelbusch, *The Railway Journey*, 174.
47. Ruskin, *The Seven Lamps of Architecture*, 221–2.
48. Simmel, *The Philosophy of Money*, 489.
49. Emile Durkheim discusses time so in *The Elementary Forms of the Religious Life*.
50. Davidoff, *The Best Circles*, 34.
51. Roger Osborne, *Iron, Steam, and Money: The Making of the Industrial Revolution* (London: The Bodley Head, 2013), 290.
52. Donald L. Miller, *Lewis Mumford: A Life* (New York: Weidenfeld and Nicolson, 1989), 328–9.
53. Mayhew, *London Labour and the London Poor*, vol. 1, 353–4. In America in the 1880s watches were available which simultaneously showed the new railroad time with steel hands and local times with brass ones.
54. Nichols, *Forty Years of American Life*, vol. 1, 1379.
55. I have always thought it a rather odd tradition—started in the 19th century—whereby the standard gift for a departing, long-serving employee should be a watch (having retired, surely that is the

last thing anybody would need or want—but perhaps I'm missing something there).

56. Porter, *Jubilee Jim and the Wizard of Wall Street*, 314.

57. Simmons, *The Victorian Railway*.

58. "Eastern Counties Railway Investigation." Likewise, Marquis Childs suggests that timekeeping on the river steamboats in America was often very poor; and that "the beautiful time schedules, patterned after railroad schedules," were "largely works of fiction." Childs, *Mighty Mississippi*, 113.

59. See Parris, *Government and the Railways*, 6, 36.

60. Advertisements for English stagecoaches before the turnpike age often said coaches would arrive in *about two days*, or at a certain time *if the road was good*. See Flanders, *Consuming Passions*, 129.

61. *Ibid.*, 195.

62. "Third-Class Railway Carriages."

63. Dunbar, *A History of Travel in America*, vol. 3, 1033–4.

64. Burrhus F. Skinner, *Particulars of My Life* (London: Jonathan Cape, 1976), 71.

65. See Hopkins, *The Poetry of Railways*, 81.

66. Carlton J. Corliss, *The Day of Two Noons* (Washington, D.C.: Association of American Railroads, 1948), 4.

67. See McKenna, *The Railway Workers*, 244; Simmons, *The Victorian Railway*, 346.

68. Apart from the benefits to railroad capitalism itself, and to the capitalist system more generally, railroad time standardization in Britain considerably enhanced the ability of companies to operate rail services safely—during the early period there had been numerous accidents attributable to "irrational" timetabling or human error in respect of timetabling (both, to some extent, a consequence of the absence of a time standard).

69. See Derek Howse, *Greenwich Time and the Discovery of the Longitude* (Oxford: Oxford University Press, 1980), 114.

70. In the late Middle Ages, an attempt was made to more widely apply *London Standard Weights and Measures*, the effect at Bury St. Edmonds (Market) to "paralyze the town"; consequently, people ceased taking their goods to that market, instead taking them to more distant markets where they could use the measures they were accustomed to. See Davis, *A History of Shopping*, 7.

71. See Richards and McKenzie, *The Railway Station*, 2.

72. Rule 16, *Erie Railroad Regulations 1854*.

73. Fried, *Appetite for America*, 96; Beatty, *Age of Betrayal*, 4–5.

74. Stilgoe, *Metropolitan Corridor*, 205.

75. Corliss, *The Day of Two Noons*, 2–4.

76. "French Opinion of English Railways," *The Leeds Mercury*, August 29, 1840.

77. "The Pace That Kills," *The Graphic* December 30, 1871.

78. Charles Dickens (ed.), *All the Year Round*, no. 15 (1866): 82.

79. Brown, *Hear That Lonesome Whistle Blow*, 227.

80. See Matteson, *Eden's Outcasts*, 317.

81. McFeely, *Grant*, 26

82. Hamlin, *Greek Revival Architecture in America*, 34.

83. Simmel, *The Philosophy of Money*, 231.

84. Emile Durkheim *The Division of Labor in Society* (New York: The Free Press, 1984), 276.

85. Schivelbusch, *The Railway Journey*, 61, 67, 69.

86. Richards and McKenzie, *The Railway Station*, 298.

87. Karl Marx, *Dispatches for the New York Tribune: Selected Journalism of Karl Marx* (London: Penguin, 2007), 143.

88. Richard D. Altick, *The English Common Reader* (Chicago: University of Chicago Press, 1957), 30.

89. Mayhew, *London Labour and the London Poor*, vol. 3, 320.

90. See Roger Chartier (ed.), *A History of Private Life*, vol. 3 (Cambridge MA: The Belknap Press, 2003), 150.

91. Mentioned in Richard Watson, *Cogito Ergo Sum: The Life of Rene Descartes* (Boston: David R. Godine, 2002), 273.

92. Glendinning, *Trollope*, 218.

93. Richard D. Altick, *Writers, Readers and Occasions* (Columbus: Ohio State University Press, 1989), 150.

94. Schivelbusch, *The Railway Journey*, 67.

95. See Cockayne, *Hubbub*, 179.

96. Faith, *The World the Railways Made*, 37.

97. Erving Goffman, *Behaviour in Public Places* (New York: The Free Press, 1963), 137–9.

98. Richards and McKenzie, *The Railway Station*, 298.

99. Mayhew, *London Labour and the London Poor*, vol. 1, 291.

100. Bovill, *The England of Nimrod and Surtees*, 19.

101. Nevett, *Advertising in Britain*, 34.

102. Faith, *The World the Railways Made*, 246–7.

103. "Travelers' Tales," *Wrexham and Denbighshire Advertiser*, January 7, 1860.

104. See W. Tuckniss in Mayhew, *London Labour and the London Poor*, vol. 4.

105. Browne, *Charles Darwin*, vol. 1, 427.

106. Alberto Manguel, *A History of Reading* (London: HarperCollins, 1996), 214.

Selected Bibliography

Acworth, William. M. *The Railways of England*. London: John Murray, 1890.

Ambrose, Stephen E. *Nothing Like It in the World: The Men Who Built the Transcontinental Railroad 1863–1869*. New York: Simon & Schuster, 2000.

Armstrong, E.L. *History of Public Works in the United States 1776–1996*. Chicago: American Public Works Association, 1976.

Bain, David H. *Empire Express: Building the Transcontinental Railroad*. New York: Viking, 1999.

Bates, Catherine. E. *A Year in the Great Republic*. London: Ward and Downey, 1887.

Berg, Walter C. *Buildings and Structures of American Railroads*. New York: John Wiley and Sons, 1893.

Bernstein, Peter L. *Wedding of the Waters: The Erie Canal and the Making of a Great Nation*. New York: W.W. Norton, 2005.

Boddam-Whetham, John W. *Western Wanderings: A Record of Travel in the Evening Land*. London: Bentley, 1874.

Brown, Dee. *Hear That Lonesome Whistle Blow*. London: Chatto and Windus, 1978.

Buckingham, James. *The Eastern and Western States of America*. London: Fisher, Son and Co., 1842.

Cavalier, Julian. *North American Railroad Stations*. Cranbury, NJ: A.S. Barnes and Co., 1979.

Childs, Marquis. *Mighty Mississippi: Biography of a River*. New Haven, CT: Ticknor and Fields, 1982.

Churton, Edward. *The Railroad Book of England 1851*. London: Sidgwick and Jackson, 1851.

Combe, George. *Notes on the United States of America*. Philadelphia: Carey and Hart, 1841.

Cunynghame, Arthur. *A Glimpse of the Great Western Republic*. London: Richard Bentley, 1851.

Curtis, Benjamin. *Dottings Round the Circle*. Boston: J.R. Osgood and Co., 1876.

Deedes, Henry. *Sketches of the South and West*. London: W. Blackwood and Sons, 1869.

Dixon, Roger, and Stefan Malthesius. *Victorian Architecture*. London: Thames and Hudson, 1985.

Dorsey, Edward B. *English and American Railroads Compared*. New York: John Wiley and Sons, 1887.

Dunbar, Seymour. *A History of Travel in America*. New York: Greenwood, 1968.

Ellis, Hamilton. *Nineteenth Century Railway Carriages in the British Isles*. London: Modern Transport Publishing, 1949.

Ferguson, William. *America by River and Rail*. London: J. Nisbet and Co., 1856.

Francis, John. *A History of the English Railway: Its Social Relations and Revelations 1820–1845*. Newton Abbot: David and Charles, 1851.

Garfield, Simon. *The Last Journey of William Huskisson*. London: Faber & Faber, 2002.

Glendinning, Victoria. *Trollope*. London: Hutchinson, 1992.

Gottschalk, Louis. *Notes of a Pianist*. New York: Alfred A. Knopf, 1964

Greeley, Horace. *An Overland Journey from New York to San Francisco in the Summer of 1859*. London: MacDonald, 1965.

Hamlin, Talbot. *Greek Revival Architecture in America*. New York: Dover, 1944.

Handlin, David P. *American Architecture*. London: Thames and Hudson, 2004.

Hardman, William A. *A Trip to America*. London: T.V. Wood, 1884.

Hardy, Duffus. *Through Cities and Prairie Lands: Sketches of an American Tour*. New York: R. Worthington, 1881.

Hogan, James F. *The Australian in London and America*. London: Ward and Downey, 1889.

Hoyt, Edwin P. *The Vanderbilts and Their Fortunes*. London: Frederick Muller, 1963.

Hudson, T.S. *A Scamper Through America*. New York: E.P. Dutton and Co., 1882.

Jennings, Humphrey. *Pandaemonium: The Coming of the Machine as Seen by Contemporary Observers*. London: Andre Deutsch, 1985.

Jensen, Oliver. *The American Heritage History of Railroads in America*. New York: American Heritage Publishing, 1975.

Jones, Edgar. *Industrial Architecture in Britain 1750–1939*. London: B.T. Batsford, 1985.

Kemble, Frances. *Journal of a Residence on a Georgian Plantation in 1838–9*. New York: Harper and Brothers, 1864.

Lee, Charles. *Passenger Class Distinctions*. London: The Railway Gazette, 1946.
Lewis, Oscar. *The Big Four*. New York: Alfred A. Knopf, 1938.
Leyendecker, Liston E. *Palace Car Prince: A Biography of George Mortimer Pullman*. Niwot: University Press of Colorado, 1992.
Lloyd, David L., and Donald W. Insall. *Railway Station Architecture*. Newton Abbot: David and Charles, 1978.
MacDermot, Edward T. *History of the Great Western Railway*. London: Great Western Railway Co., 1927.
Marshall, Walter. *Through America*. London: Sampson, Low, Marston, Searle and Rivington, 1881.
Mayhew, Henry. *London Labour and the London Poor*. New York: Dover, 1968 (facsimile of the 1861–2 edition).
McCabe, James D., Jr. *Lights and Shadows of New York Life*. London: Andre Deutsch, 1971 (facsimile of the 1872 edition).
Meeks, Carroll L. *The Railway Station: An Architectural History*. London: The Architectural Press, 1957.
Mencken, August. *The Railroad Passenger Car*. Baltimore: The Johns Hopkins University Press, 2000.
Moir, Esther. *The Discovery of Britain: The English Tourists 1540–1840*. London: Routledge and Kegan Paul, 1964.
Myers, Gustavus. *History of the Great American Fortunes*. New York: The Modern Library, 1909.
Nichols, Thomas. *Forty Years of American Life*. London: J. Maxwell and Co., 1864.
Pachter, Mark, and Frances S. Wein. *Abroad in America*. Washington, D.C.: Smithsonian Institution, 1976.
Parsons, Nicholas T. *Worth the Detour: A History of the Guidebook*. Stroud, UK: Sutton, 2007.
Pratt, Edwin A. *A History of Inland Transit and Communication in England*. London: Kegan, Paul, Trench, Trubner, 1912.
Rae, W. Fraser. *Westward by Rail: The New Route to the East*. New York: D. Appleton and Co., 1871.
Ritchie, Robert. *Railways: Their Rise, Progress and Construction*. London: Longman, Brown, Green, 1846.
Rogers, H.C. *Turnpike to Iron Road*. London: Seeley, Service and Co., 1961.
Sarmiento, Domingo. *Travels: A Selection*. Washington, D.C.: Pan American Union, 1963.
Schivelbusch, Wolfgang. *The Railway Journey*. Berkeley: University of California Press, 1986.
Smith, William A. *A Yorkshireman's Trip to the United States and Canada*. London: Longmans, Green, 1892.
Steel, Wilfred L. *The History of the London and North Western Railway*. London: The Railway and Travel Monthly, 1914.
Stevenson, Robert L. *The Amateur Emigrant: Across the Plains*. New York: Scribner's, 1895.
Stiles, T.J. *The First Tycoon: The Epic Life of Cornelius Vanderbilt*. New York: Alfred A. Knopf, 2009.
Stilgoe, John. *Metropolitan Corridor*. New Haven, CT: Yale University Press, 1983.
Stimson, Alexander L. *History of the Express Business*. New York: Baker and Godwin, 1881.
Stover, John. *American Railroads*. Chicago: University of Chicago Press, 1961.
Tarr, Lazlo. *The History of the Carriage*. London: Vision Press, 1969.
Tocqueville, Alexis de. *Democracy in America*. London: Saunders and Otley, 1838.
Trollope, Anthony. *North America*. Harmondsworth, UK: Penguin, 1968.
Trollope, Frances. *Domestic Manners of the Americans*. New York: Dodd-Mead, 1901.
Twain, Mark. *Life on the Mississippi*. New York: Harper and Brothers, 1917.
_____. *Roughing It*. London: Penguin, 1985.
Ward, James A. *Railroads and the Character of America 1820–1887*. Knoxville: University of Tennessee Press, 1986.
White, John H. *American Locomotives: An Engineering History, 1830–1880*. Baltimore: The Johns Hopkins University Press, 1968.
Williams, Henry T. *The Pacific Tourist*. New York: Henry T. Williams, 1876.
Yelverton, Therese. *Teresina in America*. London: Richard Bentley and Sons, 1875.
Zincke, Foster. *Last Winter in the United States*. London: J. Murray, 1868.

Index

accidents, railroad UK 23, 47, 55, 67–70, 74–5, 78, 85, 87–8, 198–228; US 124, 174, 182, 186, 190, 231–4, 256, 291
advertising, on railroads 34, 60, 64, 261; UK 69, 21; US 102, 152, 162
amalgamations/takeovers, of railroad companies: UK 82; US 48
American system of railroad construction 98, 100, 156–7, 162, 189–92, 213, 222–3, 271–2
anomie/alienation 107
architecture, architectural ornamentation 61–3, 150–3, 202, 248–50, 283; classical, UK 61, 63–4; compartment, UK 50; US 150, 250
aristocracy: aristocratic pretensions of Americans 103, 114–6, 241; railroad travel 29–30, 46, 65–8, 143, 159, 265, 270; UK 21, 28, 45, 50, 52–3, 65–8, 80, 84, 101, 109, 142, 250

baggage/luggage 9, 17–8, 300, 44, 46,-7, 59, 66, 69, 81–2, 86, 88, 98, 128–9, 139, 146, 153, 166, 177, 182–4, 202, 263, 275, 286
baggage smashers, US 82, 94, 166, 182–3, 263
Baltimore and Ohio Railroad, US 48, 136–8, 149, 160–1, 171, 186, 273, 275, 282, 288
Bates, Catherine (English author and traveler) 26–7, 98, 164, 168, 170, 186–7, 191
Board of Trade, UK 54, 56, 87–8, 102, 190, 193, 214, 226, 235–6
boiler explosions: locomotive 123, 202, 204–5; other industrial 203, 218, 239
brakes/braking systems 18, 162, 201, 226–7
Brunel, Isambard K. (English engineer) 22, 82, 87, 92, 153, 201–2, 219, 254

canal passenger travel 5, 6, 43, 131, 263; UK 37–8, 44, 123; US 37, 123–4, 136, 168, 184, 255

canal tolls, imposed on railroad companies, US 184
carceral, concept of and railroad travel, UK 8, 14, 27–92, 120, 269–70
carriages, passenger, UK 1, 8, 9, 11, 16, 18–9, 27–33, 43–59, 65–77, 84–92, 98, 100, 102, 113, 122, 127, 133, 138, 143, 160–1, 163, 165, 170–1, 176, 181, 189, 197–8, 201–4, 208–12, 216–7, 226, 239, 242, 249, 255, 265, 269–72
cars, passenger, US 2, 22, 51, 69–70, 75–6, 98, 112–3, 120,, 122, 126, 128–42, 144–5, 157–66, 171, 173, 176, 178, 181, 183–4, 187, 189, 191–2, 203, 206, 209, 215, 222, 228–9, 241, 255, 265, 271, 275, 281–2, 288
cattle and other livestock strikes, US 206, 246
Cheap Trains Act, 1883, UK 88
coach/stagecoach: box seat UK 23, 38; conviviality during coach travel 78; inside/outside distinction 38, 43–4, 46, 71; mail coach, UK 16, 38, 46, 80, 253, 256; speed 16
color blindness, of railroad employees 227
comfort, quest for, US 109, 132–8
compartments: UK 11, 23–5, 29–30, 38, 46–54, 65–8, 71–80, 120, 133, 139, 164, 263, 270, 272, 280; US 161
conductors 18; UK 24, 54; US 22, 25, 76, 115, 130, 141, 153, 167, 169, 172–5, 178–80, 185, 187, 206, 208, 285
Cook, Thomas (travel agent, UK) 130, 14-, 160, 170, 173

Darwin, Charles (scientist) 67, 79, 85, 258, 266
derailments 69, 187, 201, 206, 209, 215, 220, 222, 224–5, 232, 260
Dickens, Charles (author) 7, 95, 100, 112, 123, 127, 160, 175, 222, 226, 257, 261, 267

dining/refreshment while traveling: UK 22, 64, 273; US 32, 113, 122, 135, 138–40, 170–3, 176
discipline 130, 141, 152; railroad travel UK 20–4; *see also* carceral
Duke of Wellington (English statesman) 47, 66, 143, 200
Durkheim, Emile (French sociologist) 260

Edmondson's ticketing machine, UK 16, 24
egalitarianism, US 103, 114–20, 124–5, 131–2
emigrants: class 128, 130, 142, 165; cars 128–30, 176, 281; railroad conveyance of, US 1, 123–33, 154
equality of opportunity, US 117–8, 124–5
equine metaphors, in relation to railroads 239–40
etiquette/etiquette books 21, 31–7, 81, 96, 166, 253, 263–5; UK 32, 34, 187, 263–4; US 32, 113, 194

fares, passenger: canal, UK 38; Parliamentary, UK 88, 92; rail, UK 40, 65, 67, 70, 85, 92, 132–3, 213, 275, 285; steamboat, US 123; US 25, 122, 125–6, 132–3, 168, 174, 213, 222, 281, 285
fines, of passengers, UK 23–4, 207, 210
fire hazards 23, 55, 70, 75, 78, 163, 195, 205, 217, 228
first-class railroad travel, UK 40, 43–54, 61, 66–71, 77, 80, 83, 87, 122, 133, 233; US 128, 281
foot-warmers, railroad travel, UK 69
fourth-class railroad travel, UK 92
free (rail travel) pass, US 25, 175, 181–2, 285

gauge, railroad line 46, 48, 82, 133, 139, 185–6, 198, 219
Gladstone, William E. (English

statesman) 81, 85, 88–9; Act for Regulating Railways, 1844, UK 81, 85–9
global village, concept of and railroads 243
Gottschalk, Louis (composer and pianist) 131, 151, 166, 176, 181, 225, 247
Gould, Jay (American railroad capitalist) 105, 139, 173
Great Exhibition of 1851 15, 20, 34, 40, 92, 216–7
Great Western Railway Company, UK 14, 22, 47, 51, 54–5, 65, 82, 87–92, 161, 210, 218, 254, 256, 277
guidebooks 31–5, 60, 95, 141, 165, 170, 263–4

Harvey, Fred (hospitality entrepreneur, US) 171
horse 16, 18, 24, 34, 41, 59, 63, 65–7, 79, 81, 83, 105, 122, 135, 196, 206, 220, 238–9, 240–1, 263, 266, 275–6; horse-drawn trains 41, 160, 189, 239–41; horsepower, concept 18, 238–41; iron horse, metaphor 158, 239–41
hotel car, Pullman 139–40, 161, 171
hotels: UK 58, 64 US 17, 94, 103, 110, 112, 119–22, 125, 149, 168, 171, 173, 183, 187, 280
Hudson River, US 67, 102, 112, 131, 138
Huish, Mark (general manager, London and North Western Railway, UK) 74, 212, 216–7
Huskisson, William (statesman, and first fatal railroad accident victim) 200, 226

Indians, native American 117, 121, 144, 152, 165, 212, 228, 231
individualism 32–3; UK 259, 274; US 103–9, 115, 135, 180, 193, 244, 259, 271–2, 274
Industrial Revolution 5, 239
inns 46, 58, 79, 91, 110, 127, 149, 168, 282
insurance, railroad travel 149, 219, 232–34
Interstate Commerce Commission, US 227

James, Henry (author) 101, 106, 107, 171

Kemble, Frances (English actress) 117, 158, 160, 162, 191, 221–2, 239

La Trobe, Benjamin 147–8
lighting/illumination of carriages/cars 47–8, 69–70, 71, 228, 262
Lincoln, Abraham

(statesman/lawyer) 106, 139, 175–6, 181
Liverpool and Manchester Railway, UK 40–1, 43–4, 46–7, 53, 66, 158, 200, 204, 208, 211, 217–8, 226, 256, 275
livestock wagons, and passenger conveyance UK 37, 54
locomotives/engines 1, 9, 18, 241, 248, 254; UK 23, 43, 144, 197, 205, 217, 239, 254; US 46, 147, 157–9, 163, 187, 203, 206, 221, 283, 288
luggage trains, passenger conveyance by means of, UK 51, 54

management, railroad 18; UK 22, 40, 82, 86–7, 217; US 142, 152, 156, 169, 180–2, 186, 192, 243, 282
Marx, Karl (German economic historian) 32–3, 262
Marx, Leo (American author) 240, 245
mass transportation, concept of 14–7, 26
materialism: UK 274; US 101, 104–7, 150, 259, 271, 274
Mayhew, Henry (19th century English sociologist) 15, 58, 70, 205, 219–21, 252, 262, 265
military titles of civilians, as status symbols, US 114–6
Mumford, Lewis (historian/author) 56, 59
Myers, Gustavus (historian) 104, 118, 182

national identity and railroads 98–9, 120
national style, of railroad systems and travel 6, 19, 26, 50, 52, 93, 100, 144, 146, 179, 193, 236–8, 270, 272
negroes (African-Americans) railroad travel, US 5–6, 11, 110, 117, 122, 124, 126–8, 131, 133, 139, 152, 168, 177–8, 203, 230, 271, 285
neurasthenia, medical condition 196
New York and Erie Railroad, US 111, 128, 136, 138, 151, 173, 175, 180, 186, 223, 243, 257

Omaha, US 128, 130, 145, 165–7, 170, 183, 185, 192, 222, 231, 233
open carriages, UK 47, 55, 74–5, 85, 198, 201, 232

Parliamentary Carriage, UK 86
passenger class, concept of UK 43–7, 50
Peel, Sir Robert (English statesman) 29, 88
Pennsylvania Railroad Company, US 126, 129, 137, 140, 155, 172–3, 187, 192, 227

poor whites, Southern US 117–8, 280
privacy: English fetish for 28–30, 32, 39, 65, 67, 72, 75–6, 79–80, 270, 274; and poke bonnet 29; US 29, 76, 161, 274
Pugin, Augustus (English architect) 61, 63–4, 147
Pullman, George (railroad car manufacturer, US) 134, 137–43, 171, 177–8, 226, 285; Pullman brand 1, 32, 48, 111, 121, 126–33, 135–43, 145, 160, 170, 176, 265, 282, 285–8; Pullman cars 69, 112, 120, 126–43, 145; Pullman porters 32, 136, 138–43, 168, 177–8, 285
punctuality, of trains 186–7, 193, 216, 218, 237, 253–4, 258–9

railroad: concept 9; as factory-like 12–4, 18, 42, 60, 242–3, 246–7, 249–50, 254, 269; as industrial production system 6, 12–3, 18, 20, 132, 242, 247, 269; as resembling assembly-line 13–4, 132
railroad construction costs: UK 213; US 192, 213, 222
railroad gardening/landscaping 202, 237, 245, 247–50, 249, 290
railroad systems/networks 1, 6–8, 12–3, 19, 21, 41–2, 49, 51, 53, 60–1, 132, 188, 206, 234, 242–7, 260
rails: poor quality manufacture 187, 190, 214, 216–7, 222; snaking, US 192, 222, 287; track quality, US 144, 213, 222, 225
reading, while railroad traveling 9, 140, 176–7, 260–7, 279
regulations, of railroad companies, UK 22, 24, 215–6, 247; US 22, 111, 129, 169, 173–4, 179–81, 289
republicanism, US 5–6, 12, 29, 36, 98, 103, 105–6, 108–12, 114–6, 118, 121, 124–5, 131, 140, 146, 158, 163, 181, 271–2, 276
reserved passenger seats, UK 25–6, 38–9, 54, 83
rudeness, US 82, 94, 96–7, 108–12, 167, 169, 174–5
Ruskin, John (Victorian art and architectural critic) 5, 13, 42, 59, 60–4, 147–8, 150, 250

safety/security of railroad travel 21–4, 195–235
Sarmiento, Domingo (Argentinian statesman and traveler) 85, 108–9, 122, 133, 216, 222, 234, 272
Schivelbusch, Wolfgang (author) 2, 13, 48–9, 75–81, 198–202,

Index

208, 237, 240, 243, 245, 247, 250, 260–3
second-class railroad travel, UK 16, 23, 28, 31, 38–9, 44–5, 47–50, 53–5, 57, 64–5, 67–71, 81, 84–6, 89–90, 132–3, 140, 164, 233, 252, 275, 280–1
self-made man, concept of, US 103–4, 116, 138, 234, 271
service: concept of 13, 71, 99; UK 45, 54, 68, 81–2, 86, 156; US 108–13, 127, 130–2, 140–2, 144, 156, 166–71, 175–7, 181, 187, 192–4, 279, 281–2
shock, industrial/railroad accidents and medical 196–200, 281–2
Silver Palace cars, US 119–20, 142, 145
Simmel, Georg (German sociologist) 44, 244, 260
Simmons, Jack (English transportation historian) 14–5, 42–3, 252
sleeping cars, US 12, 69, 119–22, 129, 136–42, 186, 282
Smith, Sydney (English commentator and critic) 23, 51, 73–4, 87
Smith, W.H., railroad bookstalls, UK 102, 171, 262, 265
smoking cars, US 113, 140, 171
special, private train, UK 67
speed of locomotives/trains 16, 195–6, 235, 239, 255, 258–60, 262, 270; UK 22, 54–5, 74, 197, 217; US 69, 162, 196, 207, 213, 218, 234
spitting: UK 280; US 94, 111–3, 123, 166, 174, 186–7, 192, 195
station/depot/terminus: UK 9, 14, 17–20, 22, 35, 44–6, 50–64, 68, 70, 78, 80–3, 88, 91; US 48, 50, 52, 98, 102, 144–57
status space, concept of 35–7, 57
Stephenson, George (English engineer) 158, 239
Stephenson, Robert (English engineer) 54
Stevenson, Robert L. (author) 130, 142, 158, 165, 176, 231, 240
Stockton and Darlington Railway, UK 41, 43, 239

stoves, in cars, US 69–70, 75, 162–3, 205, 228
suicide, by means of railroad, UK 80, 207, 217, 220–1, 289

telegraph 18, 55, 141, 157, 170, 173, 180, 183, 186, 208–11, 213, 217, 223, 243–4, 256–8, 285
third-class railroad travel, UK 15, 18–9, 26, 31, 35, 37, 39, 41, 45–57, 69–71, 74, 76–7, 81, 83–92, 116, 125–6, 128–30, 132–3, 156, 163, 210, 232–3, 249, 265, 271
Thoreau, Henri (American author) 13, 42, 240
through travel: UK 18, 81–3; US 164, 184–6
tickets/ticketing: machines, UK 16, 24; UK 24–5; US 25
time: consciousness 251–4; discipline 21, 246, 251, 253–4; Greenwich Meantime/London Time 256–7
time standards/standardization: UK 256, 291; US 188, 258
time zones, US 257–8
timepieces (clocks/watches) 21, 126, 146, 157, 173, 188, 251–2, 255–9, 290
timetables 20–2, 186, 190, 246, 252–5, 258
tipping: UK 81, 273; US 32, 175, 178, 183, 285
tobacco chewing, US 111–3, 163–6, 280
Tocqueville, Alexis de (author and intellectual) 30, 96, 101, 105, 109, 118, 146, 150, 166, 178, 193, 204
traffic: concept 17–8; engineering 17–9; passenger/pedestrian railroads 17–20
train butch/newsboy, US 175–7
train classes: UK 50, 52; US 129
train robbers/robbery, US 141, 228–31
tramps, railroad, US 206–7, 212, 288
transcontinental railroads, US 32, 35, 101–2, 120, 128–30, 139–42, 145–6, 151–2, 162, 165, 167, 169–70, 175–6, 183, 185–6, 191, 213, 233, 244, 279, 285, 288

Trollope, Anthony (author) 80, 99, 121–2, 125–6, 131, 135, 137, 157, 166–8, 183, 187, 263
Trollope, Frances (author) 94–8, 106, 110–6, 121–2, 157, 279
Tubman, Harriet (US. antislavery activist/Underground Railroad) 29
Tuckerman, Henry T. (author) 7, 95–6, 276
tunnels: architectural ornamentation 202; fear 196, 201–2; health issues pertaining to traveling through 197, 201–2; UK 196, 201–2; US 191, 213
turnpikes, UK 46–7, 202
Twain, Mark (author) 95, 117, 153, 157, 178, 232

urban planning and railroad systems 19

vandalism/sabotage of railroads 91–2, 201, 208–12, 272
Vanderbilt, Cornelius (American railroad capitalist) 20, 25, 44, 104–5, 151, 156, 159, 172, 193, 223, 226
Vanderbilt, William K. 137, 139, 182, 188
Veblen, Thorstein (American sociologist) 13
ventilation, of carriages: UK 47–8, 69, 71, 87; US 162–3
vestibule, US 139, 164, 181

waiting-rooms: UK 16, 18–9, 57–8, 80, 91, 240; US 126–7, 151–2, 230
Weber, Max (German historical sociologist) 45, 240–1
women rail travel, UK 15, 21, 58–9, 69, 75–6, 87, 264; US 7, 162, 166–9, 183, 272; alleged assaults 76–7, 80, 167, 272

Yelverton, Therese (English aristocratic traveler and author) 76, 96–101, 112, 119–20, 123, 141–2, 145, 155, 166–7, 179, 189, 207, 225, 231